SPICE & WOLF

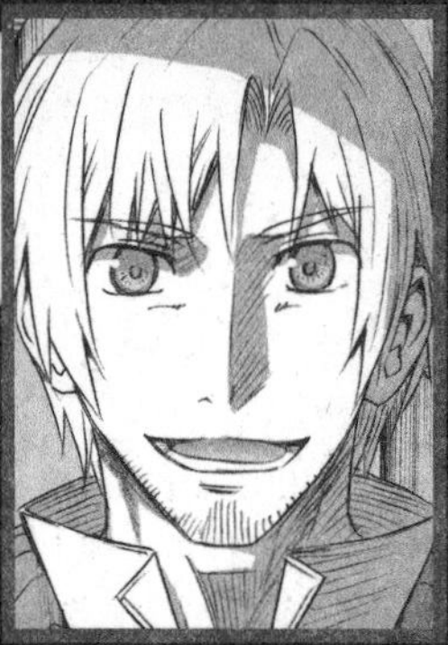

Lawrence

A clever young merchant and member of the Rowen Trade Guild. Traveling in search of Holo's homeland of Yoitsu.

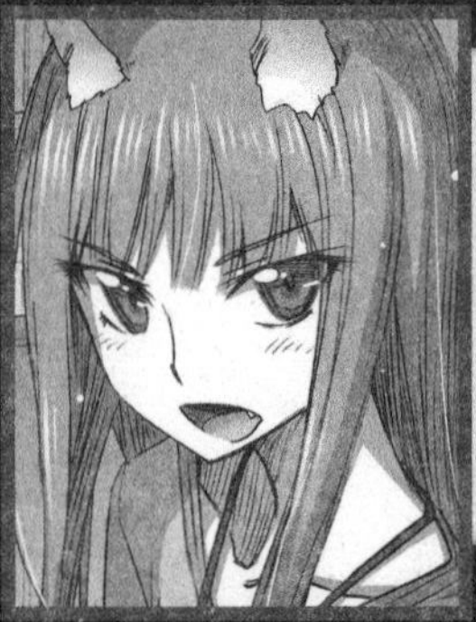

Holo

A beautiful girl traveling with Lawrence. Her true form is that of the wolf-god of the harvest.

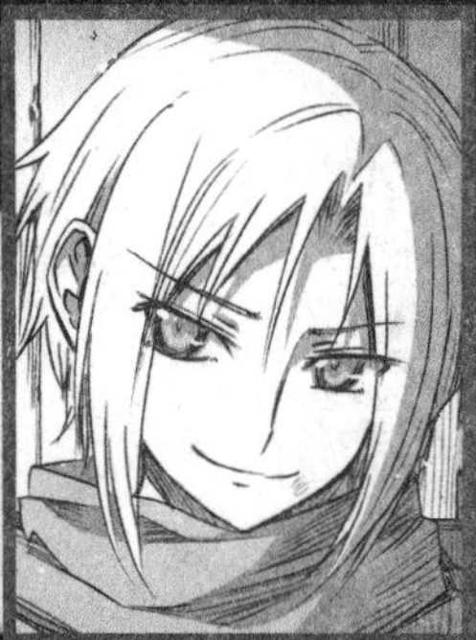

Eve

A beautiful merchant woman who hides her face and dresses like a man. She's an important figure in the north side of Kerube.

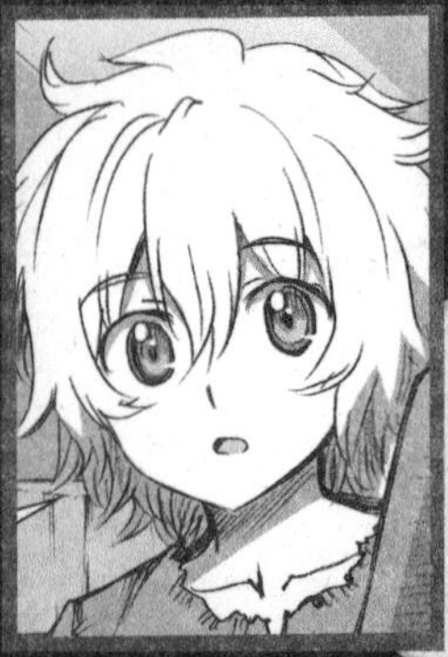

Col

A boy who Lawrence saved and who has come to travel with them. A polite and clever apprentice.

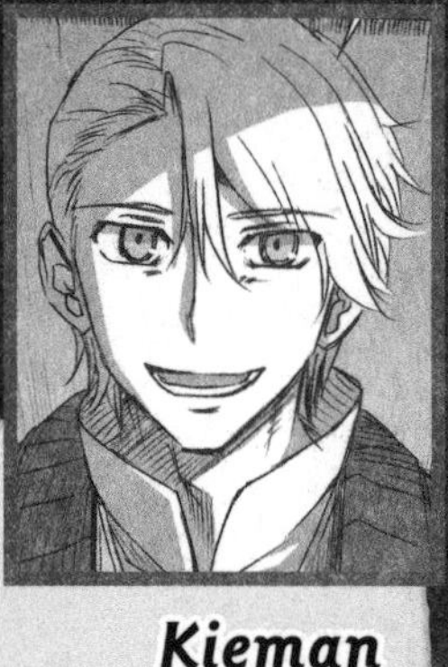

Kieman

The chief of the Kerube branch of the Rowen Trade Guild.

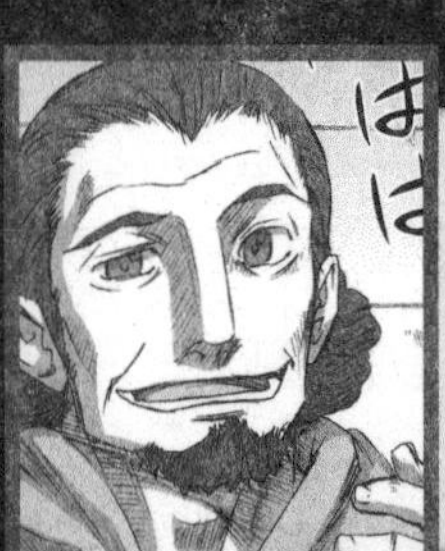
はは

Reynolds

The master of the Jean Company on the north bank of Kerube. Possesses information from a forbidden book.

Introduction

In order to protect Holo's homeland, Lawrence and company have come to the port town of Kerube in search of a forbidden book of mining techniques. The party moves through the town, which is divided into opposing north and south sides. But when a legendary creature, a narwhal, is hauled ashore, the situation changes rapidly. The narwhal is valuable enough that it could tip the precarious balance of power, and soon the town is in an uproar. Amid such danger, Lawrence and Eve the merchant woman find themselves involved in a secret deal, with the rest of the town in opposition...

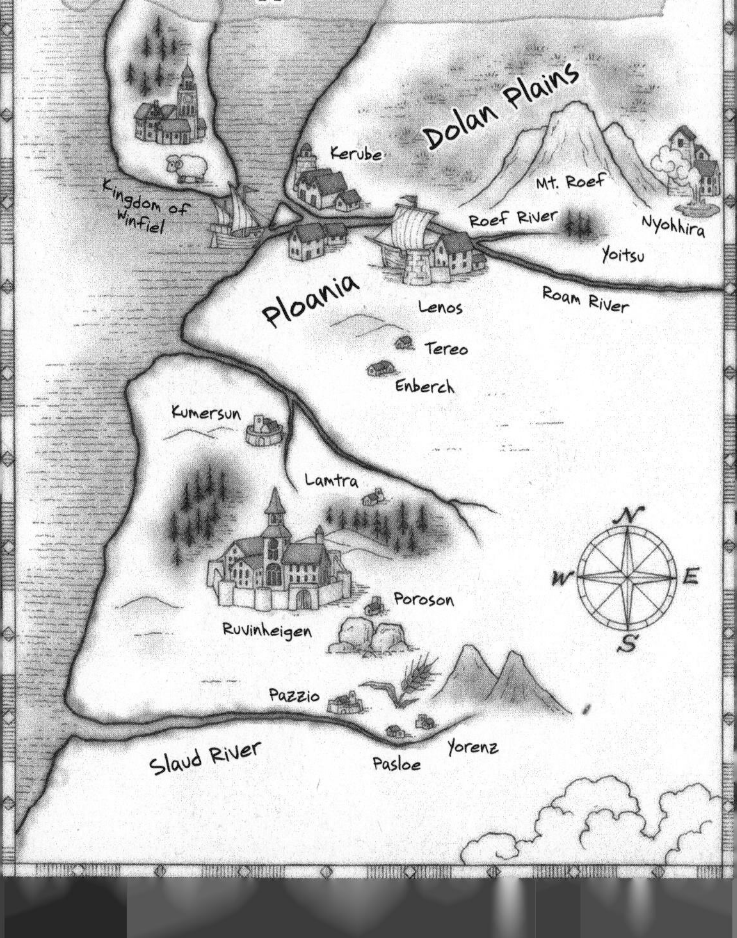

Dolan Plains
Kerube
Mt. Roef
Kingdom of Winfiel
Roef River
Nyohhira
Yoitsu
Ploania
Lenos
Roam River
Tereo
Enberch
Kumersun
Lamtra
N
W
E
S
Poroson
Ruvinheigen
Pazzio
Slaud River
Yorenz
Pasloe

SPICE & WOLF

CONTENTS

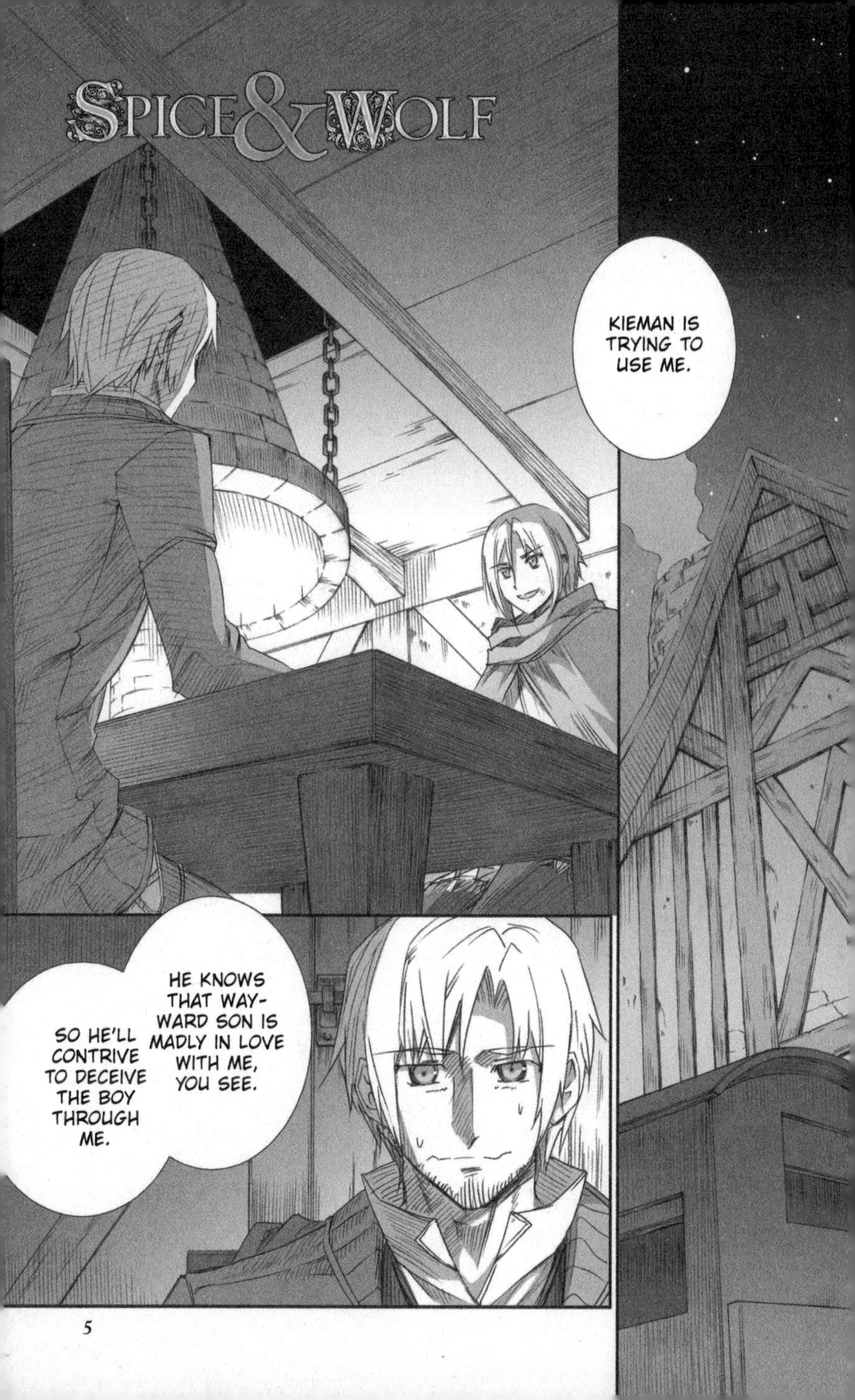
KIEMAN IS TRYING TO USE ME.
SPICE & WOLF
HE KNOWS THAT WAY-WARD SON IS MADLY IN LOVE WITH ME, YOU SEE.
SO HE'LL CONTRIVE TO DECEIVE THE BOY THROUGH ME.

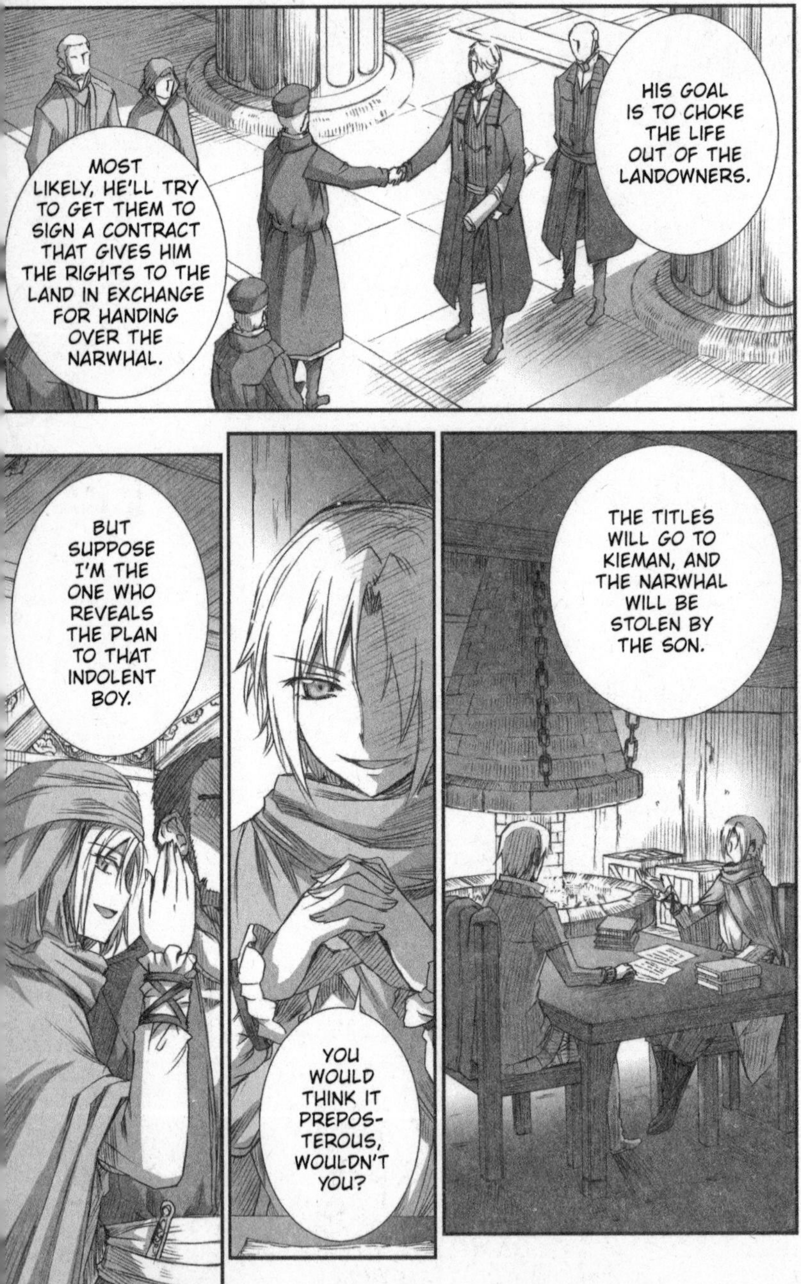
HIS GOAL IS TO CHOKE THE LIFE OUT OF THE LANDOWNERS.
MOST LIKELY, HE'LL TRY TO GET THEM TO SIGN A CONTRACT THAT GIVES HIM THE RIGHTS TO THE LAND IN EXCHANGE FOR HANDING OVER THE NARWHAL.
THE TITLES WILL GO TO KIEMAN, AND THE NARWHAL WILL BE STOLEN BY THE SON.
YOU WOULD THINK IT PREPOSTEROUS, WOULDN'T YOU?
BUT SUPPOSE I'M THE ONE WHO REVEALS THE PLAN TO THAT INDOLENT BOY.

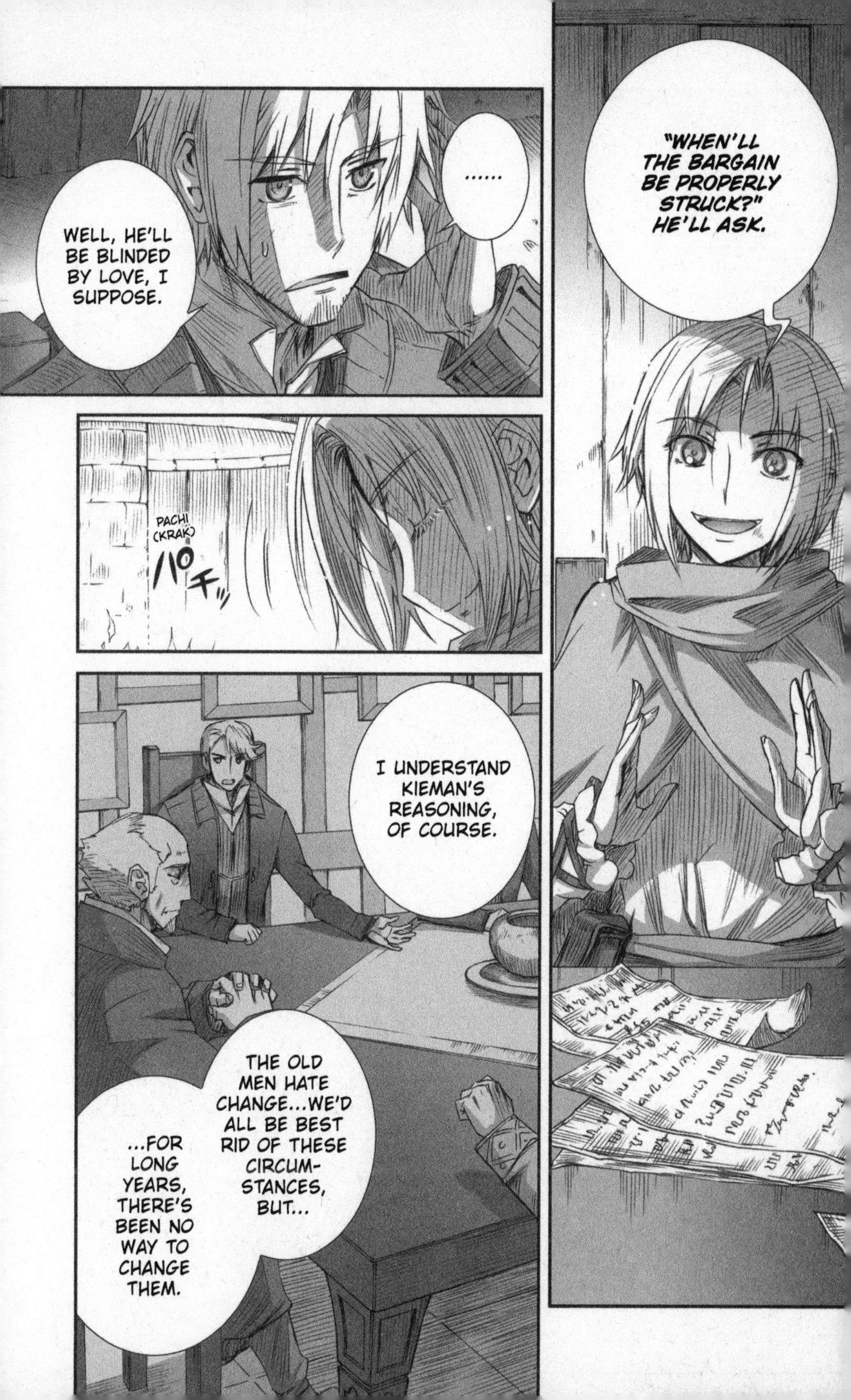
"WHEN'LL THE BARGAIN BE PROPERLY STRUCK?" HE'LL ASK.
......
WELL, HE'LL BE BLINDED BY LOVE, I SUPPOSE.
PACHI (KRAK)
パチッ
I UNDERSTAND KIEMAN'S REASONING, OF COURSE.
THE OLD MEN HATE CHANGE...WE'D ALL BE BEST RID OF THESE CIRCUM-STANCES, BUT...
...FOR LONG YEARS, THERE'S BEEN NO WAY TO CHANGE THEM.

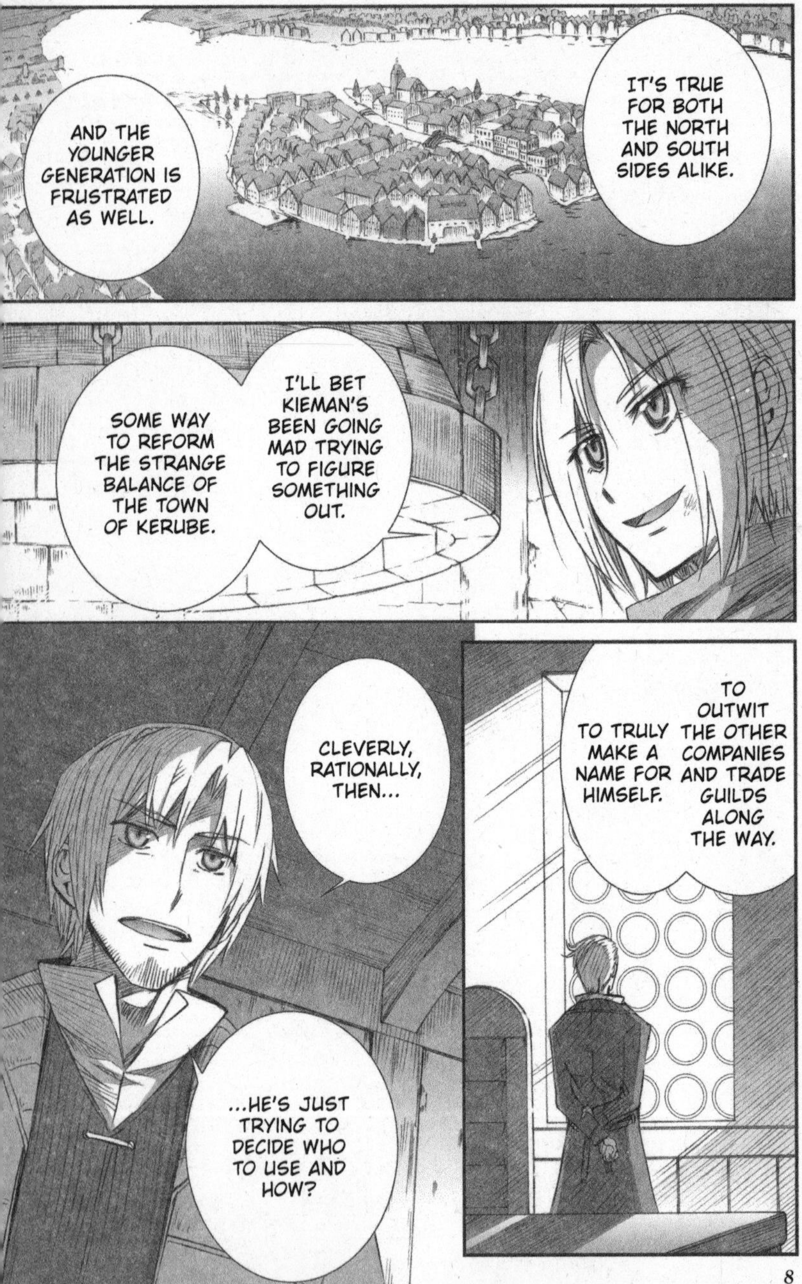
IT'S TRUE FOR BOTH THE NORTH AND SOUTH SIDES ALIKE.
AND THE YOUNGER GENERATION IS FRUSTRATED AS WELL.
I'LL BET KIEMAN'S BEEN GOING MAD TRYING TO FIGURE SOMETHING OUT.
SOME WAY TO REFORM THE STRANGE BALANCE OF THE TOWN OF KERUBE.
TO OUTWIT THE OTHER COMPANIES AND TRADE GUILDS ALONG THE WAY.
TO TRULY MAKE A NAME FOR HIMSELF.
CLEVERLY, RATIONALLY, THEN...
...HE'S JUST TRYING TO DECIDE WHO TO USE AND HOW?

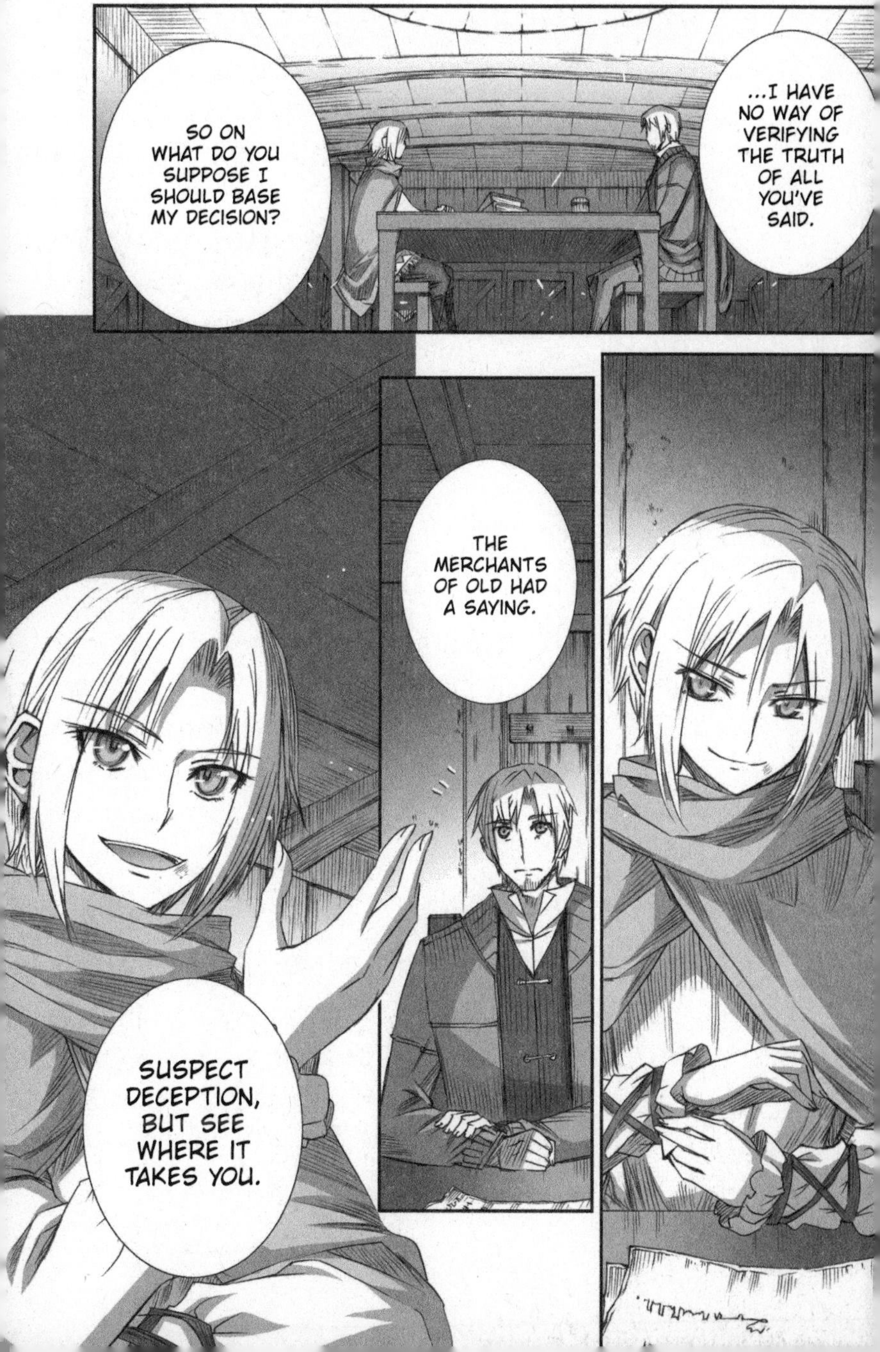
...I HAVE NO WAY OF VERIFYING THE TRUTH OF ALL YOU'VE SAID.
SO ON WHAT DO YOU SUPPOSE I SHOULD BASE MY DECISION?
THE MERCHANTS OF OLD HAD A SAYING.
SUSPECT DECEPTION, BUT SEE WHERE IT TAKES YOU.

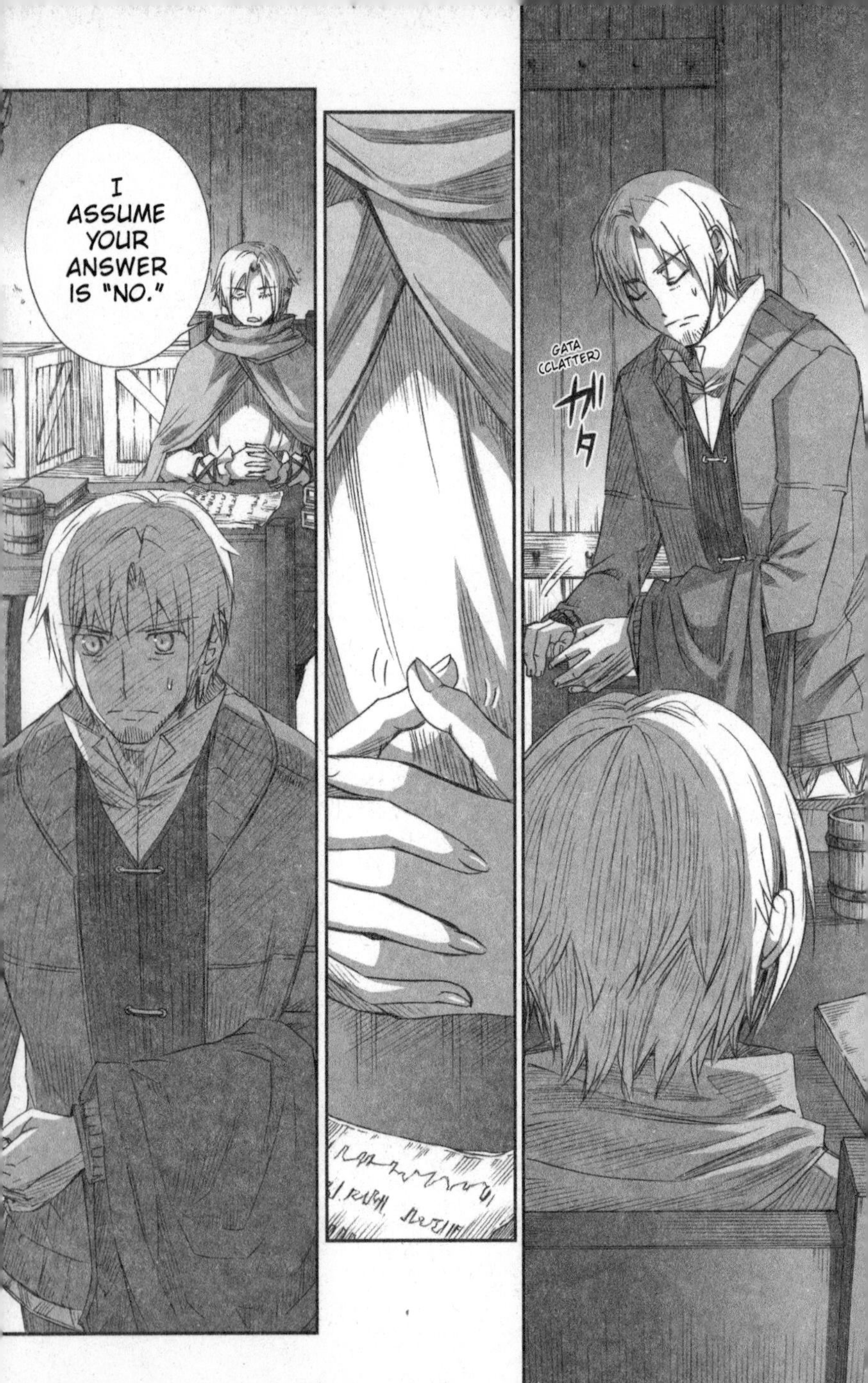
GATA (CLATTER)
ガタ
I ASSUME YOUR ANSWER IS "NO."

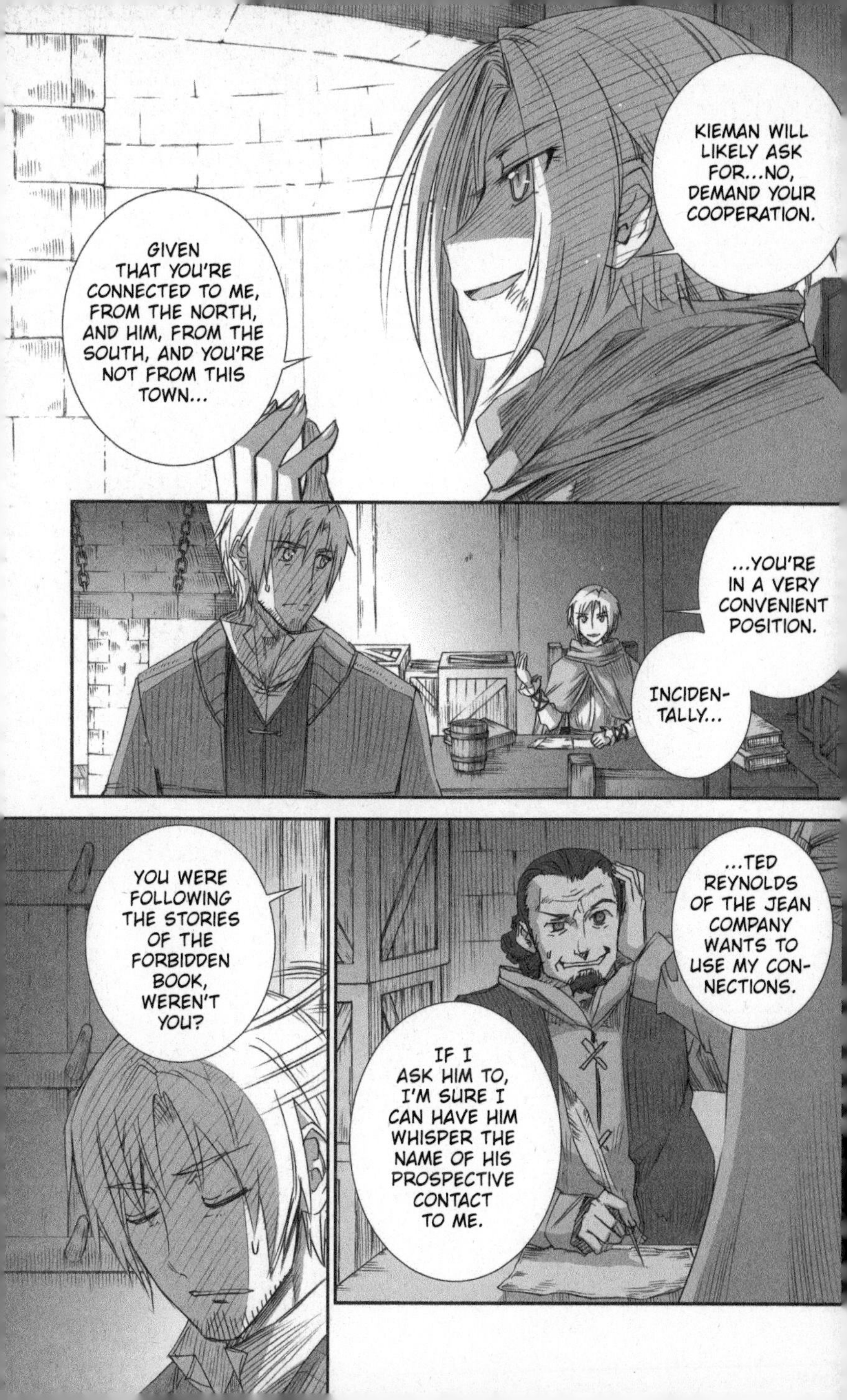
KIEMAN WILL LIKELY ASK FOR...NO, DEMAND YOUR COOPERATION.
GIVEN THAT YOU'RE CONNECTED TO ME, FROM THE NORTH, AND HIM, FROM THE SOUTH, AND YOU'RE NOT FROM THIS TOWN...
...YOU'RE IN A VERY CONVENIENT POSITION.
INCIDENTALLY...
...TED REYNOLDS OF THE JEAN COMPANY WANTS TO USE MY CONNECTIONS.
IF I ASK HIM TO, I'M SURE I CAN HAVE HIM WHISPER THE NAME OF HIS PROSPECTIVE CONTACT TO ME.
YOU WERE FOLLOWING THE STORIES OF THE FORBIDDEN BOOK, WEREN'T YOU?

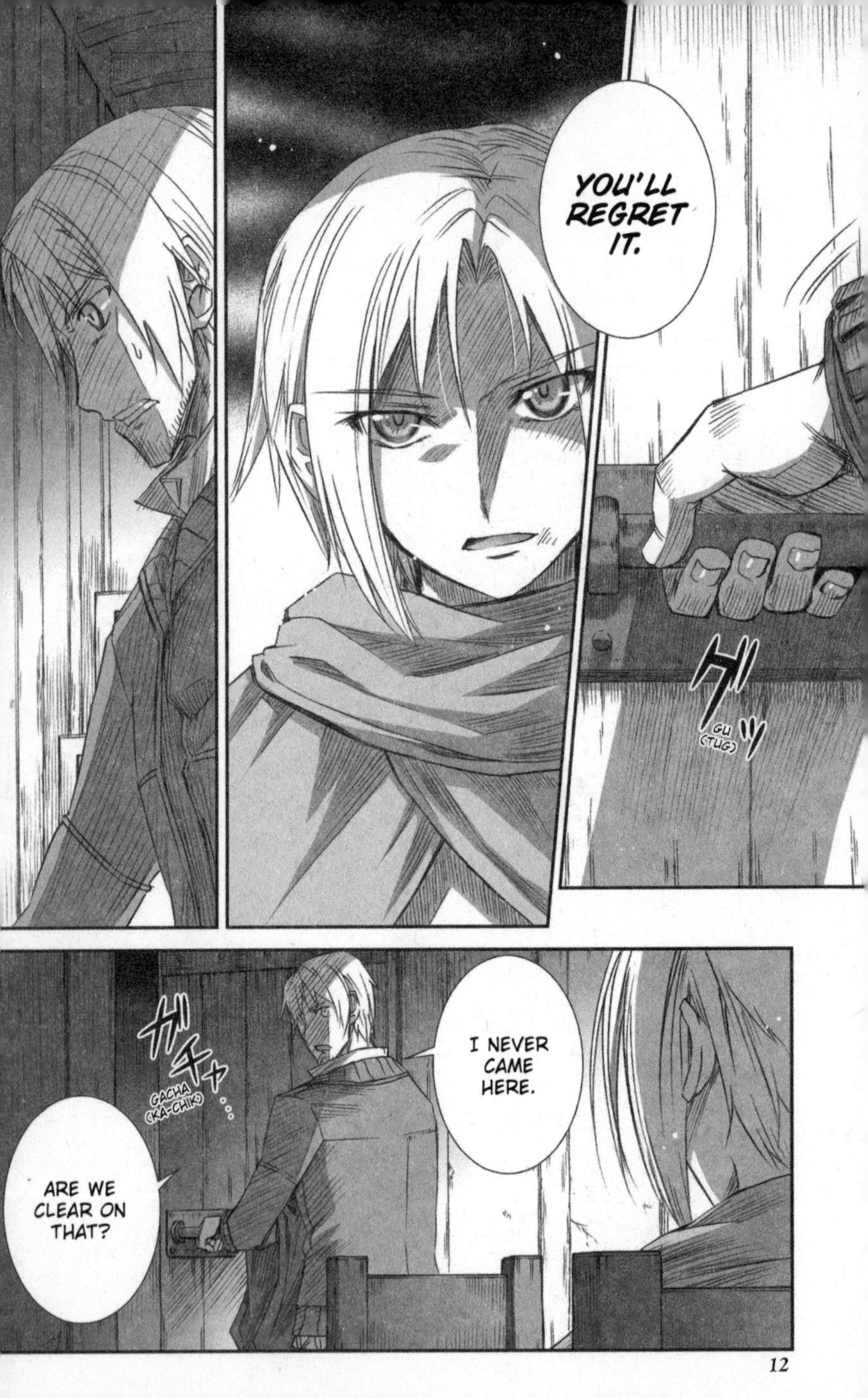
YOU'LL REGRET IT.
GU (TUG)
I NEVER CAME HERE.
GACHA (KA-CHIK)
ARE WE CLEAR ON THAT?

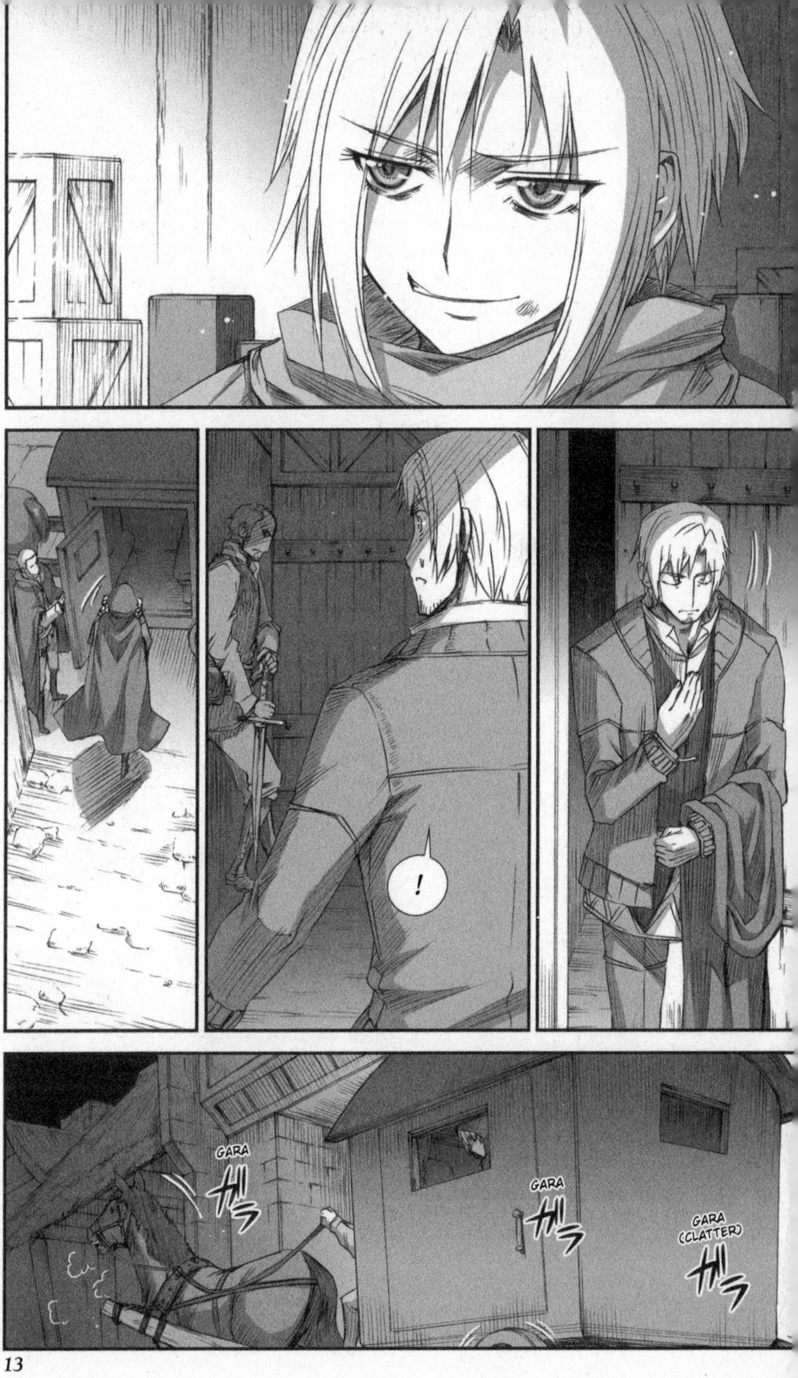
!
GARA (CLATTER)
ガラ
GARA
ガラ
GARA
ガラ

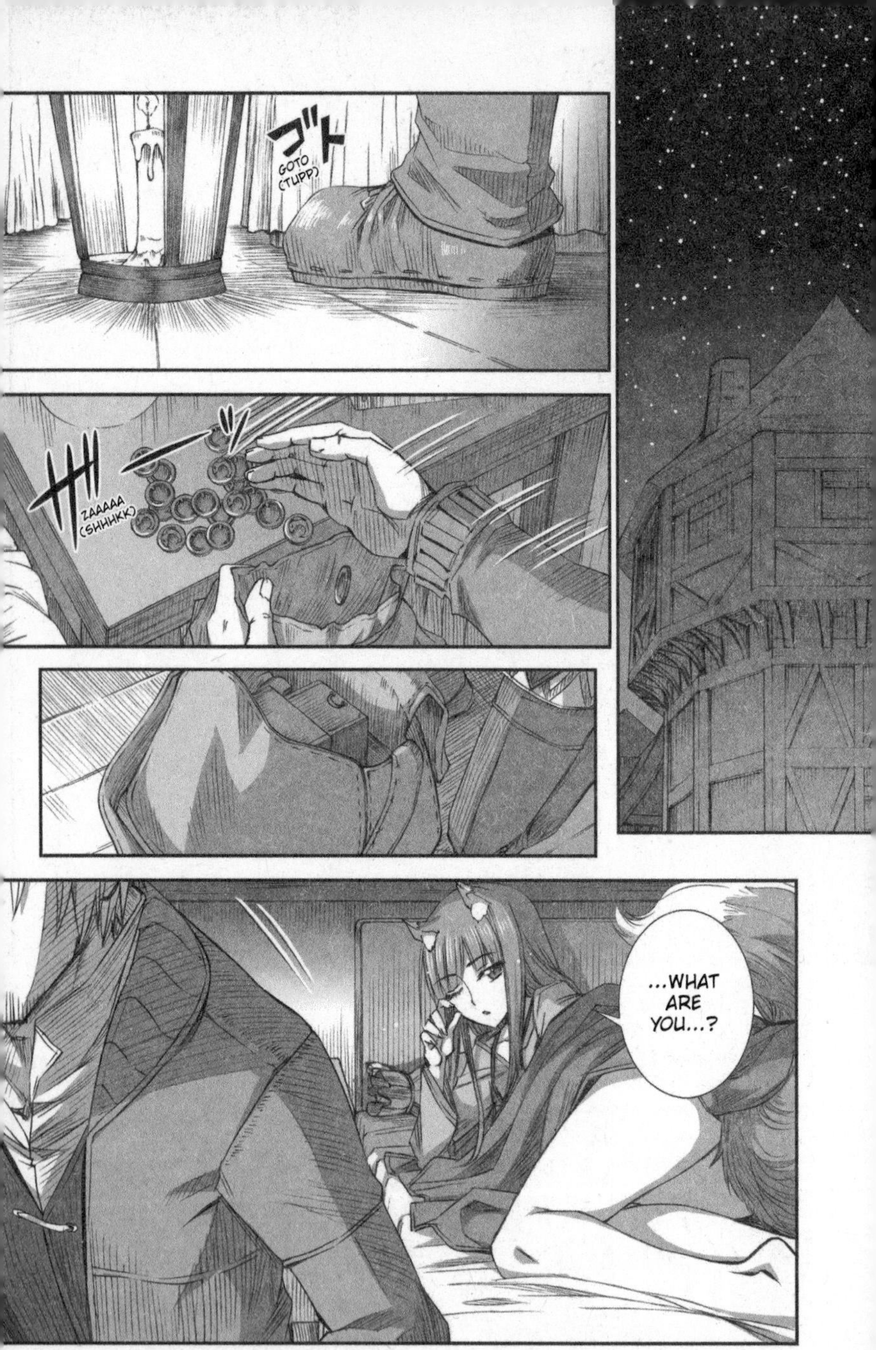
ゴト
GOTO (TUPP)
ZAAAAA (SHHHKK)
...WHAT ARE YOU...?

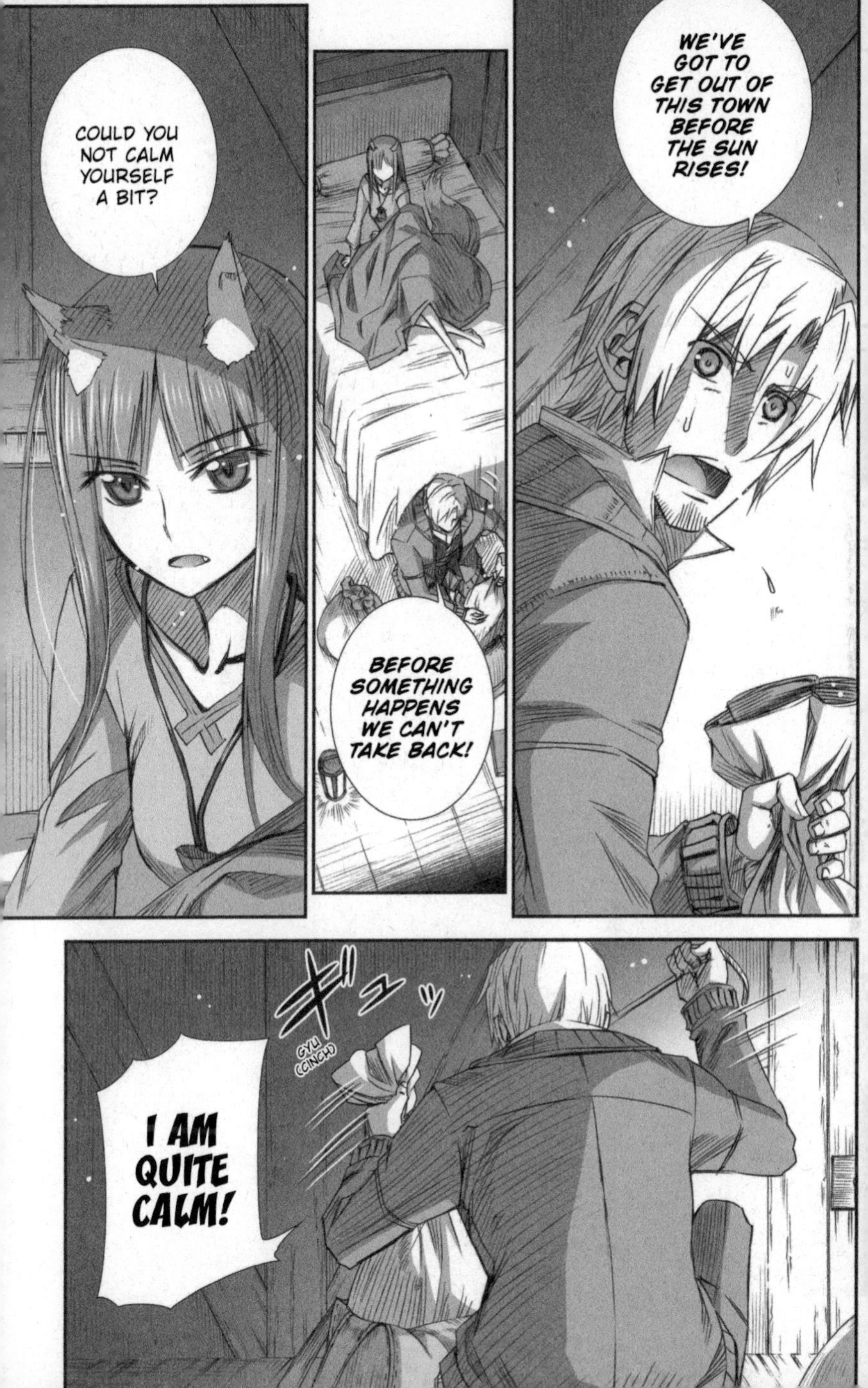
WE'VE GOT TO GET OUT OF THIS TOWN BEFORE THE SUN RISES!
BEFORE SOMETHING HAPPENS WE CAN'T TAKE BACK!
COULD YOU NOT CALM YOURSELF A BIT?
ギュッ
GYU (CINCH)
I AM QUITE CALM!

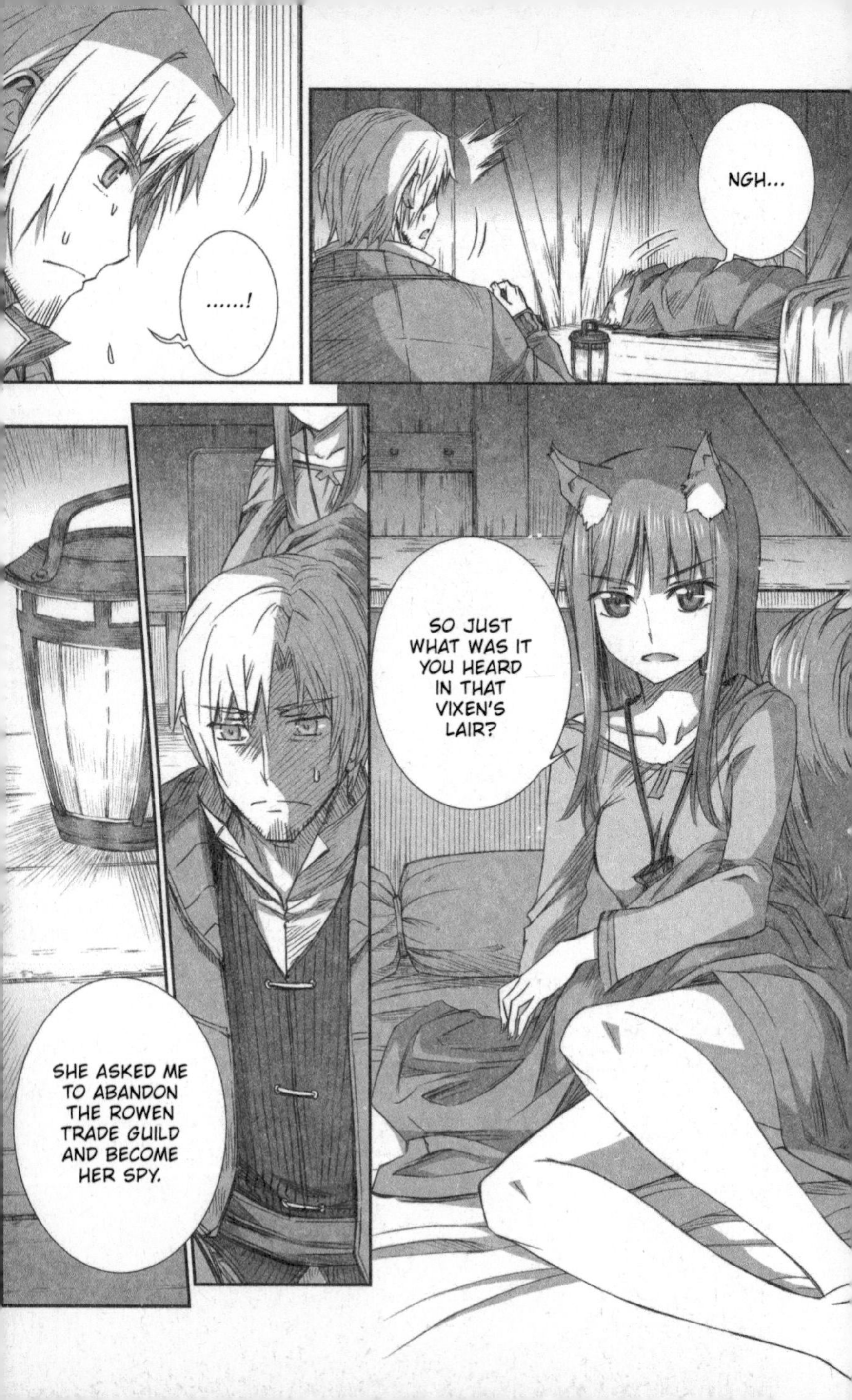
NGH...
......!
SO JUST WHAT WAS IT YOU HEARD IN THAT VIXEN'S LAIR?
SHE ASKED ME TO ABANDON THE ROWEN TRADE GUILD AND BECOME HER SPY.

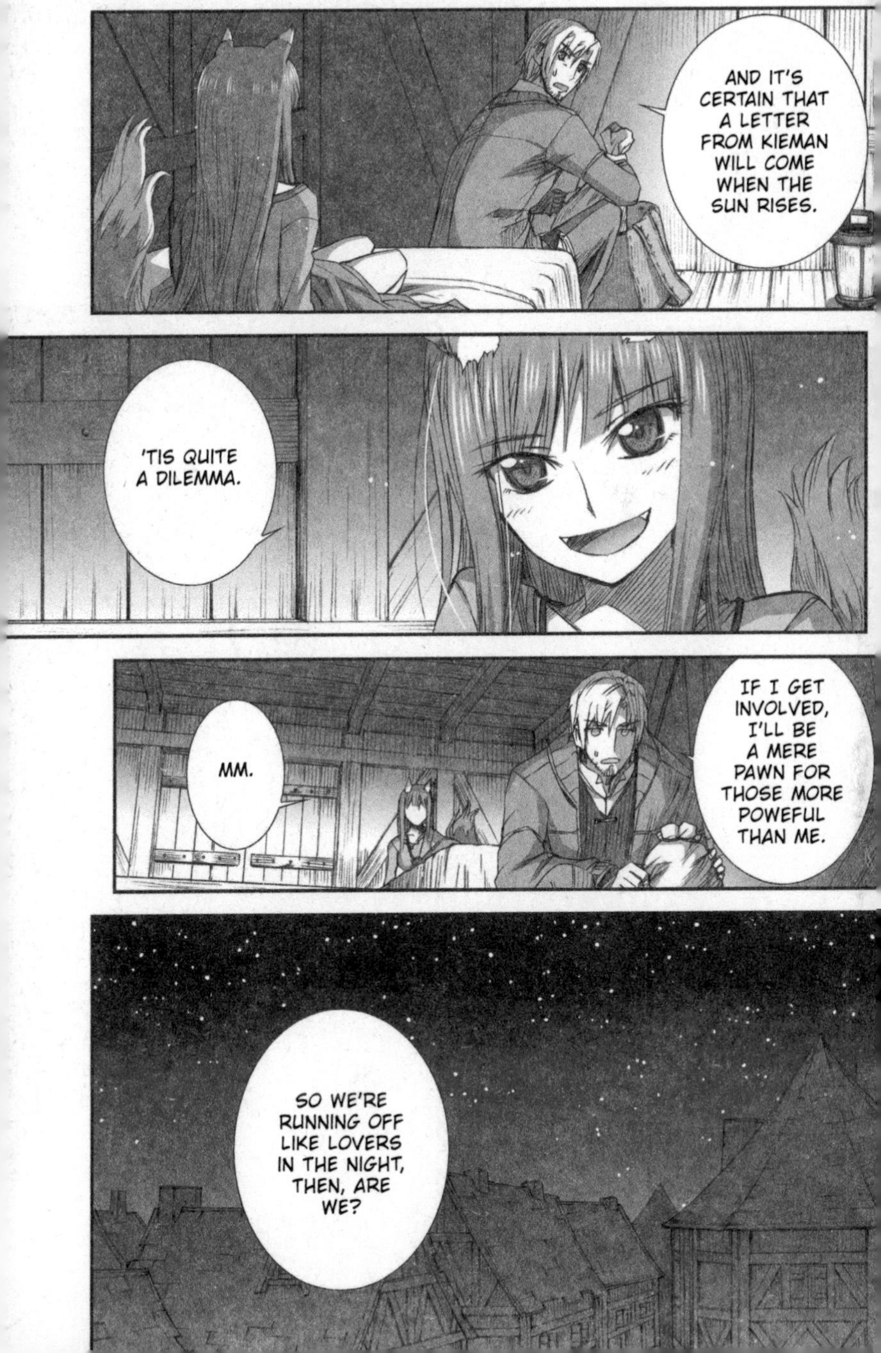
AND IT'S CERTAIN THAT A LETTER FROM KIEMAN WILL COME WHEN THE SUN RISES.
'TIS QUITE A DILEMMA.
IF I GET INVOLVED, I'LL BE A MERE PAWN FOR THOSE MORE POWEFUL THAN ME.
MM.
SO WE'RE RUNNING OFF LIKE LOVERS IN THE NIGHT, THEN, ARE WE?

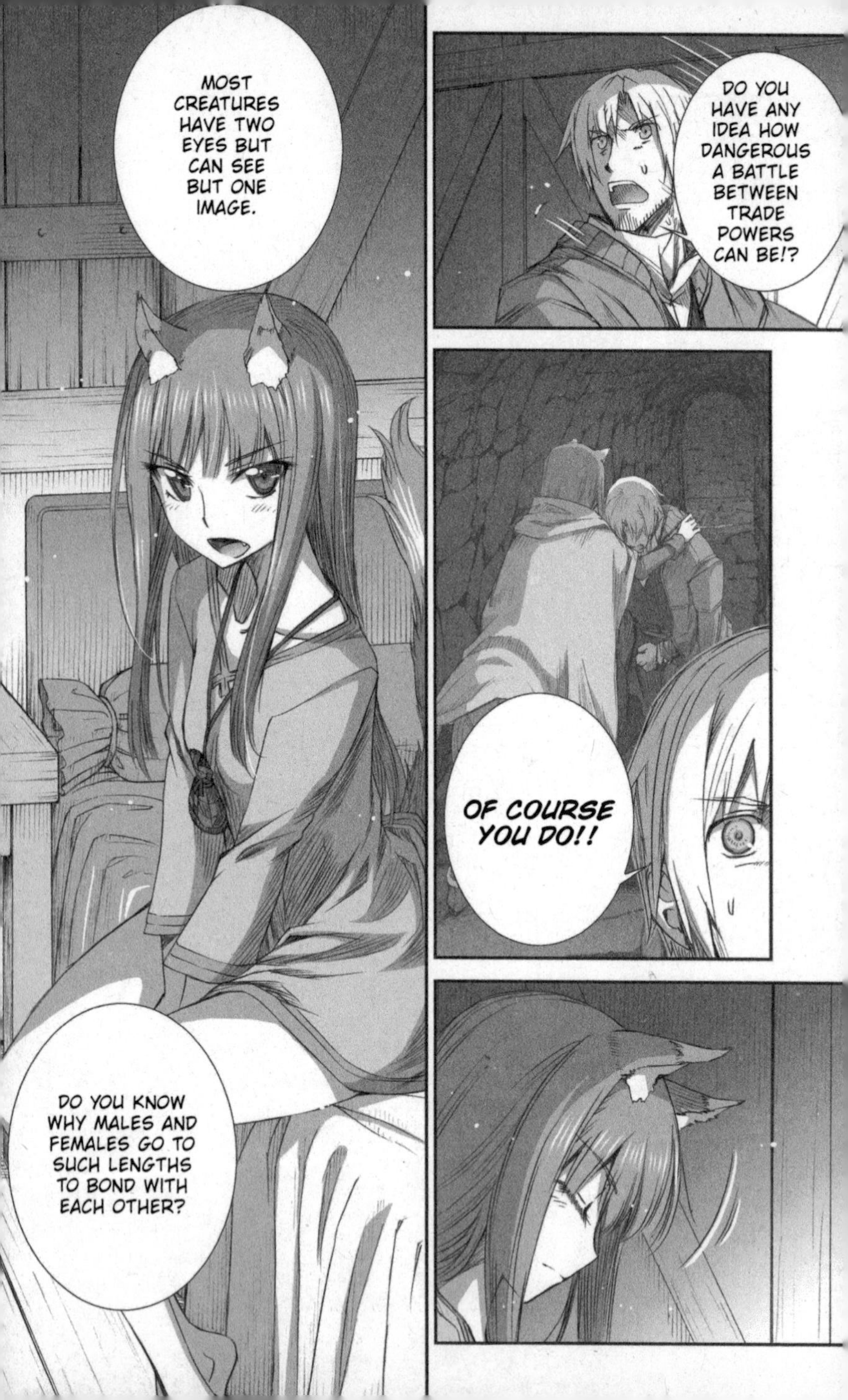
DO YOU HAVE ANY IDEA HOW DANGEROUS A BATTLE BETWEEN TRADE POWERS CAN BE!?
OF COURSE YOU DO!!
MOST CREATURES HAVE TWO EYES BUT CAN SEE BUT ONE IMAGE.
DO YOU KNOW WHY MALES AND FEMALES GO TO SUCH LENGTHS TO BOND WITH EACH OTHER?

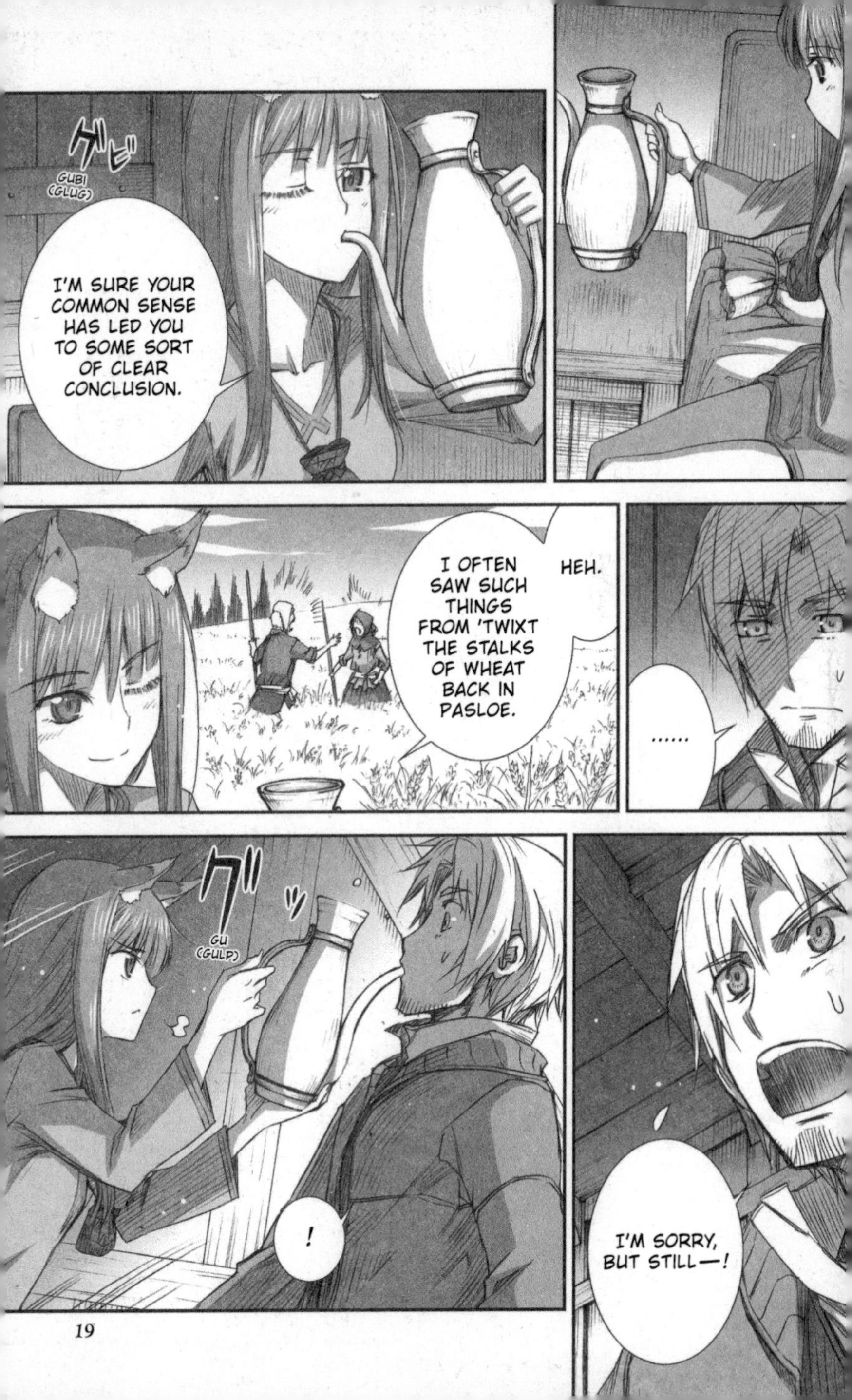

グビ
GUBI (GLUG)
I'M SURE YOUR COMMON SENSE HAS LED YOU TO SOME SORT OF CLEAR CONCLUSION.
......
HEH.
I OFTEN SAW SUCH THINGS FROM 'TWIXT THE STALKS OF WHEAT BACK IN PASLOE.
I'M SORRY, BUT STILL—!
グッ
GU (GULP)
!

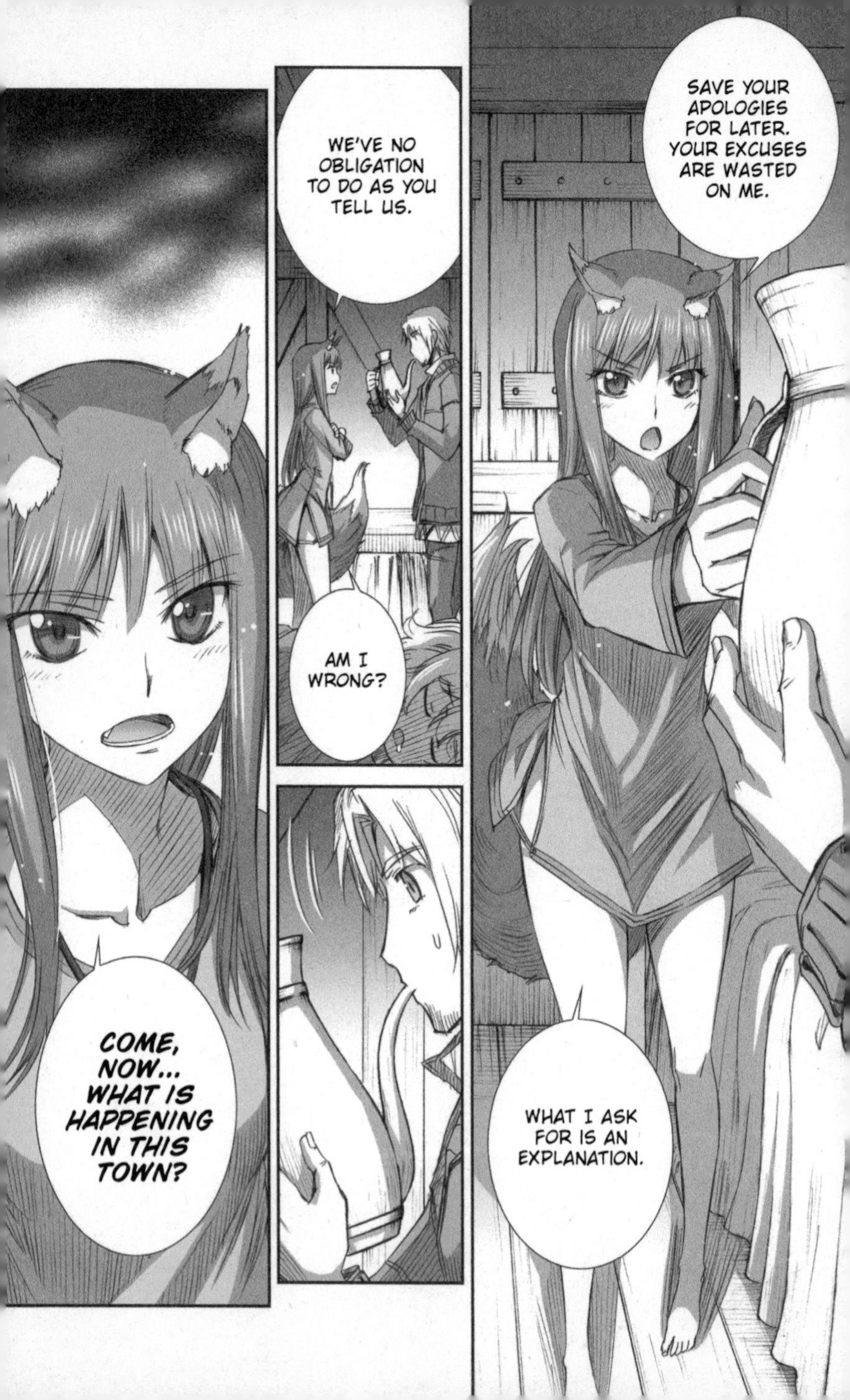
SAVE YOUR APOLOGIES FOR LATER. YOUR EXCUSES ARE WASTED ON ME.
WHAT I ASK FOR IS AN EXPLANATION.
WE'VE NO OBLIGATION TO DO AS YOU TELL US.
AM I WRONG?
COME, NOW... WHAT IS HAPPENING IN THIS TOWN?

SPICE & WOLF

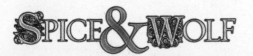

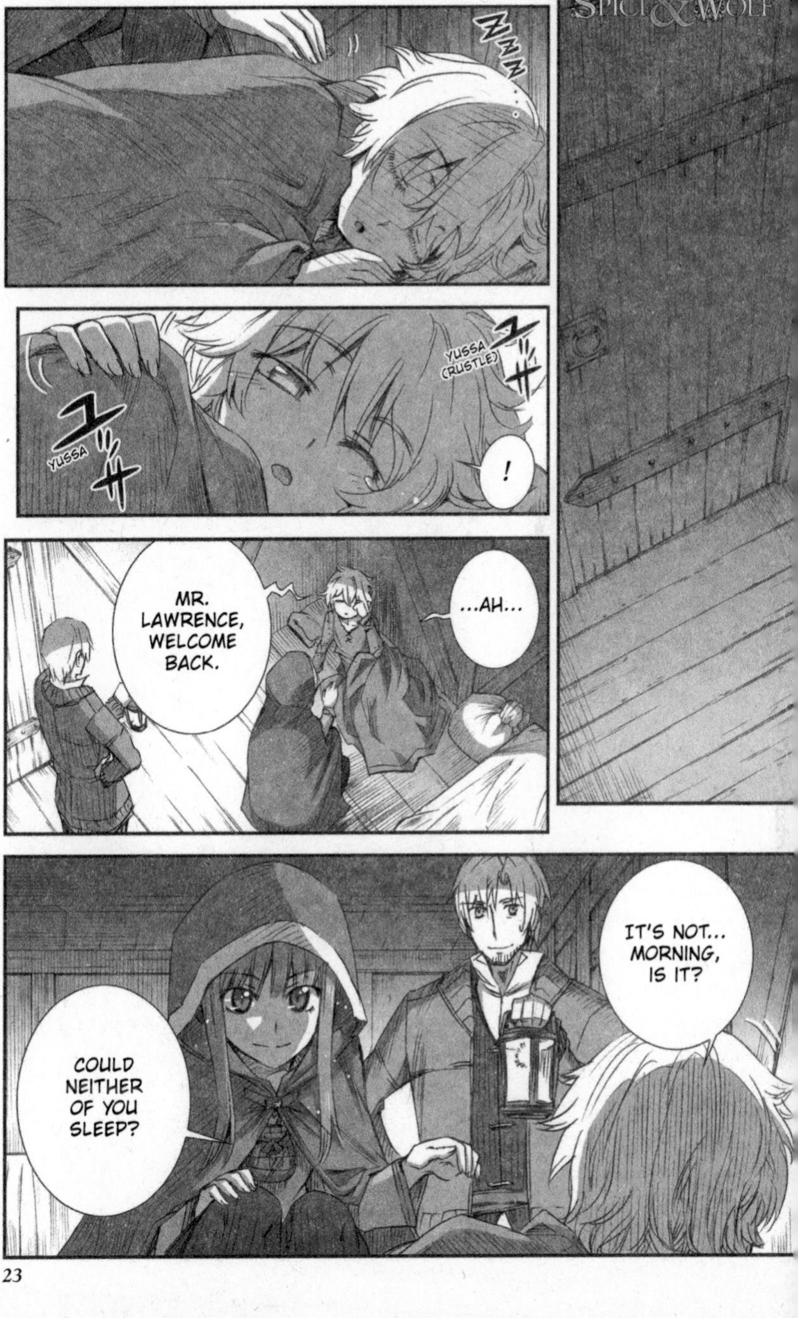
ZZZ
YUSSA (RUSTLE)
!
YUSSA
...AH...
MR. LAWRENCE, WELCOME BACK.
IT'S NOT... MORNING, IS IT?
COULD NEITHER OF YOU SLEEP?

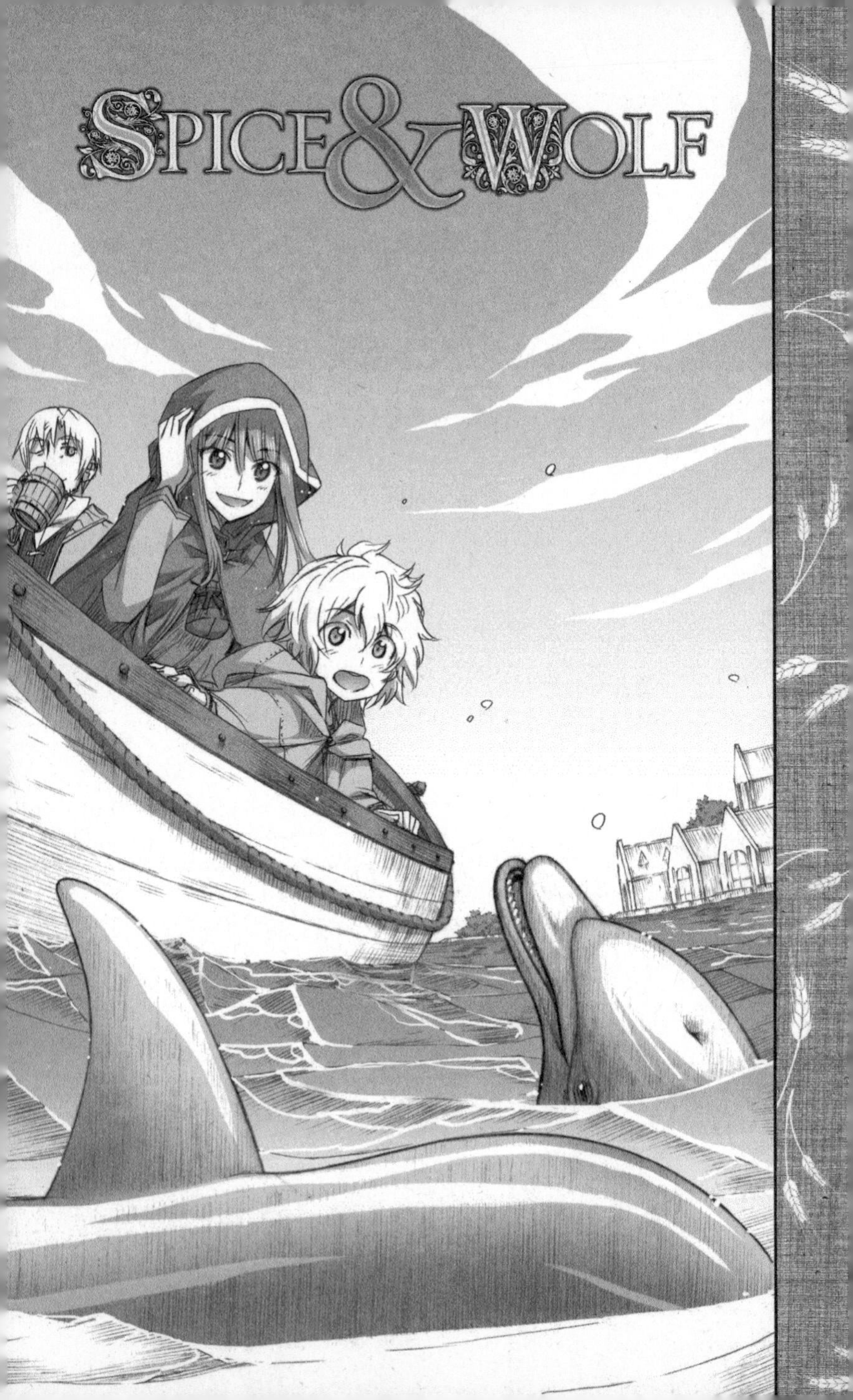
SPICE & WOLF

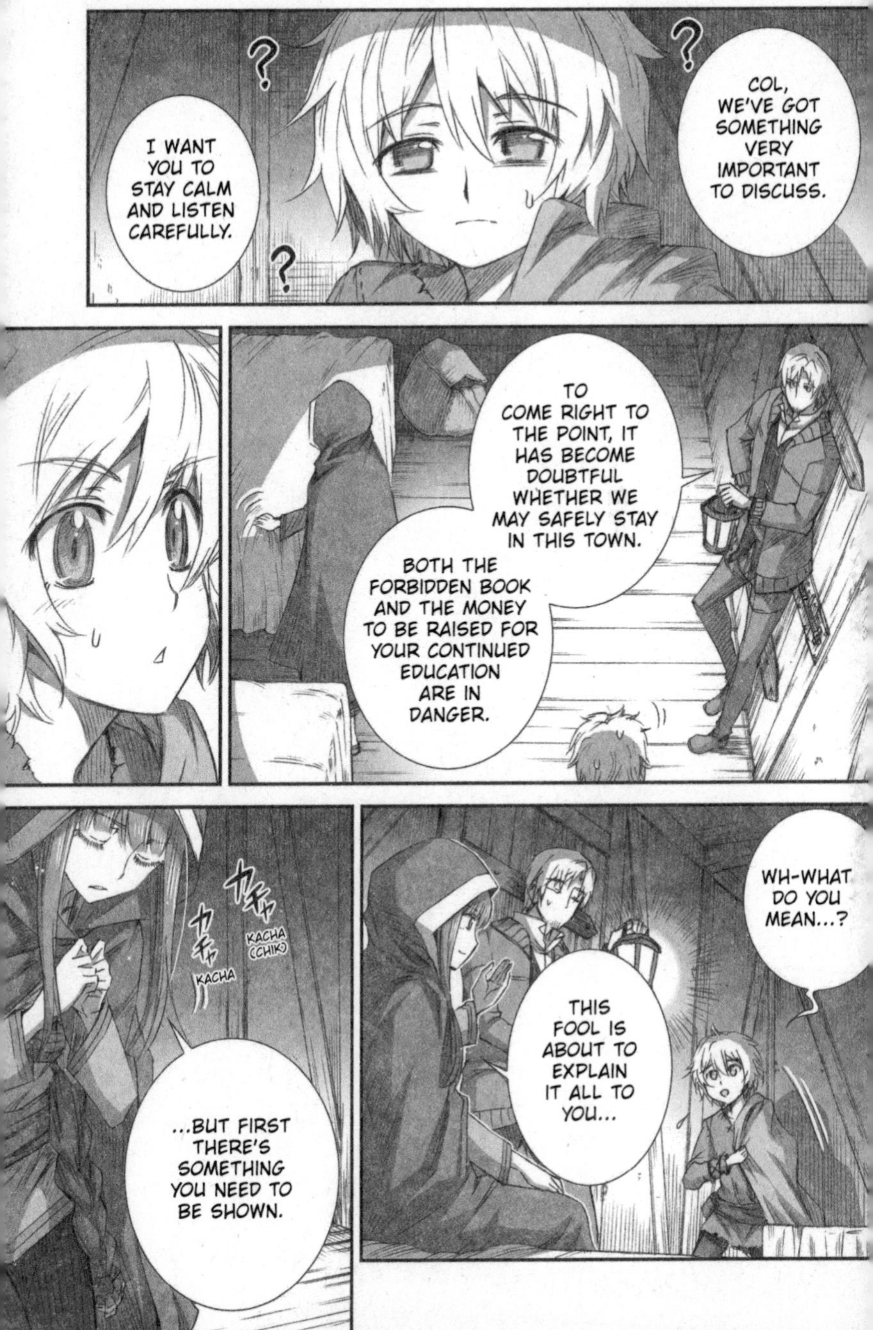
COL, WE'VE GOT SOMETHING VERY IMPORTANT TO DISCUSS.
I WANT YOU TO STAY CALM AND LISTEN CAREFULLY.
TO COME RIGHT TO THE POINT, IT HAS BECOME DOUBTFUL WHETHER WE MAY SAFELY STAY IN THIS TOWN.
BOTH THE FORBIDDEN BOOK AND THE MONEY TO BE RAISED FOR YOUR CONTINUED EDUCATION ARE IN DANGER.
WH-WHAT DO YOU MEAN...?
THIS FOOL IS ABOUT TO EXPLAIN IT ALL TO YOU...
KACHA (CHIK)
KACHA
...BUT FIRST THERE'S SOMETHING YOU NEED TO BE SHOWN.

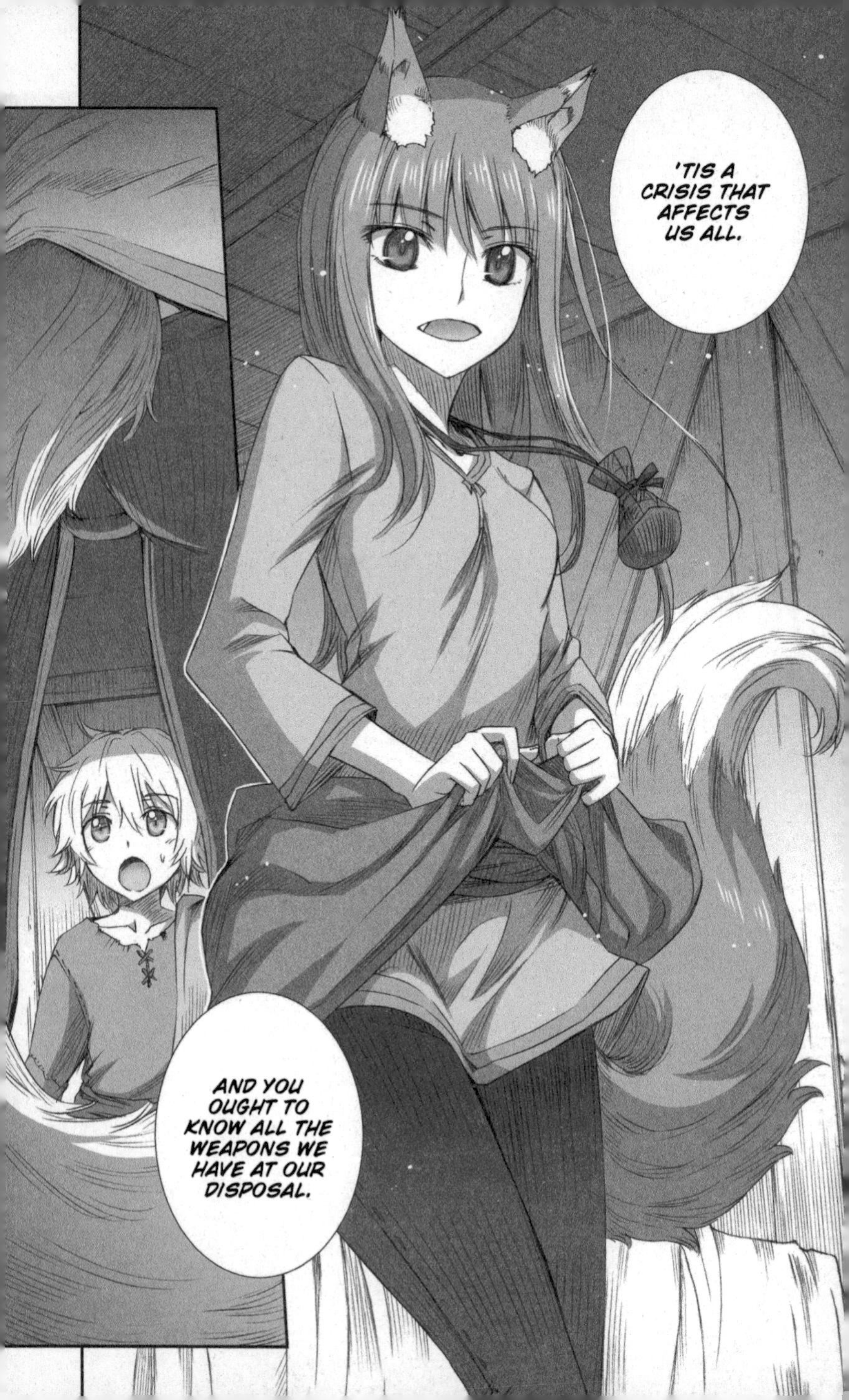
'TIS A CRISIS THAT AFFECTS US ALL.
AND YOU OUGHT TO KNOW ALL THE WEAPONS WE HAVE AT OUR DISPOSAL.

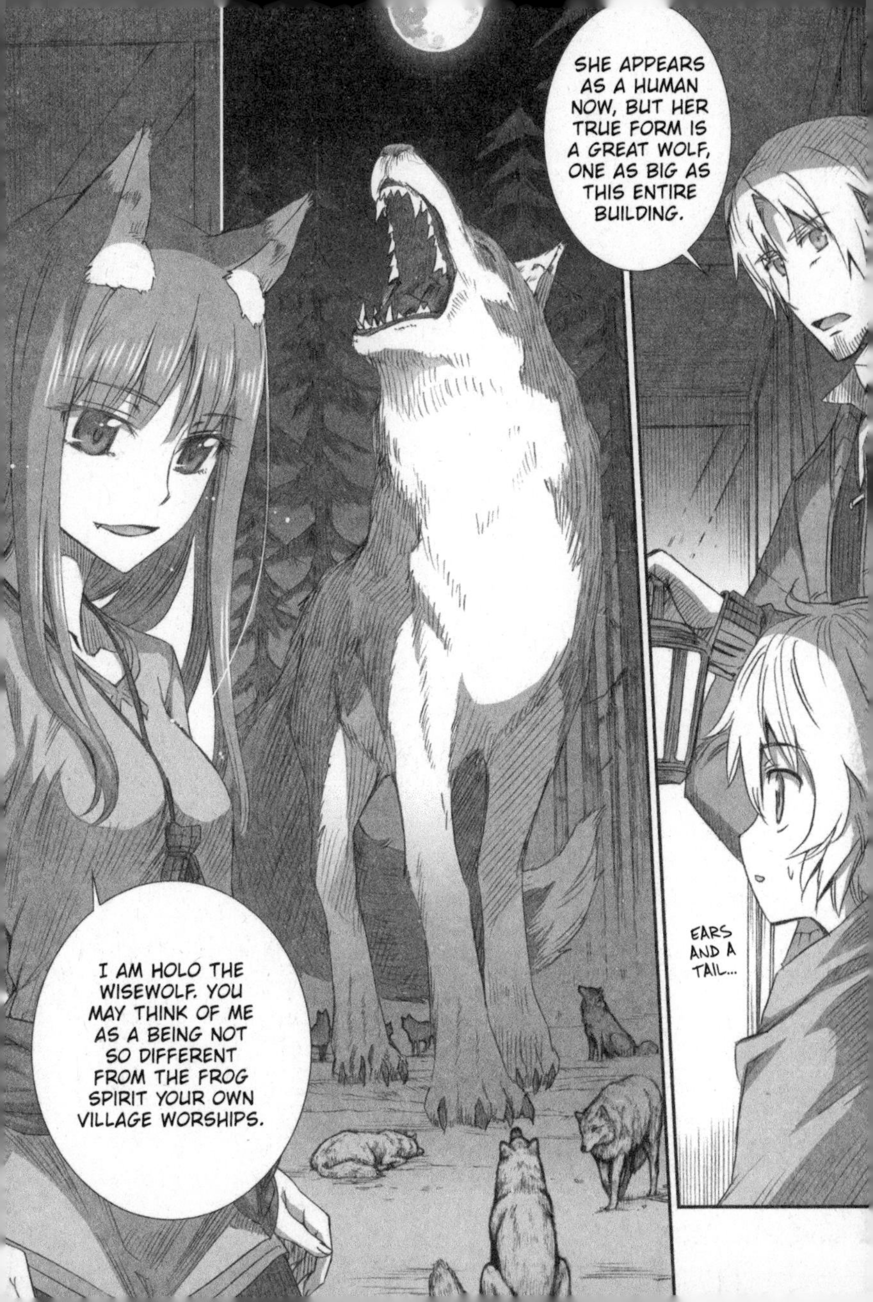
SHE APPEARS AS A HUMAN NOW, BUT HER TRUE FORM IS A GREAT WOLF, ONE AS BIG AS THIS ENTIRE BUILDING.
EARS AND A TAIL...
I AM HOLO THE WISEWOLF. YOU MAY THINK OF ME AS A BEING NOT SO DIFFERENT FROM THE FROG SPIRIT YOUR OWN VILLAGE WORSHIPS.

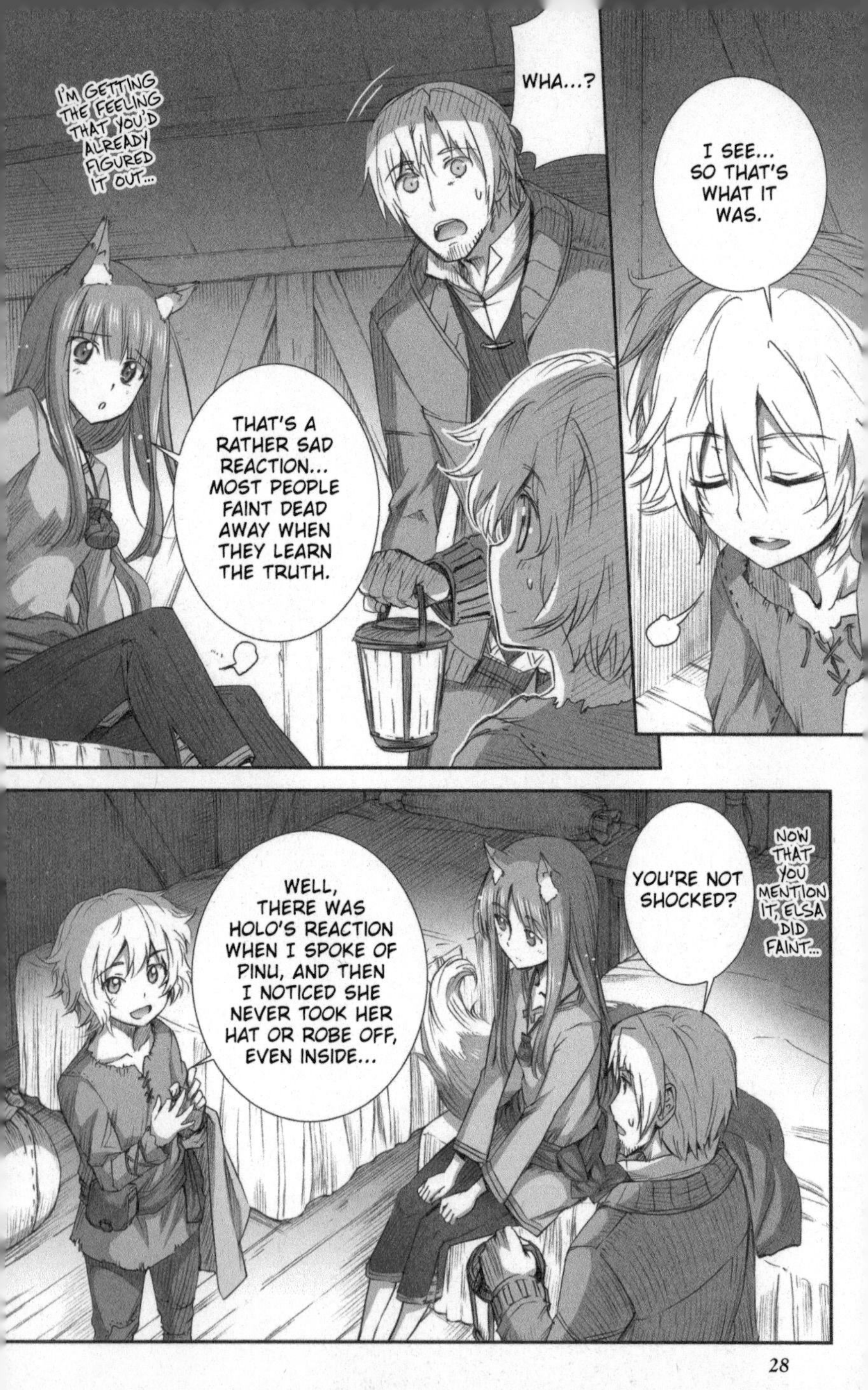
I SEE... SO THAT'S WHAT IT WAS.
WHA...?
I'M GETTING THE FEELING THAT YOU'D ALREADY FIGURED IT OUT...
THAT'S A RATHER SAD REACTION... MOST PEOPLE FAINT DEAD AWAY WHEN THEY LEARN THE TRUTH.
NOW THAT YOU MENTION IT, ELSA DID FAINT...
YOU'RE NOT SHOCKED?
WELL, THERE WAS HOLO'S REACTION WHEN I SPOKE OF PINU, AND THEN I NOTICED SHE NEVER TOOK HER HAT OR ROBE OFF, EVEN INSIDE...

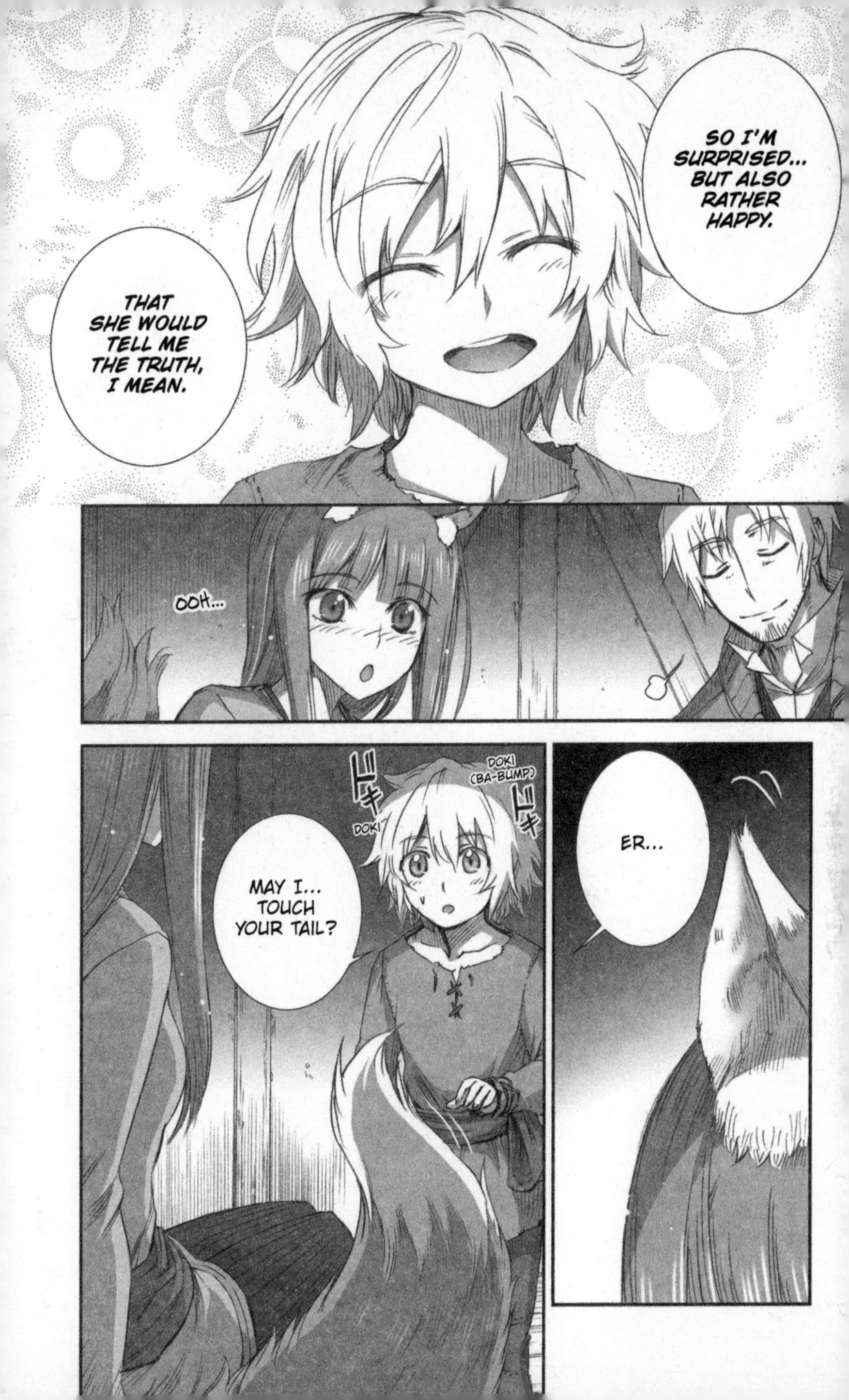
SO I'M SURPRISED... BUT ALSO RATHER HAPPY.
THAT SHE WOULD TELL ME THE TRUTH, I MEAN.
OOH...
ER...
ドキ
DOKI (BA-BUMP)
ドキ
DOKI
MAY I... TOUCH YOUR TAIL?

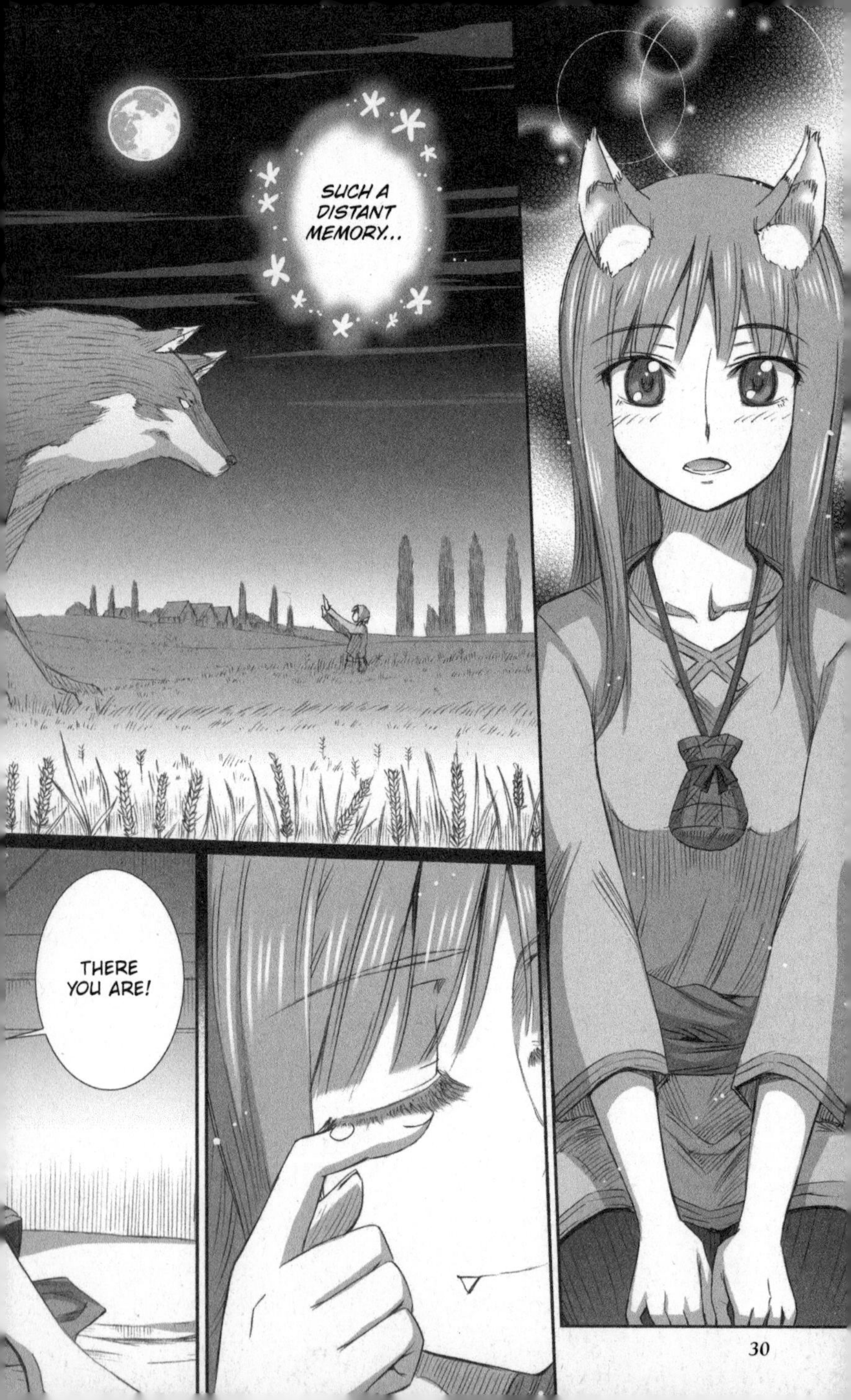
SUCH A DISTANT MEMORY...
THERE YOU ARE!

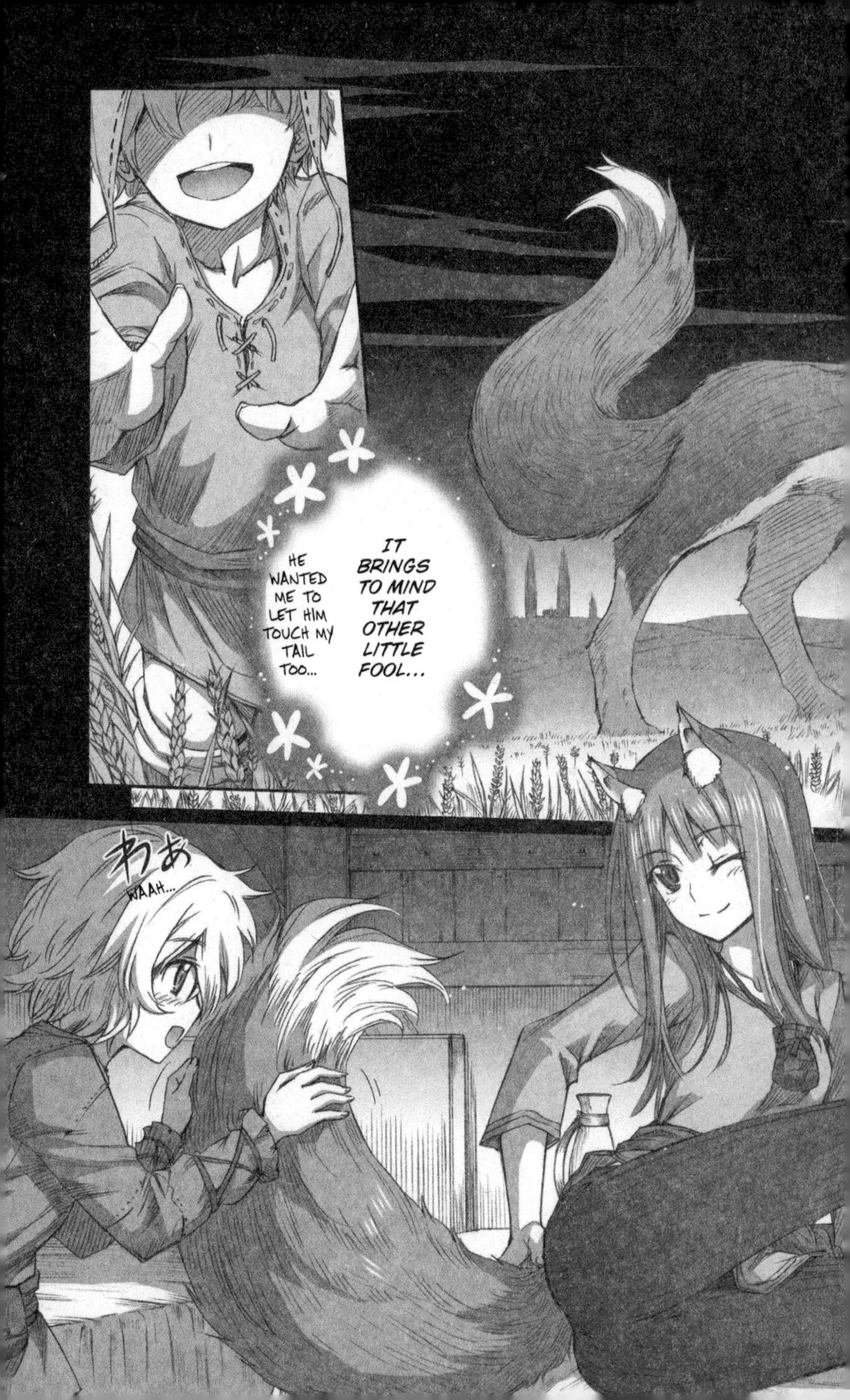
IT BRINGS TO MIND THAT OTHER LITTLE FOOL...
HE WANTED ME TO LET HIM TOUCH MY TAIL TOO...
わあ
WAAH...

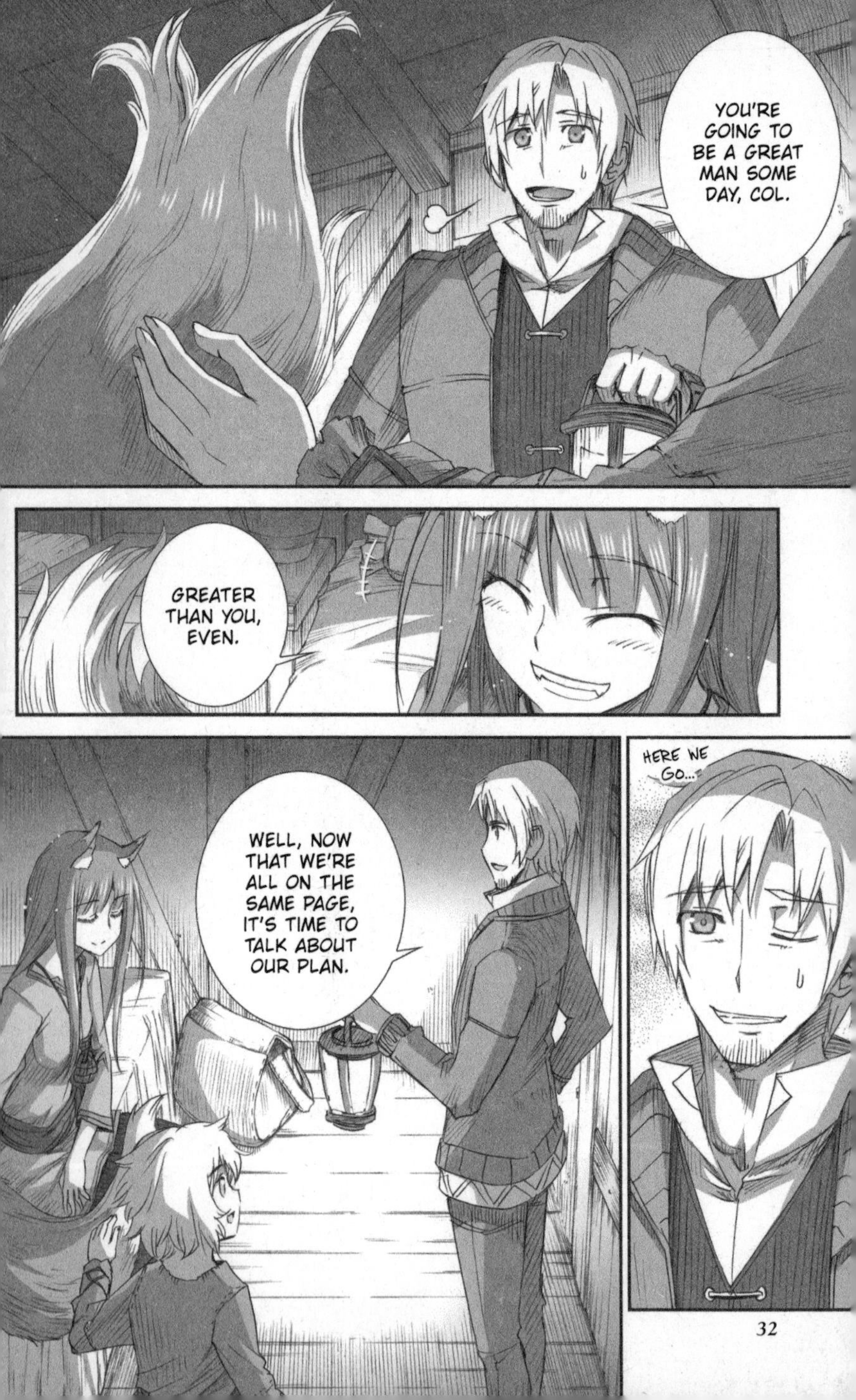
YOU'RE GOING TO BE A GREAT MAN SOME DAY, COL.
GREATER THAN YOU, EVEN.
HERE WE GO...
WELL, NOW THAT WE'RE ALL ON THE SAME PAGE, IT'S TIME TO TALK ABOUT OUR PLAN.

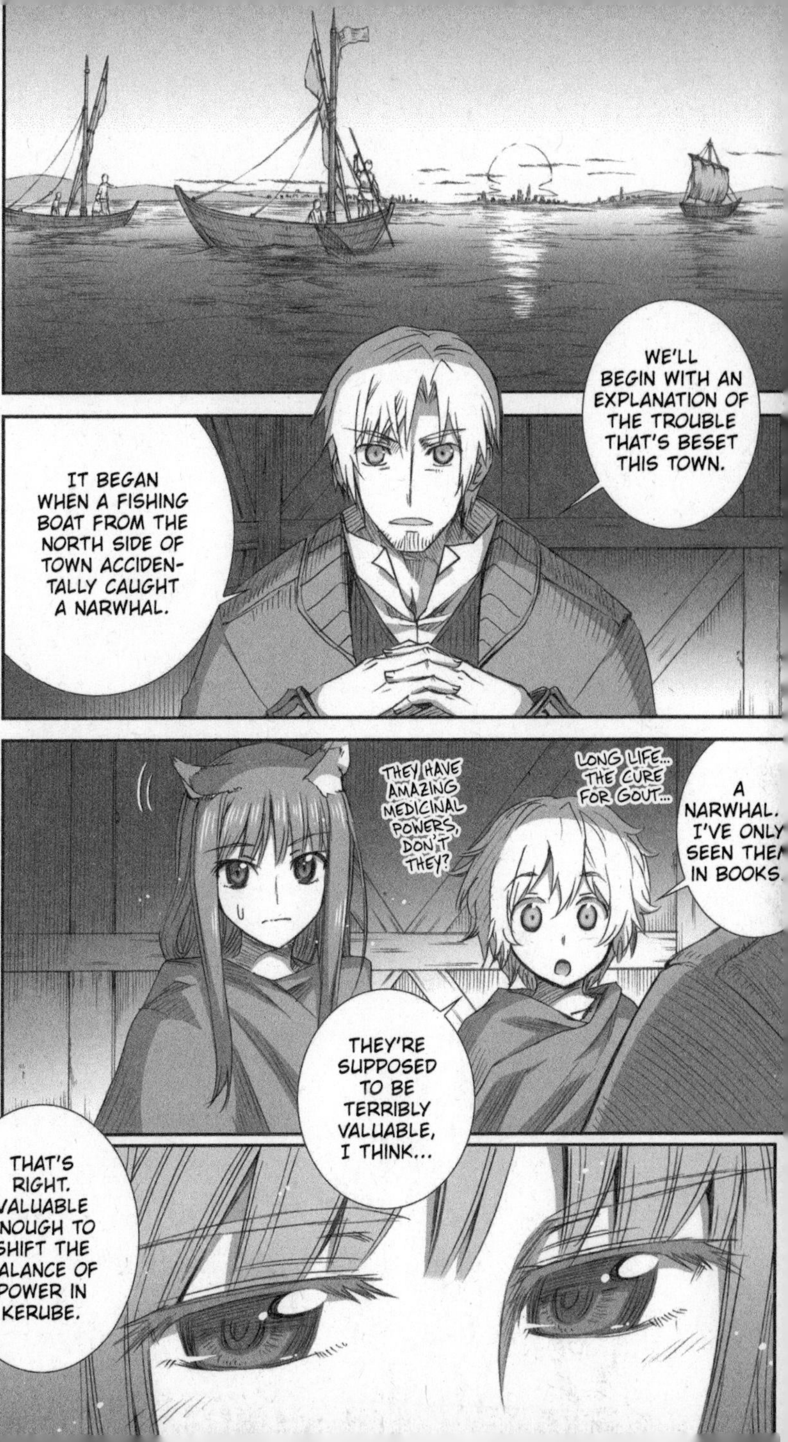
WE'LL BEGIN WITH AN EXPLANATION OF THE TROUBLE THAT'S BESET THIS TOWN.
IT BEGAN WHEN A FISHING BOAT FROM THE NORTH SIDE OF TOWN ACCIDEN-TALLY CAUGHT A NARWHAL.
A NARWHAL. I'VE ONLY SEEN THEM IN BOOKS.
LONG LIFE... THE CURE FOR GOUT...
THEY HAVE AMAZING MEDICINAL POWERS, DON'T THEY?
THEY'RE SUPPOSED TO BE TERRIBLY VALUABLE, I THINK...
THAT'S RIGHT. VALUABLE ENOUGH TO SHIFT THE BALANCE OF POWER IN KERUBE.

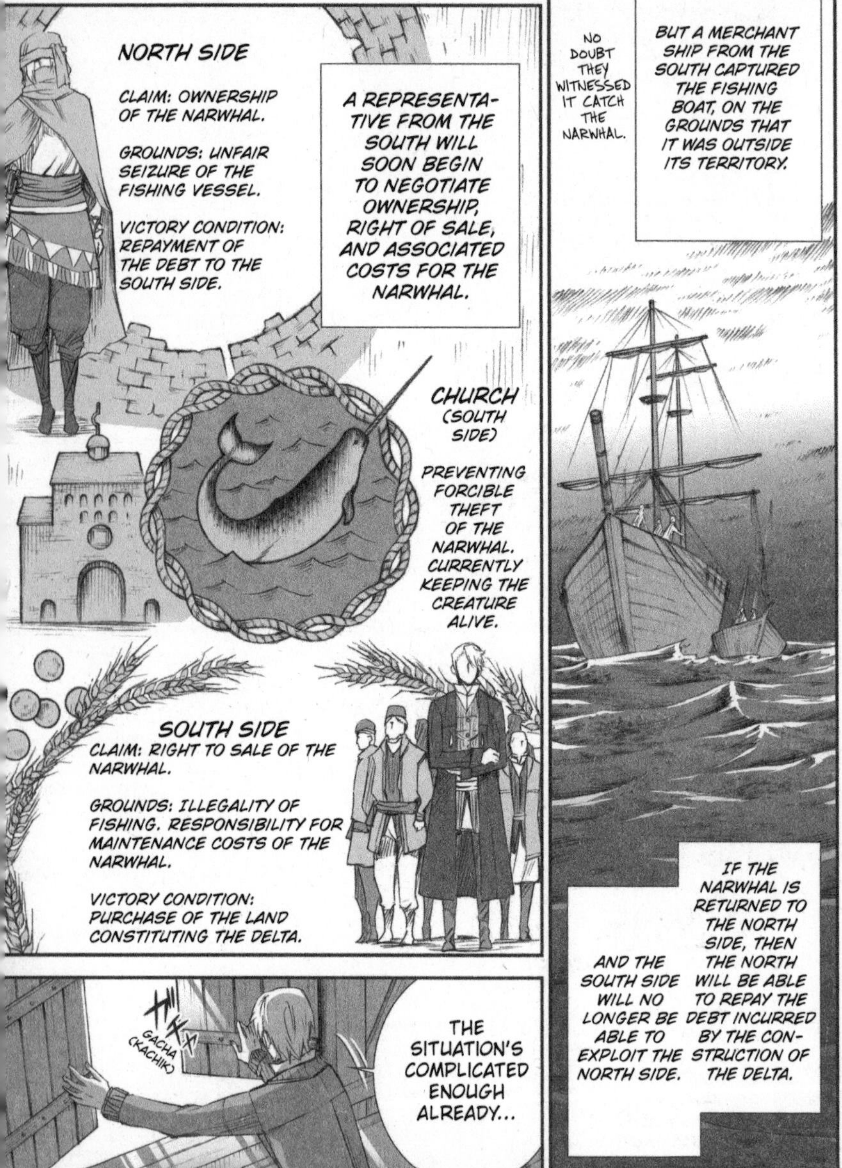

BUT A MERCHANT SHIP FROM THE SOUTH CAPTURED THE FISHING BOAT, ON THE GROUNDS THAT IT WAS OUTSIDE ITS TERRITORY.
NO DOUBT THEY WITNESSED IT CATCH THE NARWHAL.
IF THE NARWHAL IS RETURNED TO THE NORTH SIDE, THEN THE NORTH WILL BE ABLE TO REPAY THE DEBT INCURRED BY THE CONSTRUCTION OF THE DELTA.
AND THE SOUTH SIDE WILL NO LONGER BE ABLE TO EXPLOIT THE NORTH SIDE.
A REPRESENTATIVE FROM THE SOUTH WILL SOON BEGIN TO NEGOTIATE OWNERSHIP, RIGHT OF SALE, AND ASSOCIATED COSTS FOR THE NARWHAL.
NORTH SIDE
CLAIM: OWNERSHIP OF THE NARWHAL.
GROUNDS: UNFAIR SEIZURE OF THE FISHING VESSEL.
VICTORY CONDITION: REPAYMENT OF THE DEBT TO THE SOUTH SIDE.
CHURCH (SOUTH SIDE)
PREVENTING FORCIBLE THEFT OF THE NARWHAL. CURRENTLY KEEPING THE CREATURE ALIVE.
SOUTH SIDE
CLAIM: RIGHT TO SALE OF THE NARWHAL.
GROUNDS: ILLEGALITY OF FISHING. RESPONSIBILITY FOR MAINTENANCE COSTS OF THE NARWHAL.
VICTORY CONDITION: PURCHASE OF THE LAND CONSTITUTING THE DELTA.
THE SITUATION'S COMPLICATED ENOUGH ALREADY...
GACHA (KACHIK)

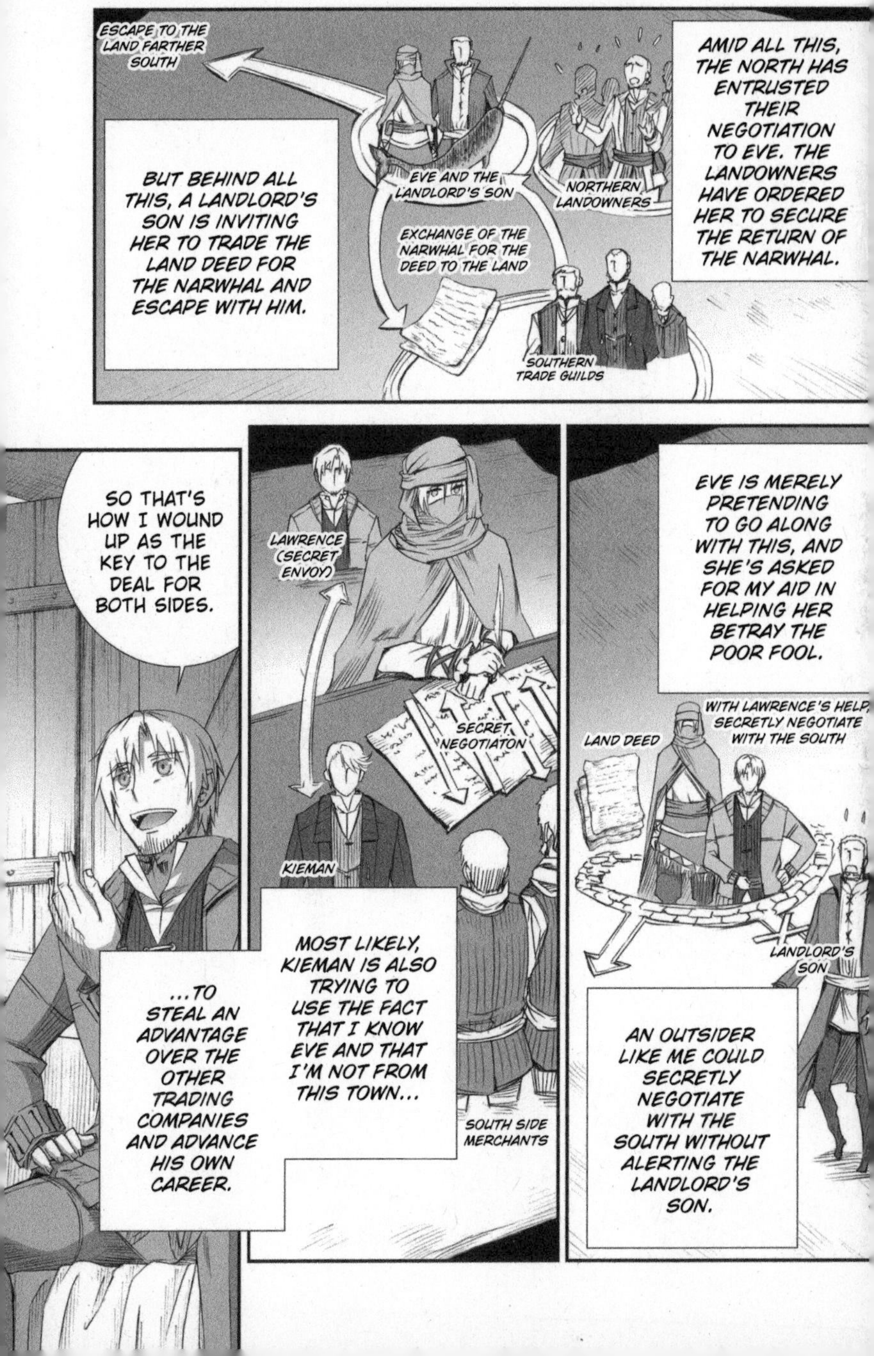
AMID ALL THIS, THE NORTH HAS ENTRUSTED THEIR NEGOTIATION TO EVE. THE LANDOWNERS HAVE ORDERED HER TO SECURE THE RETURN OF THE NARWHAL.
NORTHERN LANDOWNERS
EVE AND THE LANDLORD'S SON
ESCAPE TO THE LAND FARTHER SOUTH
EXCHANGE OF THE NARWHAL FOR THE DEED TO THE LAND
SOUTHERN TRADE GUILDS
BUT BEHIND ALL THIS, A LANDLORD'S SON IS INVITING HER TO TRADE THE LAND DEED FOR THE NARWHAL AND ESCAPE WITH HIM.
EVE IS MERELY PRETENDING TO GO ALONG WITH THIS, AND SHE'S ASKED FOR MY AID IN HELPING HER BETRAY THE POOR FOOL.
WITH LAWRENCE'S HELP, SECRETLY NEGOTIATE WITH THE SOUTH
LAND DEED
LANDLORD'S SON
AN OUTSIDER LIKE ME COULD SECRETLY NEGOTIATE WITH THE SOUTH WITHOUT ALERTING THE LANDLORD'S SON.
LAWRENCE (SECRET ENVOY)
SECRET NEGOTIATON
KIEMAN
MOST LIKELY, KIEMAN IS ALSO TRYING TO USE THE FACT THAT I KNOW EVE AND THAT I'M NOT FROM THIS TOWN...
SOUTH SIDE MERCHANTS
SO THAT'S HOW I WOUND UP AS THE KEY TO THE DEAL FOR BOTH SIDES.
...TO STEAL AN ADVANTAGE OVER THE OTHER TRADING COMPANIES AND ADVANCE HIS OWN CAREER.

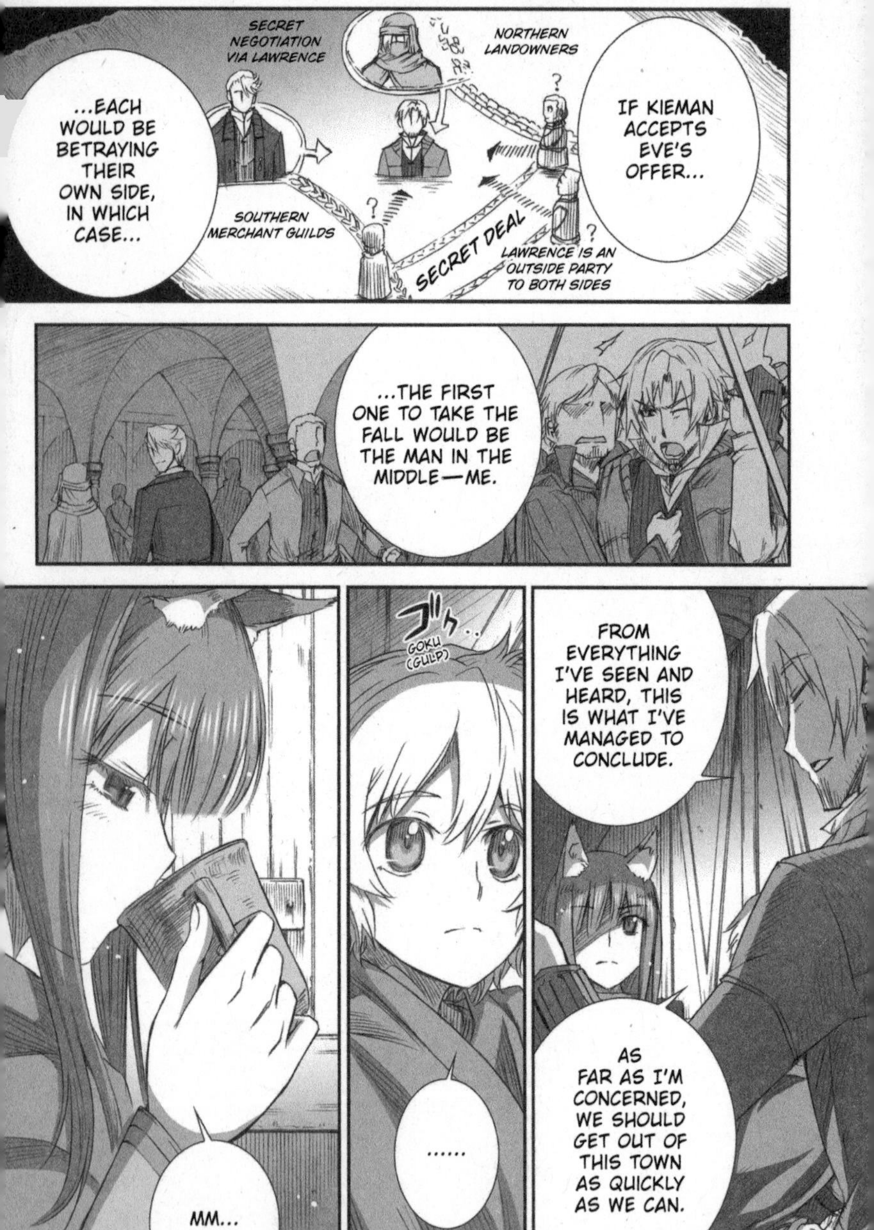
IF KIEMAN ACCEPTS EVE'S OFFER...
NORTHERN LANDOWNERS
SECRET NEGOTIATION VIA LAWRENCE
LAWRENCE IS AN OUTSIDE PARTY TO BOTH SIDES
SECRET DEAL
SOUTHERN MERCHANT GUILDS
...EACH WOULD BE BETRAYING THEIR OWN SIDE, IN WHICH CASE...
...THE FIRST ONE TO TAKE THE FALL WOULD BE THE MAN IN THE MIDDLE—ME.
FROM EVERYTHING I'VE SEEN AND HEARD, THIS IS WHAT I'VE MANAGED TO CONCLUDE.
AS FAR AS I'M CONCERNED, WE SHOULD GET OUT OF THIS TOWN AS QUICKLY AS WE CAN.
GOKU (GULP)
......
MM...

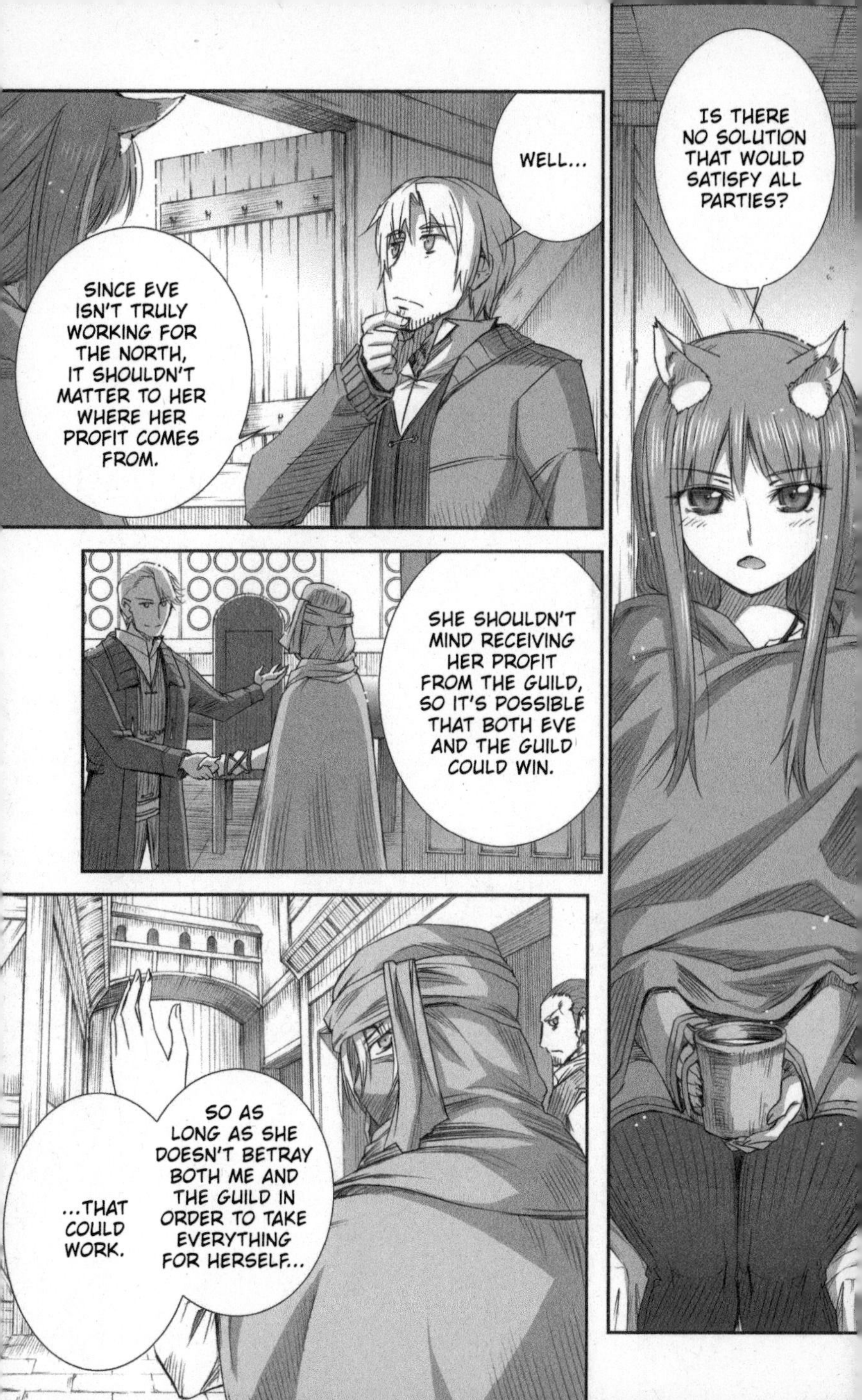
IS THERE NO SOLUTION THAT WOULD SATISFY ALL PARTIES?
WELL...
SINCE EVE ISN'T TRULY WORKING FOR THE NORTH, IT SHOULDN'T MATTER TO HER WHERE HER PROFIT COMES FROM.
SHE SHOULDN'T MIND RECEIVING HER PROFIT FROM THE GUILD, SO IT'S POSSIBLE THAT BOTH EVE AND THE GUILD COULD WIN.
SO AS LONG AS SHE DOESN'T BETRAY BOTH ME AND THE GUILD IN ORDER TO TAKE EVERYTHING FOR HERSELF...
...THAT COULD WORK.

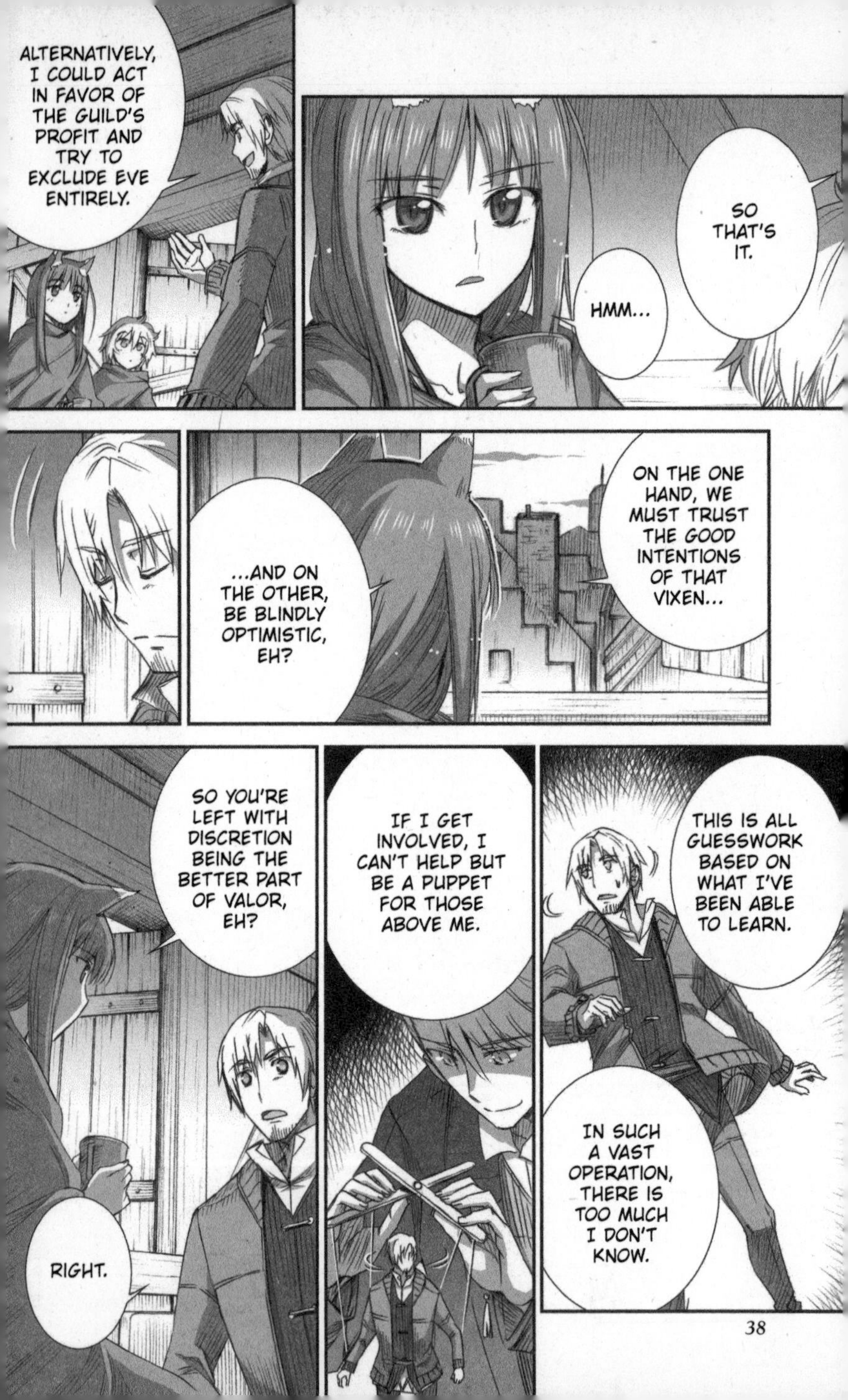
SO THAT'S IT.
HMM...
ALTERNATIVELY, I COULD ACT IN FAVOR OF THE GUILD'S PROFIT AND TRY TO EXCLUDE EVE ENTIRELY.
ON THE ONE HAND, WE MUST TRUST THE GOOD INTENTIONS OF THAT VIXEN...
...AND ON THE OTHER, BE BLINDLY OPTIMISTIC, EH?
THIS IS ALL GUESSWORK BASED ON WHAT I'VE BEEN ABLE TO LEARN.
IN SUCH A VAST OPERATION, THERE IS TOO MUCH I DON'T KNOW.
IF I GET INVOLVED, I CAN'T HELP BUT BE A PUPPET FOR THOSE ABOVE ME.
SO YOU'RE LEFT WITH DISCRETION BEING THE BETTER PART OF VALOR, EH?
RIGHT.

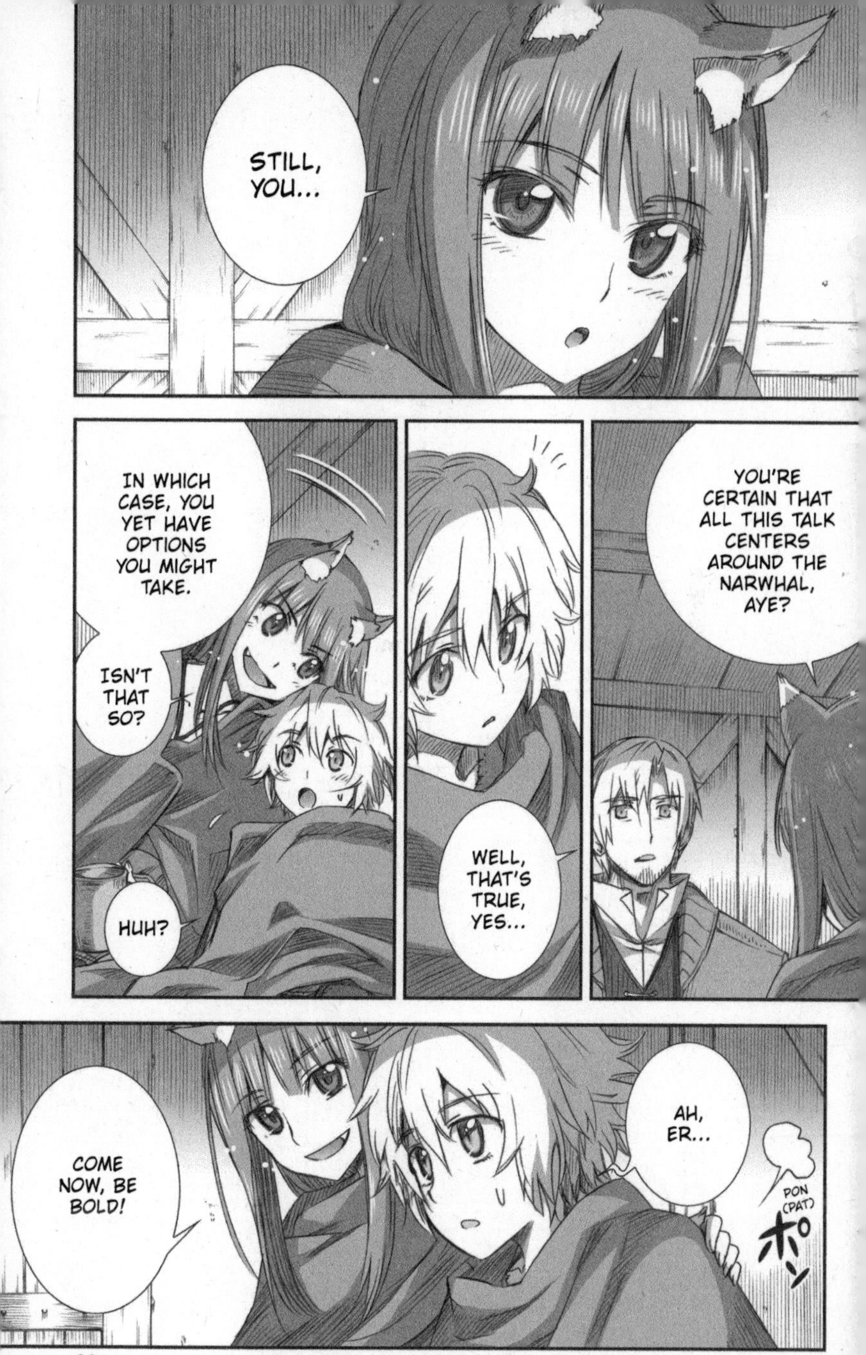
STILL, YOU...
YOU'RE CERTAIN THAT ALL THIS TALK CENTERS AROUND THE NARWHAL, AYE?
WELL, THAT'S TRUE, YES...
IN WHICH CASE, YOU YET HAVE OPTIONS YOU MIGHT TAKE.
ISN'T THAT SO?
HUH?
PON (PAT)
AH, ER...
COME NOW, BE BOLD!

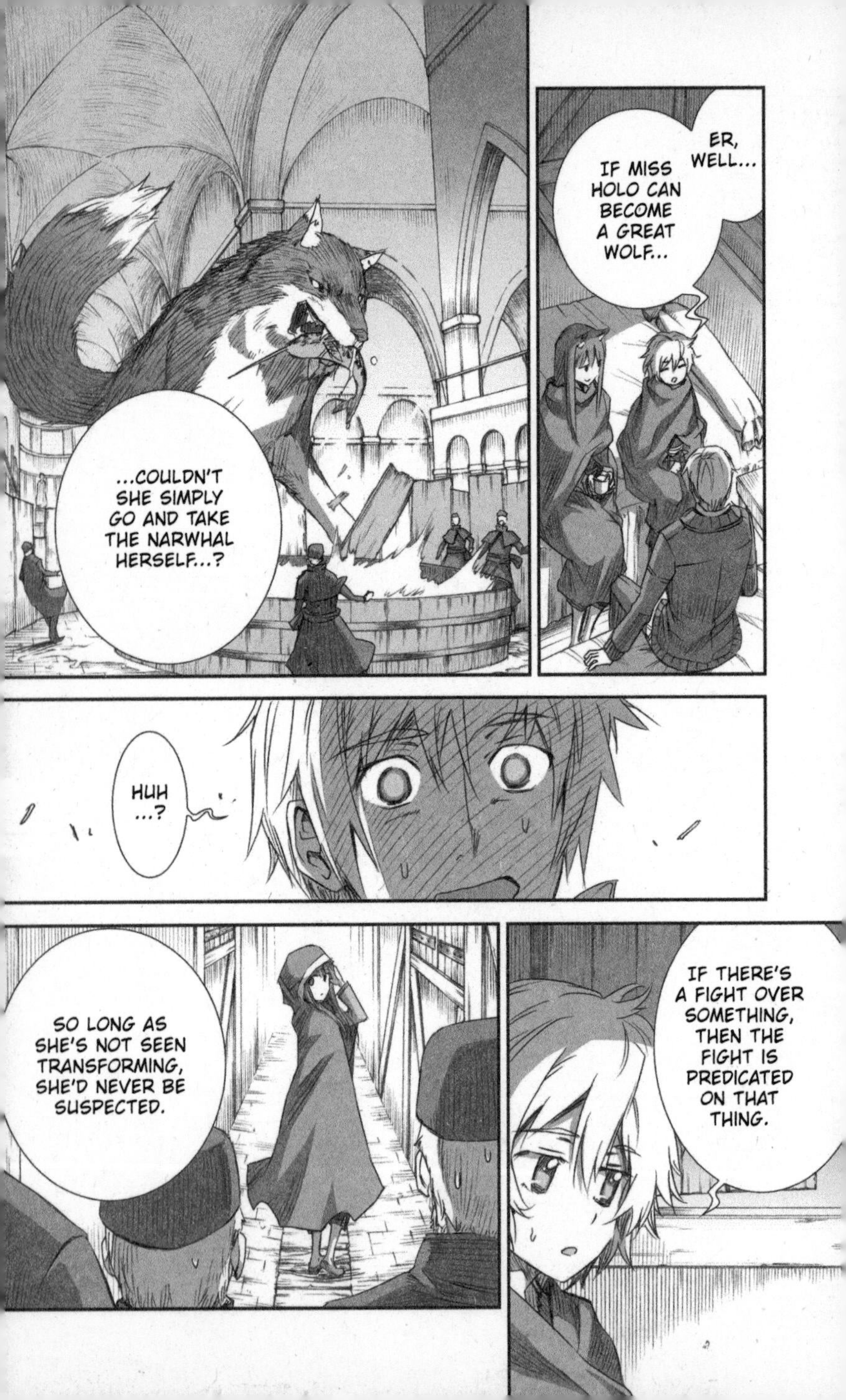
ER, WELL...
IF MISS HOLO CAN BECOME A GREAT WOLF...
...COULDN'T SHE SIMPLY GO AND TAKE THE NARWHAL HERSELF...?
HUH ...?
IF THERE'S A FIGHT OVER SOMETHING, THEN THE FIGHT IS PREDICATED ON THAT THING.
SO LONG AS SHE'S NOT SEEN TRANSFORMING, SHE'D NEVER BE SUSPECTED.

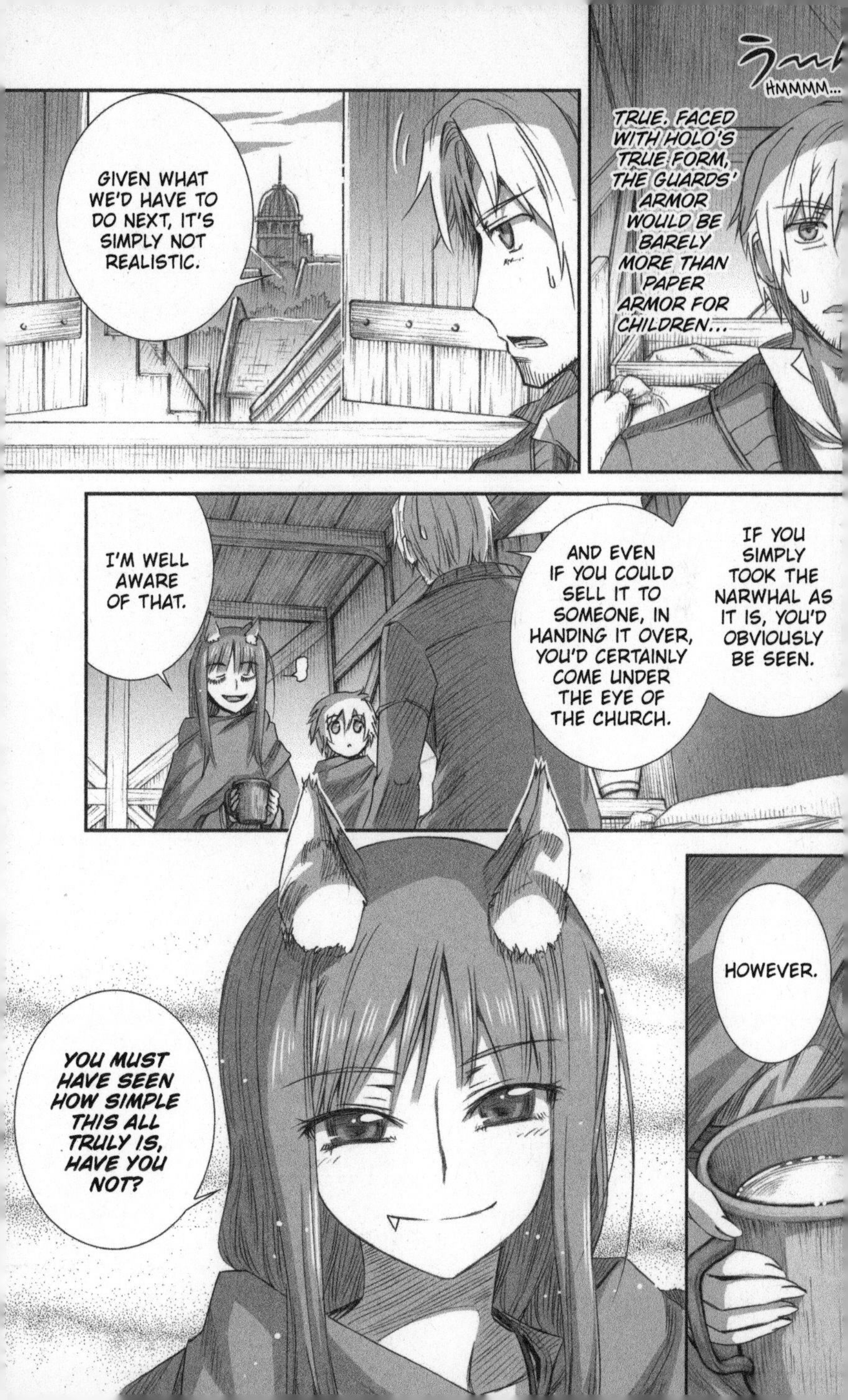
HMMMM...
TRUE. FACED WITH HOLO'S TRUE FORM, THE GUARDS' ARMOR WOULD BE BARELY MORE THAN PAPER ARMOR FOR CHILDREN...
GIVEN WHAT WE'D HAVE TO DO NEXT, IT'S SIMPLY NOT REALISTIC.
IF YOU SIMPLY TOOK THE NARWHAL AS IT IS, YOU'D OBVIOUSLY BE SEEN.
AND EVEN IF YOU COULD SELL IT TO SOMEONE, IN HANDING IT OVER, YOU'D CERTAINLY COME UNDER THE EYE OF THE CHURCH.
I'M WELL AWARE OF THAT.
HOWEVER.
YOU MUST HAVE SEEN HOW SIMPLE THIS ALL TRULY IS, HAVE YOU NOT?

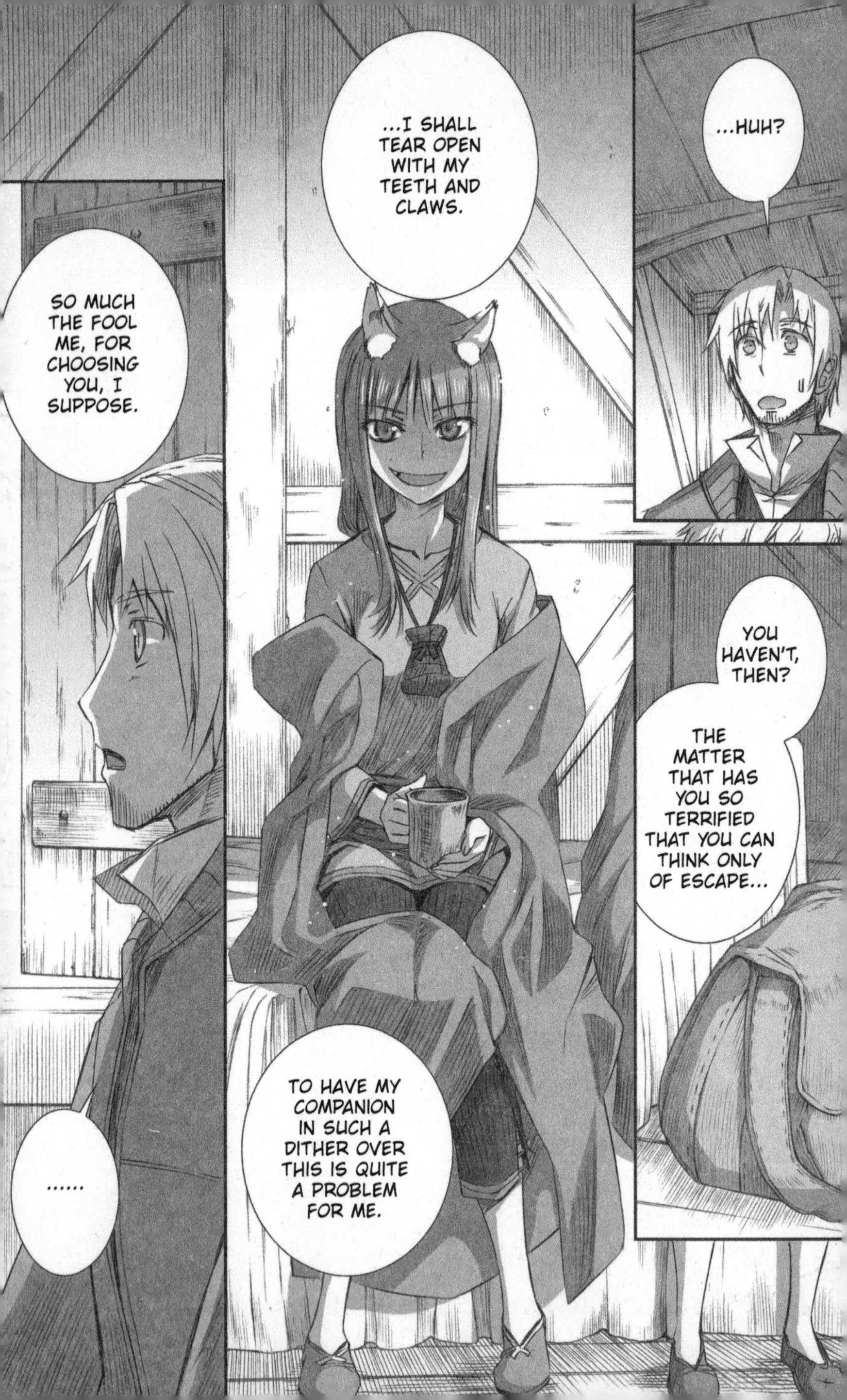
...HUH?
YOU HAVEN'T, THEN?
THE MATTER THAT HAS YOU SO TERRIFIED THAT YOU CAN THINK ONLY OF ESCAPE...
...I SHALL TEAR OPEN WITH MY TEETH AND CLAWS.
TO HAVE MY COMPANION IN SUCH A DITHER OVER THIS IS QUITE A PROBLEM FOR ME.
SO MUCH THE FOOL ME, FOR CHOOSING YOU, I SUPPOSE.
......

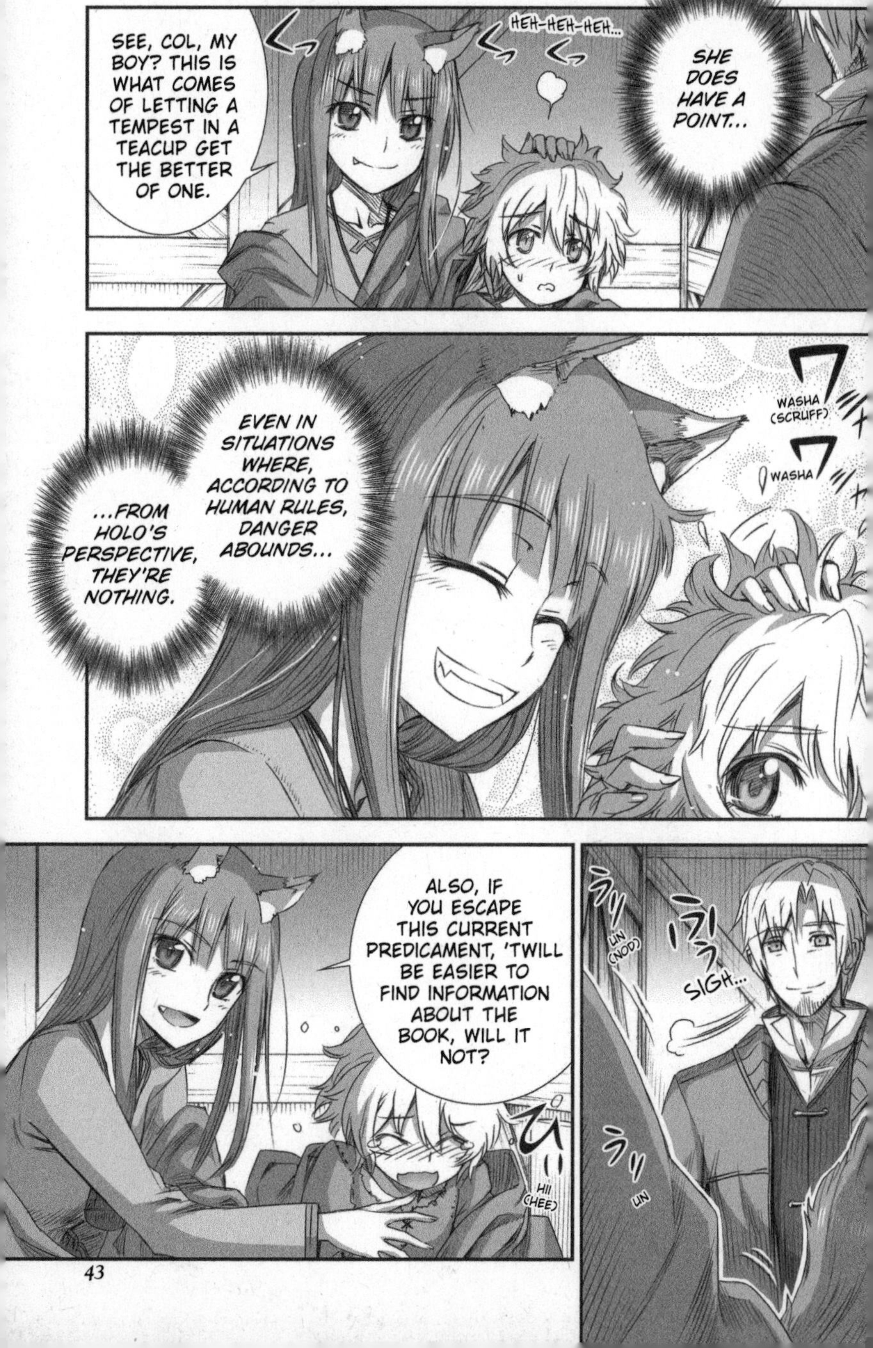
HEH-HEH-HEH...
SHE DOES HAVE A POINT...
SEE, COL, MY BOY? THIS IS WHAT COMES OF LETTING A TEMPEST IN A TEACUP GET THE BETTER OF ONE.
WASHA (SCRUFF)
WASHA
EVEN IN SITUATIONS WHERE, ACCORDING TO HUMAN RULES, DANGER ABOUNDS...
...FROM HOLO'S PERSPECTIVE, THEY'RE NOTHING.
UN (NOD)
SIGH...
UN
ALSO, IF YOU ESCAPE THIS CURRENT PREDICAMENT, 'TWILL BE EASIER TO FIND INFORMATION ABOUT THE BOOK, WILL IT NOT?
HII (CHEE)

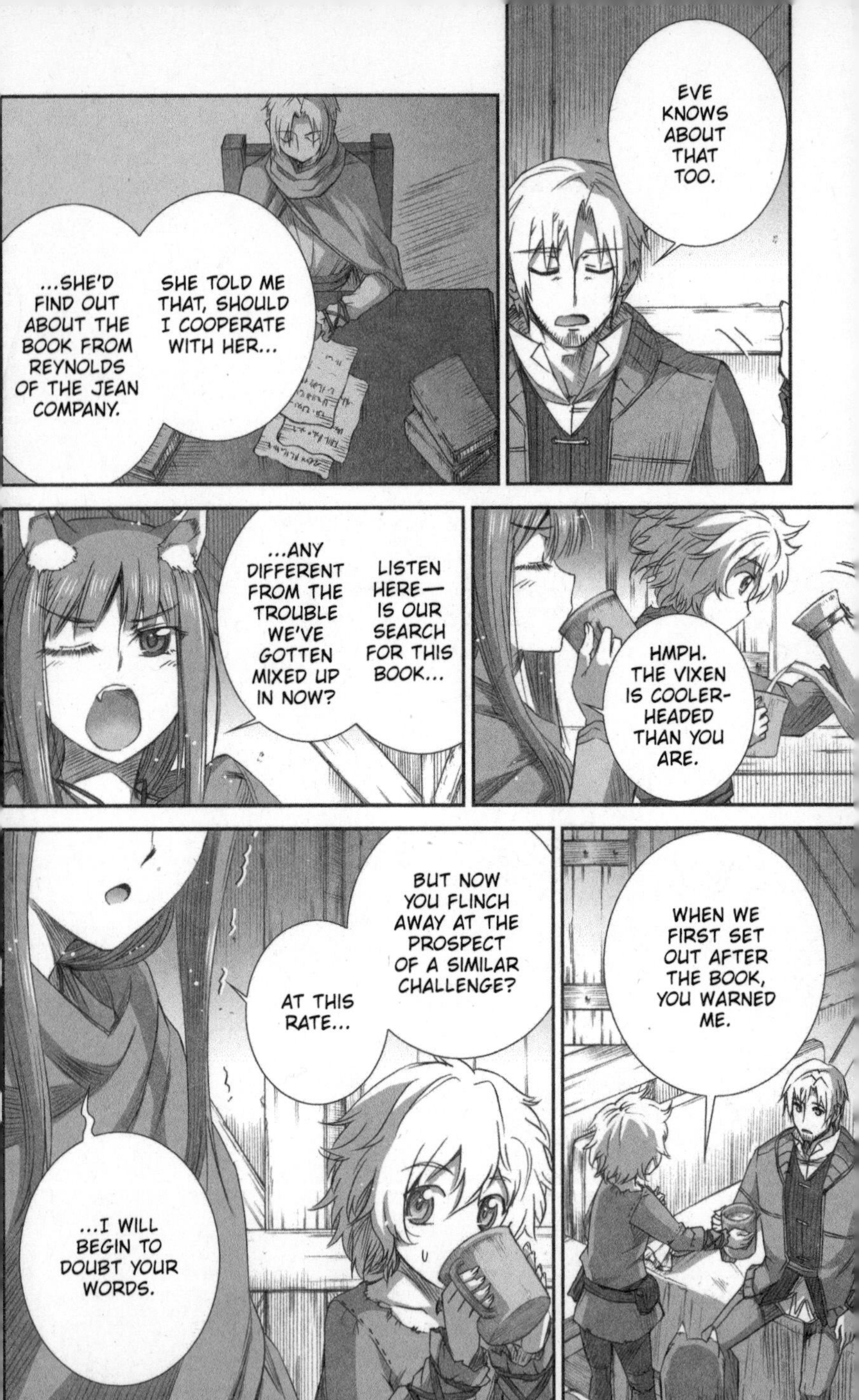
EVE KNOWS ABOUT THAT TOO.
SHE TOLD ME THAT, SHOULD I COOPERATE WITH HER...
...SHE'D FIND OUT ABOUT THE BOOK FROM REYNOLDS OF THE JEAN COMPANY.
HMPH. THE VIXEN IS COOLER-HEADED THAN YOU ARE.
LISTEN HERE— IS OUR SEARCH FOR THIS BOOK...
...ANY DIFFERENT FROM THE TROUBLE WE'VE GOTTEN MIXED UP IN NOW?
WHEN WE FIRST SET OUT AFTER THE BOOK, YOU WARNED ME.
BUT NOW YOU FLINCH AWAY AT THE PROSPECT OF A SIMILAR CHALLENGE?
AT THIS RATE...
...I WILL BEGIN TO DOUBT YOUR WORDS.

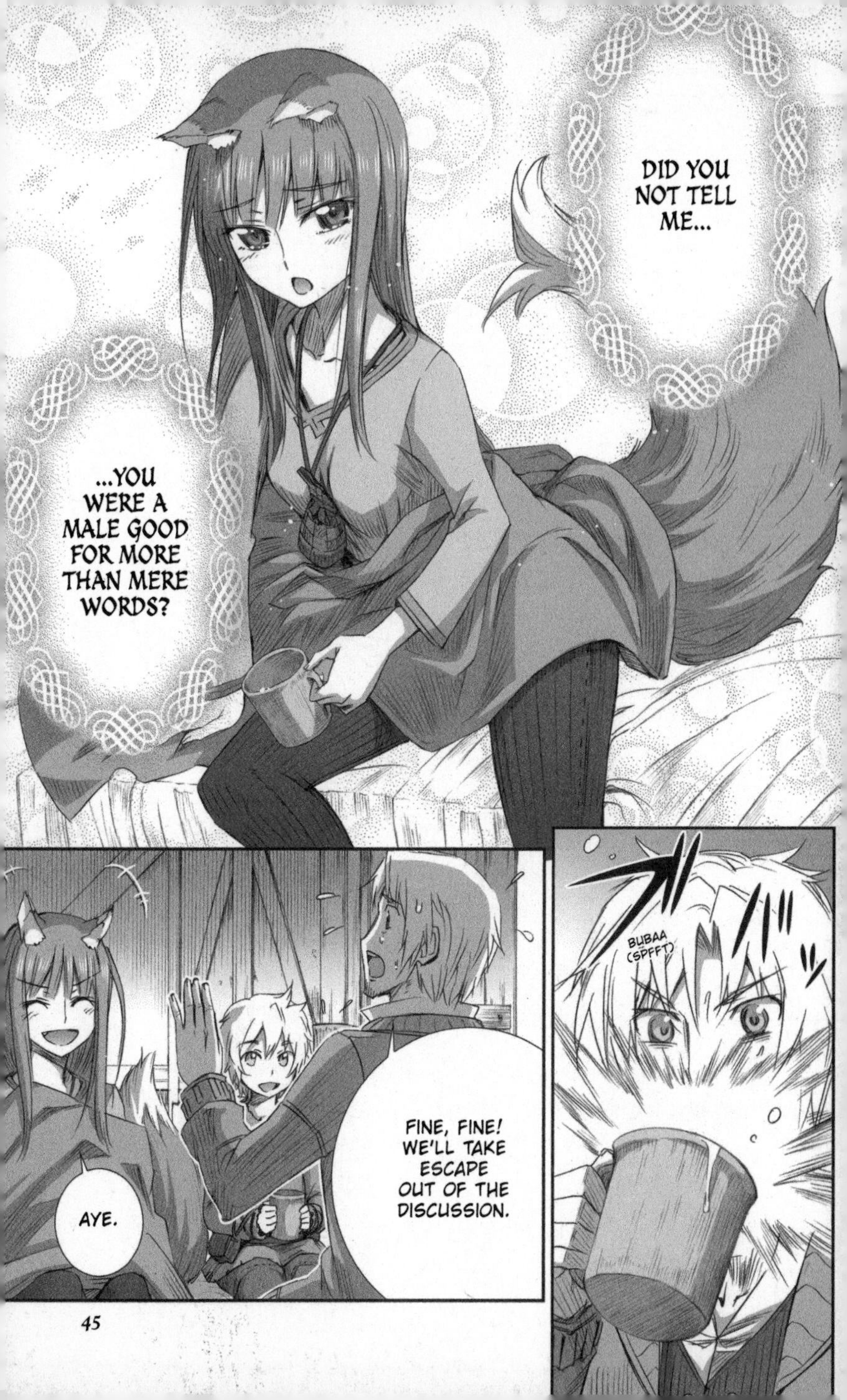
DID YOU NOT TELL ME...
...YOU WERE A MALE GOOD FOR MORE THAN MERE WORDS?
BUBAA (SPFFT)
FINE, FINE! WE'LL TAKE ESCAPE OUT OF THE DISCUSSION.
AYE.

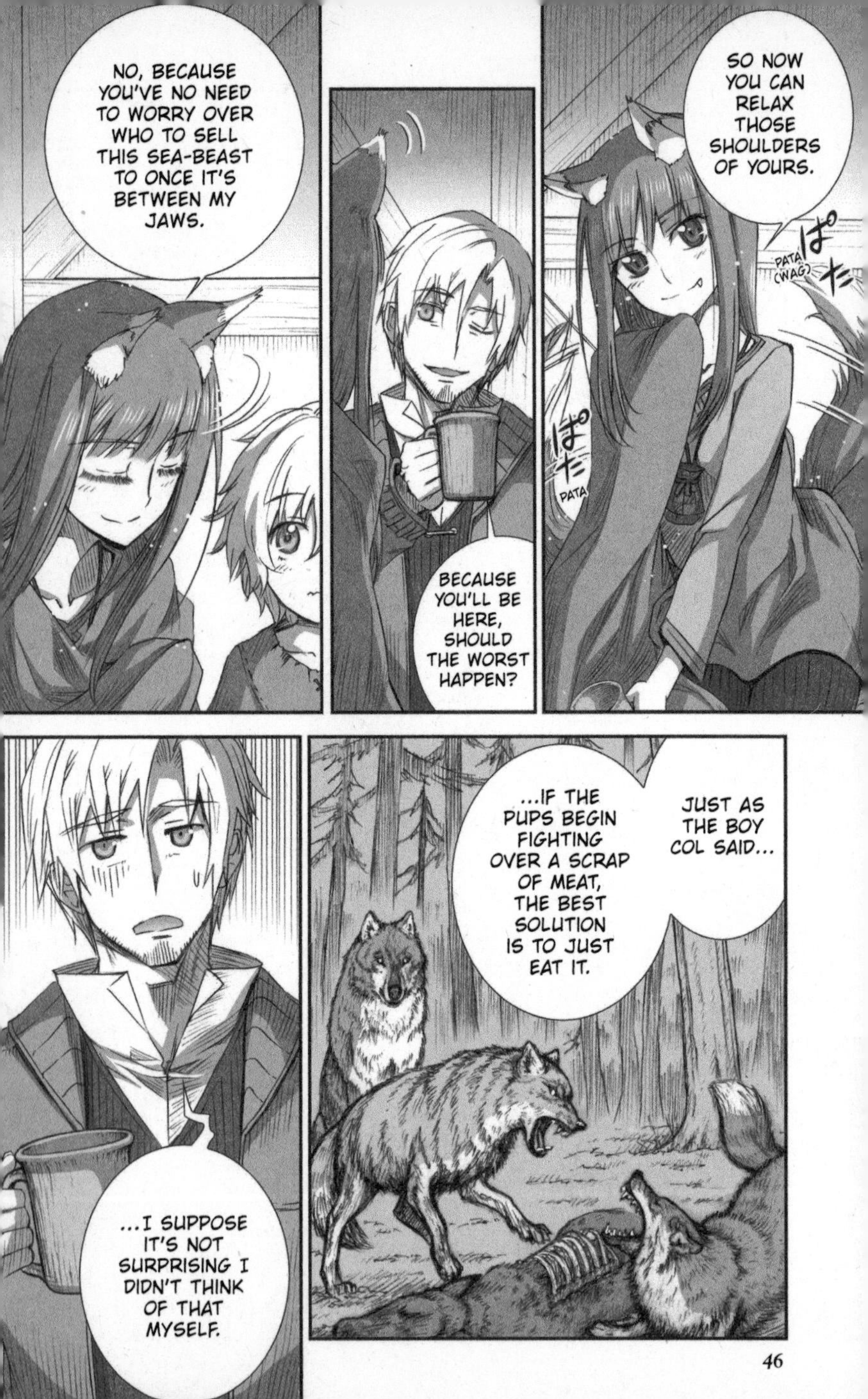
SO NOW YOU CAN RELAX THOSE SHOULDERS OF YOURS.
ぱた
PATA (WAG)
ぱた
PATA
BECAUSE YOU'LL BE HERE, SHOULD THE WORST HAPPEN?
NO, BECAUSE YOU'VE NO NEED TO WORRY OVER WHO TO SELL THIS SEA-BEAST TO ONCE IT'S BETWEEN MY JAWS.
JUST AS THE BOY COL SAID...
...IF THE PUPS BEGIN FIGHTING OVER A SCRAP OF MEAT, THE BEST SOLUTION IS TO JUST EAT IT.
...I SUPPOSE IT'S NOT SURPRISING I DIDN'T THINK OF THAT MYSELF.

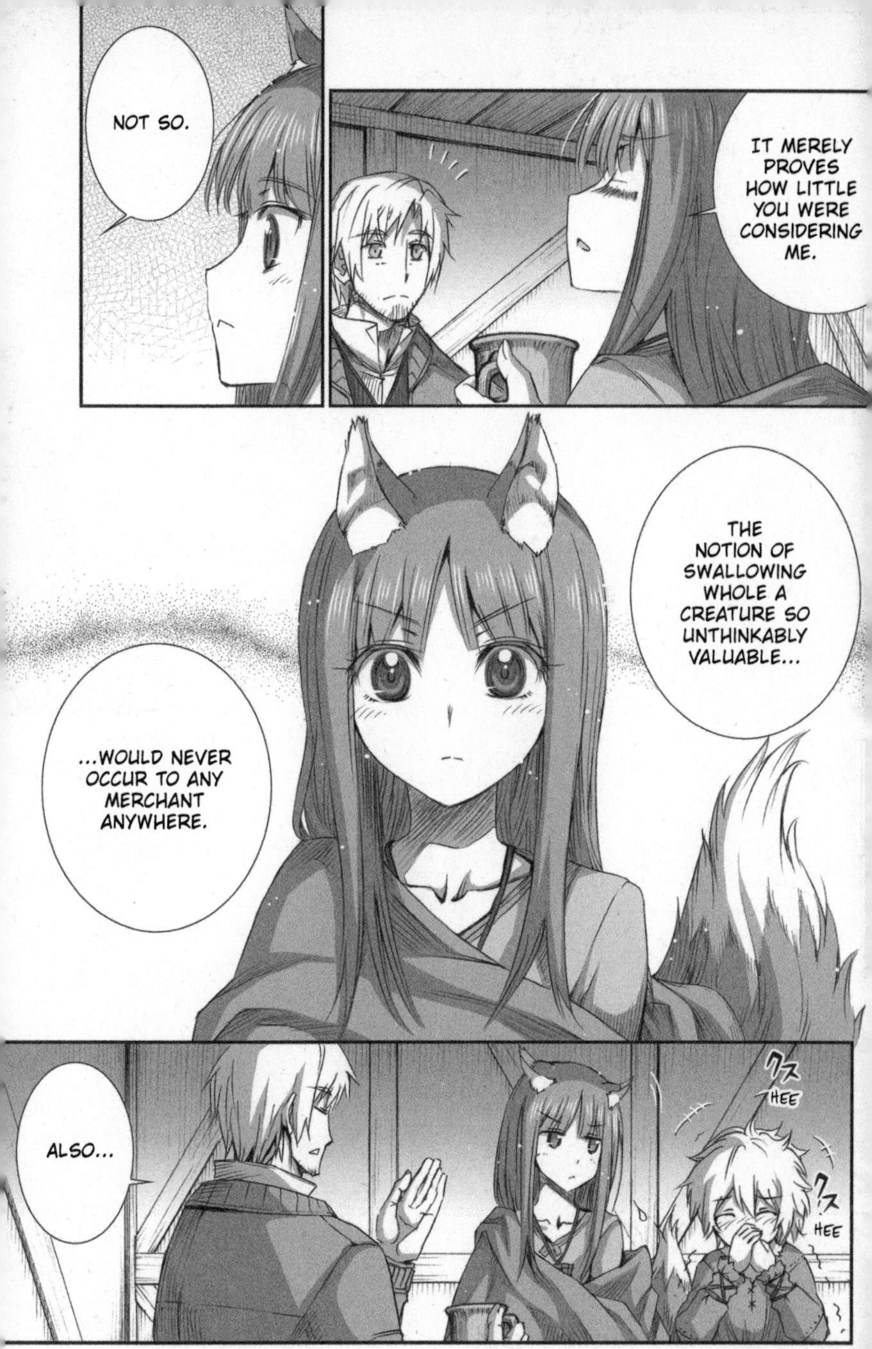
IT MERELY PROVES HOW LITTLE YOU WERE CONSIDERING ME.
NOT SO.
THE NOTION OF SWALLOWING WHOLE A CREATURE SO UNTHINKABLY VALUABLE...
...WOULD NEVER OCCUR TO ANY MERCHANT ANYWHERE.
クス HEE
クス HEE
ALSO...

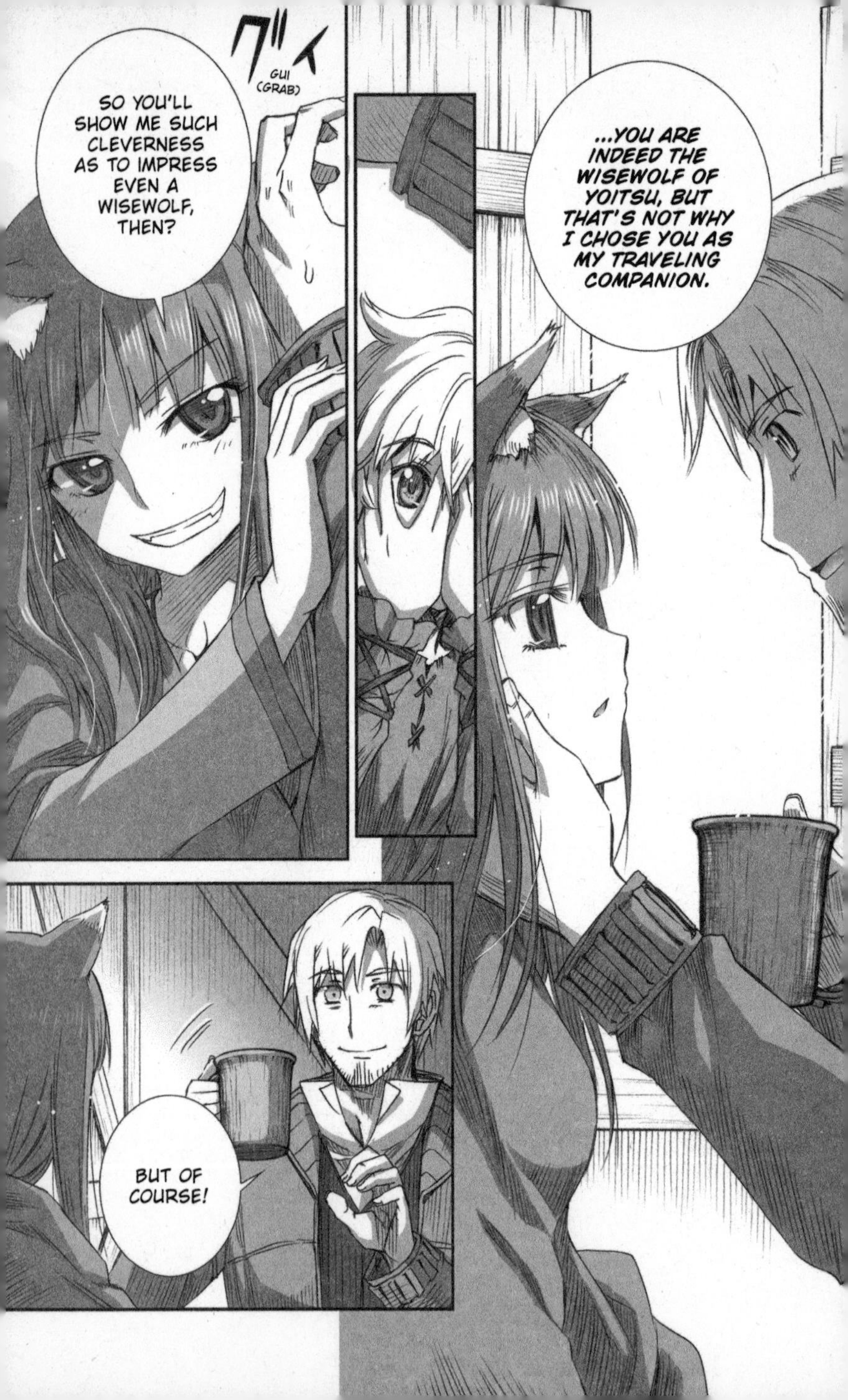
...YOU ARE INDEED THE WISEWOLF OF YOITSU, BUT THAT'S NOT WHY I CHOSE YOU AS MY TRAVELING COMPANION.
グイ
GUI (GRAB)
SO YOU'LL SHOW ME SUCH CLEVERNESS AS TO IMPRESS EVEN A WISEWOLF, THEN?
BUT OF COURSE!

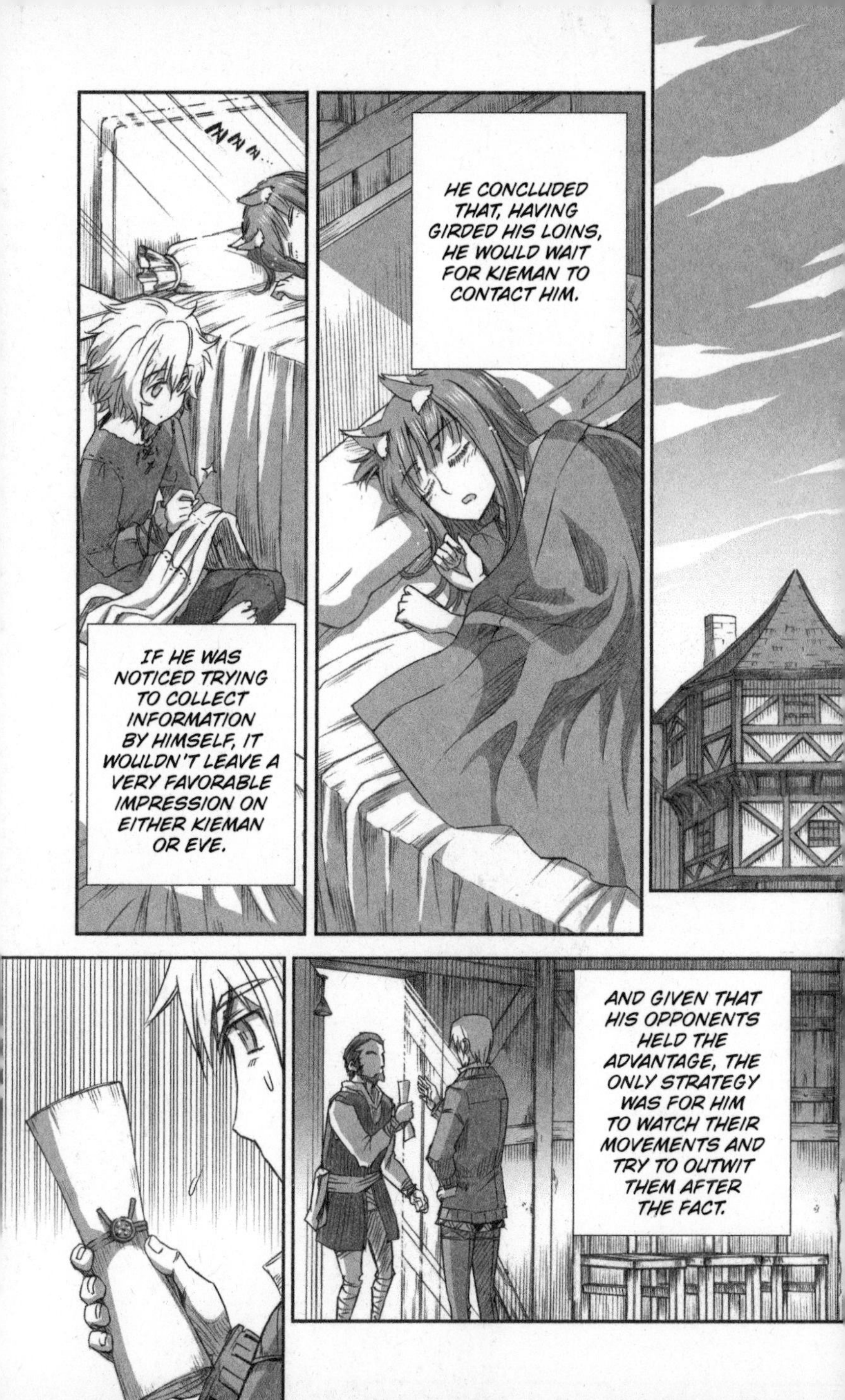
HE CONCLUDED THAT, HAVING GIRDED HIS LOINS, HE WOULD WAIT FOR KIEMAN TO CONTACT HIM.
ZZZ...
IF HE WAS NOTICED TRYING TO COLLECT INFORMATION BY HIMSELF, IT WOULDN'T LEAVE A VERY FAVORABLE IMPRESSION ON EITHER KIEMAN OR EVE.
AND GIVEN THAT HIS OPPONENTS HELD THE ADVANTAGE, THE ONLY STRATEGY WAS FOR HIM TO WATCH THEIR MOVEMENTS AND TRY TO OUTWIT THEM AFTER THE FACT.

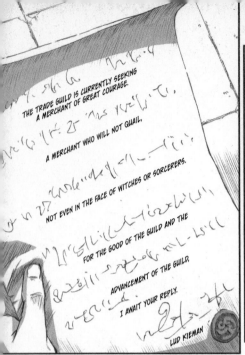

THE TRADE GUILD IS CURRENTLY SEEKING A MERCHANT OF GREAT COURAGE.

A MERCHANT WHO WILL NOT QUAIL,

NOT EVEN IN THE FACE OF WITCHES OR SORCERERS.

FOR THE GOOD OF THE GUILD AND THE

ADVANCEMENT OF THE GUILD,

I AWAIT YOUR REPLY.

LUD KIEMAN

KASA
(RUSTLE)

HE WROTE "GUILD" THREE TIMES... IT WOULD HAVE BEEN REFRESHING TO SEE HIM WRITE "I," FOR ONCE.

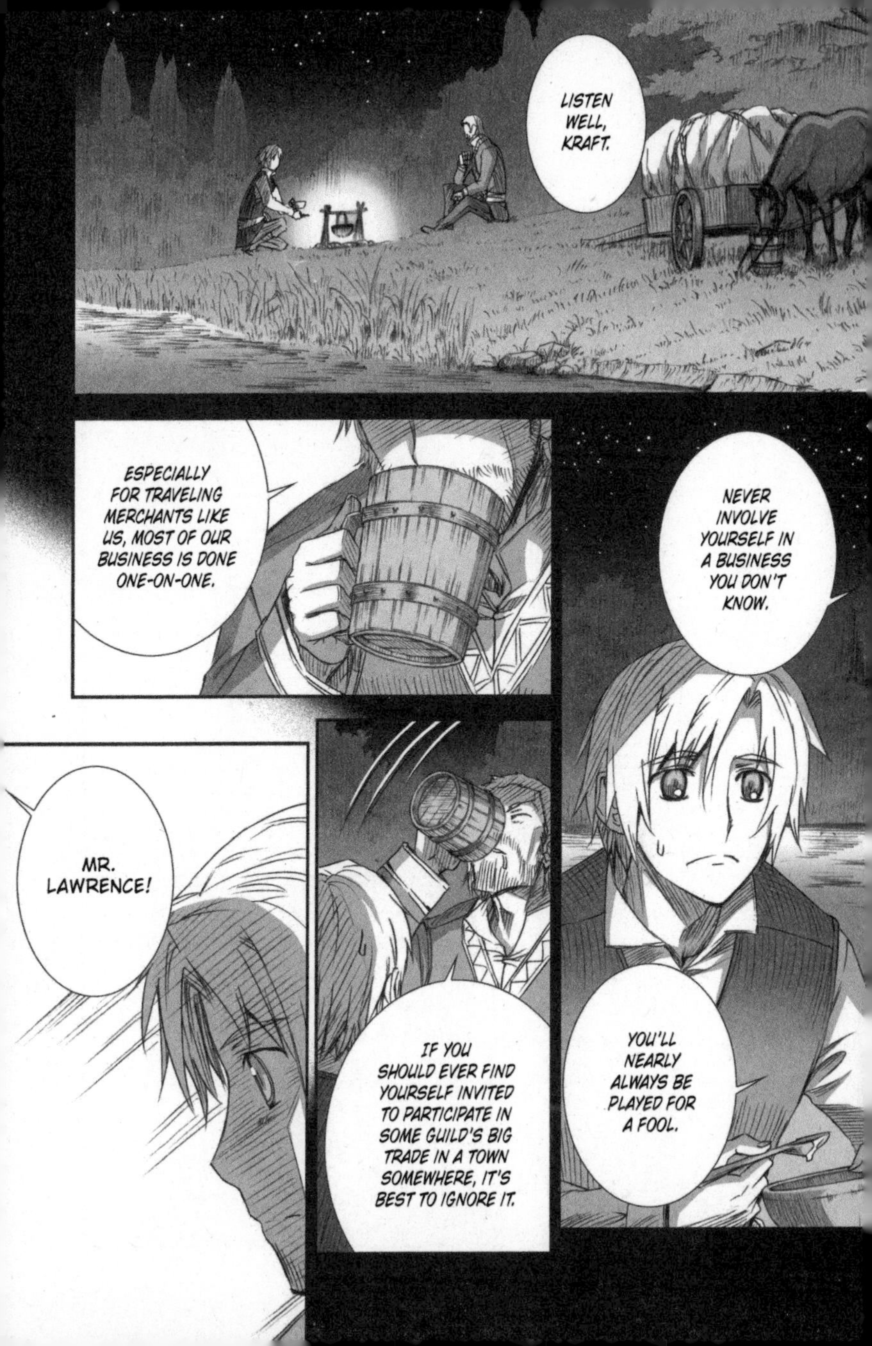
LISTEN WELL, KRAFT.
NEVER INVOLVE YOURSELF IN A BUSINESS YOU DON'T KNOW.
YOU'LL NEARLY ALWAYS BE PLAYED FOR A FOOL.
ESPECIALLY FOR TRAVELING MERCHANTS LIKE US, MOST OF OUR BUSINESS IS DONE ONE-ON-ONE.
IF YOU SHOULD EVER FIND YOURSELF INVITED TO PARTICIPATE IN SOME GUILD'S BIG TRADE IN A TOWN SOMEWHERE, IT'S BEST TO IGNORE IT.
MR. LAWRENCE!

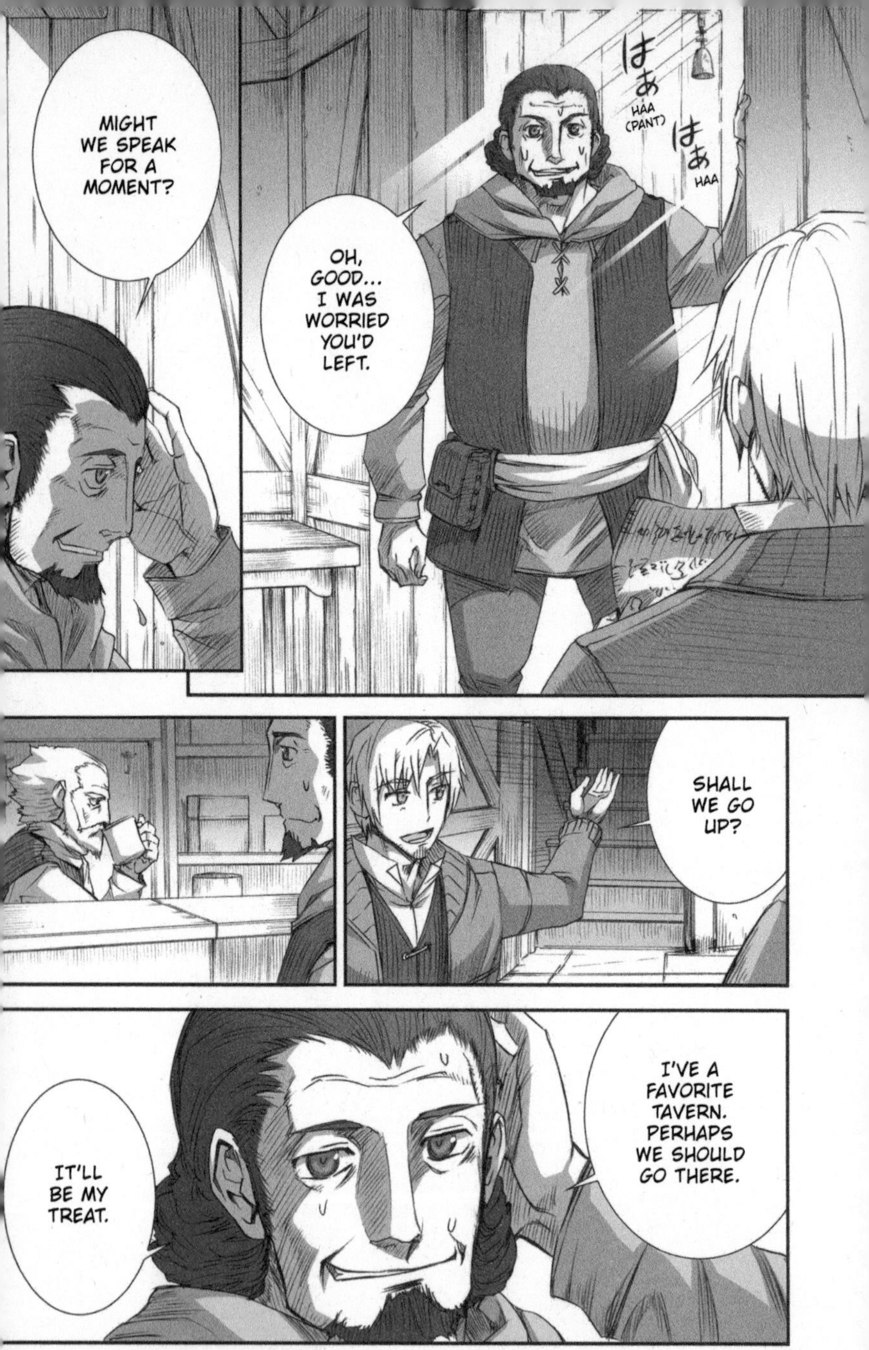
はあ
HAA (PANT)
はあ
HAA
OH, GOOD... I WAS WORRIED YOU'D LEFT.
MIGHT WE SPEAK FOR A MOMENT?
SHALL WE GO UP?
I'VE A FAVORITE TAVERN. PERHAPS WE SHOULD GO THERE.
IT'LL BE MY TREAT.

SPICE & WOLF

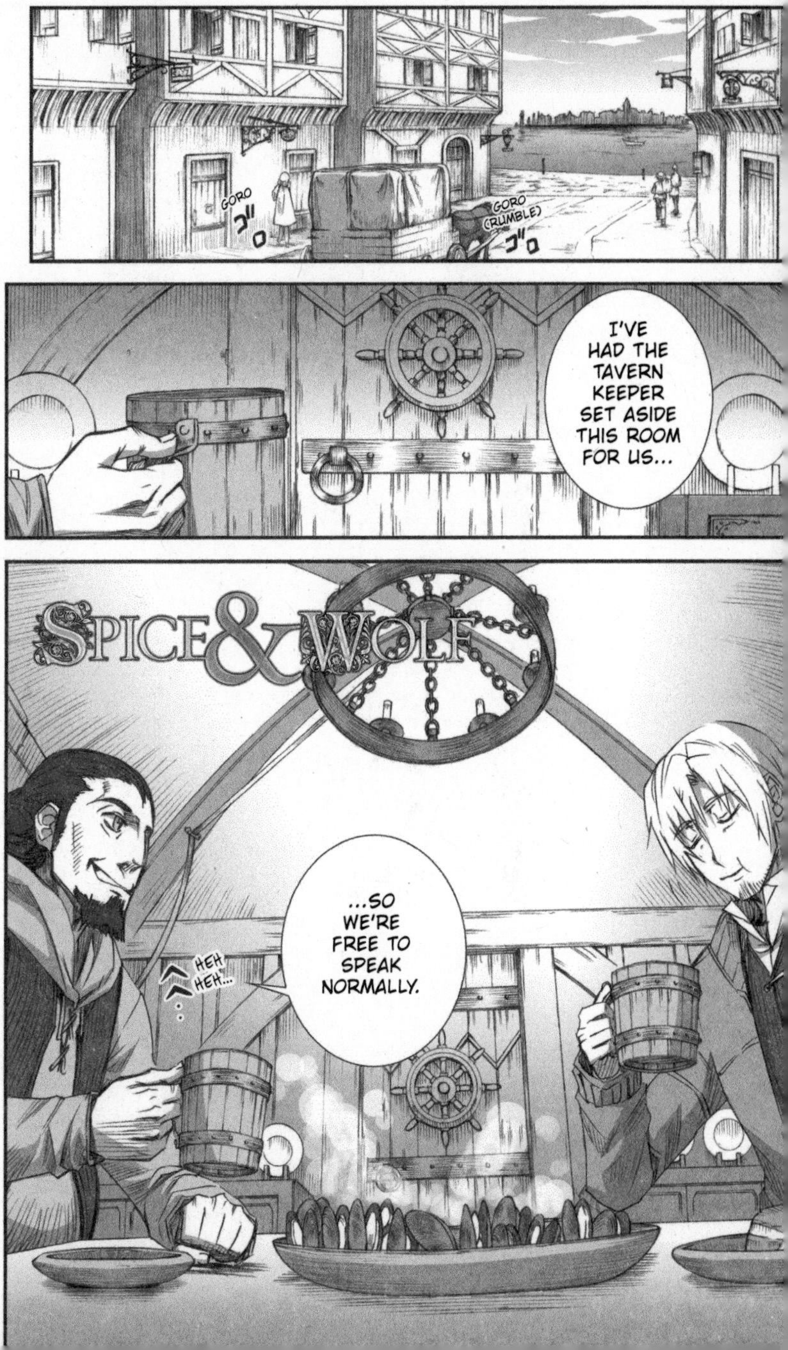
GORO (RUMBLE)
ゴロ
GORO
ゴロ
I'VE HAD THE TAVERN KEEPER SET ASIDE THIS ROOM FOR US...
SPICE & WOLF
...SO WE'RE FREE TO SPEAK NORMALLY.
HEH HEH...

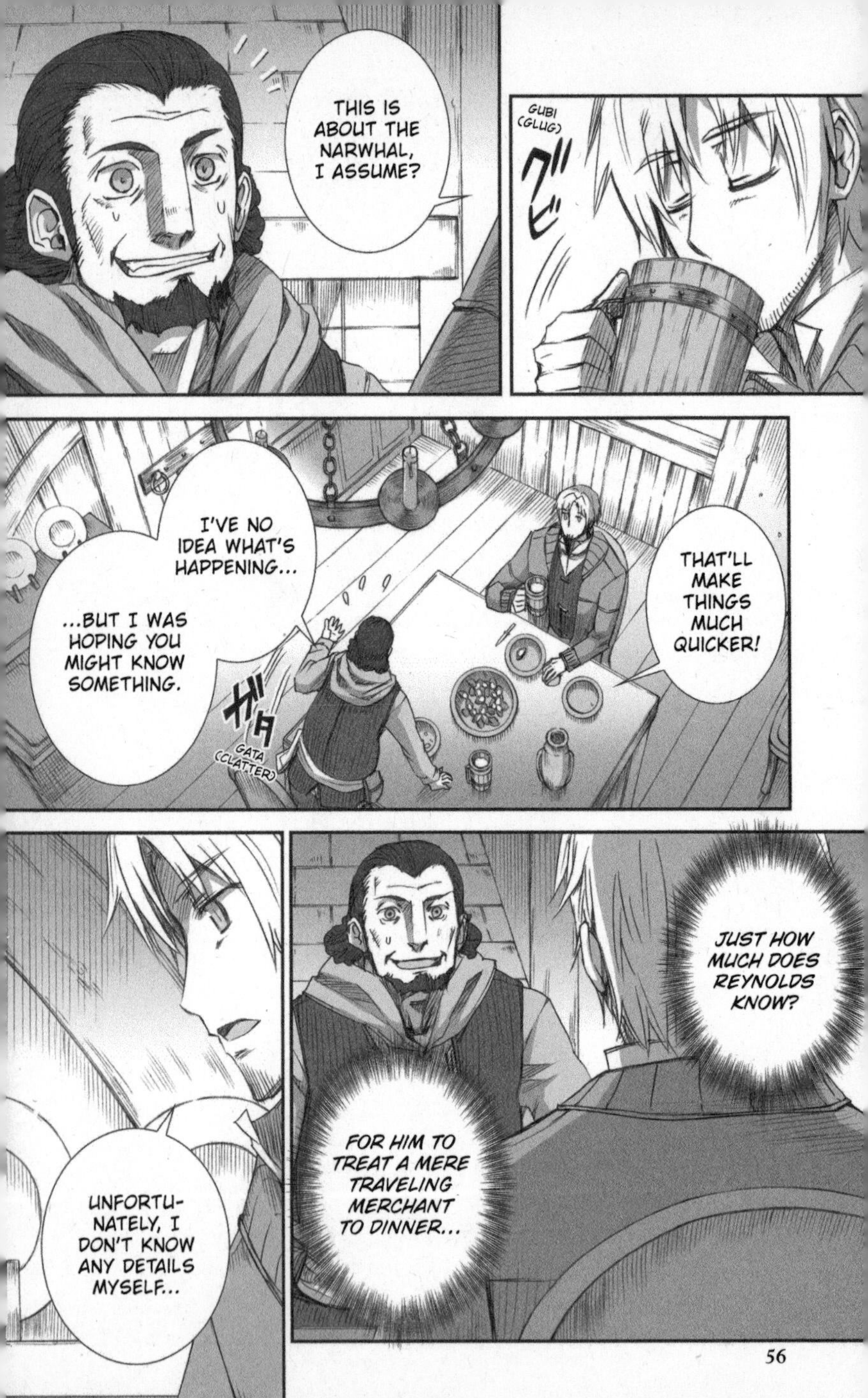
GUBI (GLUG)
THIS IS ABOUT THE NARWHAL, I ASSUME?
THAT'LL MAKE THINGS MUCH QUICKER!
I'VE NO IDEA WHAT'S HAPPENING...
...BUT I WAS HOPING YOU MIGHT KNOW SOMETHING.
GATA (CLATTER)
JUST HOW MUCH DOES REYNOLDS KNOW?
FOR HIM TO TREAT A MERE TRAVELING MERCHANT TO DINNER...
UNFORTU-NATELY, I DON'T KNOW ANY DETAILS MYSELF...

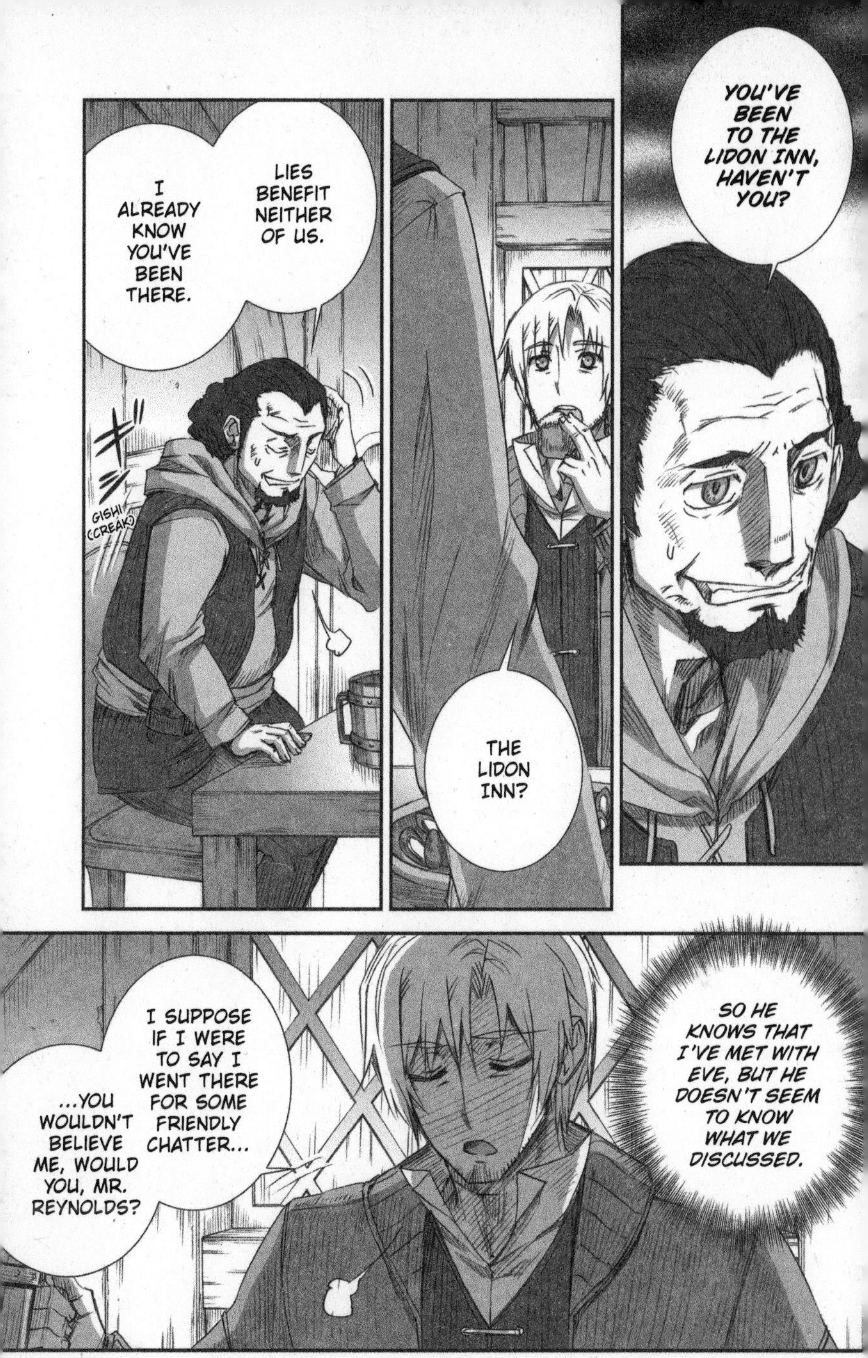
YOU'VE BEEN TO THE LIDON INN, HAVEN'T YOU?
THE LIDON INN?
LIES BENEFIT NEITHER OF US.
I ALREADY KNOW YOU'VE BEEN THERE.
GISHI (CREAK)
SO HE KNOWS THAT I'VE MET WITH EVE, BUT HE DOESN'T SEEM TO KNOW WHAT WE DISCUSSED.
I SUPPOSE IF I WERE TO SAY I WENT THERE FOR SOME FRIENDLY CHATTER...
...YOU WOULDN'T BELIEVE ME, WOULD YOU, MR. REYNOLDS?

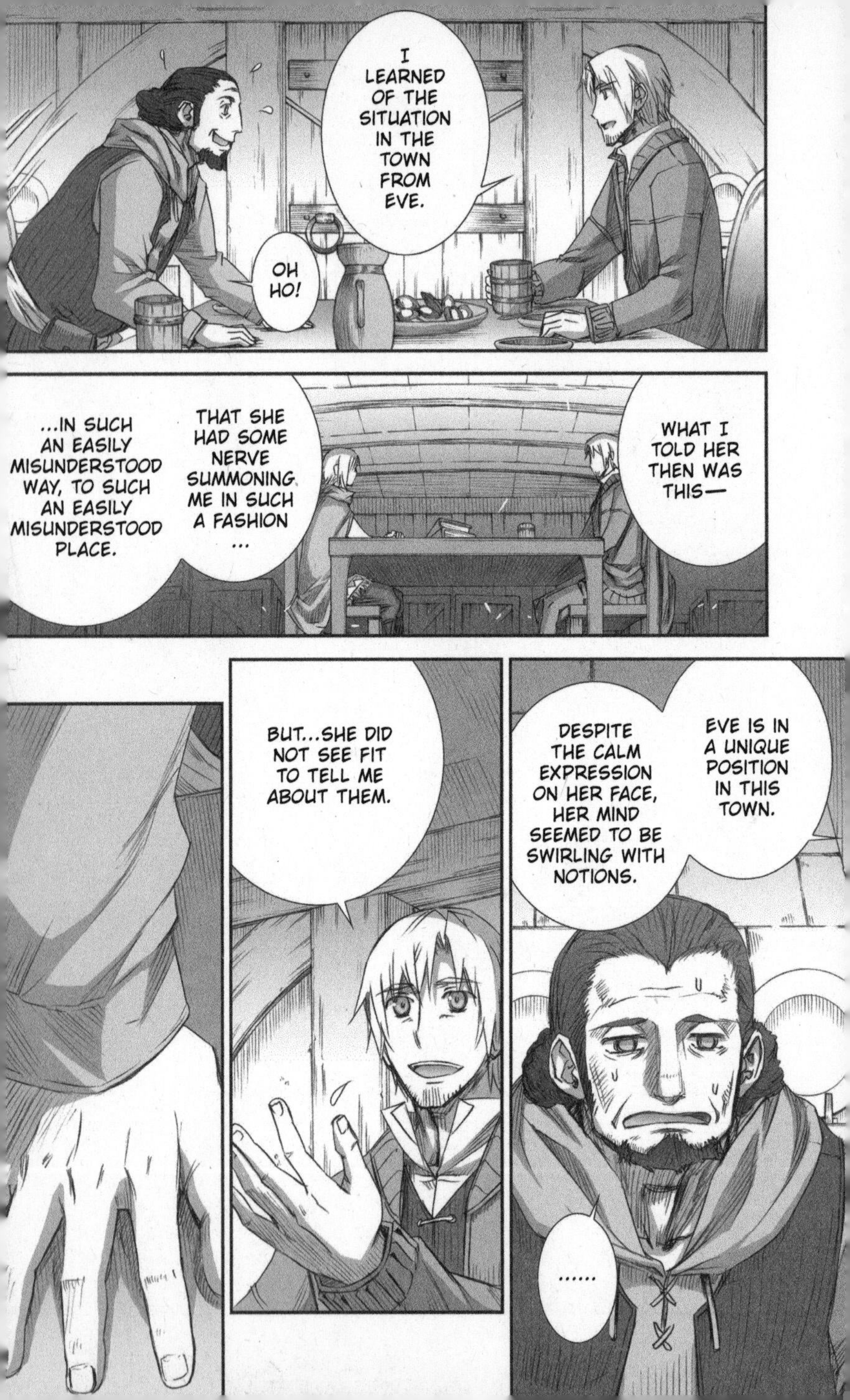
I LEARNED OF THE SITUATION IN THE TOWN FROM EVE.
OH HO!
WHAT I TOLD HER THEN WAS THIS—
THAT SHE HAD SOME NERVE SUMMONING ME IN SUCH A FASHION…
…IN SUCH AN EASILY MISUNDERSTOOD WAY, TO SUCH AN EASILY MISUNDERSTOOD PLACE.
EVE IS IN A UNIQUE POSITION IN THIS TOWN.
DESPITE THE CALM EXPRESSION ON HER FACE, HER MIND SEEMED TO BE SWIRLING WITH NOTIONS.
……
BUT…SHE DID NOT SEE FIT TO TELL ME ABOUT THEM.

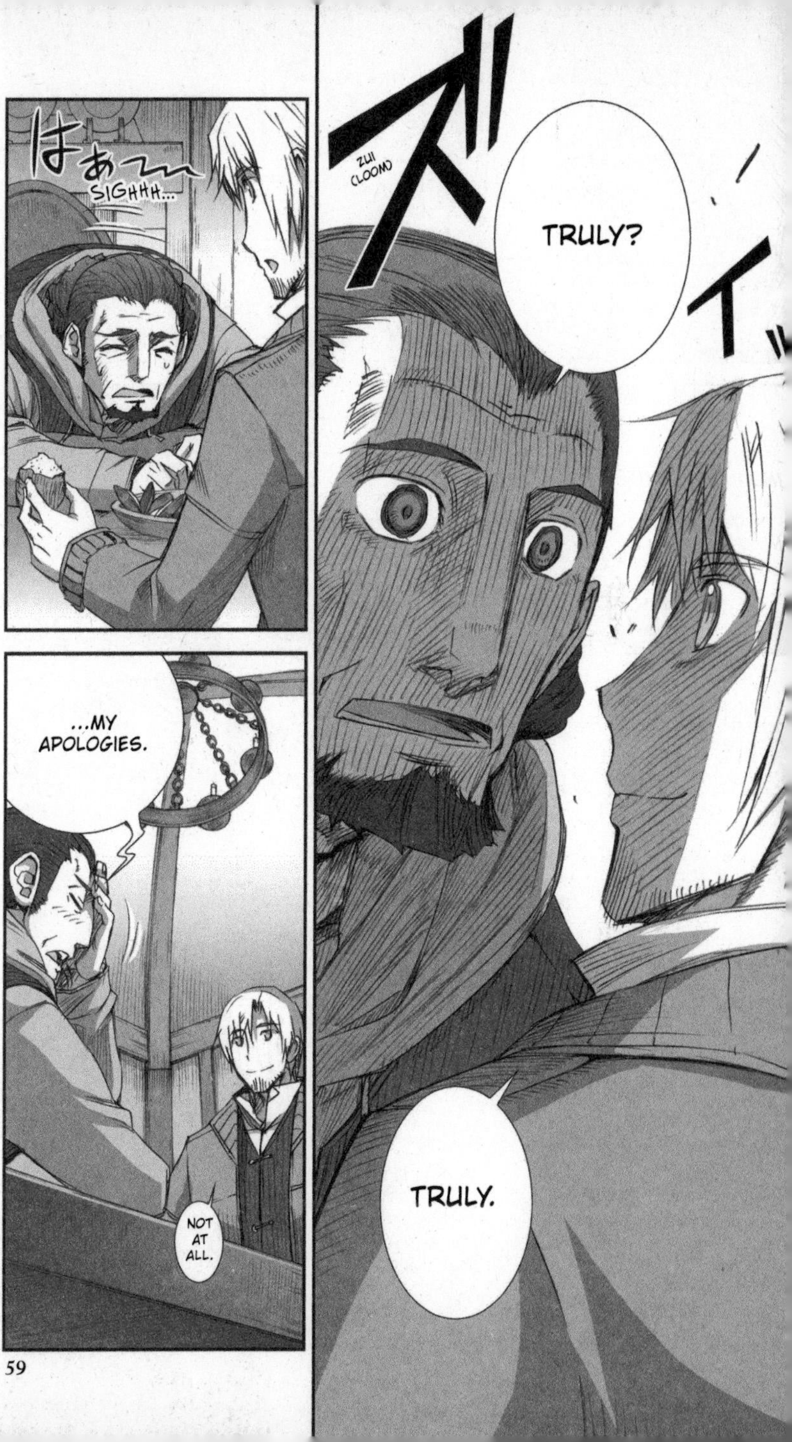
ZUI (LOOM)
TRULY?
TRULY.
SIGHHH...
...MY APOLOGIES.
NOT AT ALL.

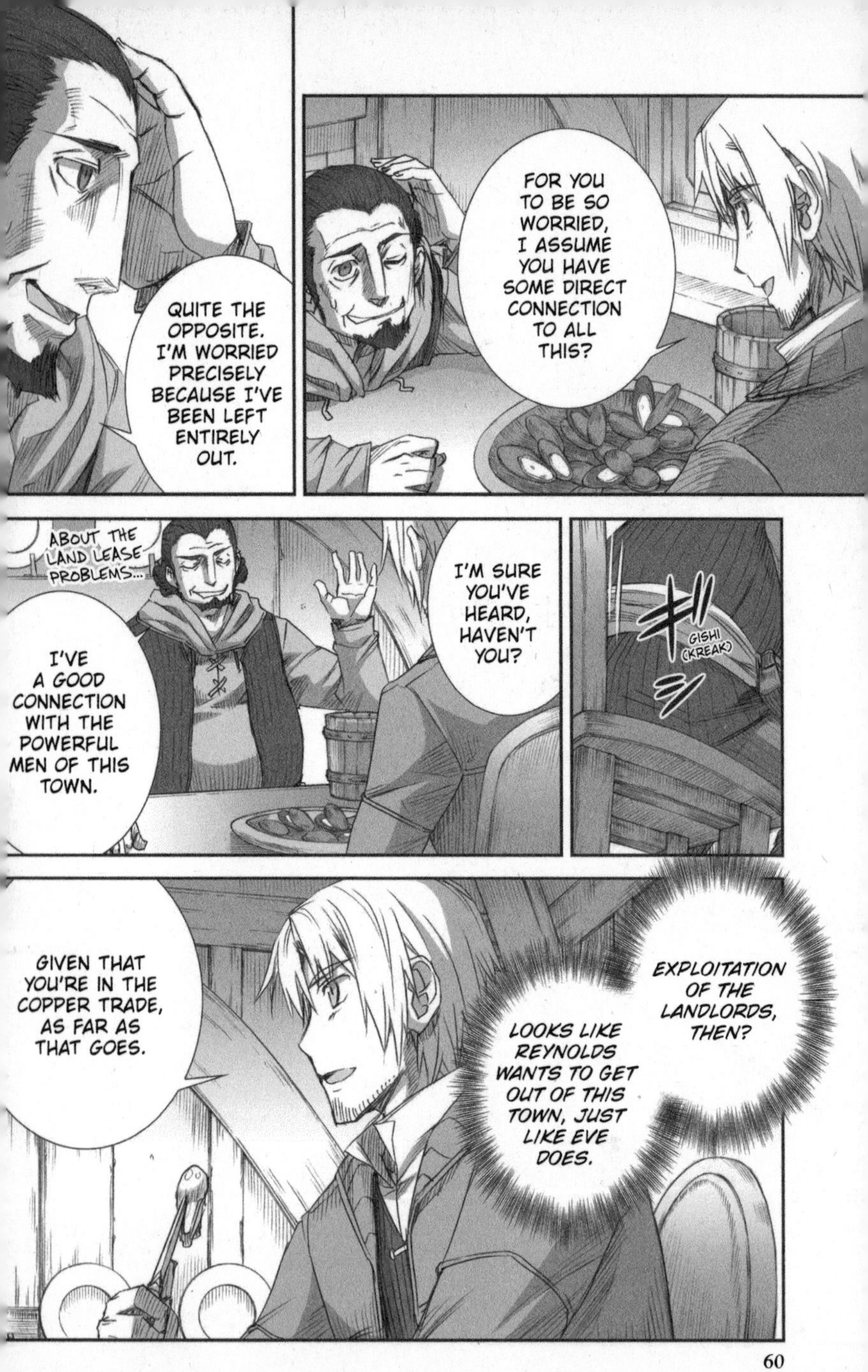
FOR YOU TO BE SO WORRIED, I ASSUME YOU HAVE SOME DIRECT CONNECTION TO ALL THIS?
QUITE THE OPPOSITE. I'M WORRIED PRECISELY BECAUSE I'VE BEEN LEFT ENTIRELY OUT.
GISHI (KREAK)
I'M SURE YOU'VE HEARD, HAVEN'T YOU?
ABOUT THE LAND LEASE PROBLEMS...
I'VE A GOOD CONNECTION WITH THE POWERFUL MEN OF THIS TOWN.
EXPLOITATION OF THE LANDLORDS, THEN?
LOOKS LIKE REYNOLDS WANTS TO GET OUT OF THIS TOWN, JUST LIKE EVE DOES.
GIVEN THAT YOU'RE IN THE COPPER TRADE, AS FAR AS THAT GOES.

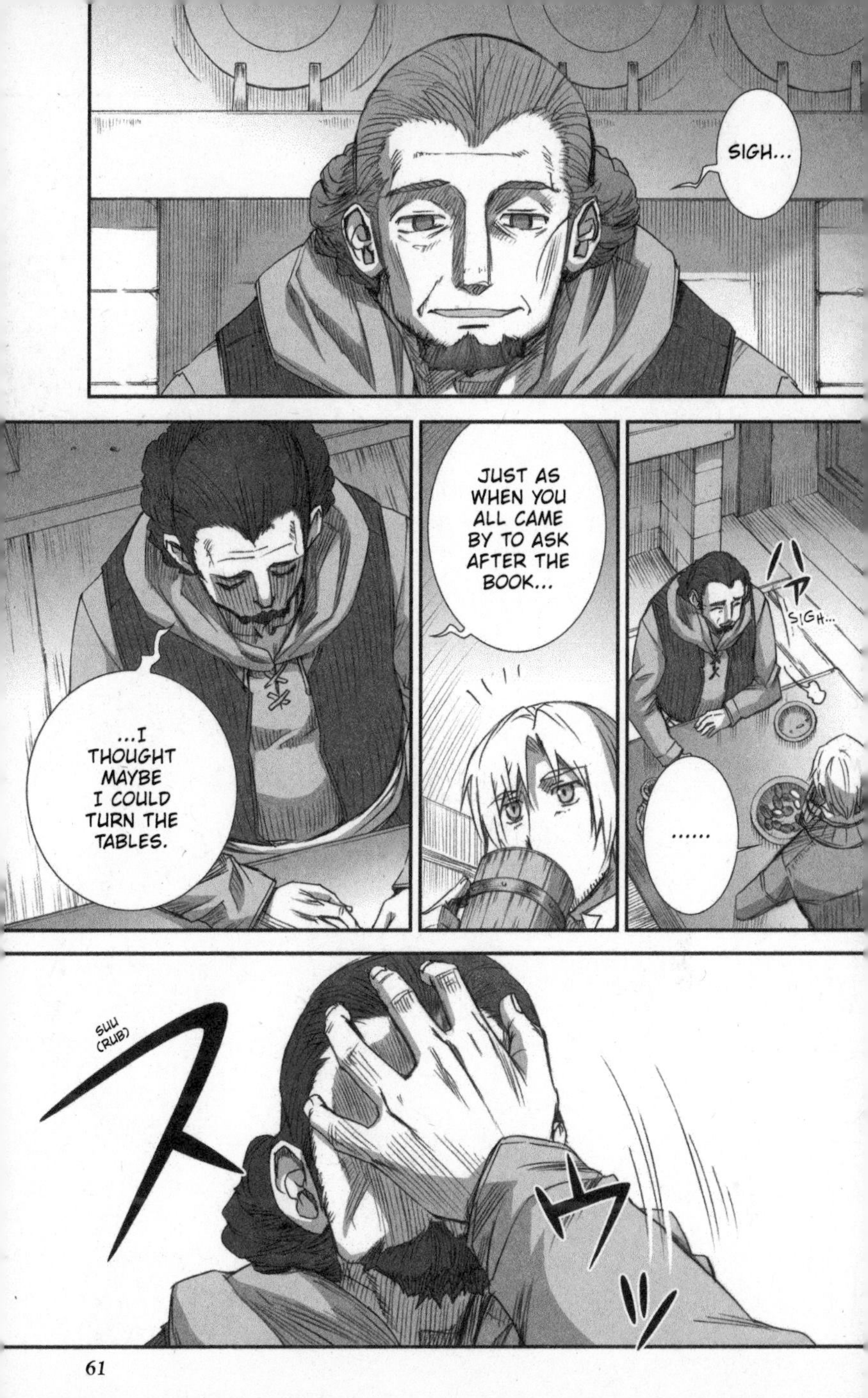
SIGH...
SIGH...
......
JUST AS WHEN YOU ALL CAME BY TO ASK AFTER THE BOOK...
...I THOUGHT MAYBE I COULD TURN THE TABLES.
SUU (RUB)

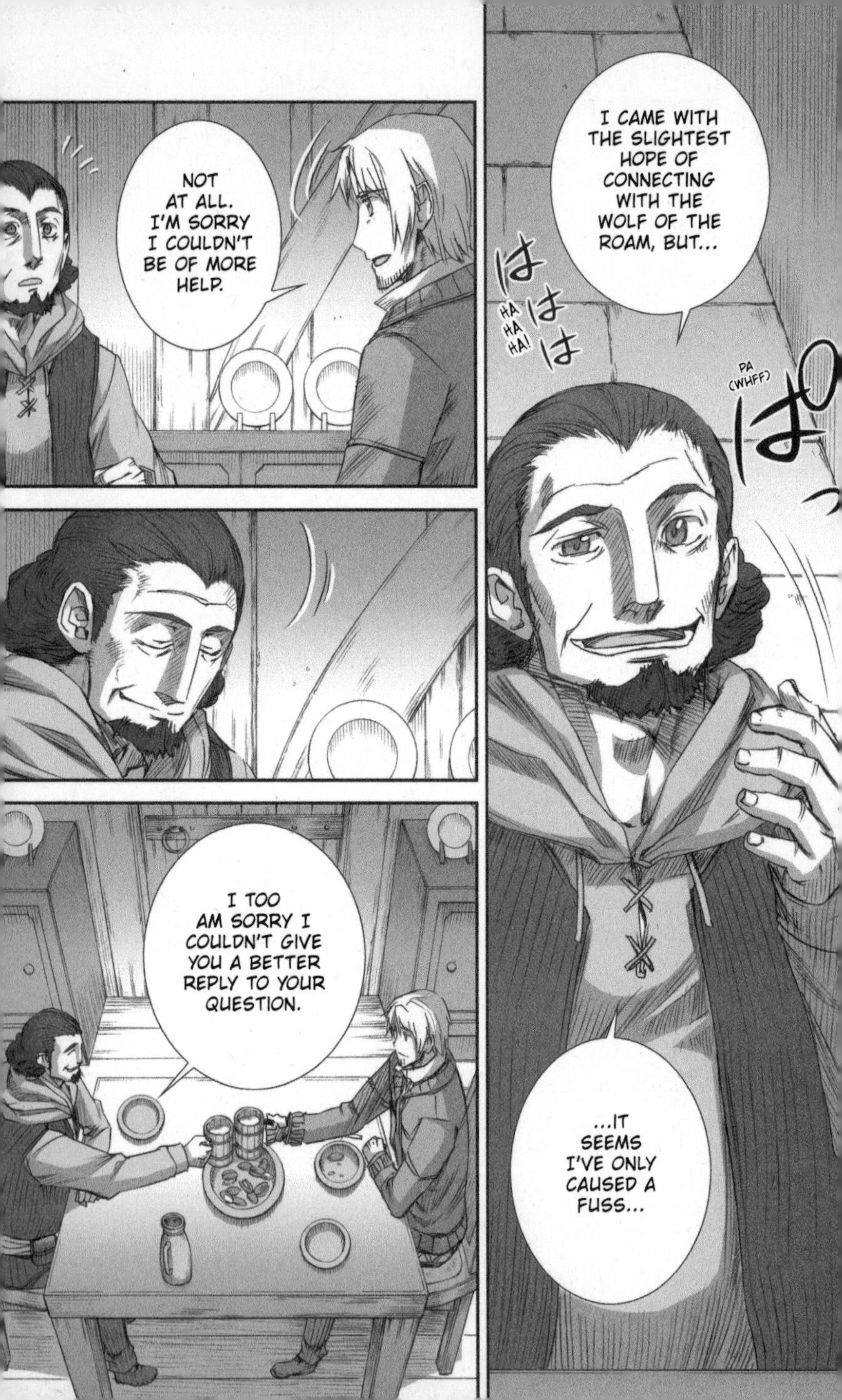
I CAME WITH THE SLIGHTEST HOPE OF CONNECTING WITH THE WOLF OF THE ROAM, BUT...
ははは
HA HA HA!
ぱっ
PA (WHFF)
...IT SEEMS I'VE ONLY CAUSED A FUSS...
NOT AT ALL. I'M SORRY I COULDN'T BE OF MORE HELP.
I TOO AM SORRY I COULDN'T GIVE YOU A BETTER REPLY TO YOUR QUESTION.

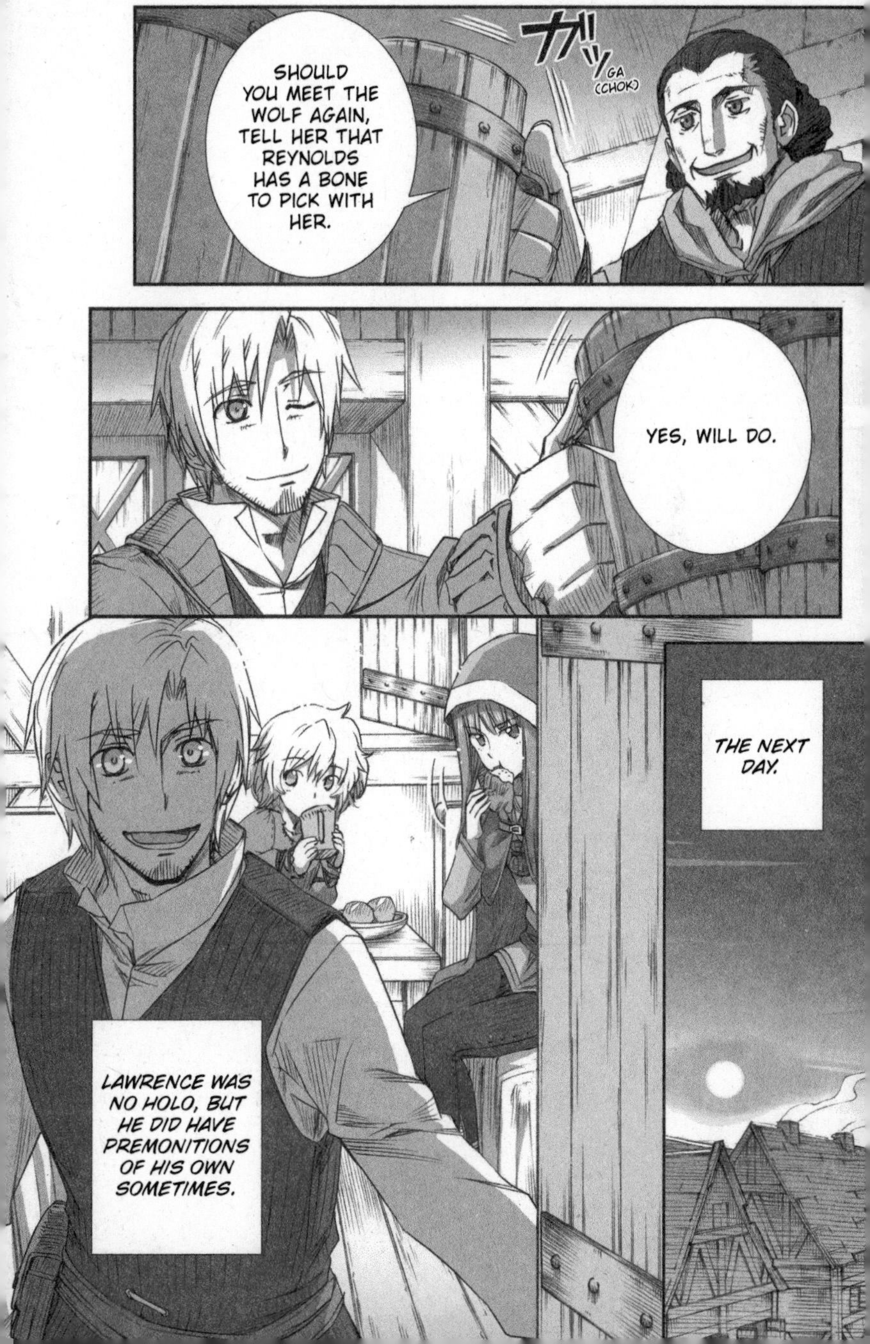
ガッ GA (CHOK)
SHOULD YOU MEET THE WOLF AGAIN, TELL HER THAT REYNOLDS HAS A BONE TO PICK WITH HER.
YES, WILL DO.
THE NEXT DAY.
LAWRENCE WAS NO HOLO, BUT HE DID HAVE PREMONITIONS OF HIS OWN SOMETIMES.

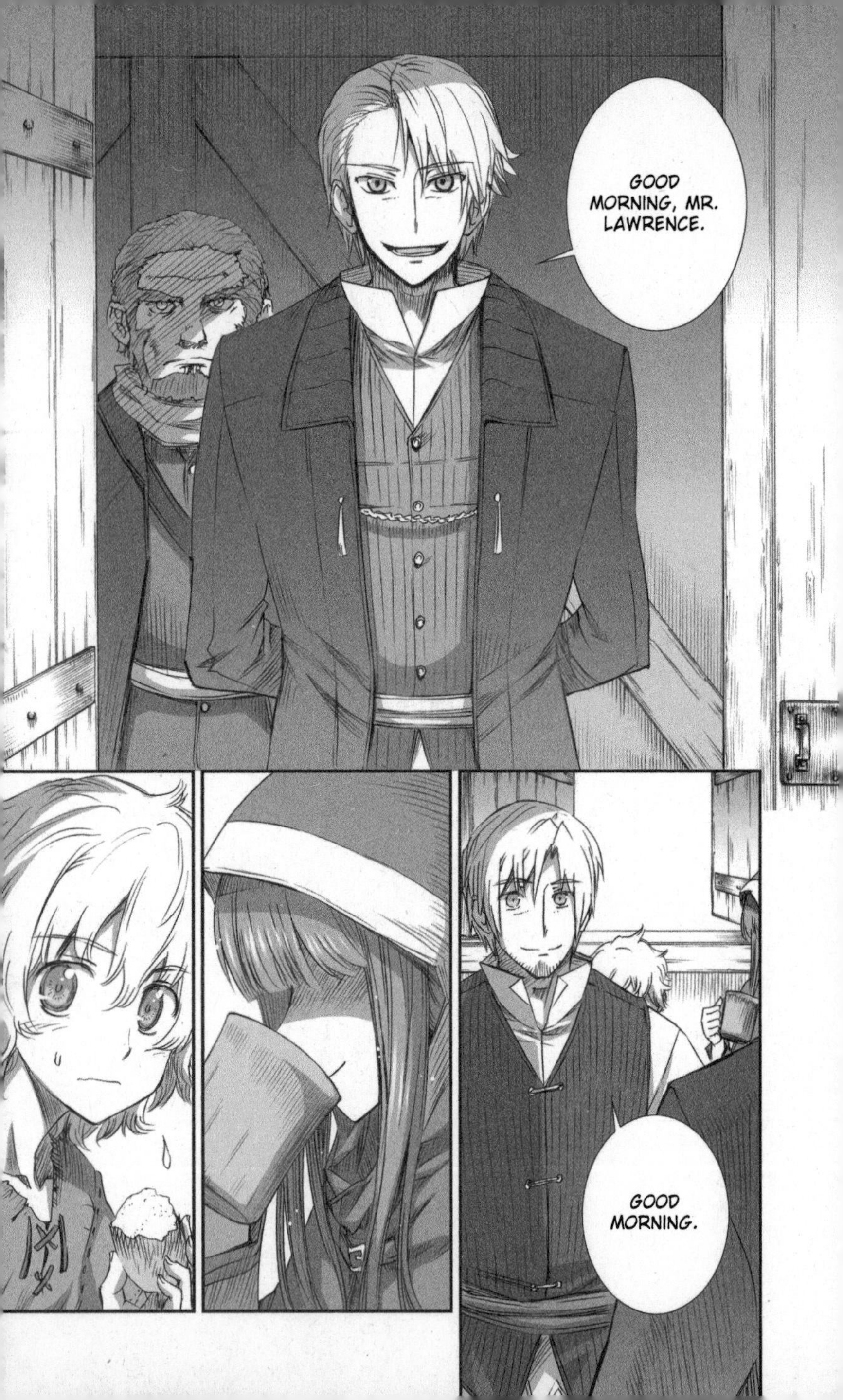
GOOD MORNING, MR. LAWRENCE.
GOOD MORNING.

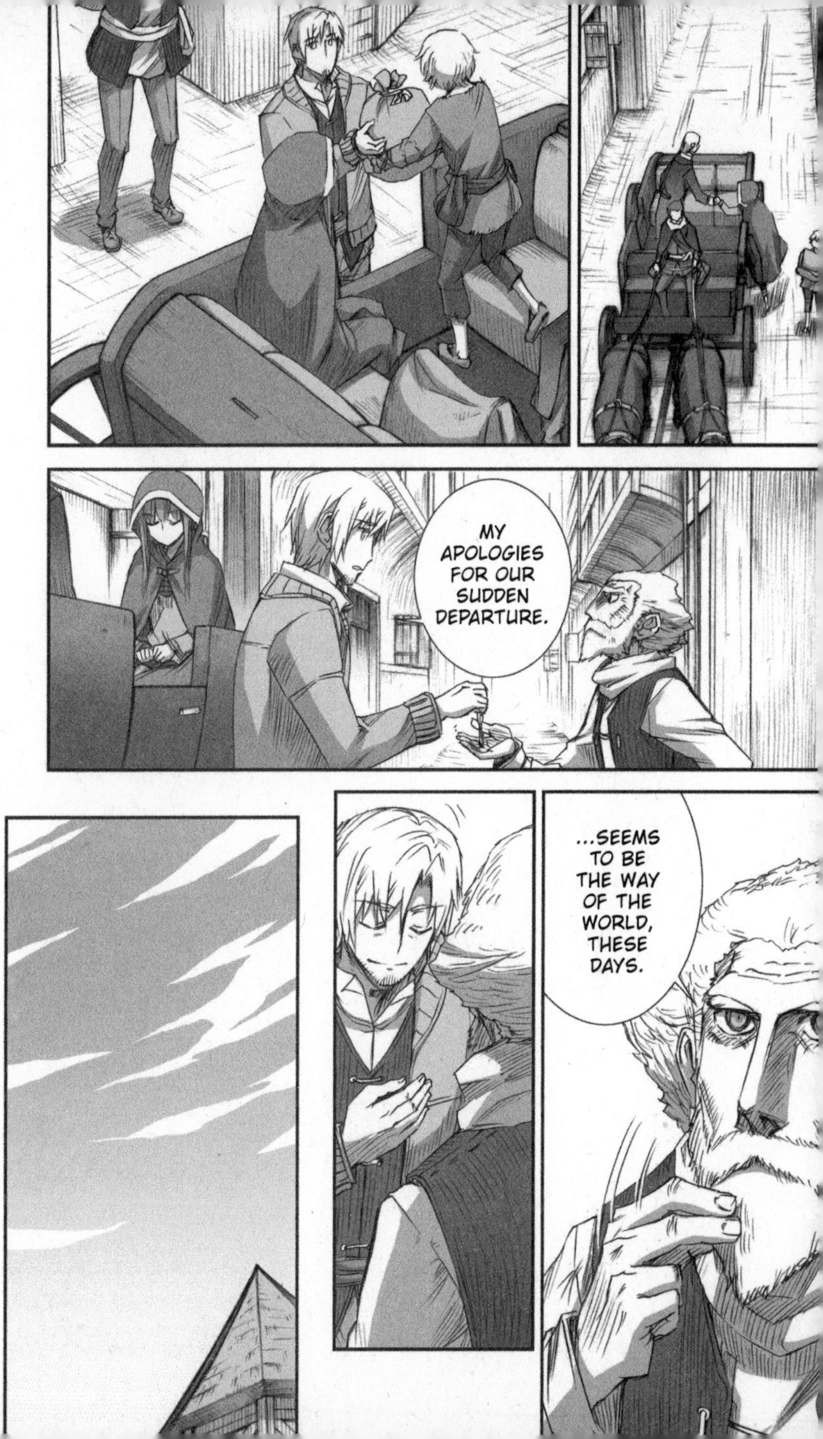
MY APOLOGIES FOR OUR SUDDEN DEPARTURE.
...SEEMS TO BE THE WAY OF THE WORLD, THESE DAYS.

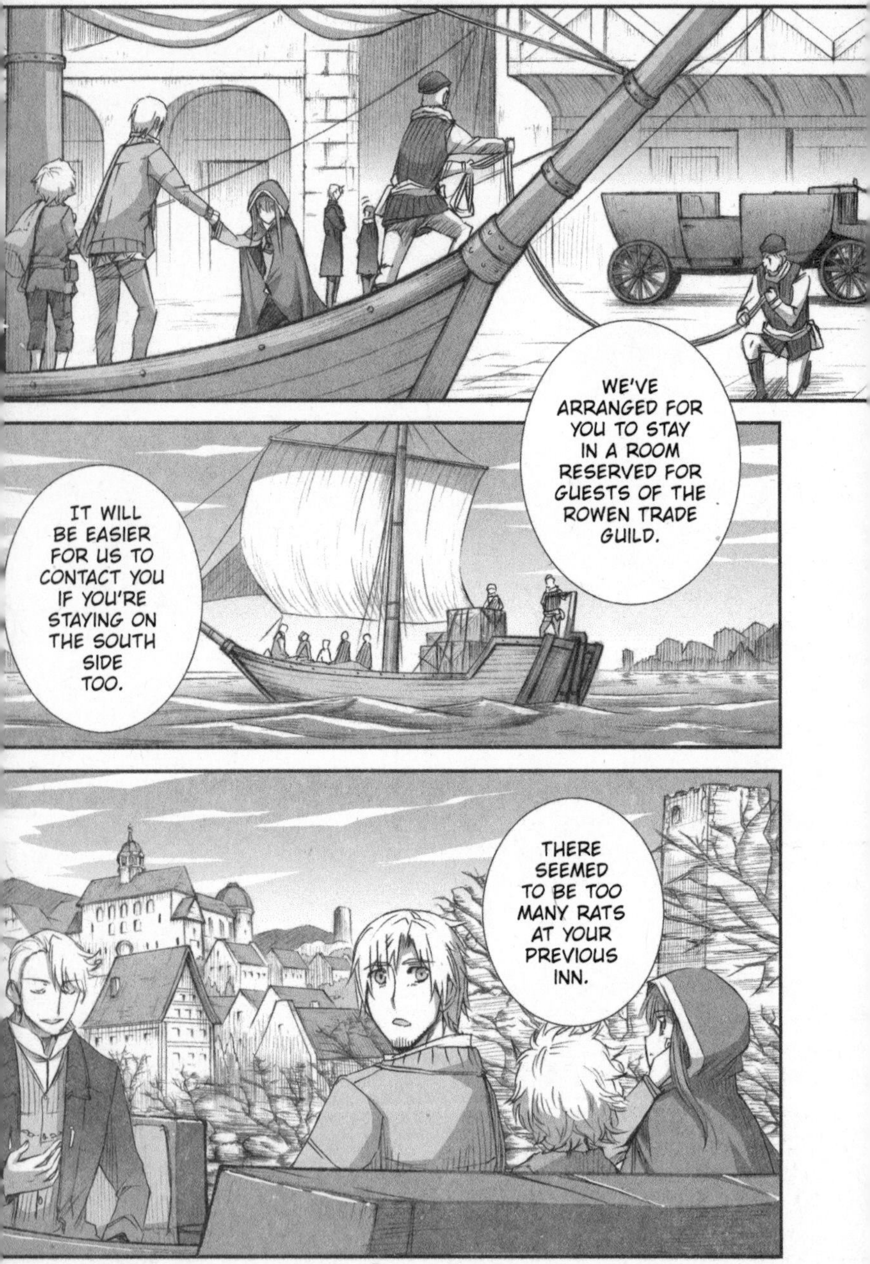
WE'VE ARRANGED FOR YOU TO STAY IN A ROOM RESERVED FOR GUESTS OF THE ROWEN TRADE GUILD.
IT WILL BE EASIER FOR US TO CONTACT YOU IF YOU'RE STAYING ON THE SOUTH SIDE TOO.
THERE SEEMED TO BE TOO MANY RATS AT YOUR PREVIOUS INN.

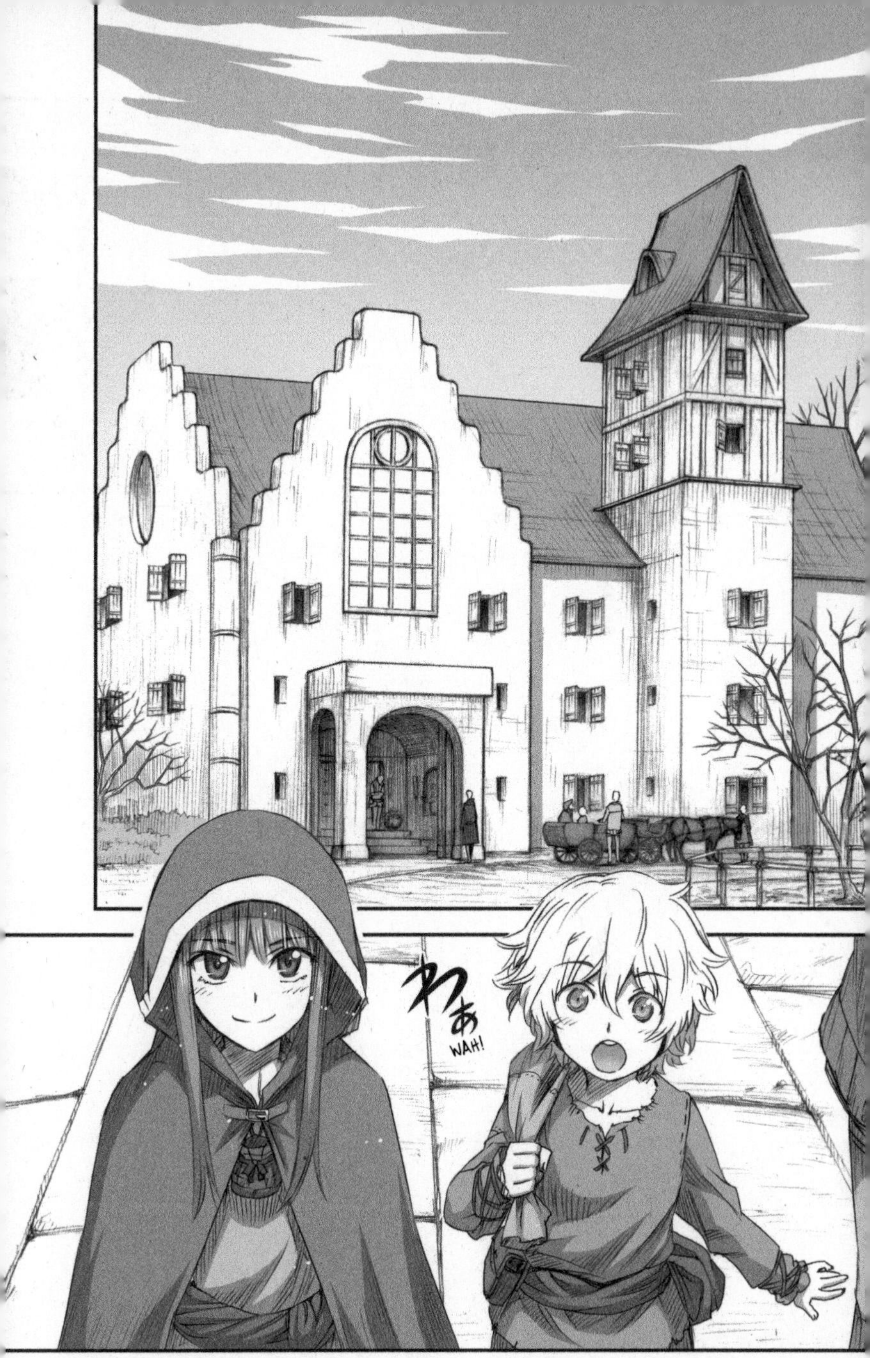
わあ
WAH!

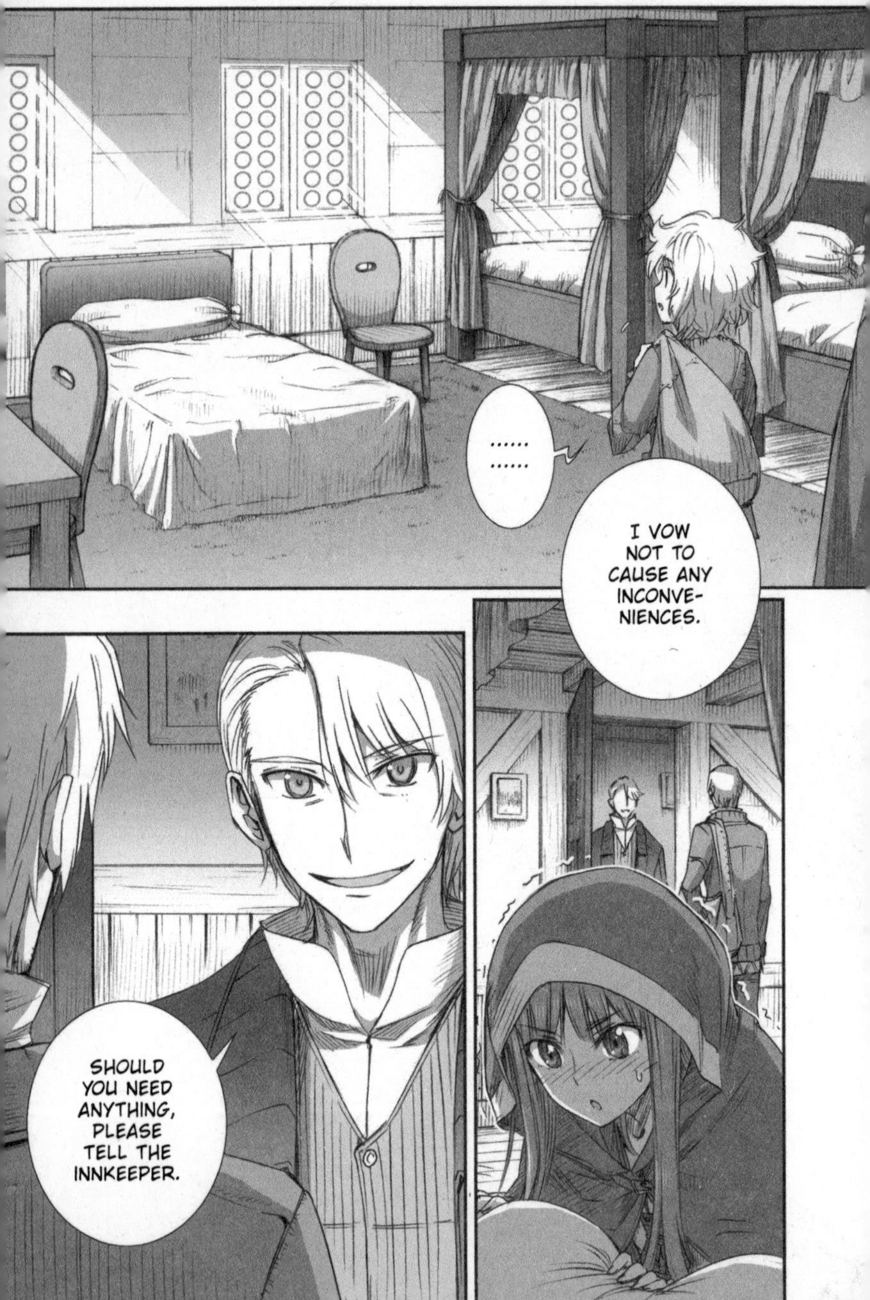
......
......
I VOW NOT TO CAUSE ANY INCONVE-NIENCES.
SHOULD YOU NEED ANYTHING, PLEASE TELL THE INNKEEPER.

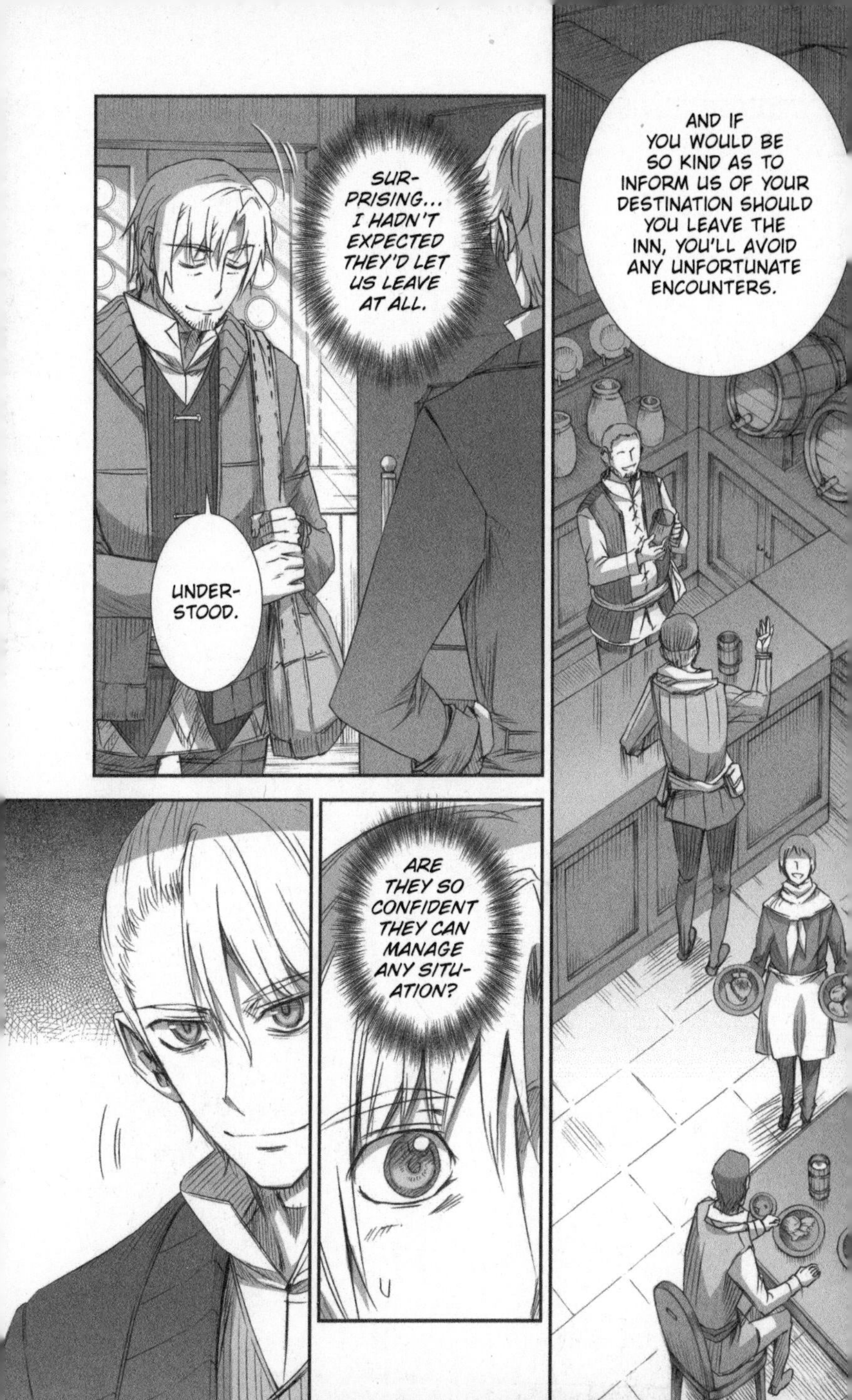
AND IF YOU WOULD BE SO KIND AS TO INFORM US OF YOUR DESTINATION SHOULD YOU LEAVE THE INN, YOU'LL AVOID ANY UNFORTUNATE ENCOUNTERS.
SUR-PRISING... I HADN'T EXPECTED THEY'D LET US LEAVE AT ALL.
UNDER-STOOD.
ARE THEY SO CONFIDENT THEY CAN MANAGE ANY SITU-ATION?

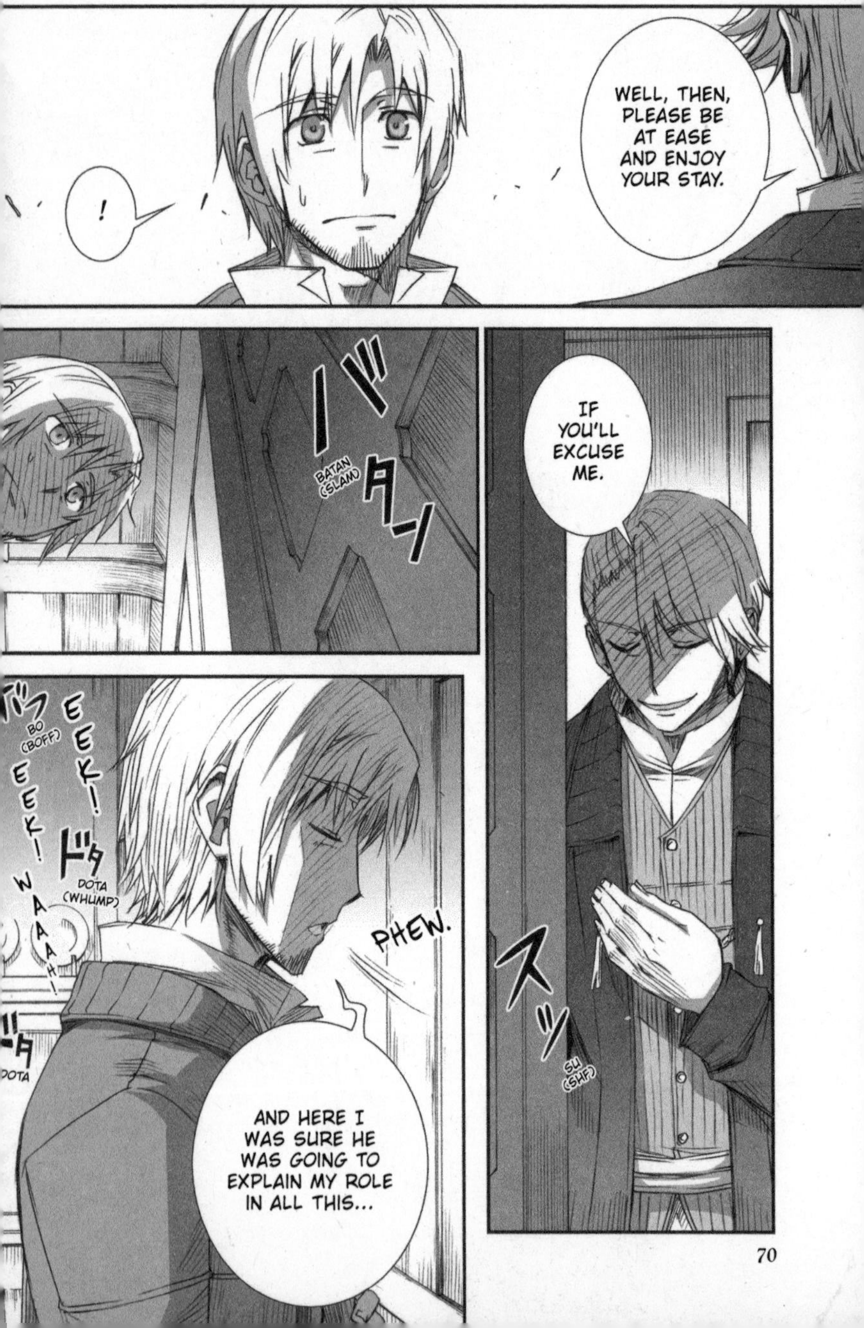
WELL, THEN, PLEASE BE AT EASE AND ENJOY YOUR STAY.
!
IF YOU'LL EXCUSE ME.
SU (SHF)
BATAN (SLAM)
PHEW.
EEEK!
BO (BOFF)
EEEK!
DOTA (WHUMP)
WAAAH!
DOTA
AND HERE I WAS SURE HE WAS GOING TO EXPLAIN MY ROLE IN ALL THIS...

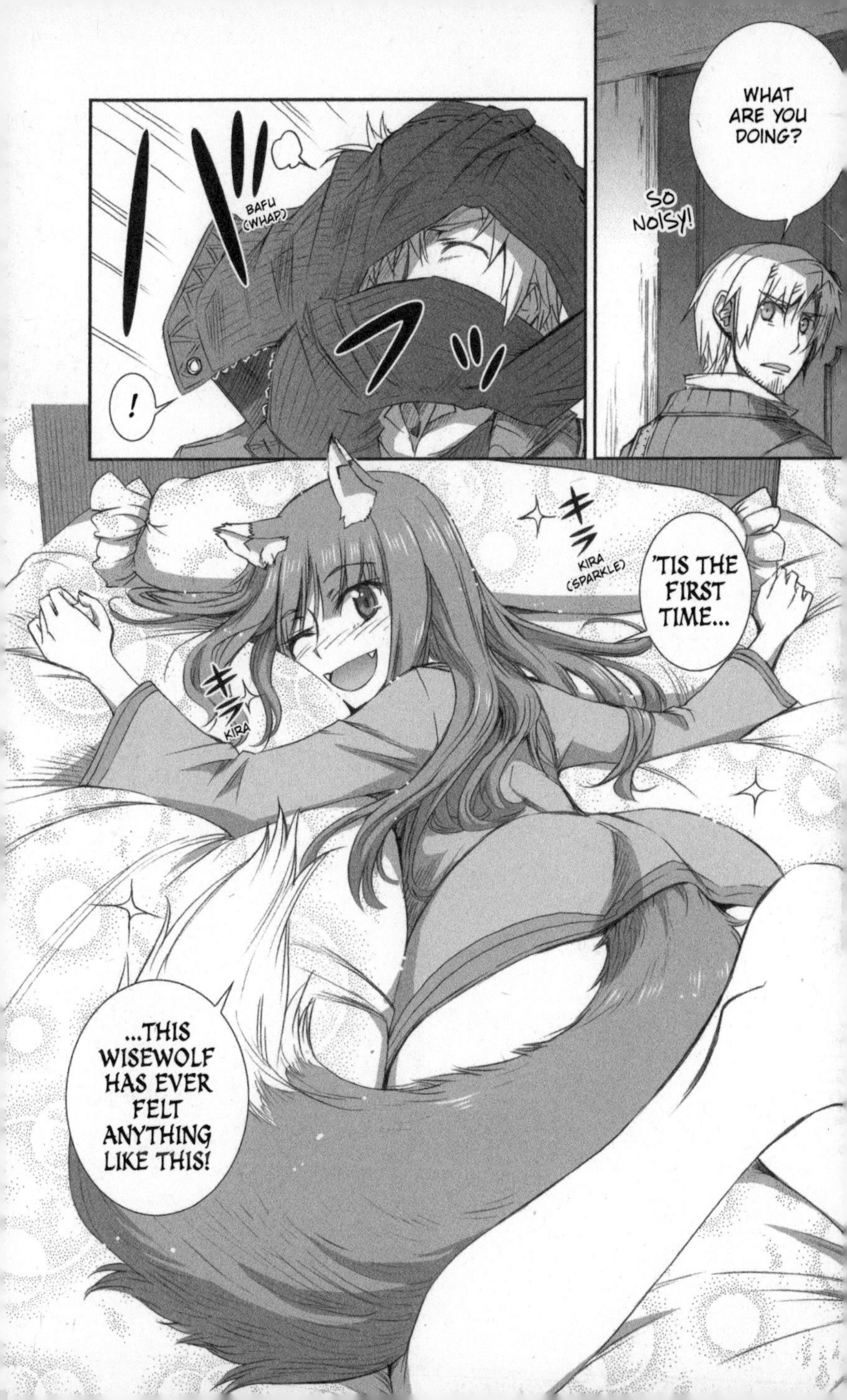
WHAT ARE YOU DOING?
SO NOISY!
BAFU (WHAP)
!
'TIS THE FIRST TIME...
キラ
KIRA (SPARKLE)
キラ
KIRA
...THIS WISEWOLF HAS EVER FELT ANYTHING LIKE THIS!

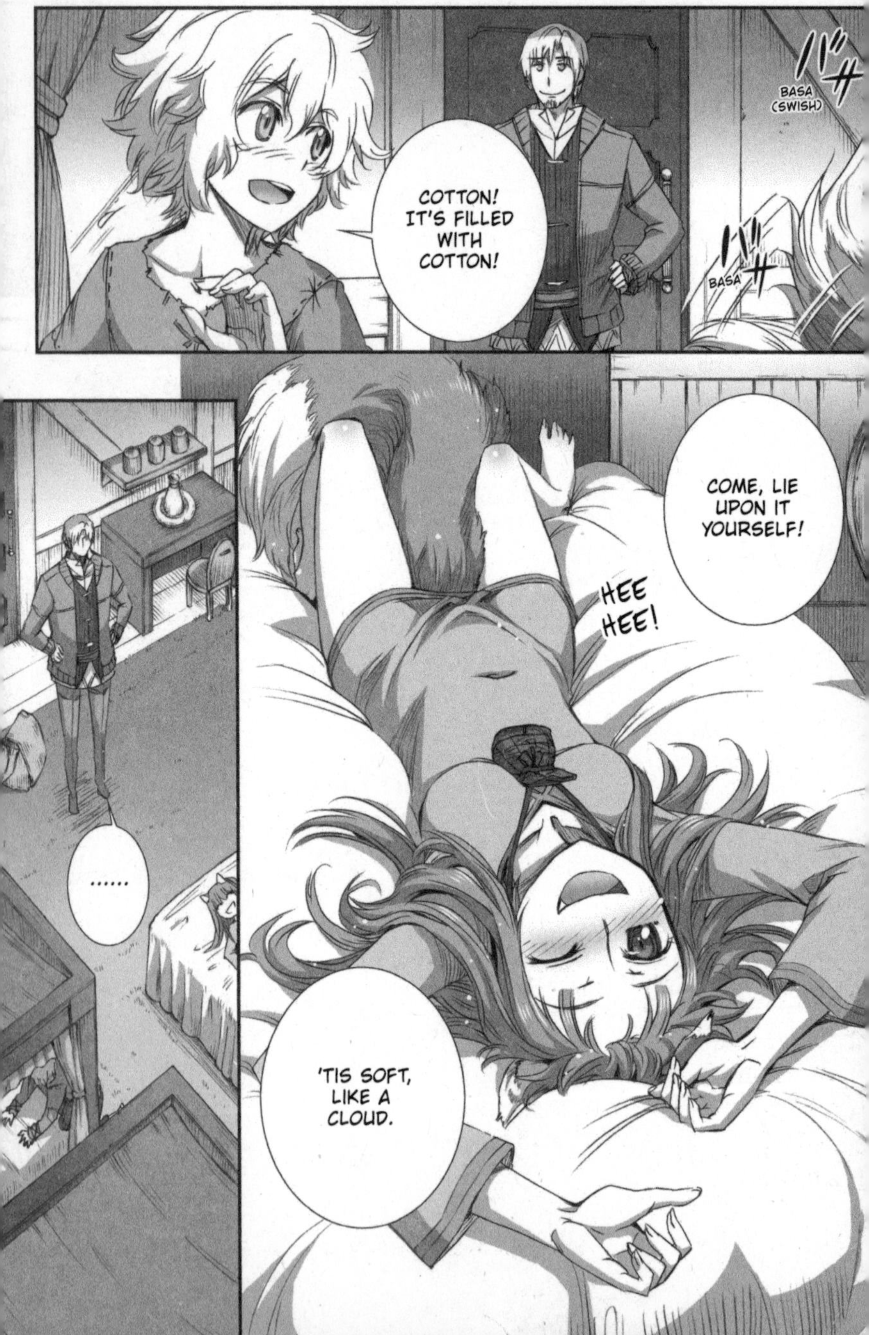

BASA (SWISH)
BASA
COTTON! IT'S FILLED WITH COTTON!
COME, LIE UPON IT YOURSELF!
HEE HEE!
'TIS SOFT, LIKE A CLOUD.
......

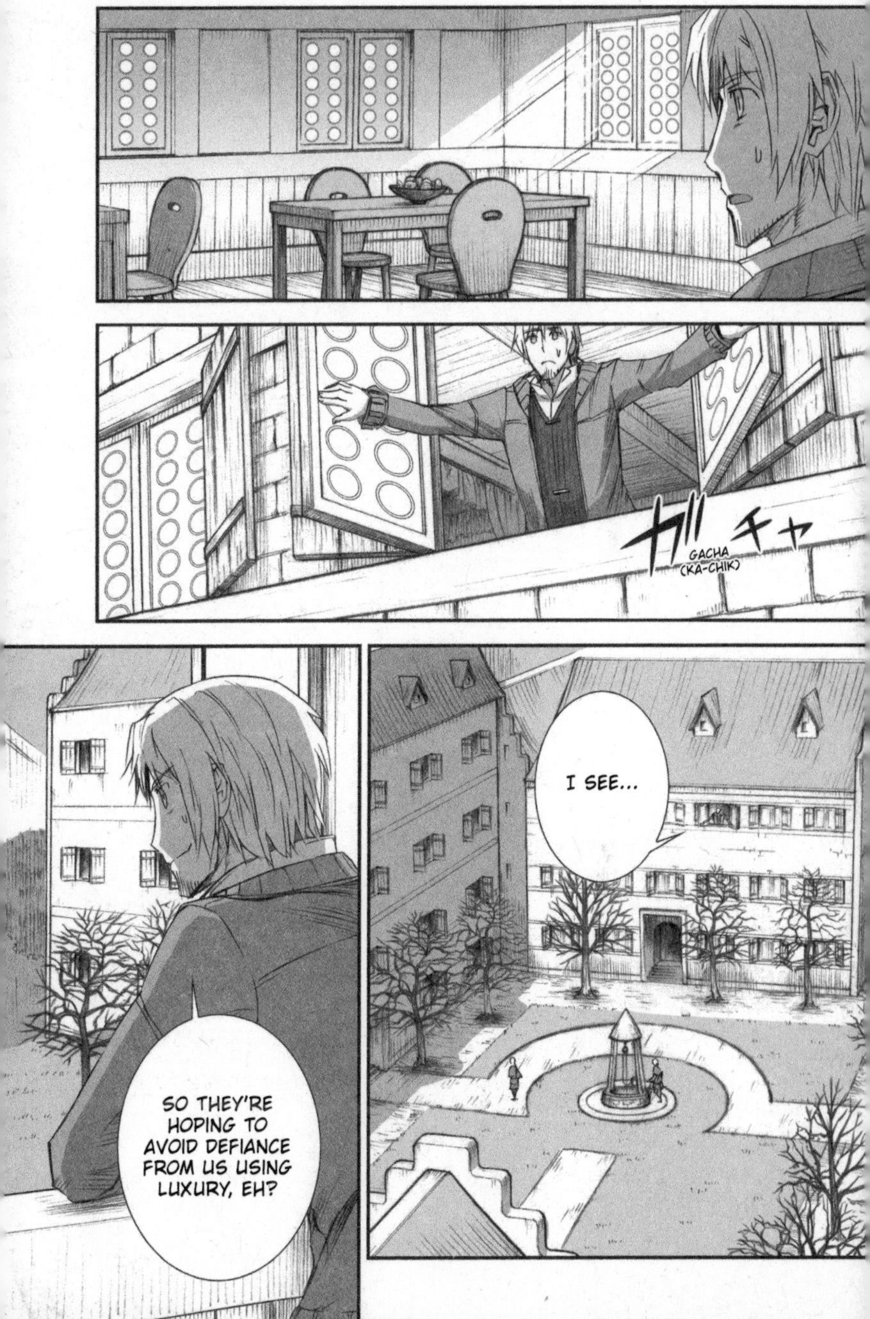
ガチャ
GACHA
(KA-CHIK)
I SEE...
SO THEY'RE HOPING TO AVOID DEFIANCE FROM US USING LUXURY, EH?

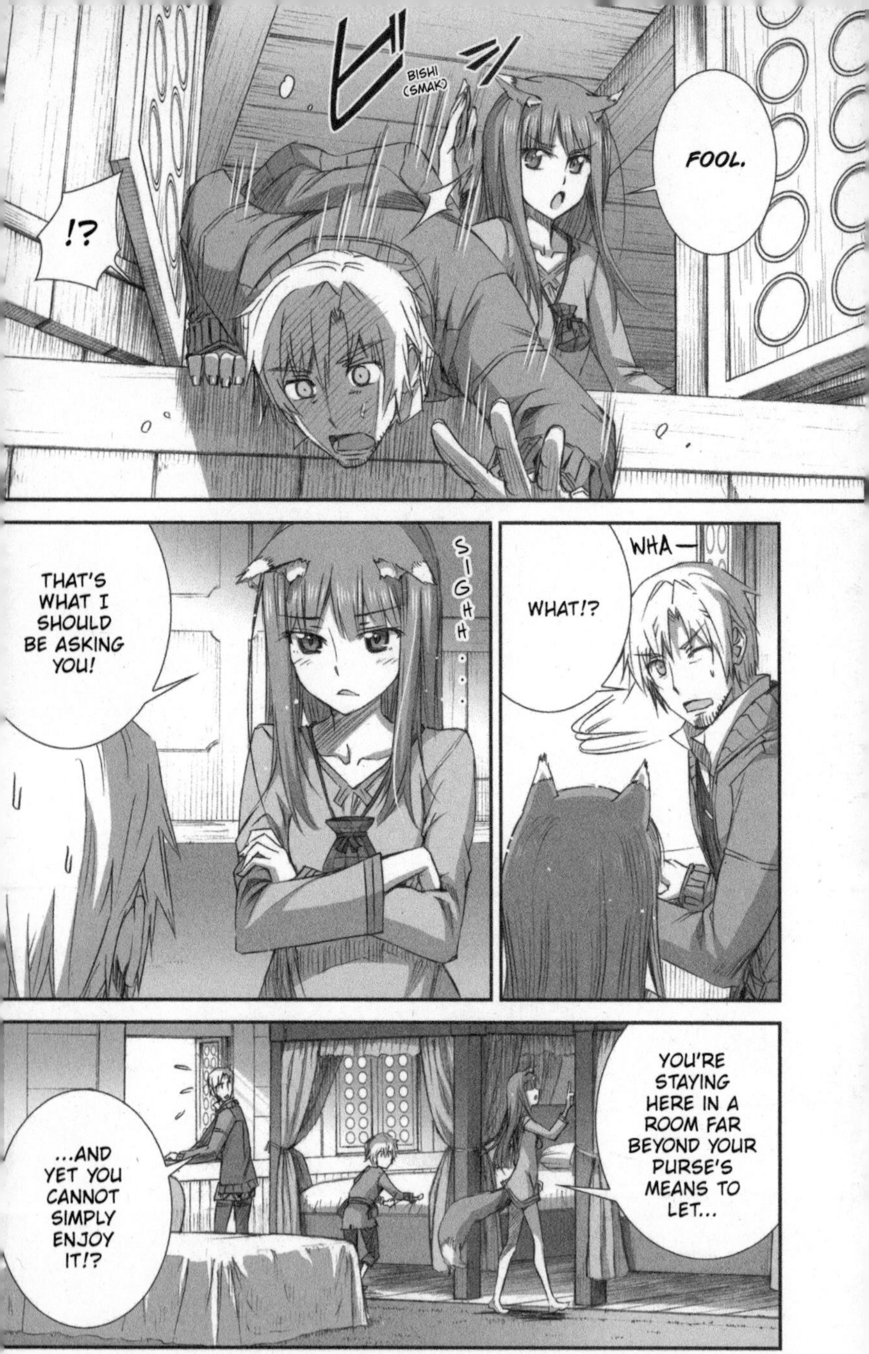
FOOL.
BISHI (SMAK)
!?
WHA—
WHAT!?
SIGH...
THAT'S WHAT I SHOULD BE ASKING YOU!
YOU'RE STAYING HERE IN A ROOM FAR BEYOND YOUR PURSE'S MEANS TO LET...
...AND YET YOU CANNOT SIMPLY ENJOY IT!?

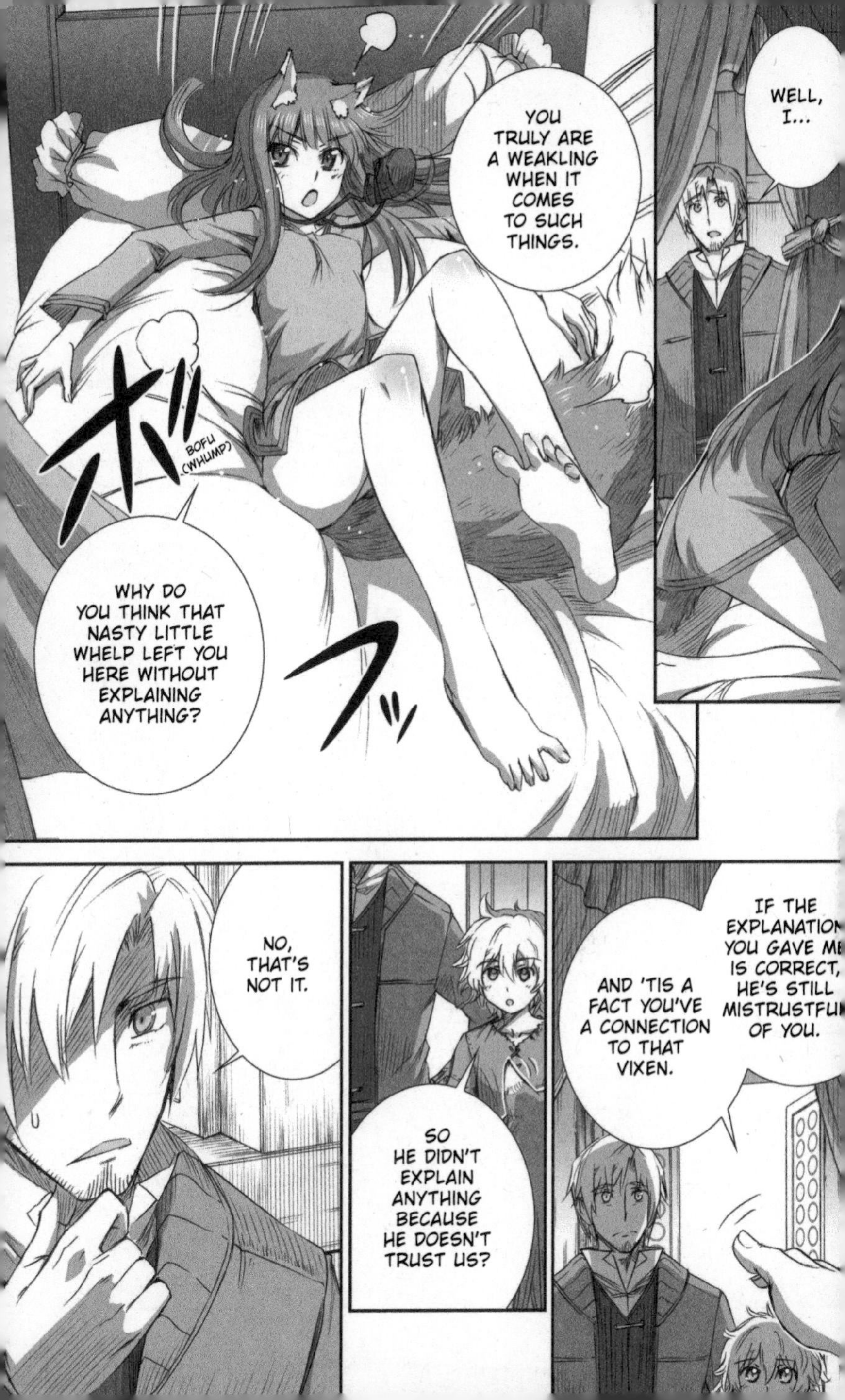
WELL, I...
YOU TRULY ARE A WEAKLING WHEN IT COMES TO SUCH THINGS.
ボフ
BOFU (WHUMP)
WHY DO YOU THINK THAT NASTY LITTLE WHELP LEFT YOU HERE WITHOUT EXPLAINING ANYTHING?
IF THE EXPLANATIO YOU GAVE ME IS CORRECT, HE'S STILL MISTRUSTFU OF YOU.
AND 'TIS A FACT YOU'VE A CONNECTION TO THAT VIXEN.
SO HE DIDN'T EXPLAIN ANYTHING BECAUSE HE DOESN'T TRUST US?
NO, THAT'S NOT IT.

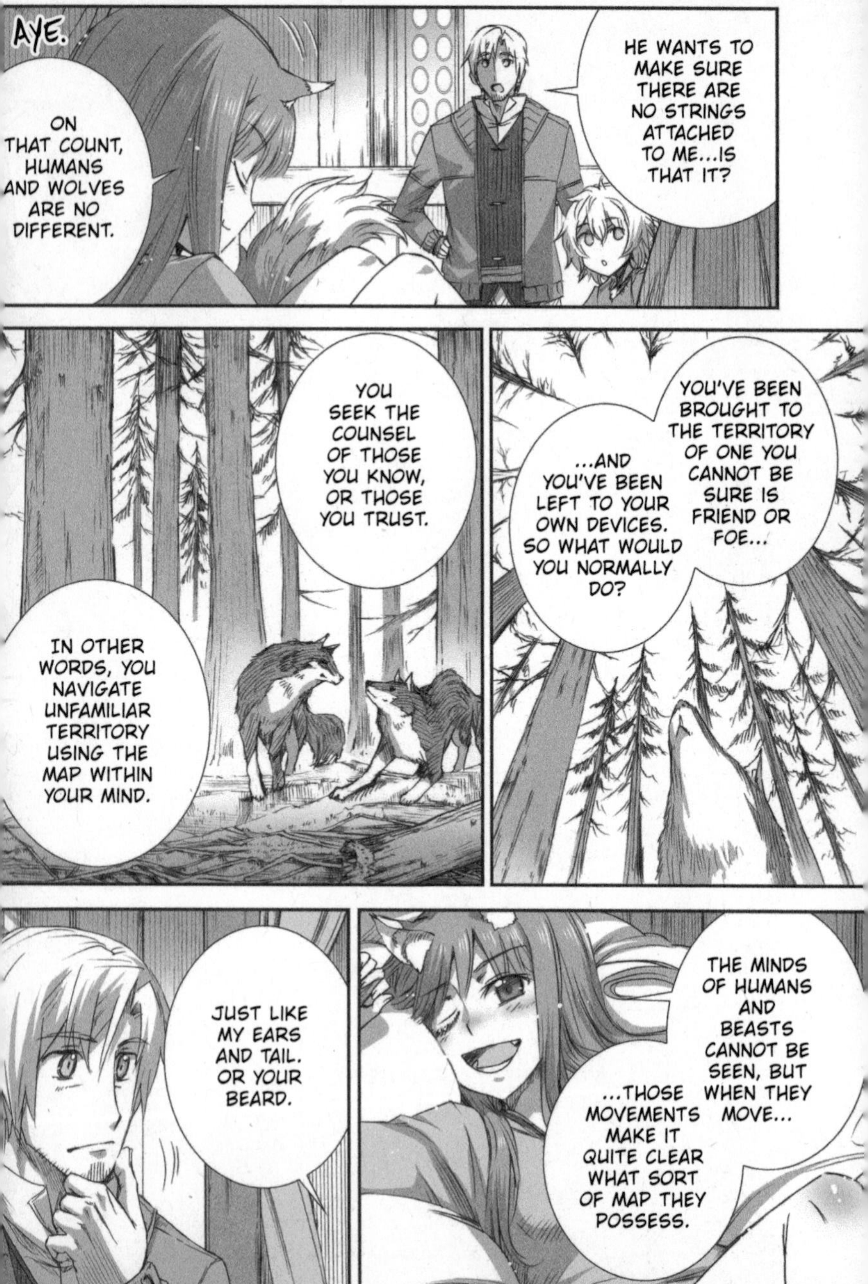
HE WANTS TO MAKE SURE THERE ARE NO STRINGS ATTACHED TO ME...IS THAT IT?
AYE.
ON THAT COUNT, HUMANS AND WOLVES ARE NO DIFFERENT.
YOU'VE BEEN BROUGHT TO THE TERRITORY OF ONE YOU CANNOT BE SURE IS FRIEND OR FOE...
...AND YOU'VE BEEN LEFT TO YOUR OWN DEVICES. SO WHAT WOULD YOU NORMALLY DO?
YOU SEEK THE COUNSEL OF THOSE YOU KNOW, OR THOSE YOU TRUST.
IN OTHER WORDS, YOU NAVIGATE UNFAMILIAR TERRITORY USING THE MAP WITHIN YOUR MIND.
THE MINDS OF HUMANS AND BEASTS CANNOT BE SEEN, BUT WHEN THEY MOVE...
...THOSE MOVEMENTS MAKE IT QUITE CLEAR WHAT SORT OF MAP THEY POSSESS.
JUST LIKE MY EARS AND TAIL. OR YOUR BEARD.

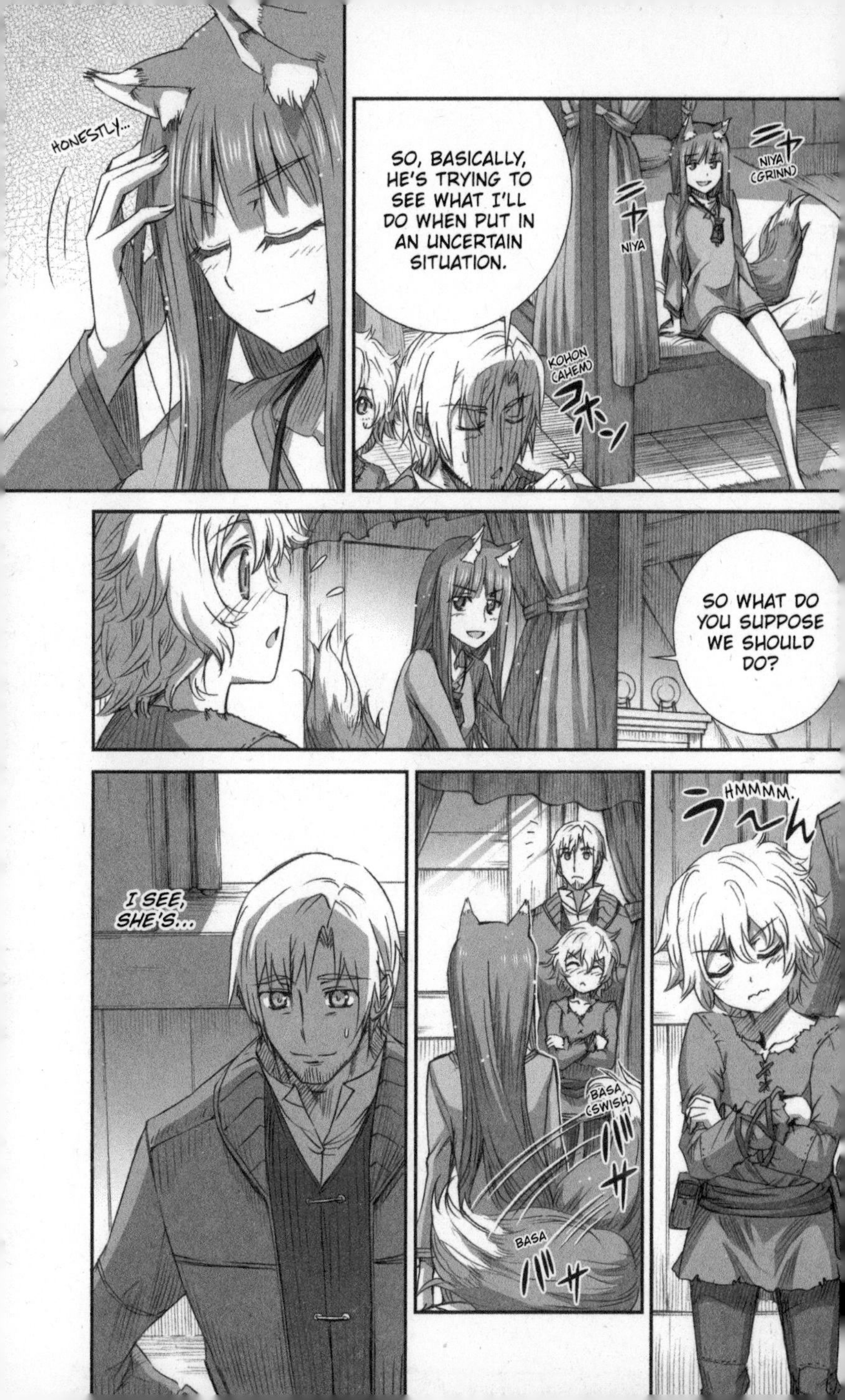
ニヤ
NIYA (GRINN)
ニヤ
NIYA
SO, BASICALLY, HE'S TRYING TO SEE WHAT I'LL DO WHEN PUT IN AN UNCERTAIN SITUATION.
KOHON (AHEM)
コホン
HONESTLY...
SO WHAT DO YOU SUPPOSE WE SHOULD DO?
HMMMM.
う〜ん
BASA (SWISH)
バサ
BASA
バサ
I SEE, SHE'S...

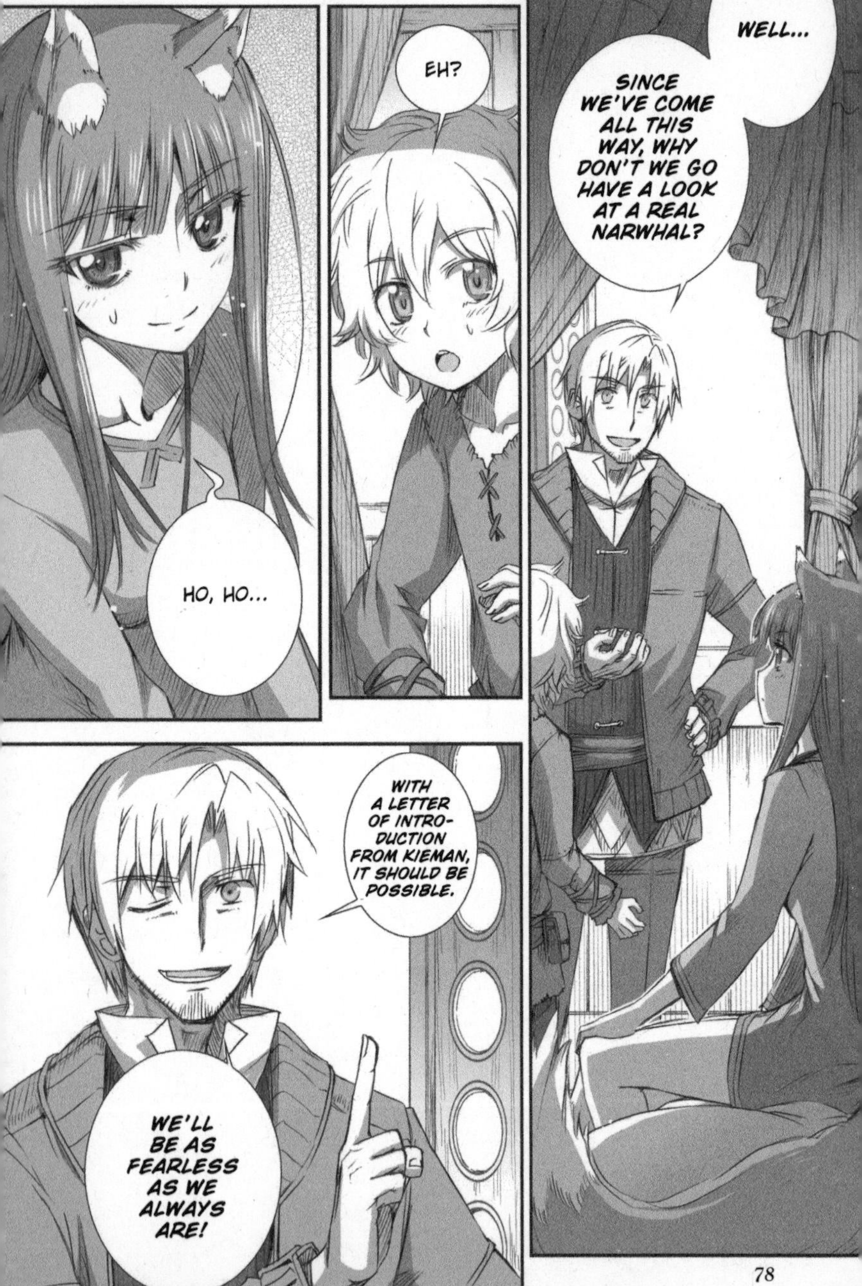
WELL...
SINCE WE'VE COME ALL THIS WAY, WHY DON'T WE GO HAVE A LOOK AT A REAL NARWHAL?
EH?
HO, HO...
WITH A LETTER OF INTRO-DUCTION FROM KIEMAN, IT SHOULD BE POSSIBLE.
WE'LL BE AS FEARLESS AS WE ALWAYS ARE!

SPICE & WOLF

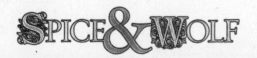

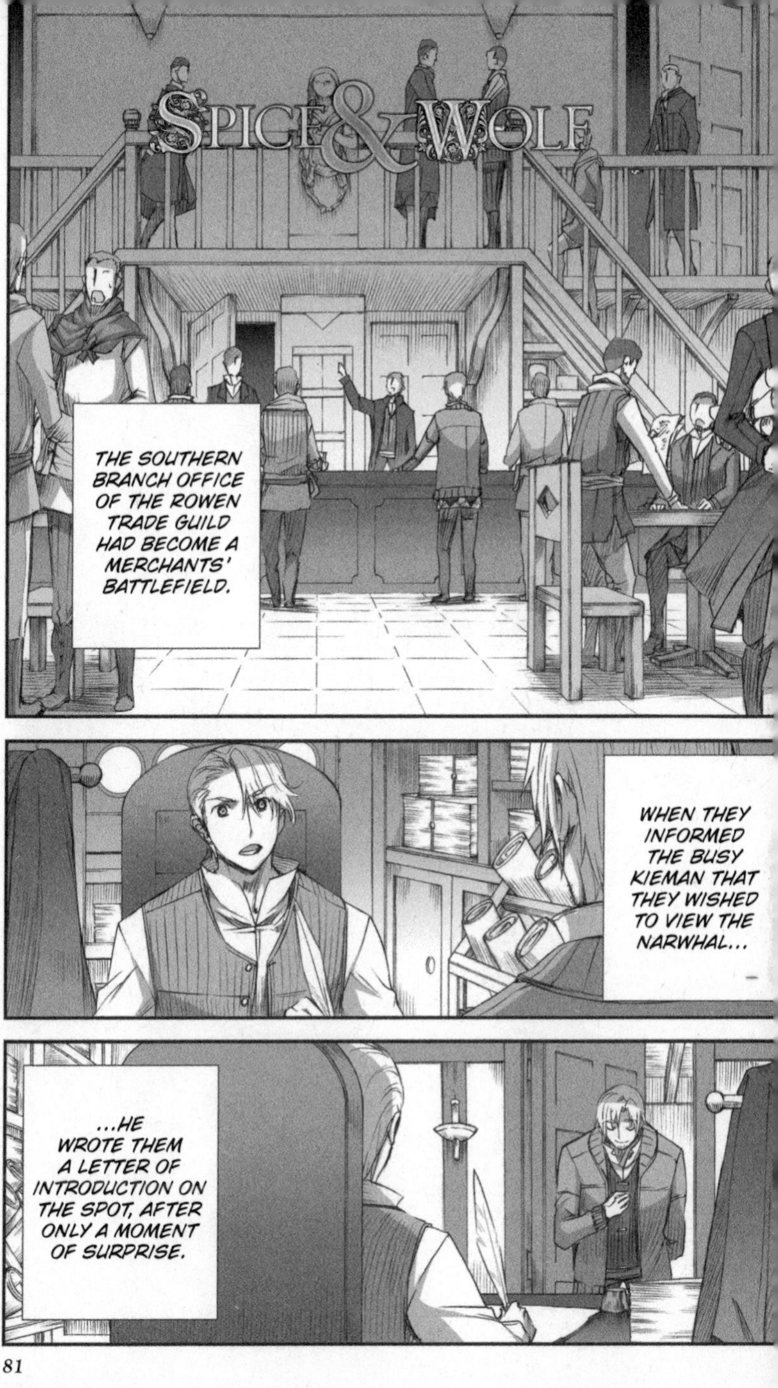
SPICE & WOLF
THE SOUTHERN BRANCH OFFICE OF THE ROWEN TRADE GUILD HAD BECOME A MERCHANTS' BATTLEFIELD.
WHEN THEY INFORMED THE BUSY KIEMAN THAT THEY WISHED TO VIEW THE NARWHAL...
...HE WROTE THEM A LETTER OF INTRODUCTION ON THE SPOT, AFTER ONLY A MOMENT OF SURPRISE.

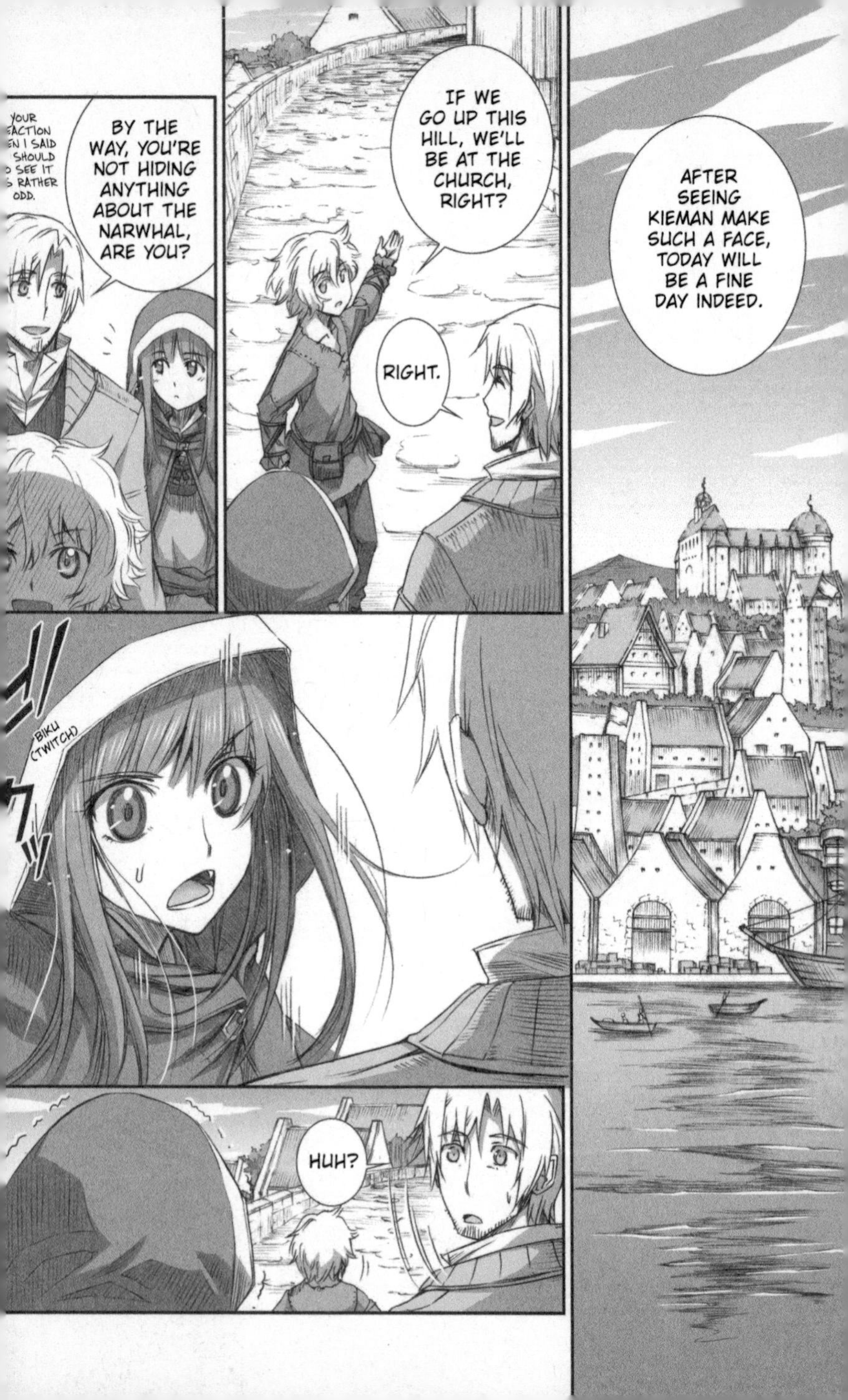
AFTER SEEING KIEMAN MAKE SUCH A FACE, TODAY WILL BE A FINE DAY INDEED.
IF WE GO UP THIS HILL, WE'LL BE AT THE CHURCH, RIGHT?
RIGHT.
BY THE WAY, YOU'RE NOT HIDING ANYTHING ABOUT THE NARWHAL, ARE YOU?
YOUR ACTION EN I SAID SHOULD O SEE IT S RATHER ODD.
BIKU (TWITCH)
HUH?

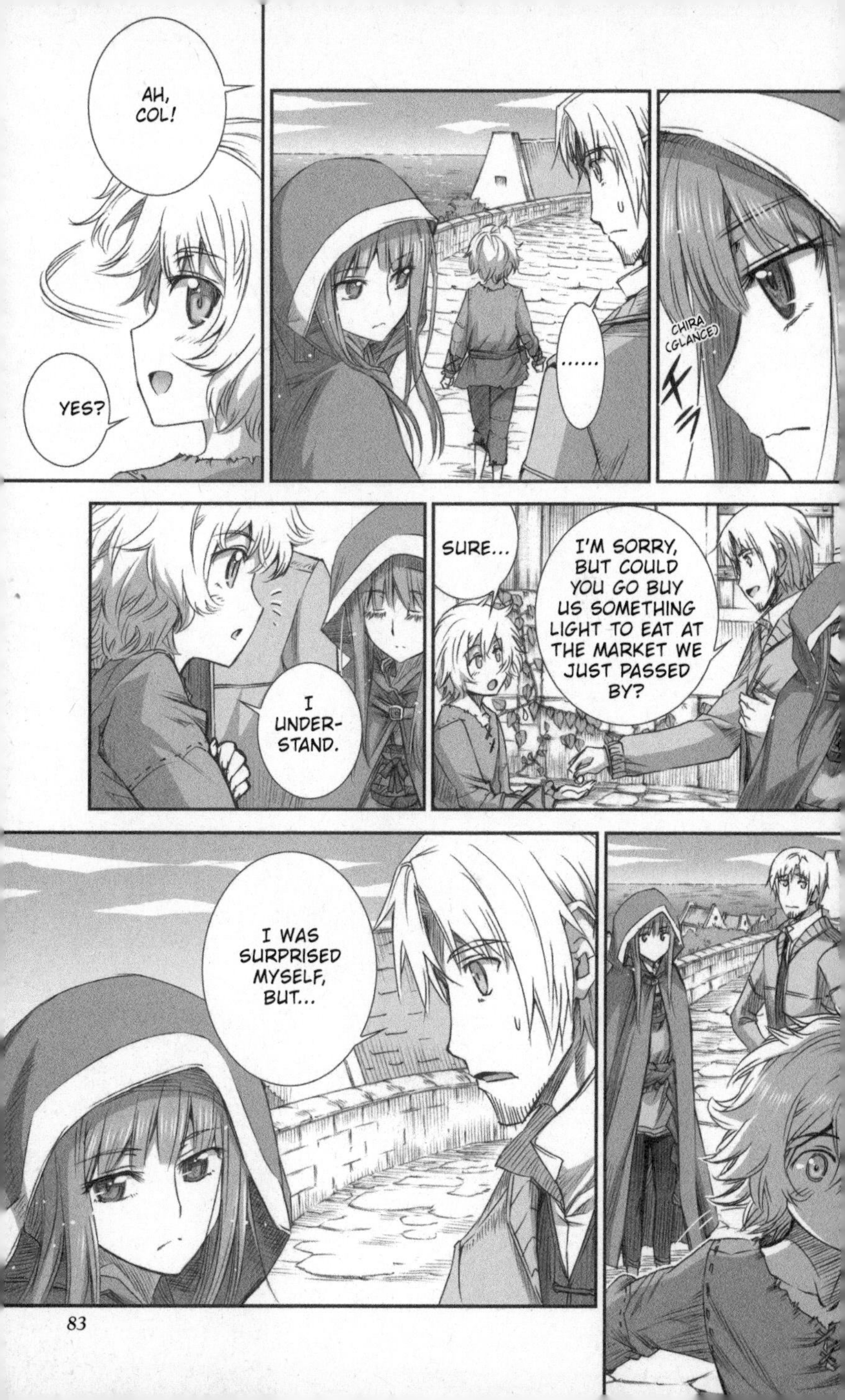
CHIRA (GLANCE)
......
AH, COL!
YES?
I'M SORRY, BUT COULD YOU GO BUY US SOMETHING LIGHT TO EAT AT THE MARKET WE JUST PASSED BY?
SURE...
I UNDER-STAND.
I WAS SURPRISED MYSELF, BUT...

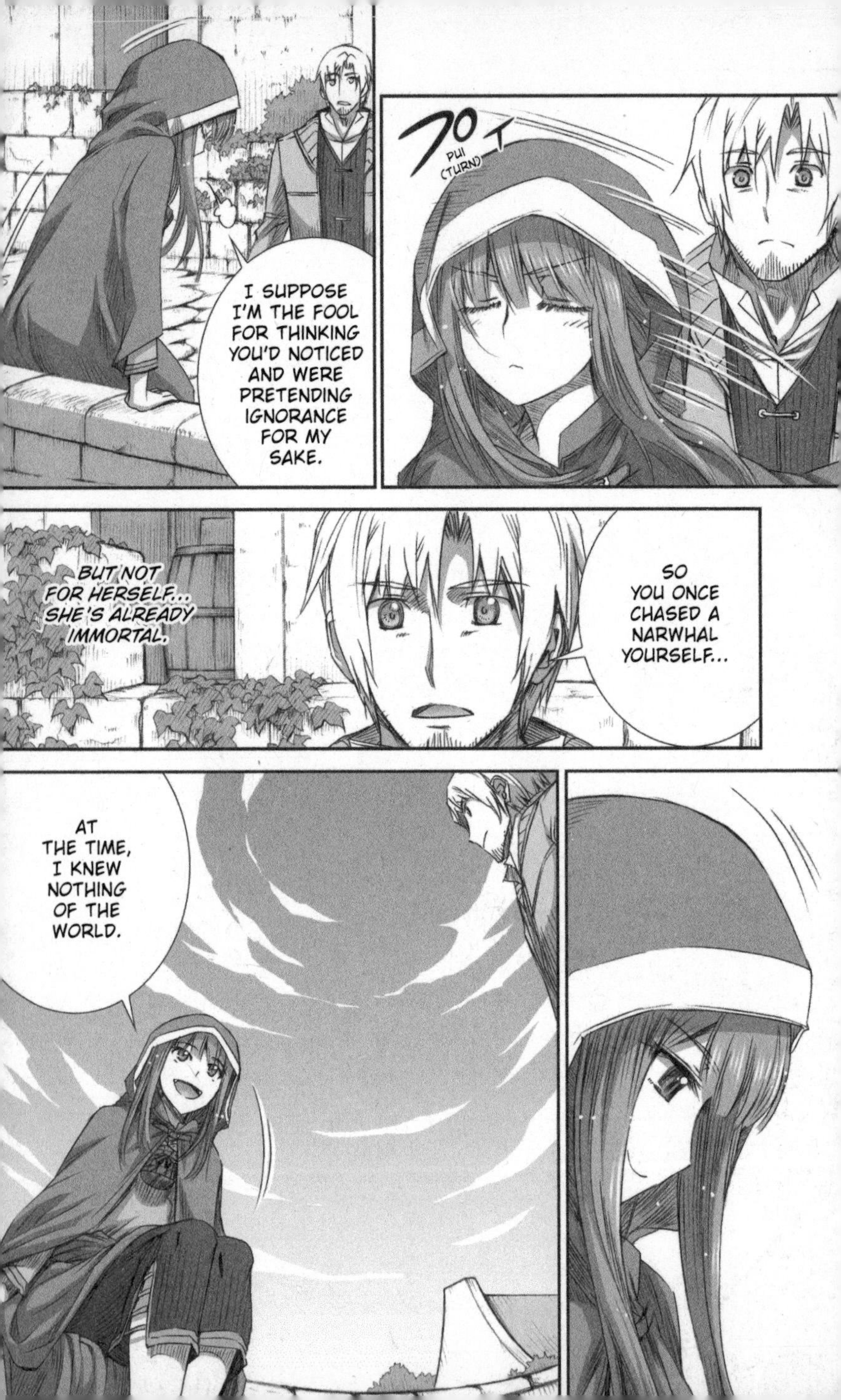
PUI (TURN)
I SUPPOSE I'M THE FOOL FOR THINKING YOU'D NOTICED AND WERE PRETENDING IGNORANCE FOR MY SAKE.
SO YOU ONCE CHASED A NARWHAL YOURSELF...
BUT NOT FOR HERSELF... SHE'S ALREADY IMMORTAL.
AT THE TIME, I KNEW NOTHING OF THE WORLD.

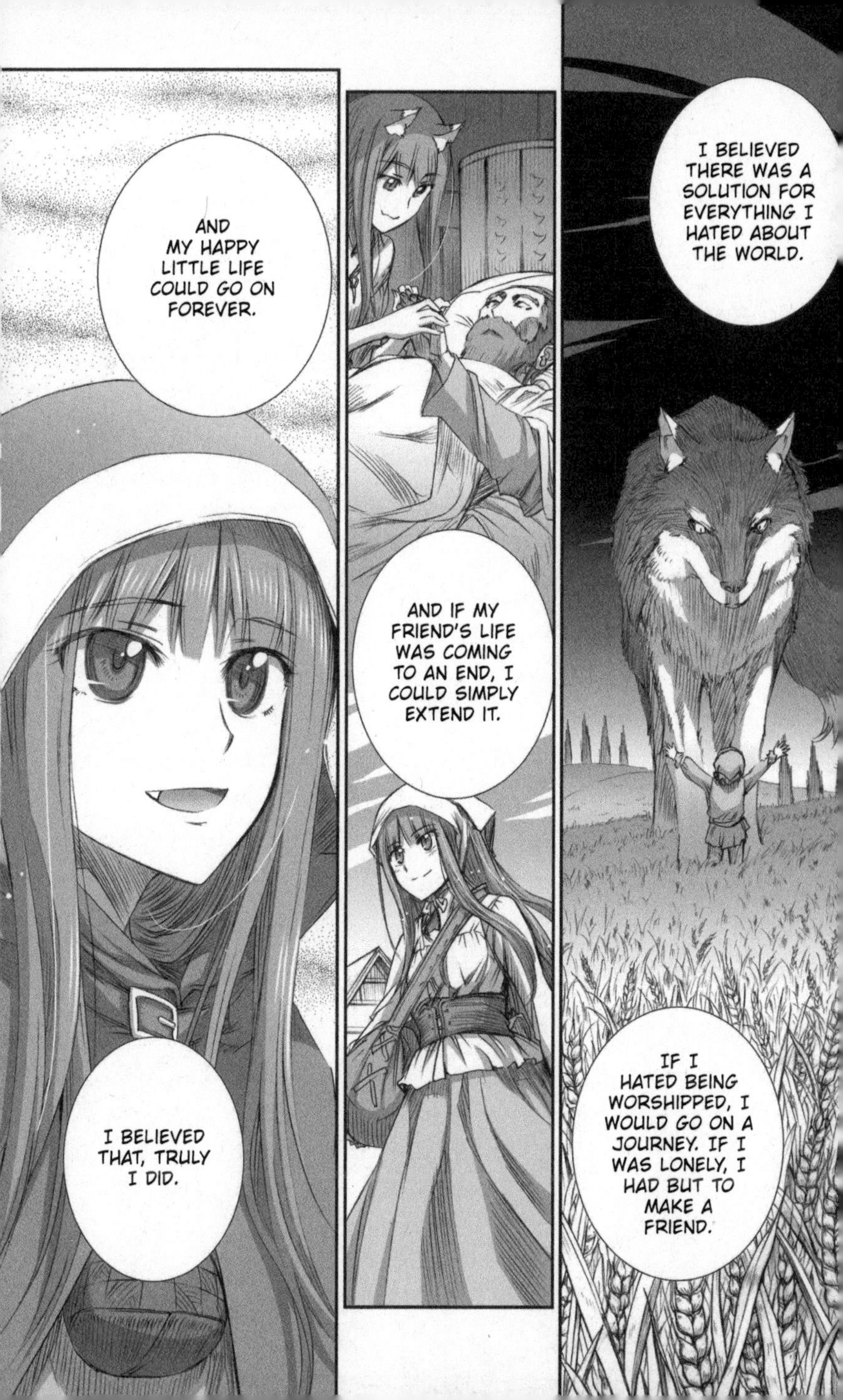
I BELIEVED THERE WAS A SOLUTION FOR EVERYTHING I HATED ABOUT THE WORLD.
IF I HATED BEING WORSHIPPED, I WOULD GO ON A JOURNEY. IF I WAS LONELY, I HAD BUT TO MAKE A FRIEND.
AND IF MY FRIEND'S LIFE WAS COMING TO AN END, I COULD SIMPLY EXTEND IT.
AND MY HAPPY LITTLE LIFE COULD GO ON FOREVER.
I BELIEVED THAT, TRULY I DID.

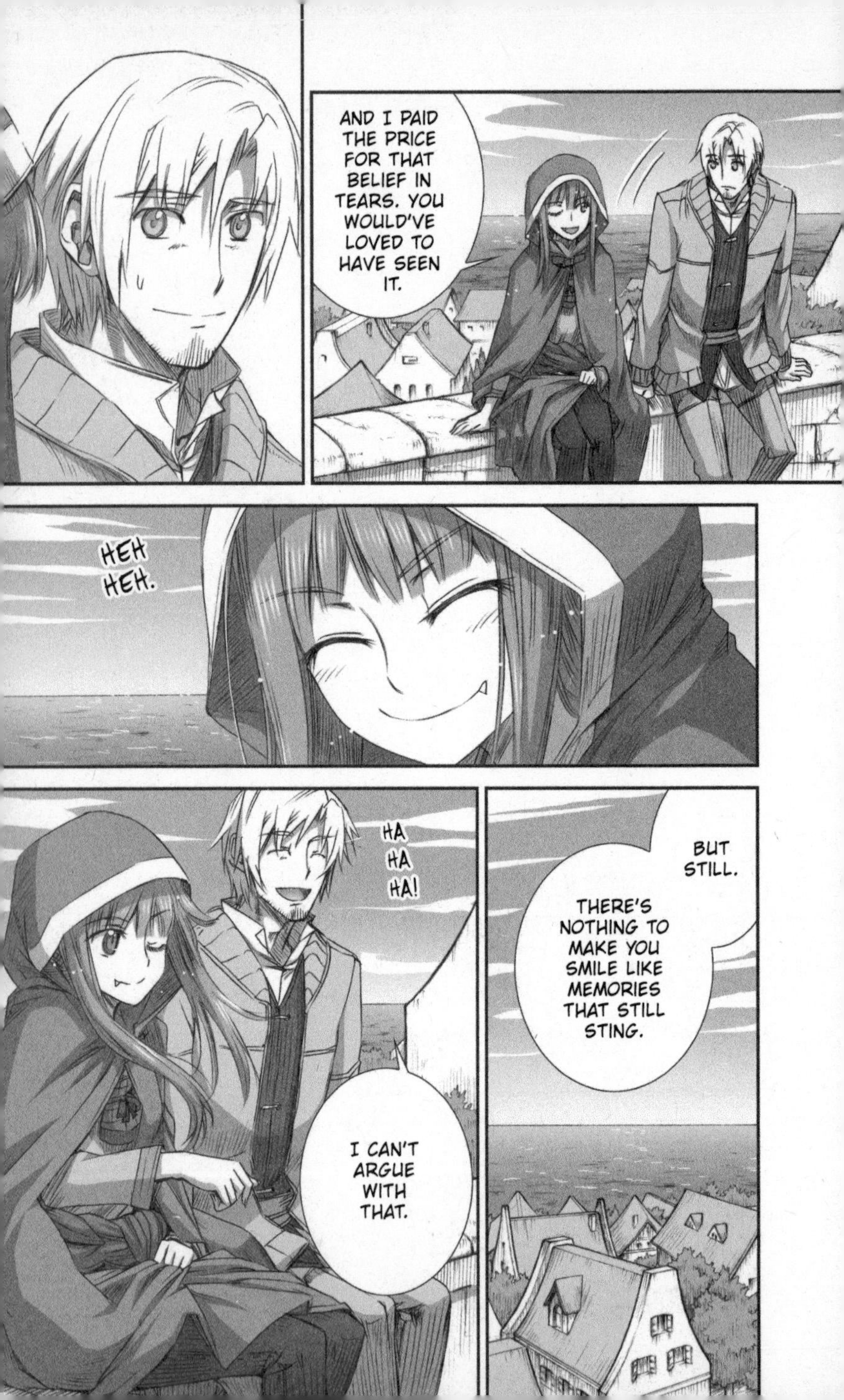
AND I PAID THE PRICE FOR THAT BELIEF IN TEARS. YOU WOULD'VE LOVED TO HAVE SEEN IT.
HEH HEH.
BUT STILL.
THERE'S NOTHING TO MAKE YOU SMILE LIKE MEMORIES THAT STILL STING.
HA HA HA!
I CAN'T ARGUE WITH THAT.

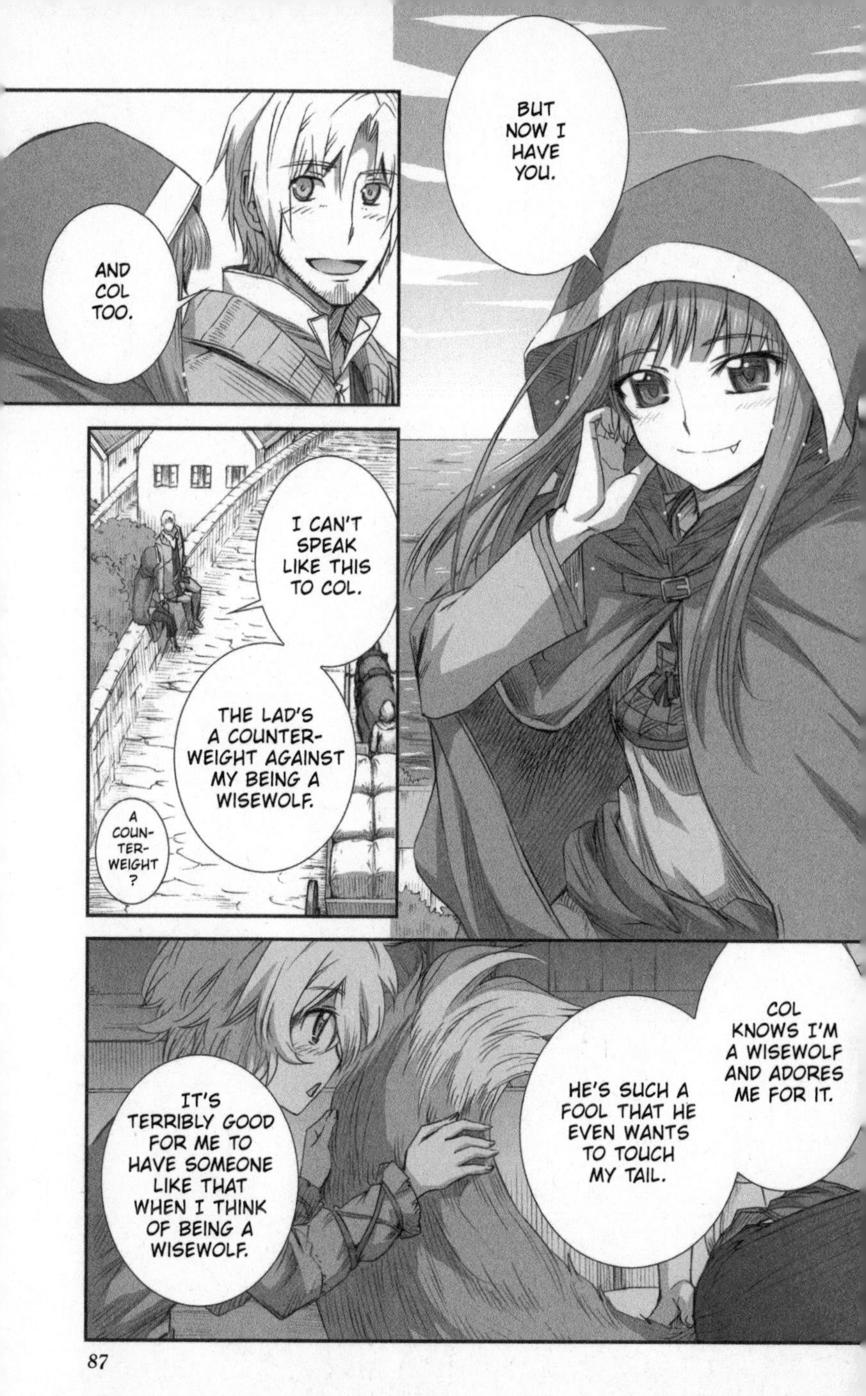
BUT NOW I HAVE YOU.
AND COL TOO.
I CAN'T SPEAK LIKE THIS TO COL.
THE LAD'S A COUNTER-WEIGHT AGAINST MY BEING A WISEWOLF.
A COUNTER-WEIGHT?
COL KNOWS I'M A WISEWOLF AND ADORES ME FOR IT.
HE'S SUCH A FOOL THAT HE EVEN WANTS TO TOUCH MY TAIL.
IT'S TERRIBLY GOOD FOR ME TO HAVE SOMEONE LIKE THAT WHEN I THINK OF BEING A WISEWOLF.

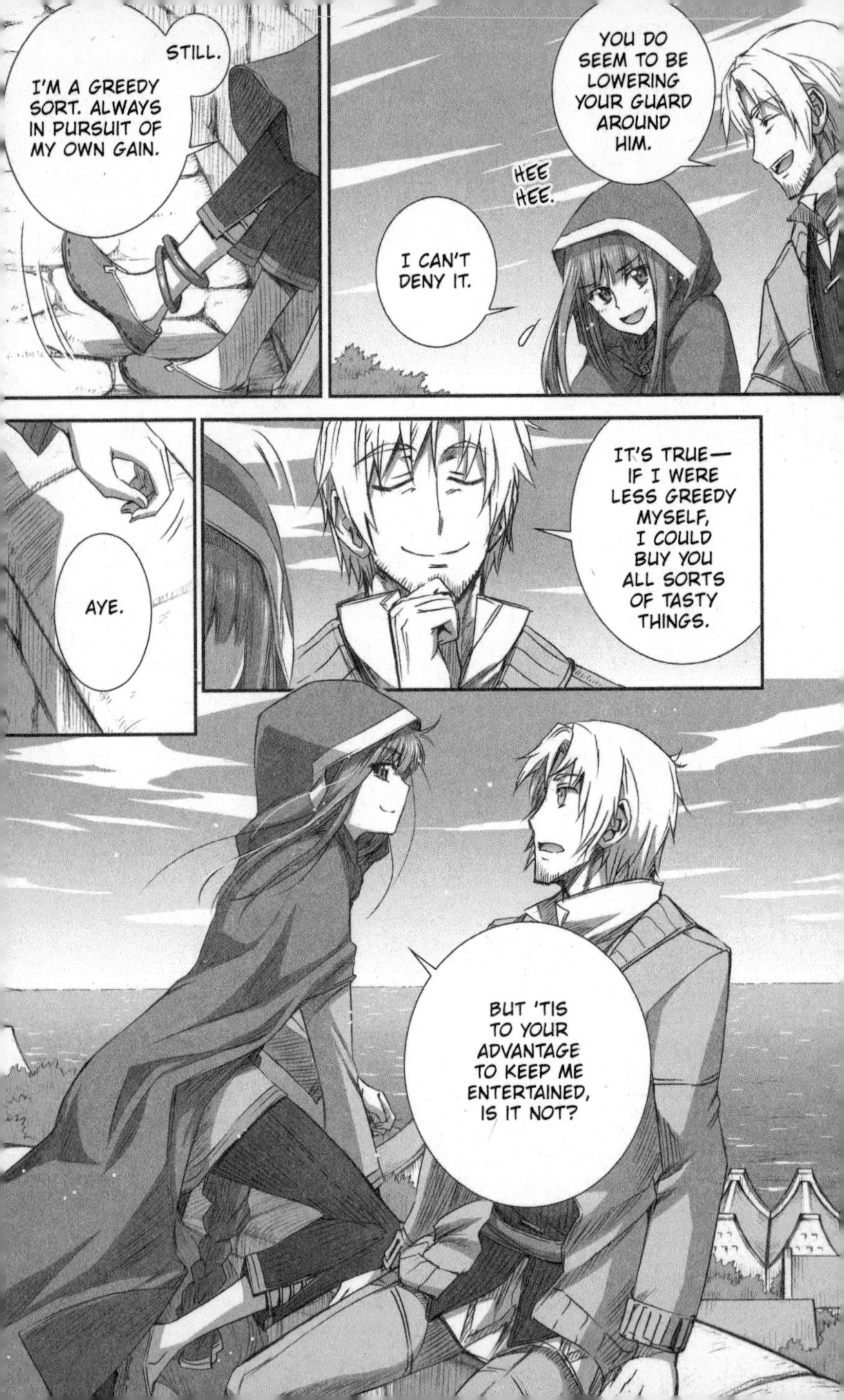
YOU DO SEEM TO BE LOWERING YOUR GUARD AROUND HIM.
HEE HEE.
I CAN'T DENY IT.
STILL.
I'M A GREEDY SORT. ALWAYS IN PURSUIT OF MY OWN GAIN.
IT'S TRUE— IF I WERE LESS GREEDY MYSELF, I COULD BUY YOU ALL SORTS OF TASTY THINGS.
AYE.
BUT 'TIS TO YOUR ADVANTAGE TO KEEP ME ENTERTAINED, IS IT NOT?

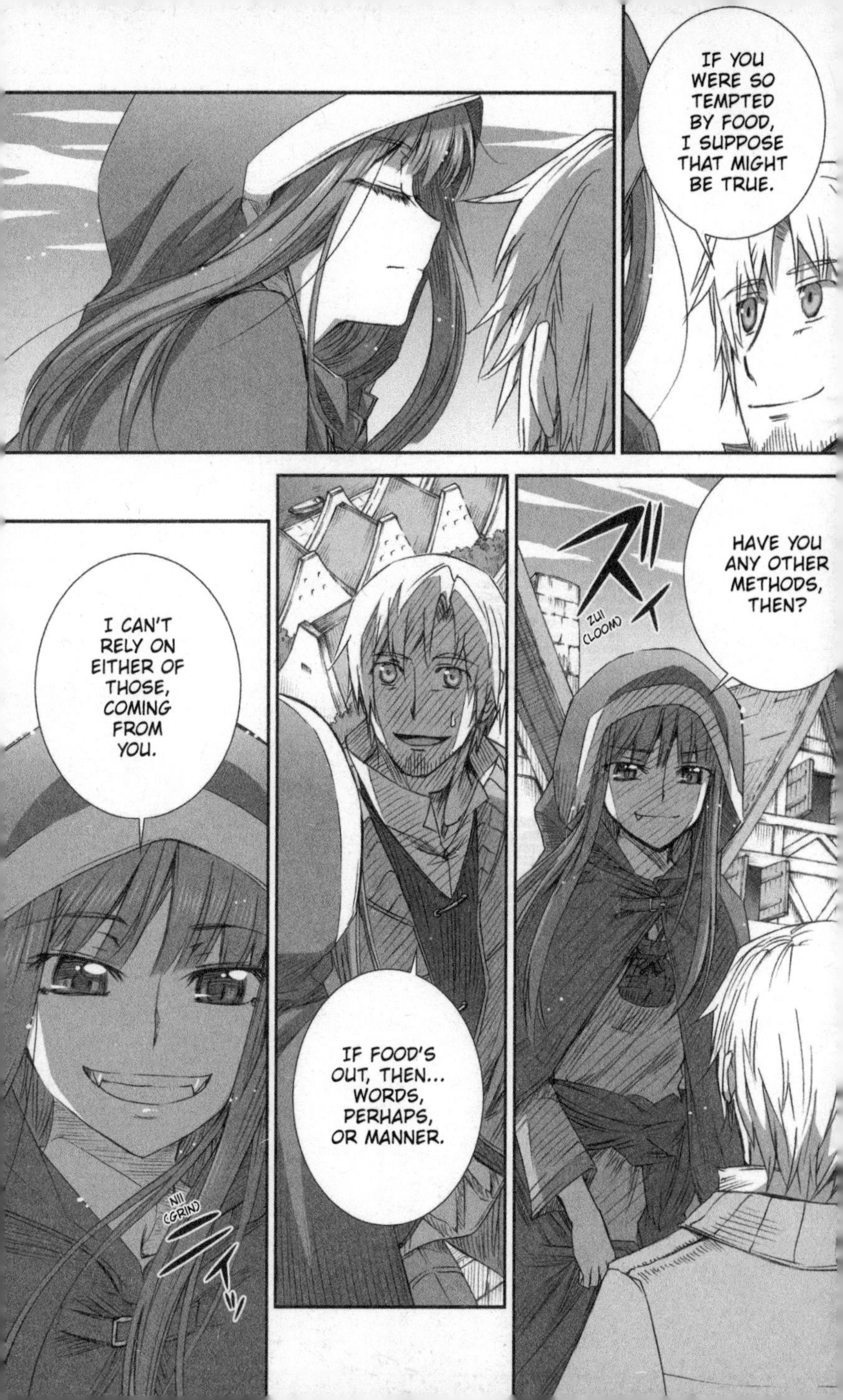
IF YOU WERE SO TEMPTED BY FOOD, I SUPPOSE THAT MIGHT BE TRUE.
HAVE YOU ANY OTHER METHODS, THEN?
ZUI (LOOM)
IF FOOD'S OUT, THEN... WORDS, PERHAPS, OR MANNER.
I CAN'T RELY ON EITHER OF THOSE, COMING FROM YOU.
NII (GRIN)

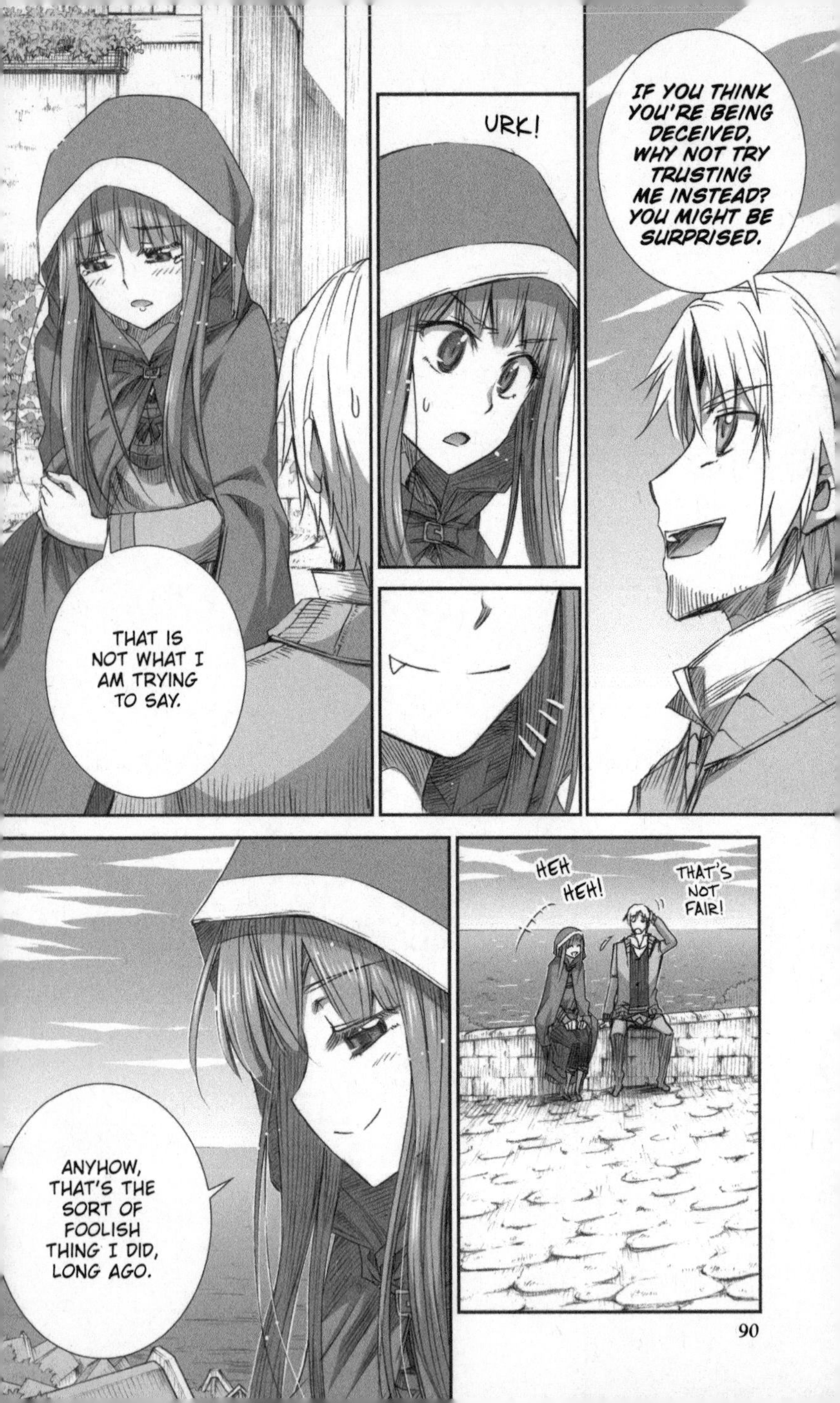
IF YOU THINK YOU'RE BEING DECEIVED, WHY NOT TRY TRUSTING ME INSTEAD? YOU MIGHT BE SURPRISED.
URK!
THAT IS NOT WHAT I AM TRYING TO SAY.
THAT'S NOT FAIR!
HEH HEH!
ANYHOW, THAT'S THE SORT OF FOOLISH THING I DID, LONG AGO.

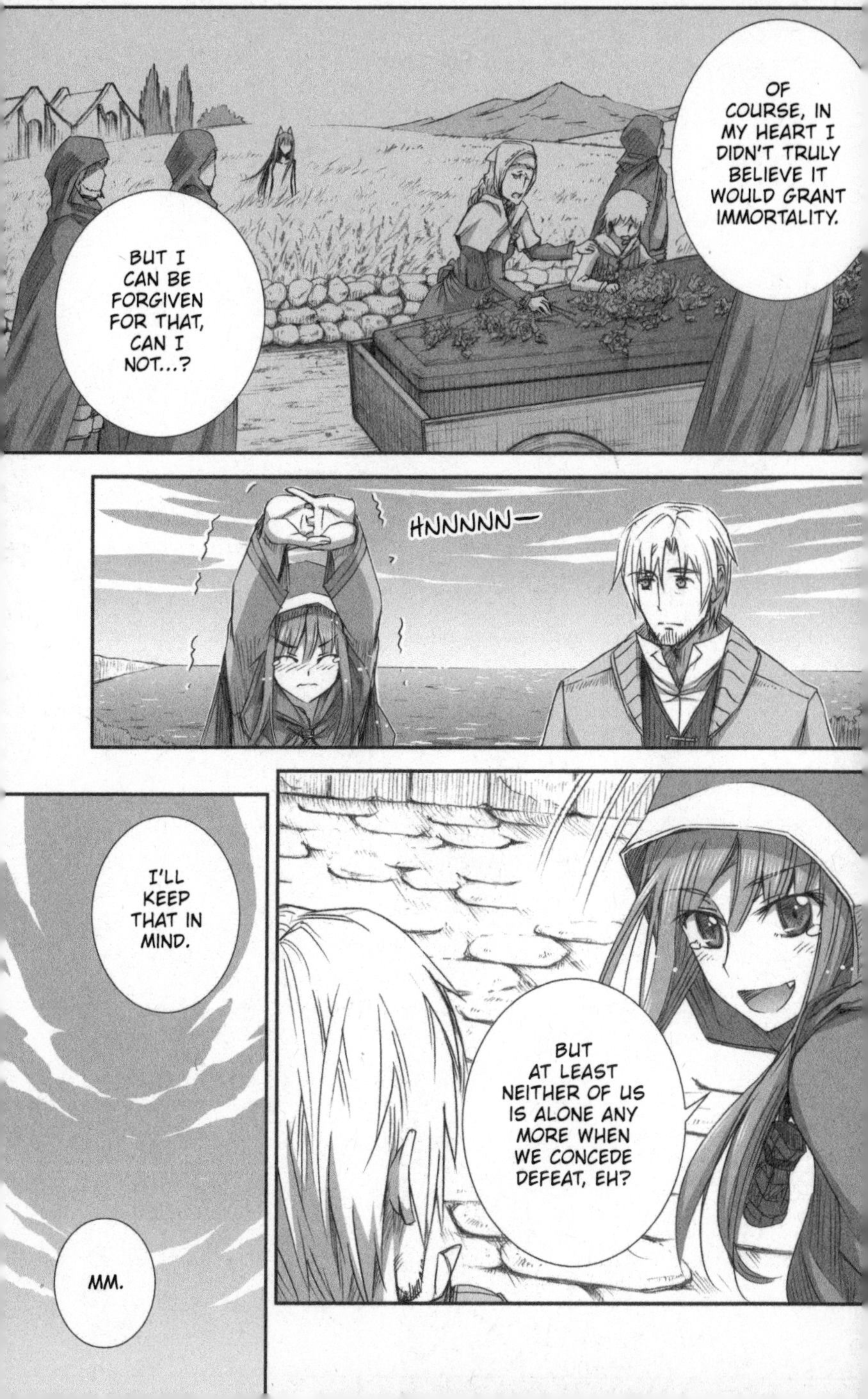
OF COURSE, IN MY HEART I DIDN'T TRULY BELIEVE IT WOULD GRANT IMMORTALITY.
BUT I CAN BE FORGIVEN FOR THAT, CAN I NOT...?
HNNNNN—
BUT AT LEAST NEITHER OF US IS ALONE ANY MORE WHEN WE CONCEDE DEFEAT, EH?
I'LL KEEP THAT IN MIND.
MM.

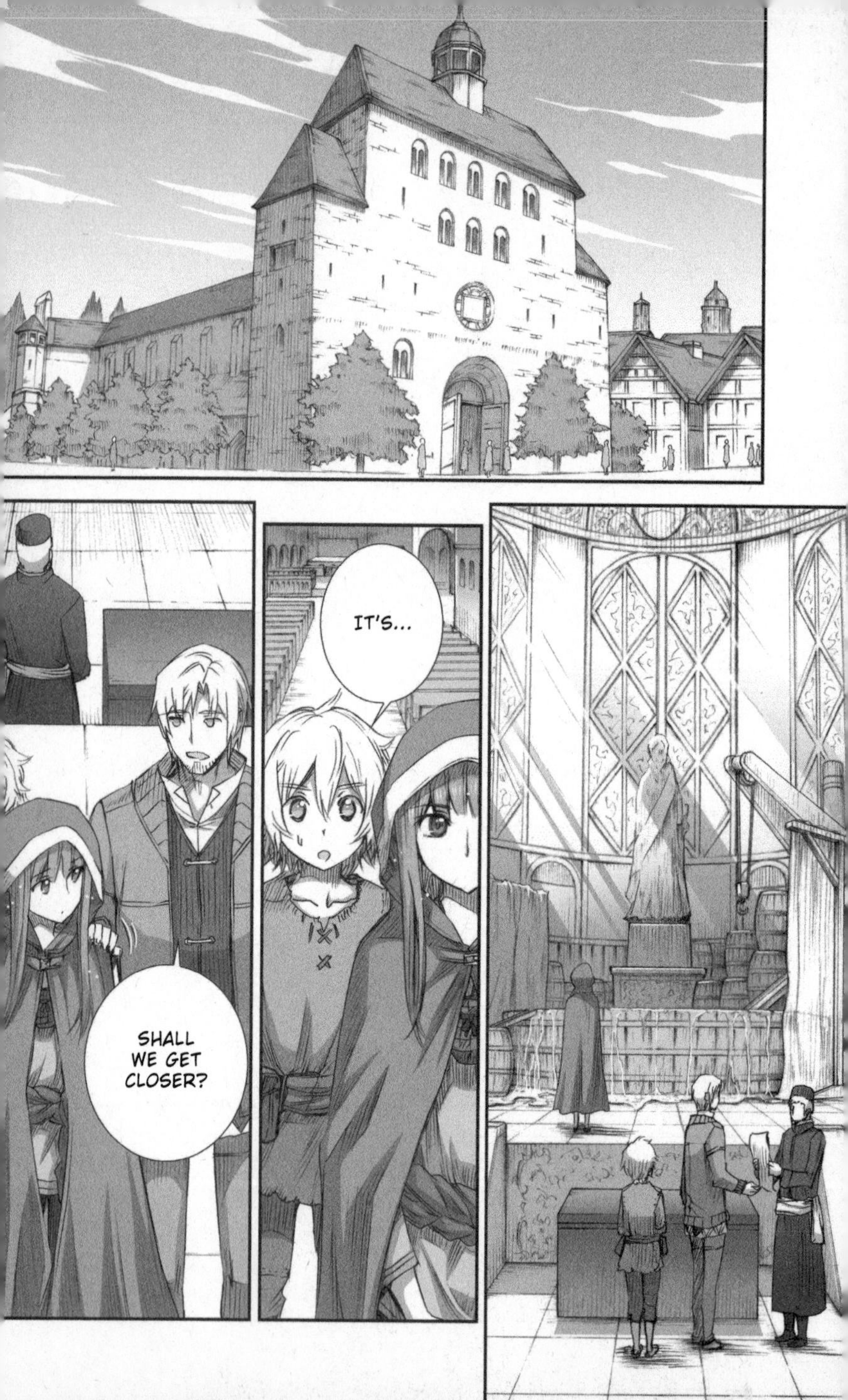
IT'S...
SHALL WE GET CLOSER?

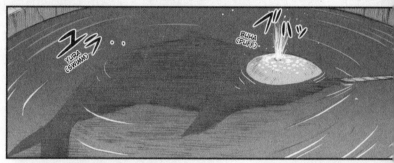

YURA
(SWIMMM)

BUHA
(PUFF)

MMM
MMM...

!

IS IT
A GOD
TOO...?

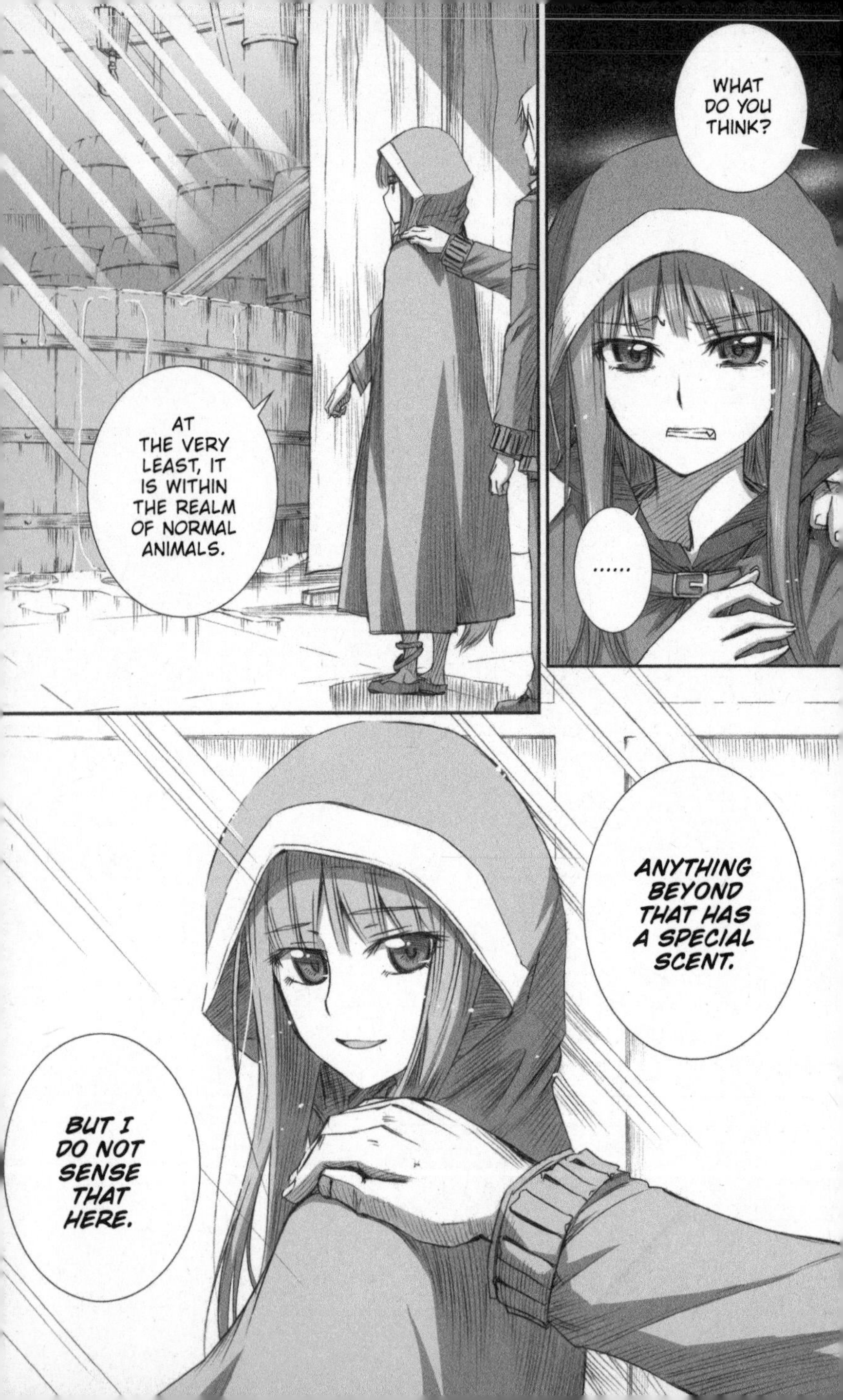
WHAT DO YOU THINK?
......
AT THE VERY LEAST, IT IS WITHIN THE REALM OF NORMAL ANIMALS.
ANYTHING BEYOND THAT HAS A SPECIAL SCENT.
BUT I DO NOT SENSE THAT HERE.

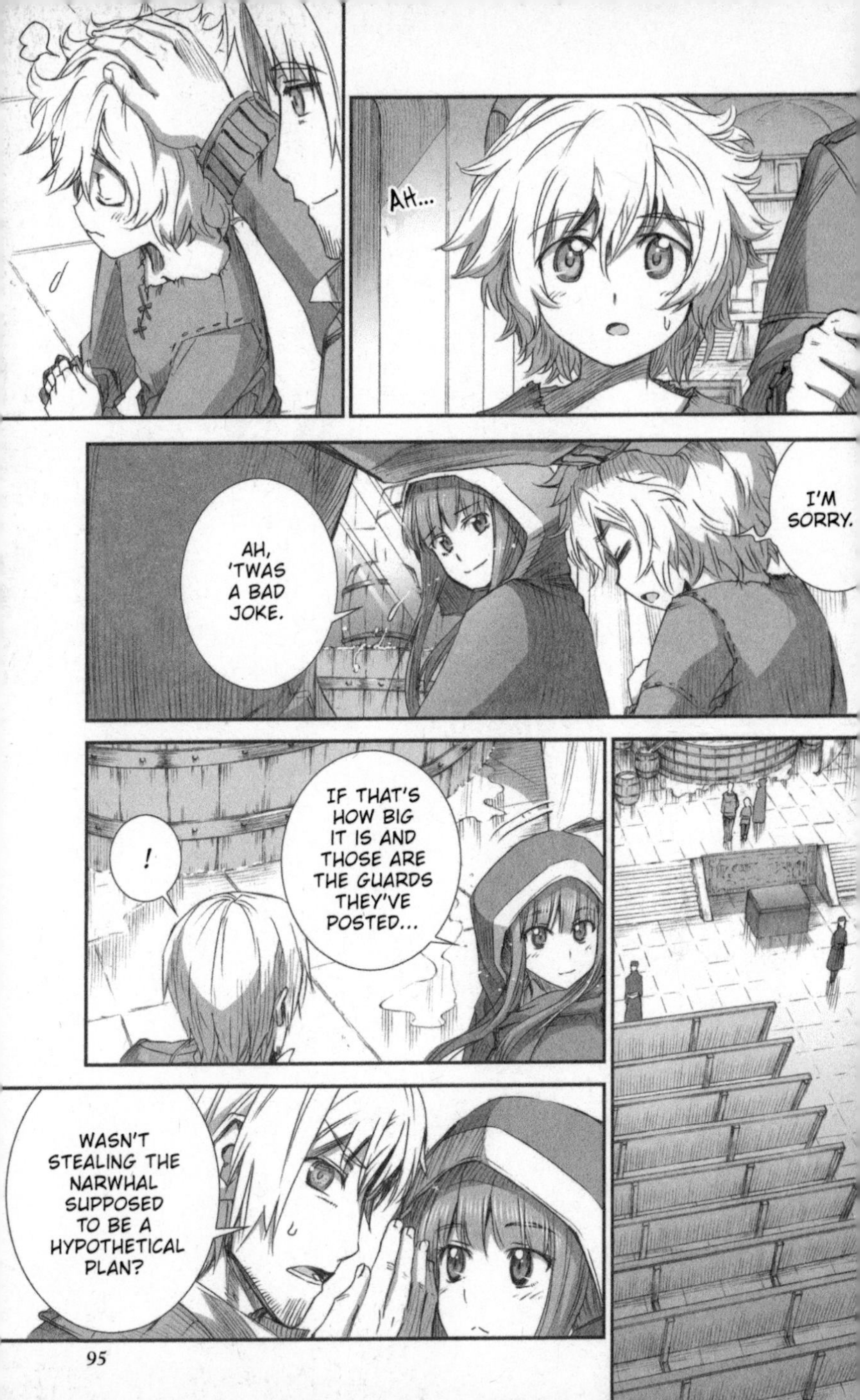
AH...
I'M SORRY.
AH, 'TWAS A BAD JOKE.
IF THAT'S HOW BIG IT IS AND THOSE ARE THE GUARDS THEY'VE POSTED...
!
WASN'T STEALING THE NARWHAL SUPPOSED TO BE A HYPOTHETICAL PLAN?

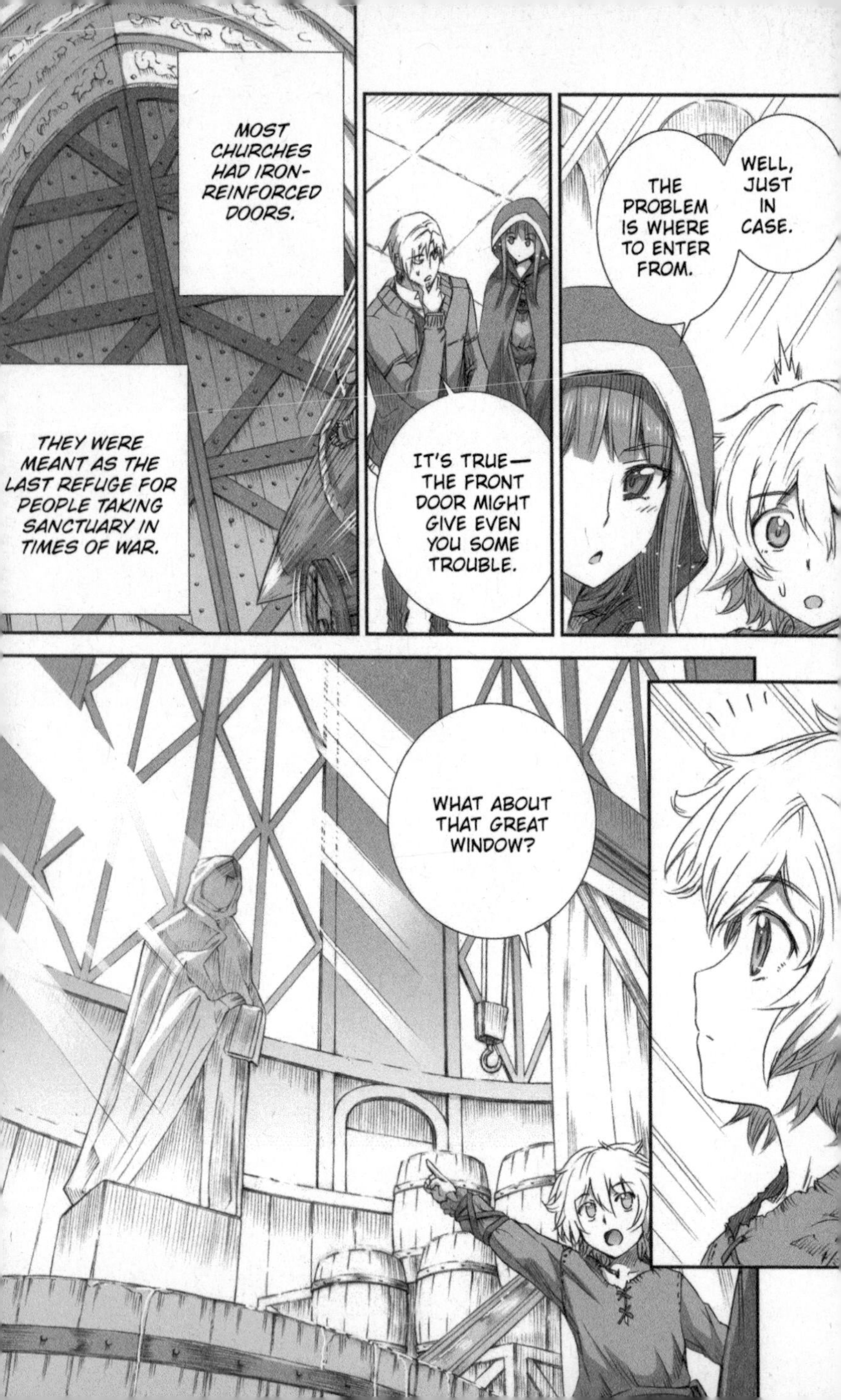
WELL, JUST IN CASE.
THE PROBLEM IS WHERE TO ENTER FROM.
IT'S TRUE—THE FRONT DOOR MIGHT GIVE EVEN YOU SOME TROUBLE.
MOST CHURCHES HAD IRON-REINFORCED DOORS.
THEY WERE MEANT AS THE LAST REFUGE FOR PEOPLE TAKING SANCTUARY IN TIMES OF WAR.
WHAT ABOUT THAT GREAT WINDOW?

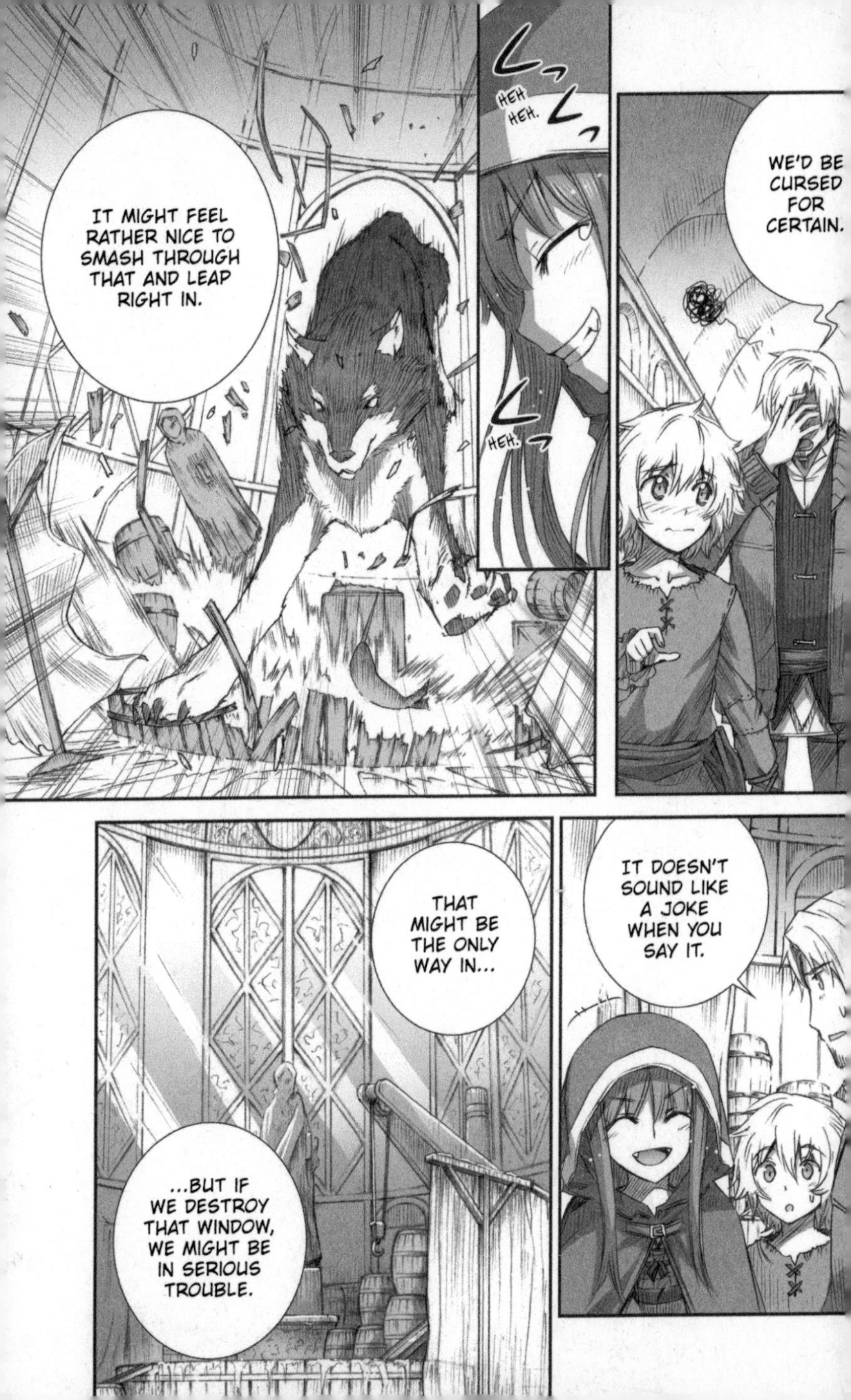
WE'D BE CURSED FOR CERTAIN.
HEH HEH.
HEH.
IT MIGHT FEEL RATHER NICE TO SMASH THROUGH THAT AND LEAP RIGHT IN.
IT DOESN'T SOUND LIKE A JOKE WHEN YOU SAY IT.
THAT MIGHT BE THE ONLY WAY IN...
...BUT IF WE DESTROY THAT WINDOW, WE MIGHT BE IN SERIOUS TROUBLE.

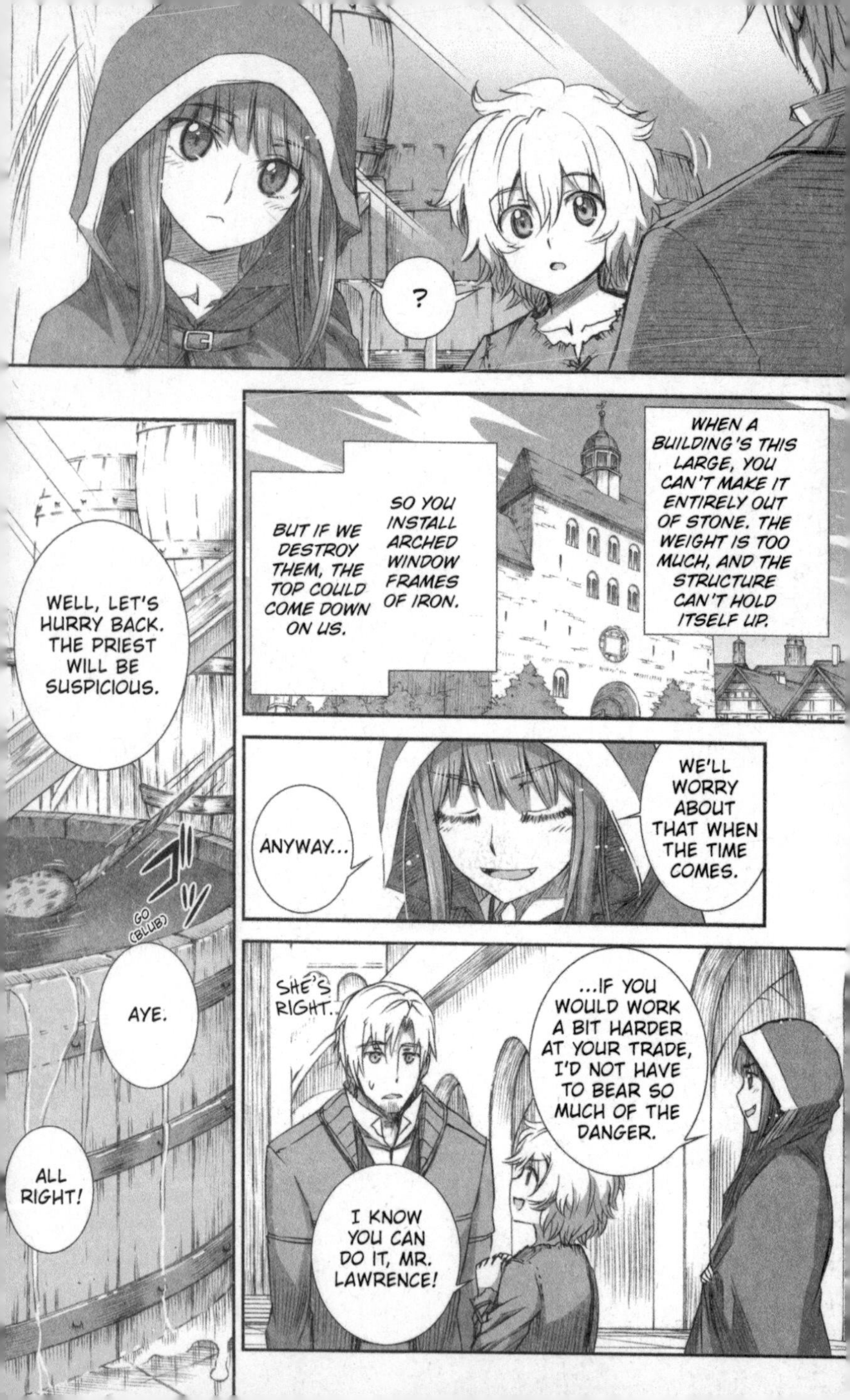
?
WHEN A BUILDING'S THIS LARGE, YOU CAN'T MAKE IT ENTIRELY OUT OF STONE. THE WEIGHT IS TOO MUCH, AND THE STRUCTURE CAN'T HOLD ITSELF UP.
SO YOU INSTALL ARCHED WINDOW FRAMES OF IRON.
BUT IF WE DESTROY THEM, THE TOP COULD COME DOWN ON US.
WE'LL WORRY ABOUT THAT WHEN THE TIME COMES.
ANYWAY...
...IF YOU WOULD WORK A BIT HARDER AT YOUR TRADE, I'D NOT HAVE TO BEAR SO MUCH OF THE DANGER.
SHE'S RIGHT...
I KNOW YOU CAN DO IT, MR. LAWRENCE!
WELL, LET'S HURRY BACK. THE PRIEST WILL BE SUSPICIOUS.
GO (BLUB)
AYE.
ALL RIGHT!

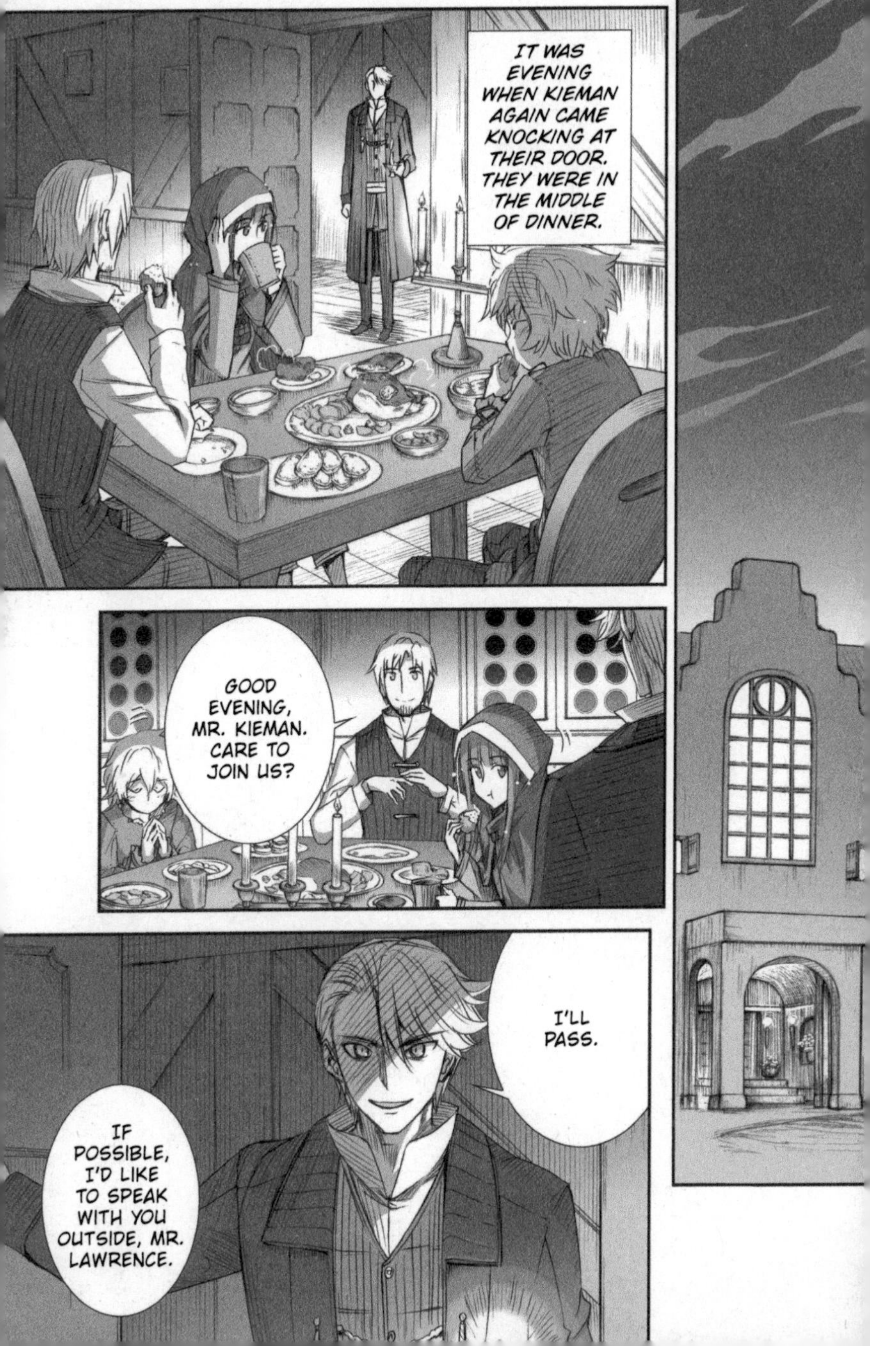
IT WAS EVENING WHEN KIEMAN AGAIN CAME KNOCKING AT THEIR DOOR. THEY WERE IN THE MIDDLE OF DINNER.
GOOD EVENING, MR. KIEMAN. CARE TO JOIN US?
I'LL PASS.
IF POSSIBLE, I'D LIKE TO SPEAK WITH YOU OUTSIDE, MR. LAWRENCE.

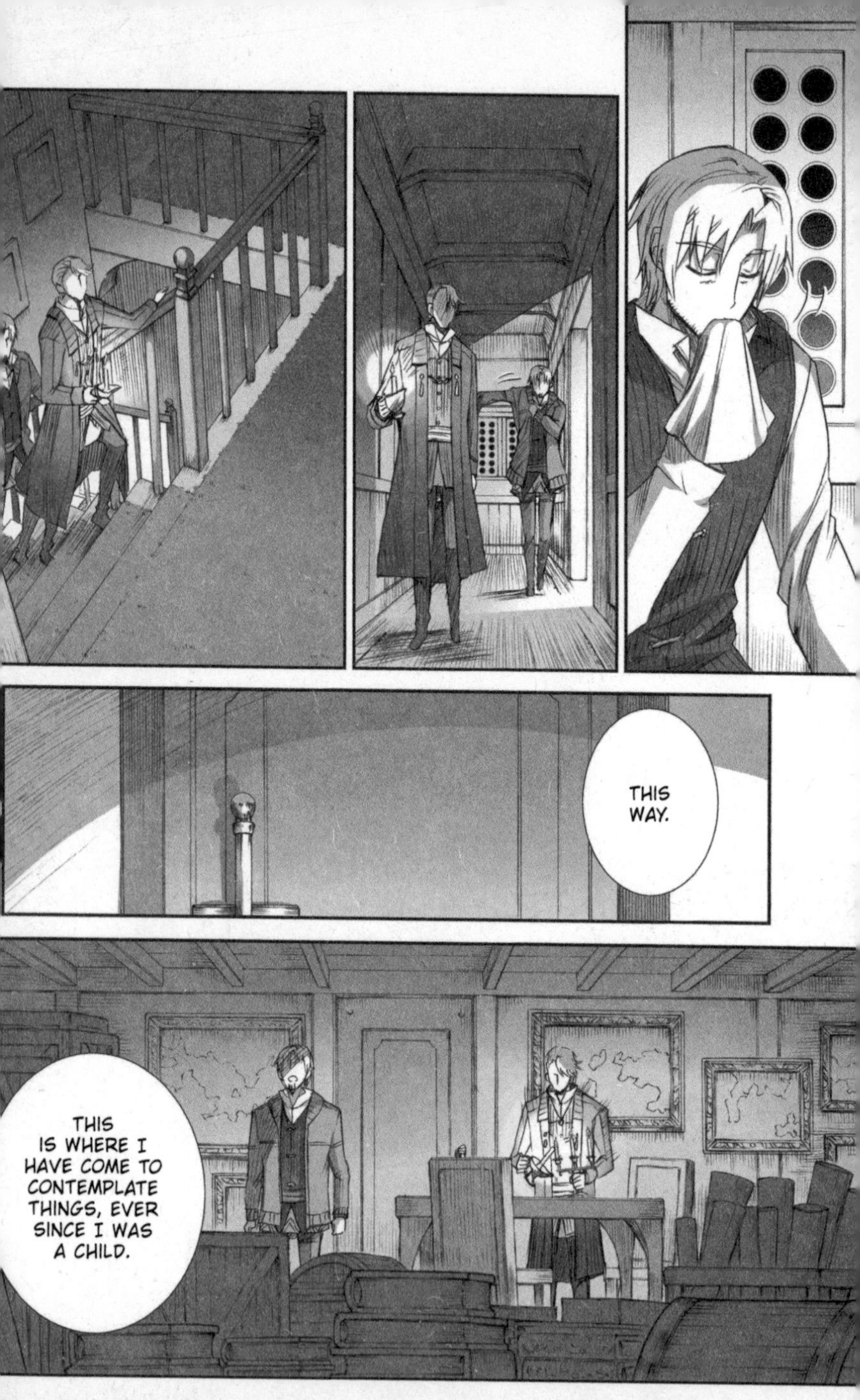
THIS WAY.
THIS IS WHERE I HAVE COME TO CONTEMPLATE THINGS, EVER SINCE I WAS A CHILD.

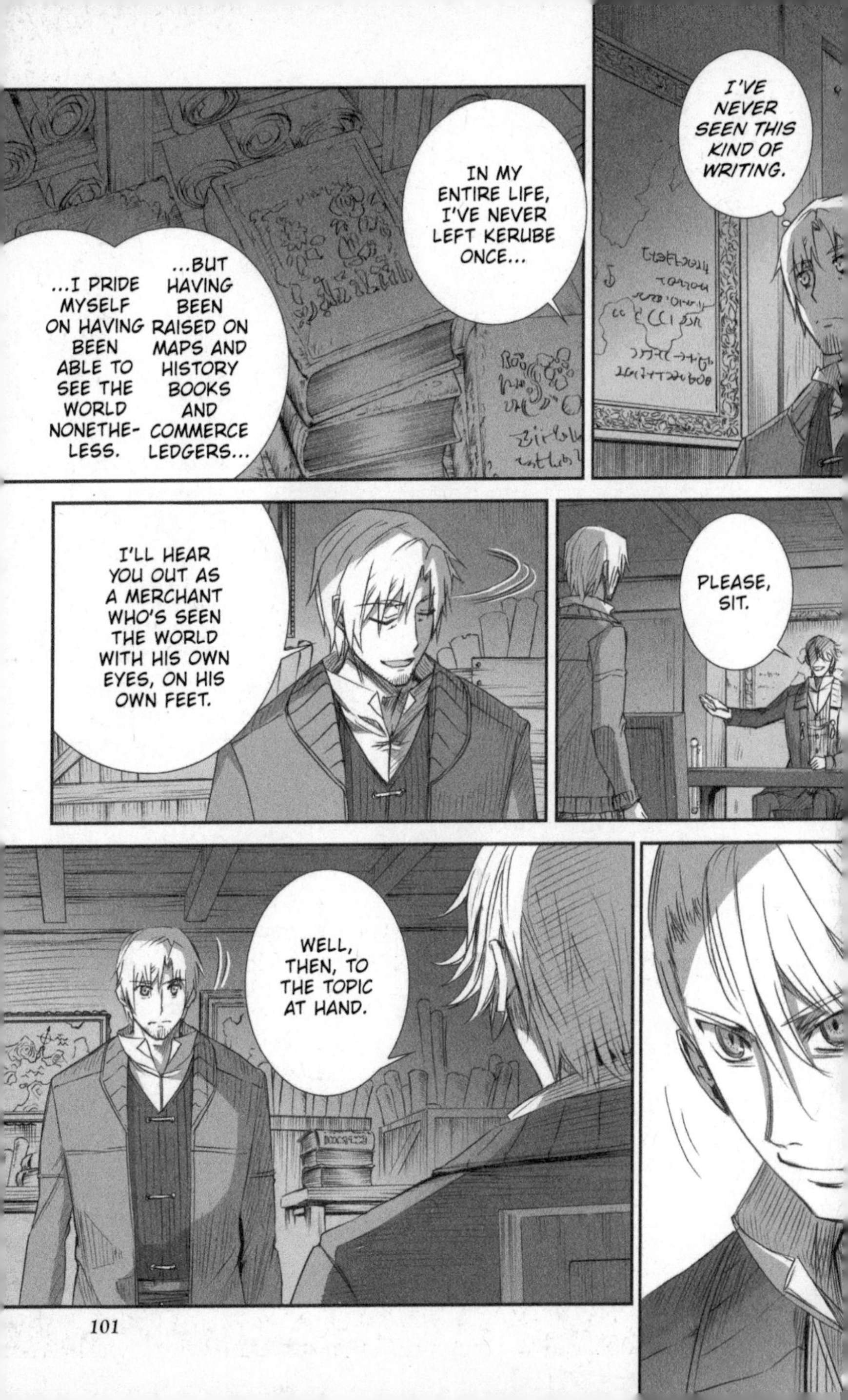
I'VE NEVER SEEN THIS KIND OF WRITING.
IN MY ENTIRE LIFE, I'VE NEVER LEFT KERUBE ONCE...
...BUT HAVING BEEN RAISED ON MAPS AND HISTORY BOOKS AND COMMERCE LEDGERS...
...I PRIDE MYSELF ON HAVING BEEN ABLE TO SEE THE WORLD NONETHELESS.
PLEASE, SIT.
I'LL HEAR YOU OUT AS A MERCHANT WHO'S SEEN THE WORLD WITH HIS OWN EYES, ON HIS OWN FEET.
WELL, THEN, TO THE TOPIC AT HAND.

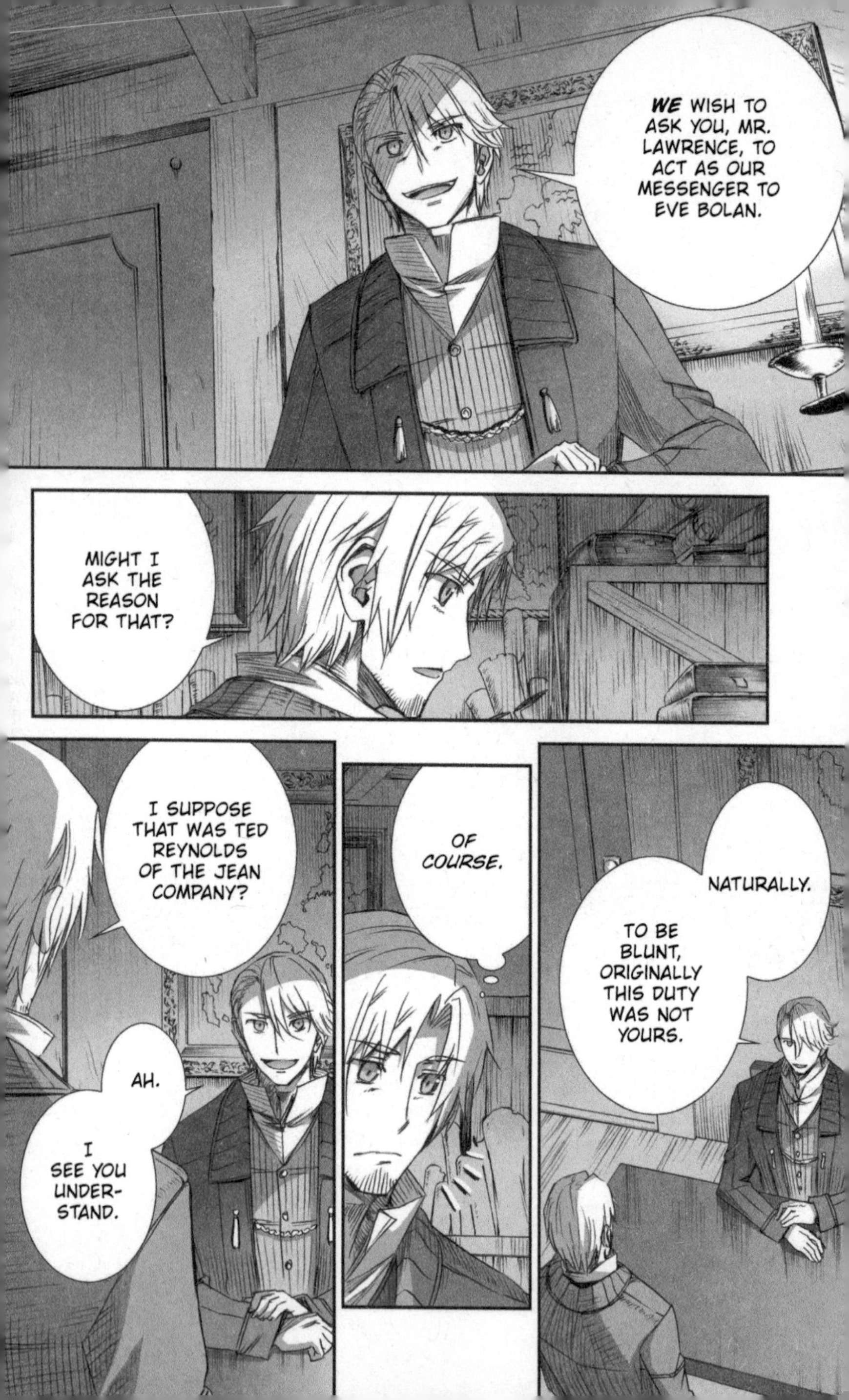

WE WISH TO ASK YOU, MR. LAWRENCE, TO ACT AS OUR MESSENGER TO EVE BOLAN.
MIGHT I ASK THE REASON FOR THAT?
NATURALLY.
TO BE BLUNT, ORIGINALLY THIS DUTY WAS NOT YOURS.
OF COURSE.
I SUPPOSE THAT WAS TED REYNOLDS OF THE JEAN COMPANY?
AH.
I SEE YOU UNDER-STAND.

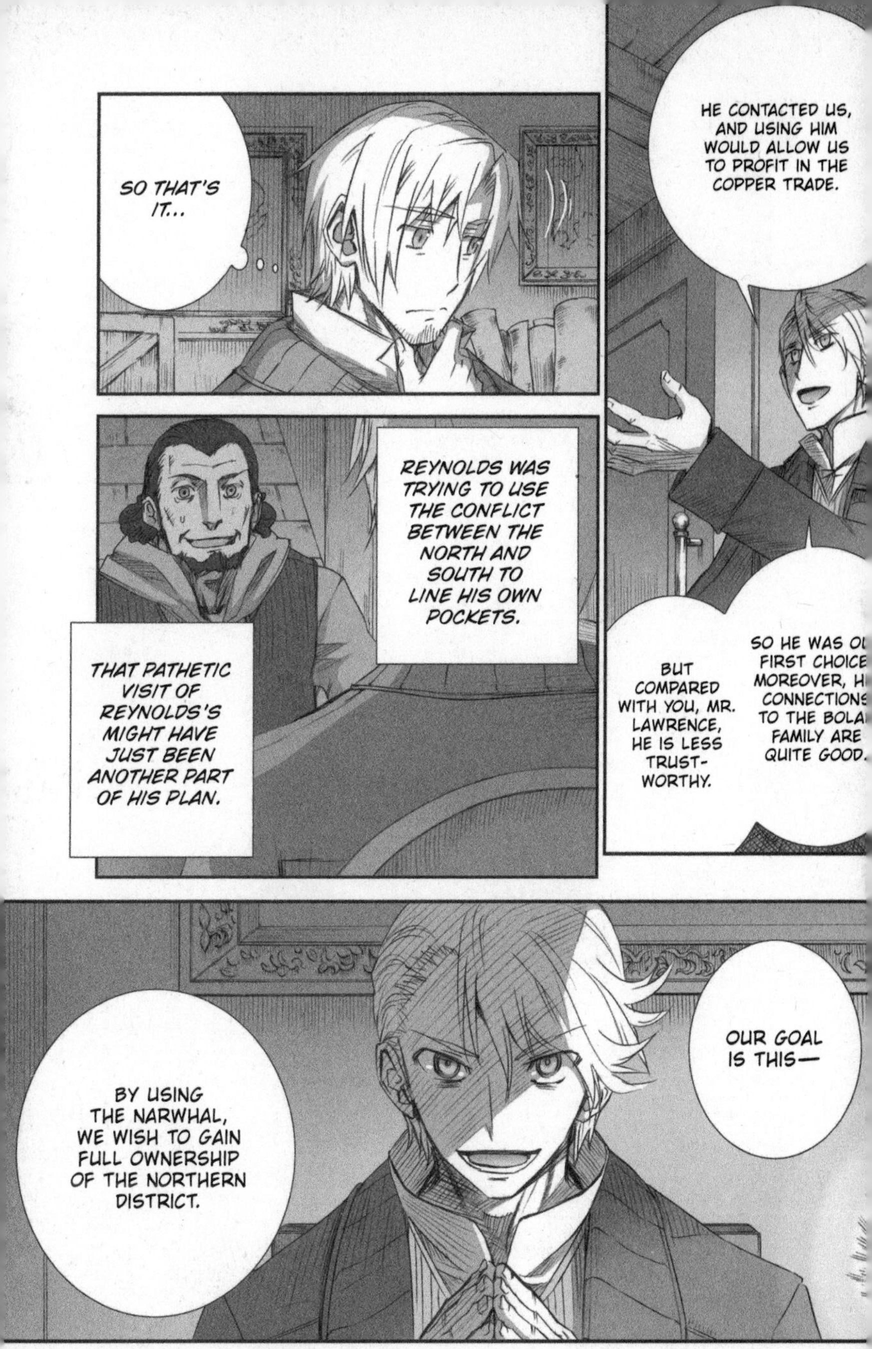
HE CONTACTED US, AND USING HIM WOULD ALLOW US TO PROFIT IN THE COPPER TRADE.
SO HE WAS OU FIRST CHOICE MOREOVER, HI CONNECTIONS TO THE BOLA FAMILY ARE QUITE GOOD.
BUT COMPARED WITH YOU, MR. LAWRENCE, HE IS LESS TRUST-WORTHY.
SO THAT'S IT...
REYNOLDS WAS TRYING TO USE THE CONFLICT BETWEEN THE NORTH AND SOUTH TO LINE HIS OWN POCKETS.
THAT PATHETIC VISIT OF REYNOLDS'S MIGHT HAVE JUST BEEN ANOTHER PART OF HIS PLAN.
OUR GOAL IS THIS—
BY USING THE NARWHAL, WE WISH TO GAIN FULL OWNERSHIP OF THE NORTHERN DISTRICT.

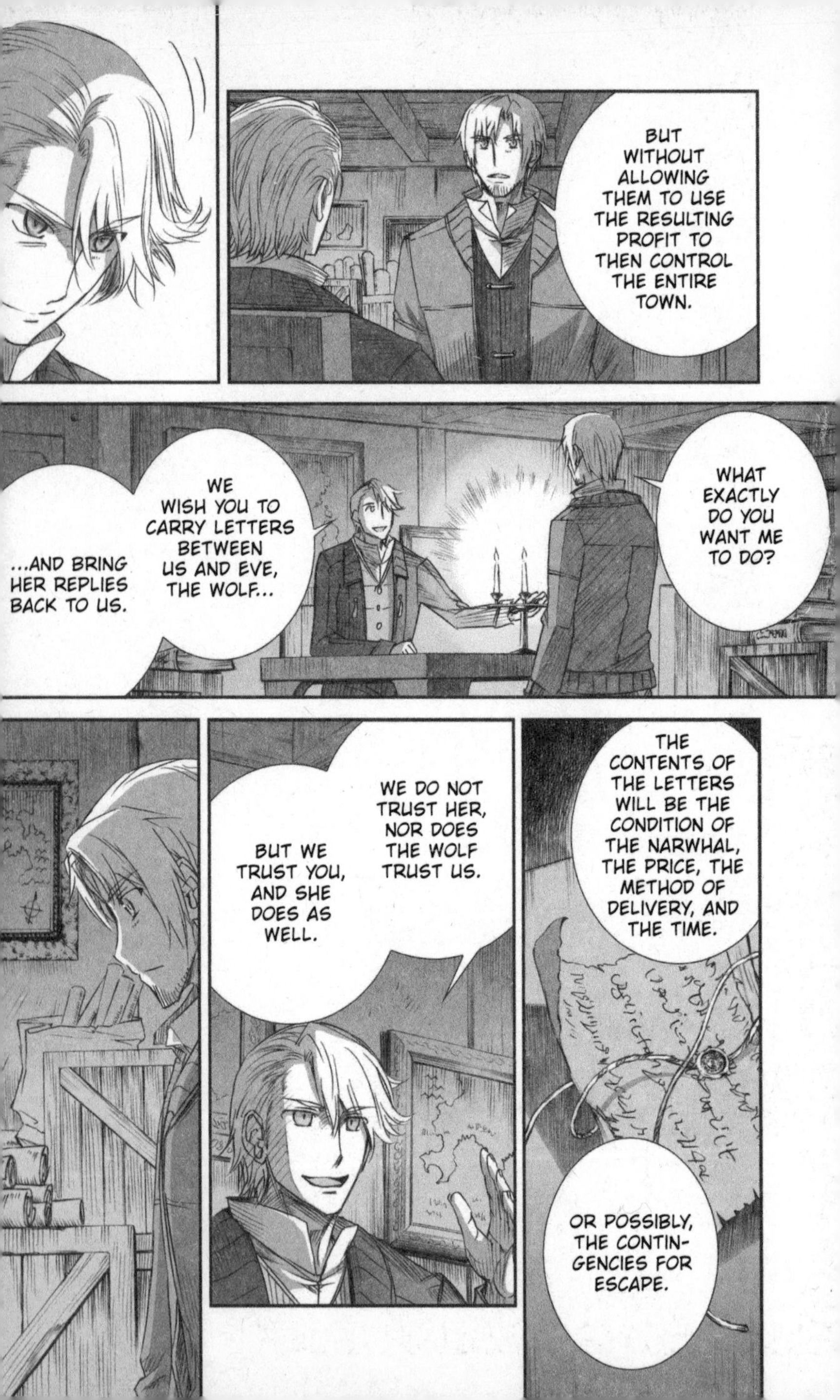
BUT WITHOUT ALLOWING THEM TO USE THE RESULTING PROFIT TO THEN CONTROL THE ENTIRE TOWN.
WHAT EXACTLY DO YOU WANT ME TO DO?
WE WISH YOU TO CARRY LETTERS BETWEEN US AND EVE, THE WOLF...
...AND BRING HER REPLIES BACK TO US.
THE CONTENTS OF THE LETTERS WILL BE THE CONDITION OF THE NARWHAL, THE PRICE, THE METHOD OF DELIVERY, AND THE TIME.
OR POSSIBLY, THE CONTIN-GENCIES FOR ESCAPE.
WE DO NOT TRUST HER, NOR DOES THE WOLF TRUST US.
BUT WE TRUST YOU, AND SHE DOES AS WELL.

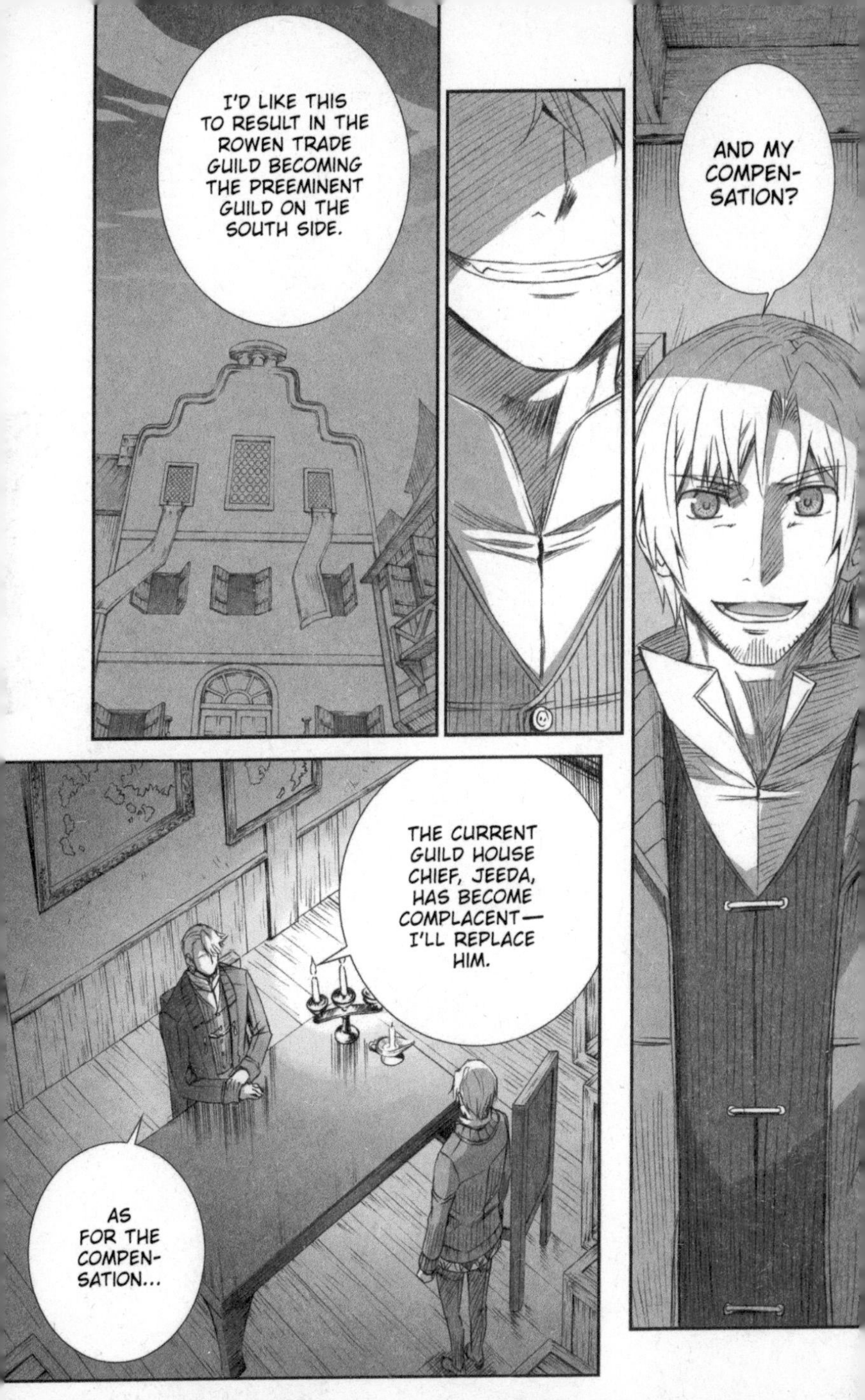
AND MY COMPENSATION?
I'D LIKE THIS TO RESULT IN THE ROWEN TRADE GUILD BECOMING THE PREEMINENT GUILD ON THE SOUTH SIDE.
THE CURRENT GUILD HOUSE CHIEF, JEEDA, HAS BECOME COMPLACENT—I'LL REPLACE HIM.
AS FOR THE COMPENSATION...

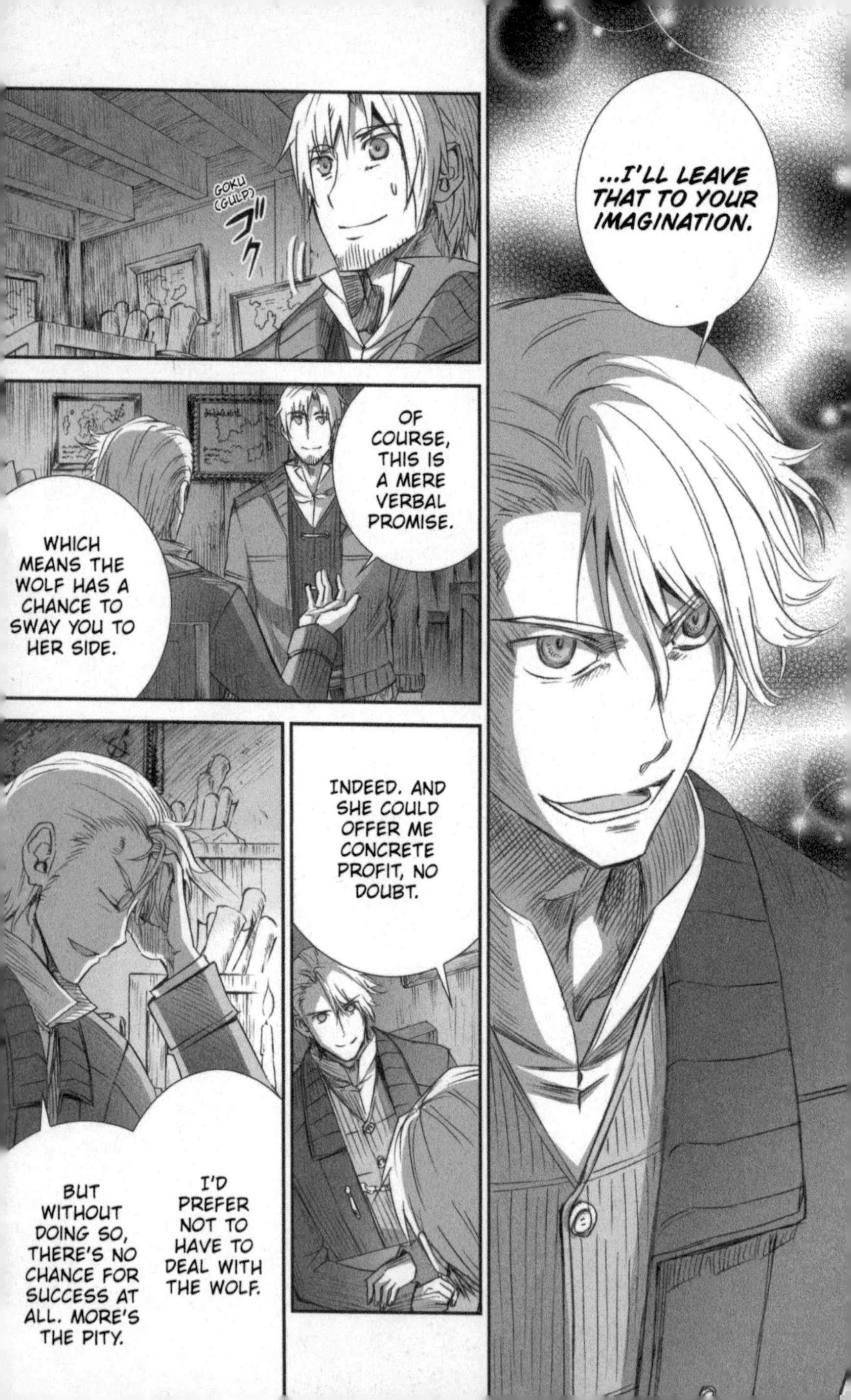
...I'LL LEAVE THAT TO YOUR IMAGINATION.
GOKU (GULP)
ゴク
OF COURSE, THIS IS A MERE VERBAL PROMISE.
WHICH MEANS THE WOLF HAS A CHANCE TO SWAY YOU TO HER SIDE.
INDEED. AND SHE COULD OFFER ME CONCRETE PROFIT, NO DOUBT.
I'D PREFER NOT TO HAVE TO DEAL WITH THE WOLF.
BUT WITHOUT DOING SO, THERE'S NO CHANCE FOR SUCCESS AT ALL. MORE'S THE PITY.

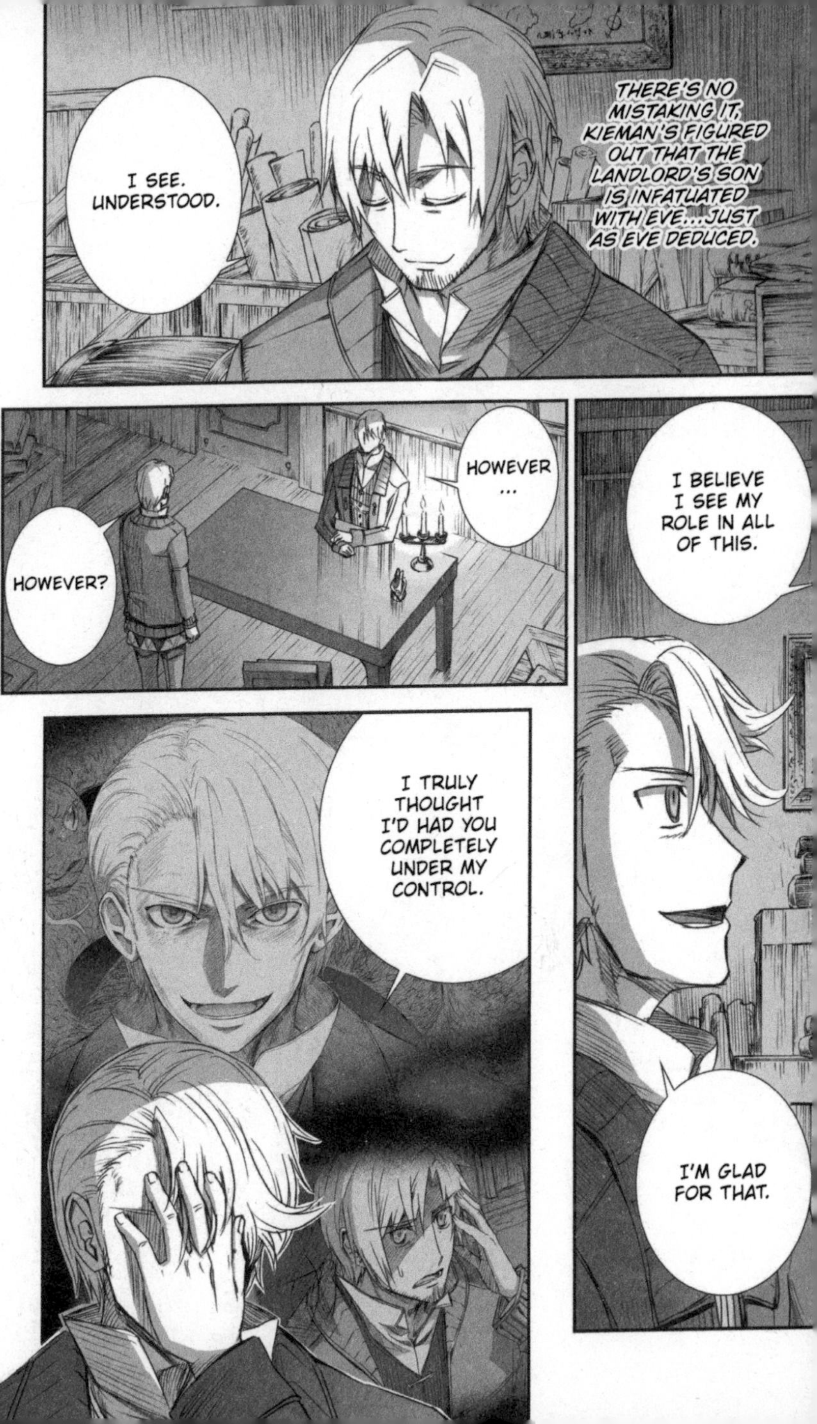
THERE'S NO MISTAKING IT, KIEMAN'S FIGURED OUT THAT THE LANDLORD'S SON IS INFATUATED WITH EVE...JUST AS EVE DEDUCED.
I SEE. UNDERSTOOD.
I BELIEVE I SEE MY ROLE IN ALL OF THIS.
I'M GLAD FOR THAT.
HOWEVER ...
HOWEVER?
I TRULY THOUGHT I'D HAD YOU COMPLETELY UNDER MY CONTROL.

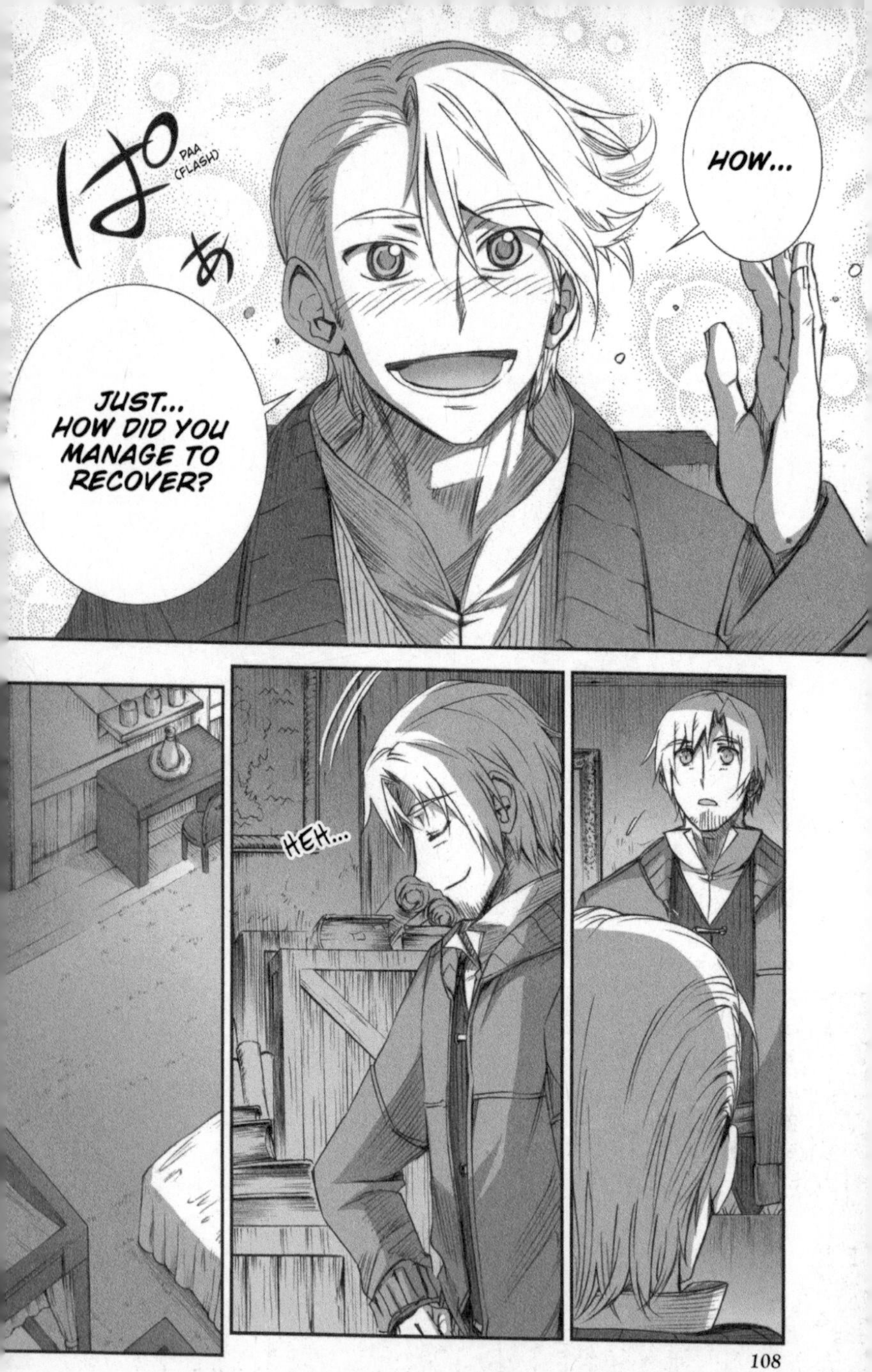
HOW...
ぱぁ
PAA (FLASH)
JUST... HOW DID YOU MANAGE TO RECOVER?
HEH...

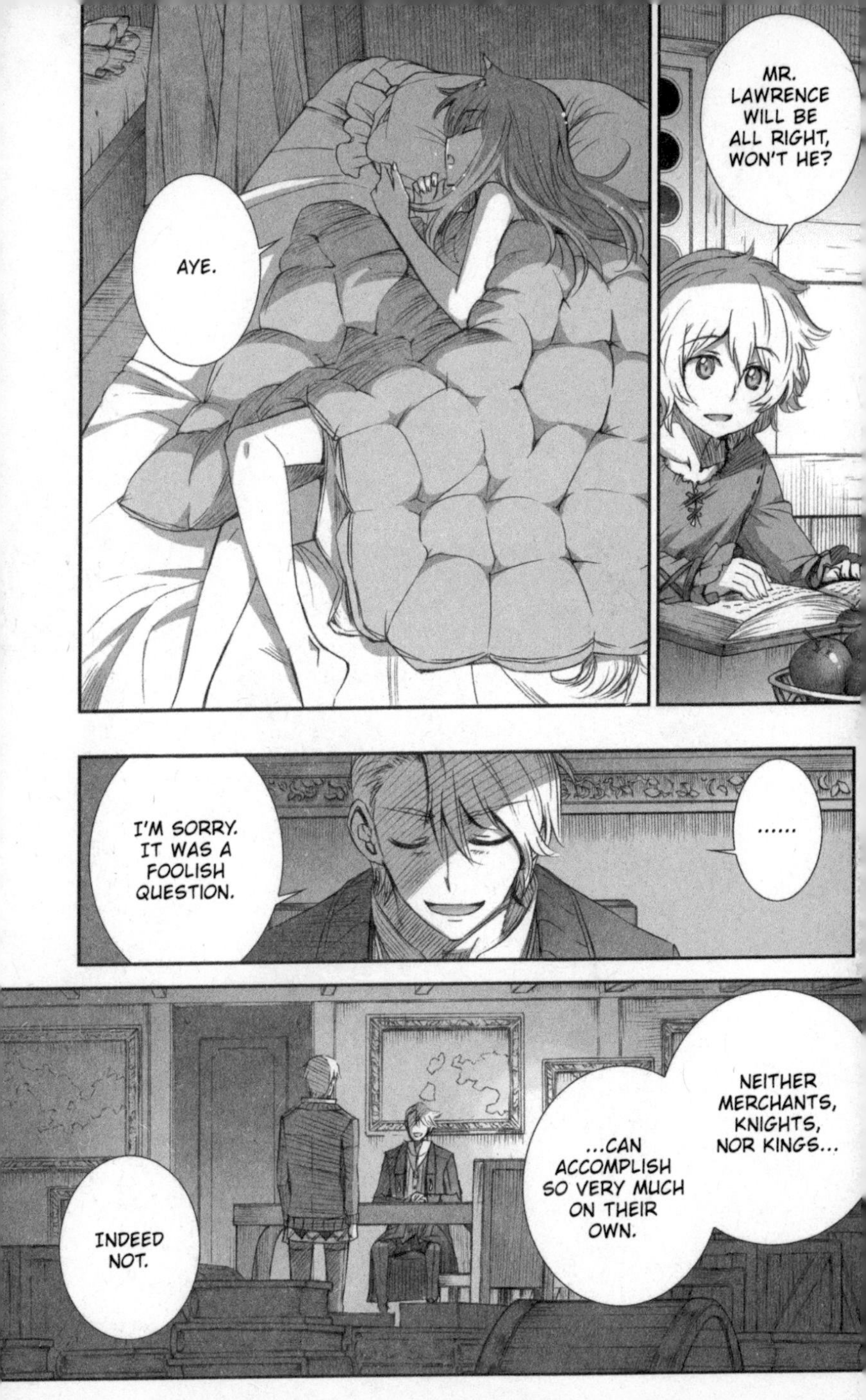
MR. LAWRENCE WILL BE ALL RIGHT, WON'T HE?
AYE.
......
I'M SORRY. IT WAS A FOOLISH QUESTION.
NEITHER MERCHANTS, KNIGHTS, NOR KINGS...
...CAN ACCOMPLISH SO VERY MUCH ON THEIR OWN.
INDEED NOT.

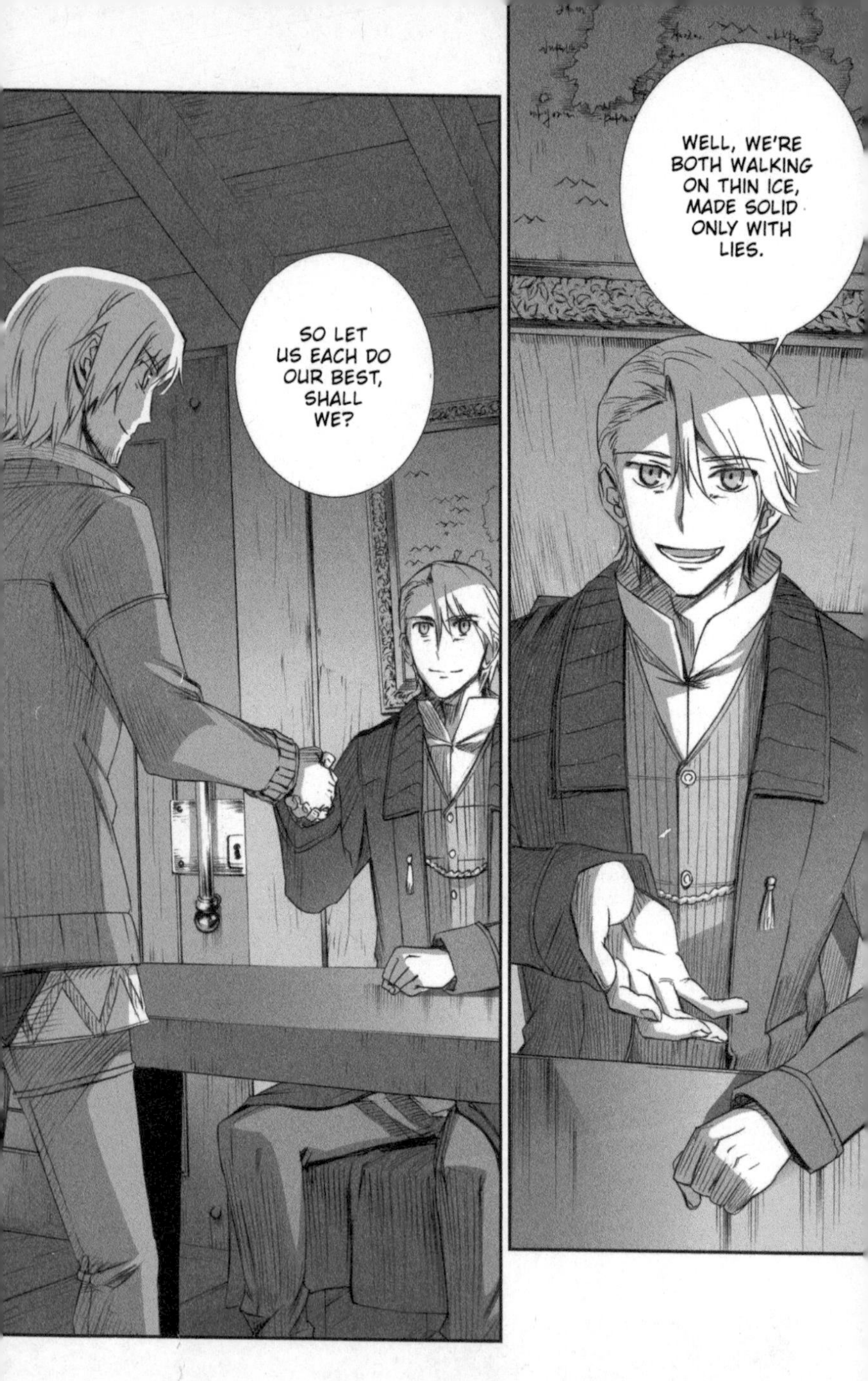
WELL, WE'RE BOTH WALKING ON THIN ICE, MADE SOLID ONLY WITH LIES.
SO LET US EACH DO OUR BEST, SHALL WE?

SPICE & WOLF

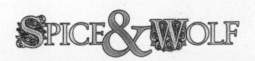

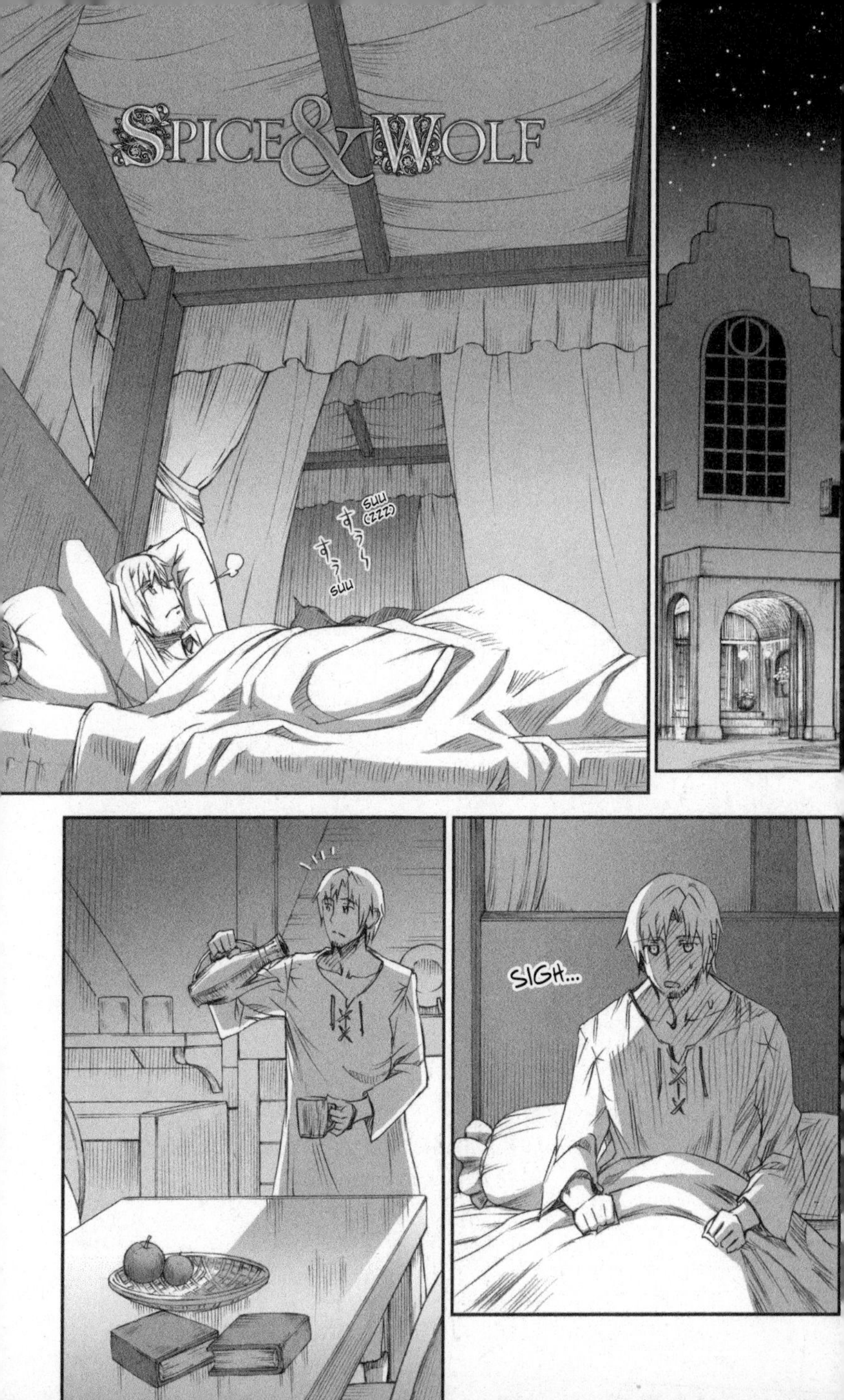
SPICE & WOLF
SUU (ZZZ)
すぅ〜
すぅ〜
SUU
SIGH...

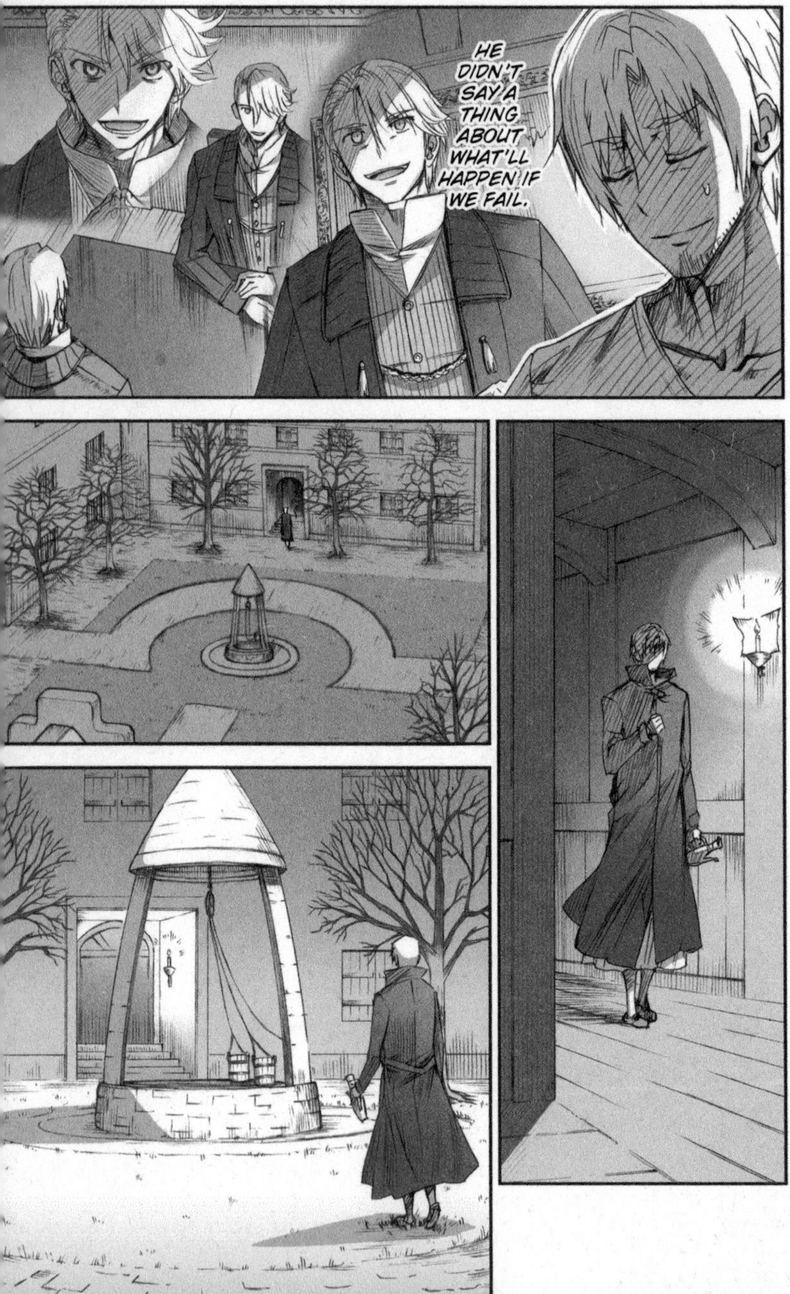
HE DIDN'T SAY A THING ABOUT WHAT'LL HAPPEN IF WE FAIL.

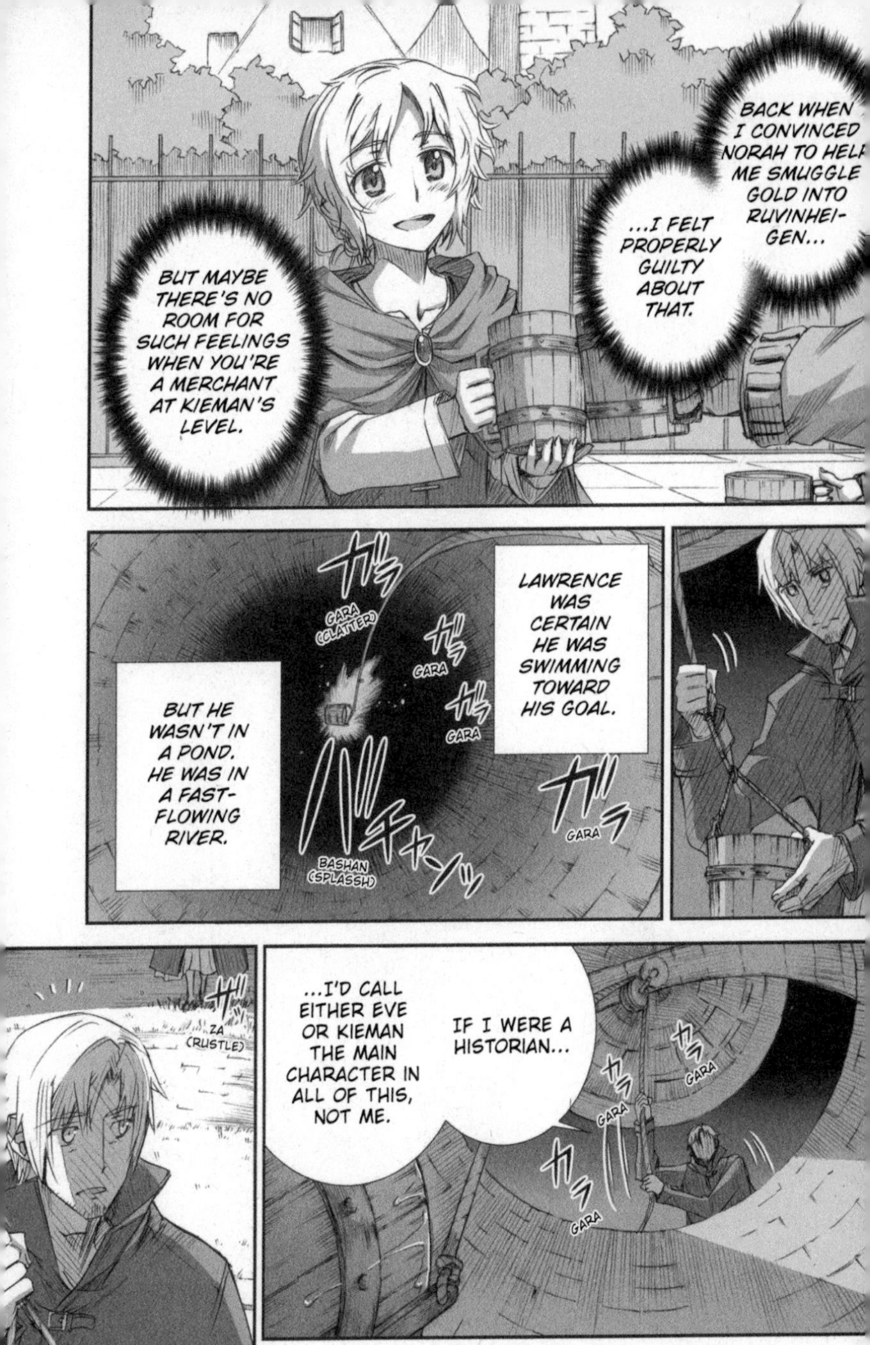
BACK WHEN I CONVINCED NORAH TO HELP ME SMUGGLE GOLD INTO RUVINHEI-GEN...
...I FELT PROPERLY GUILTY ABOUT THAT.
BUT MAYBE THERE'S NO ROOM FOR SUCH FEELINGS WHEN YOU'RE A MERCHANT AT KIEMAN'S LEVEL.
LAWRENCE WAS CERTAIN HE WAS SWIMMING TOWARD HIS GOAL.
GARA
GARA
GARA
GARA (CLATTER)
BASHAN (SPLASSH)
BUT HE WASN'T IN A POND. HE WAS IN A FAST-FLOWING RIVER.
IF I WERE A HISTORIAN...
...I'D CALL EITHER EVE OR KIEMAN THE MAIN CHARACTER IN ALL OF THIS, NOT ME.
GARA
GARA
GARA
ZA (RUSTLE)

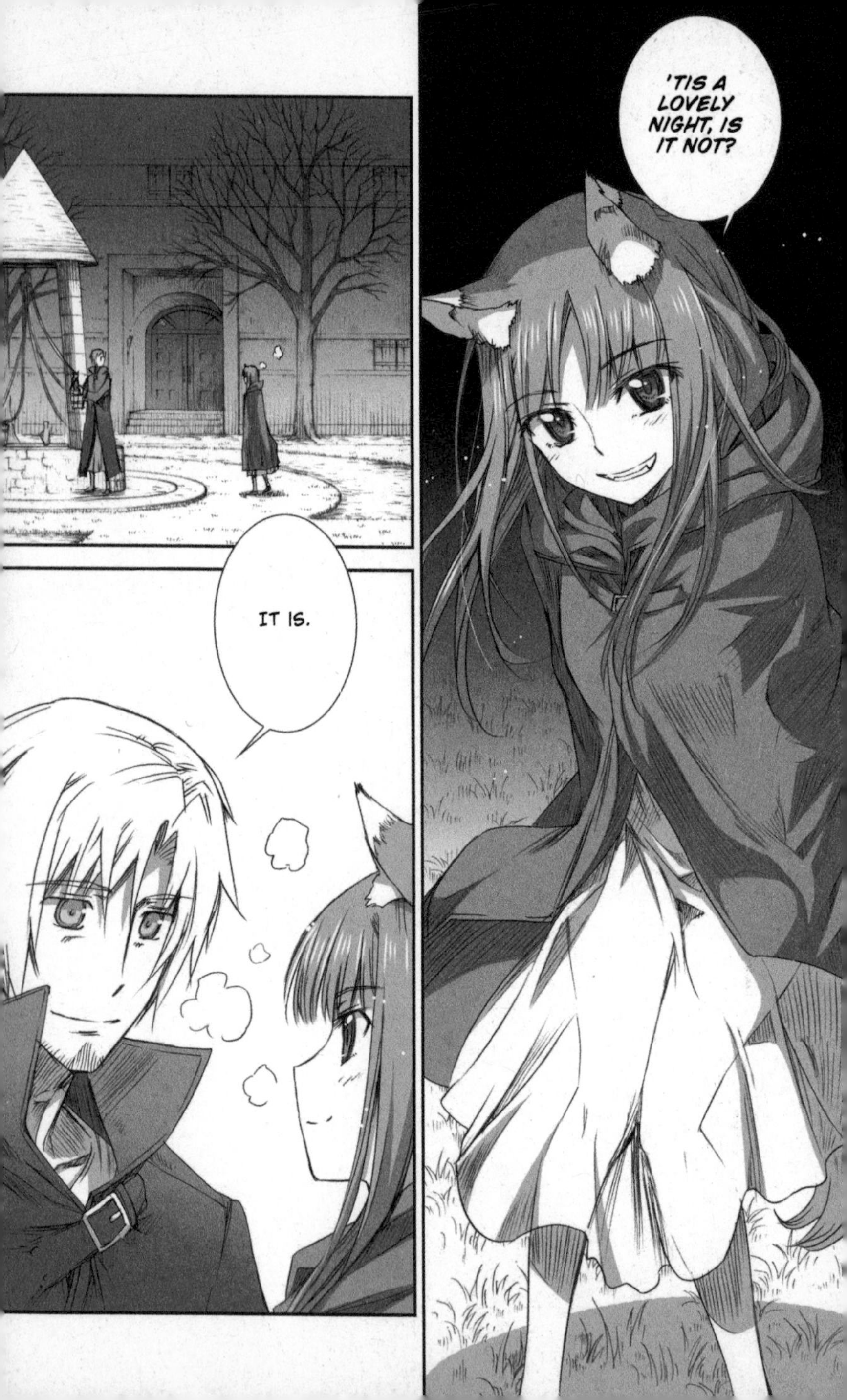
'TIS A LOVELY NIGHT, IS IT NOT?
IT IS.

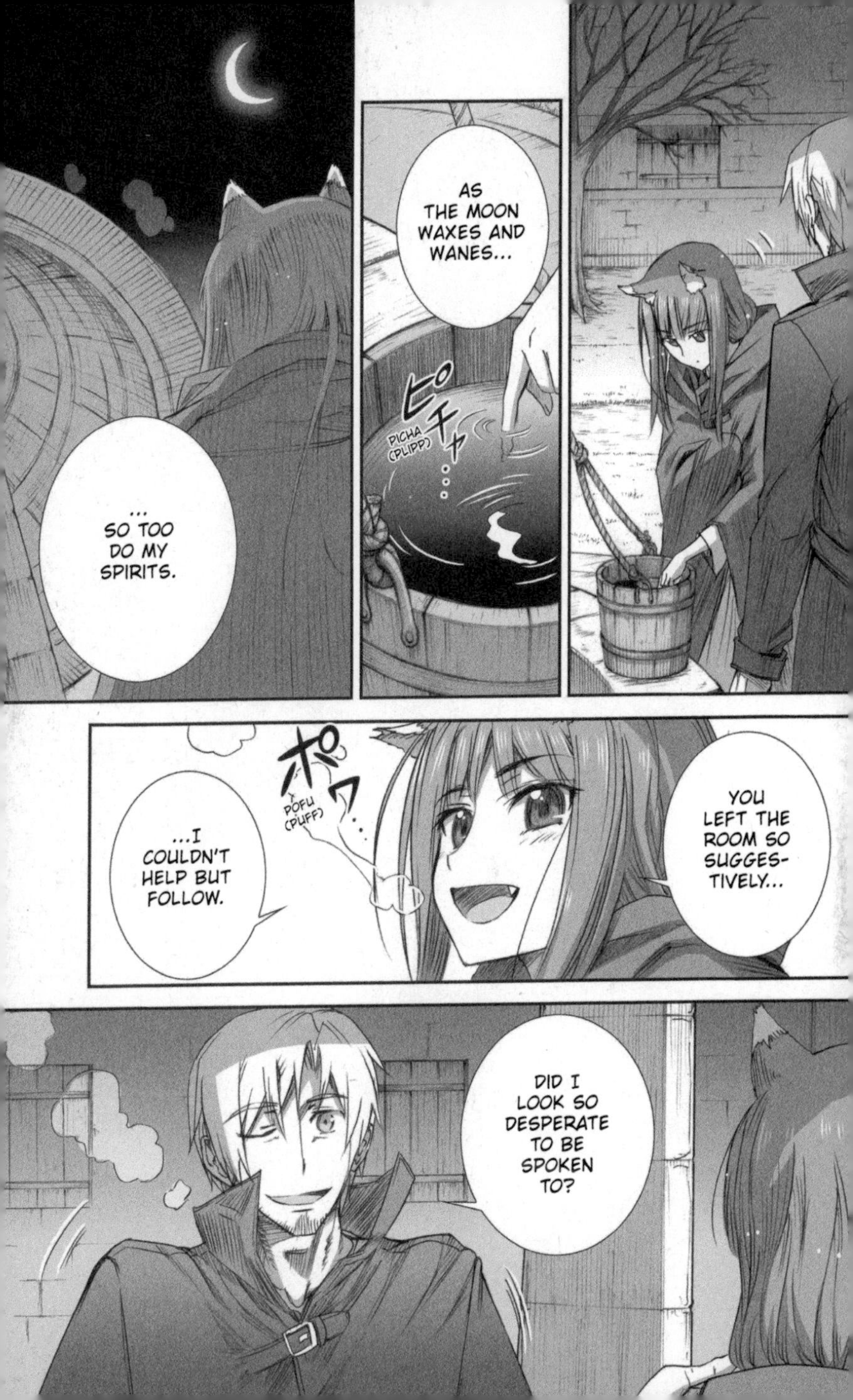
AS THE MOON WAXES AND WANES...
ピチャ...
PICHA (PLIPP)
...SO TOO DO MY SPIRITS.
YOU LEFT THE ROOM SO SUGGES-TIVELY...
ポフ...
POFU (PUFF)
...I COULDN'T HELP BUT FOLLOW.
DID I LOOK SO DESPERATE TO BE SPOKEN TO?

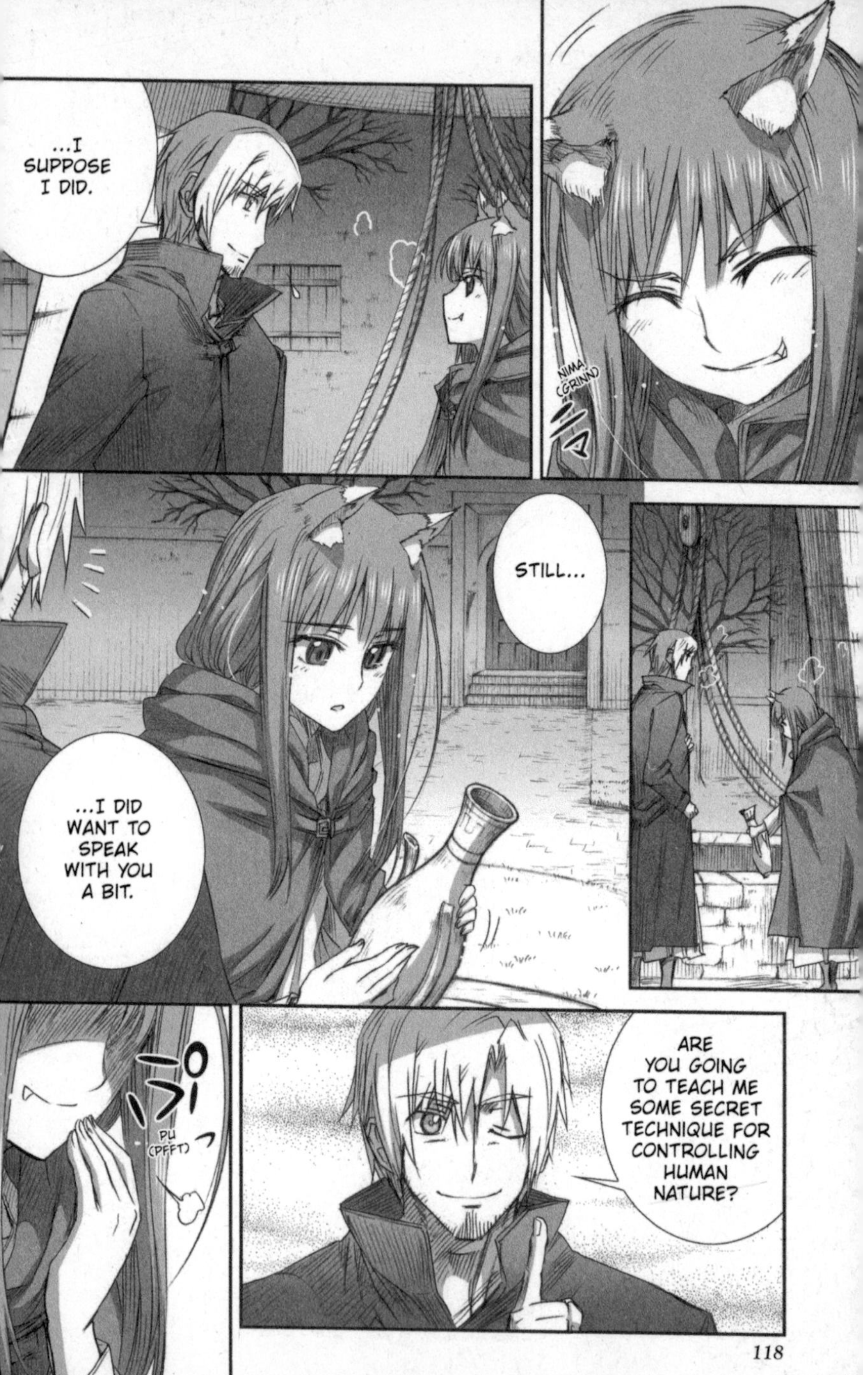
NIMA (GRINN)
...I SUPPOSE I DID.
STILL...
...I DID WANT TO SPEAK WITH YOU A BIT.
ARE YOU GOING TO TEACH ME SOME SECRET TECHNIQUE FOR CONTROLLING HUMAN NATURE?
PU (PFFT)

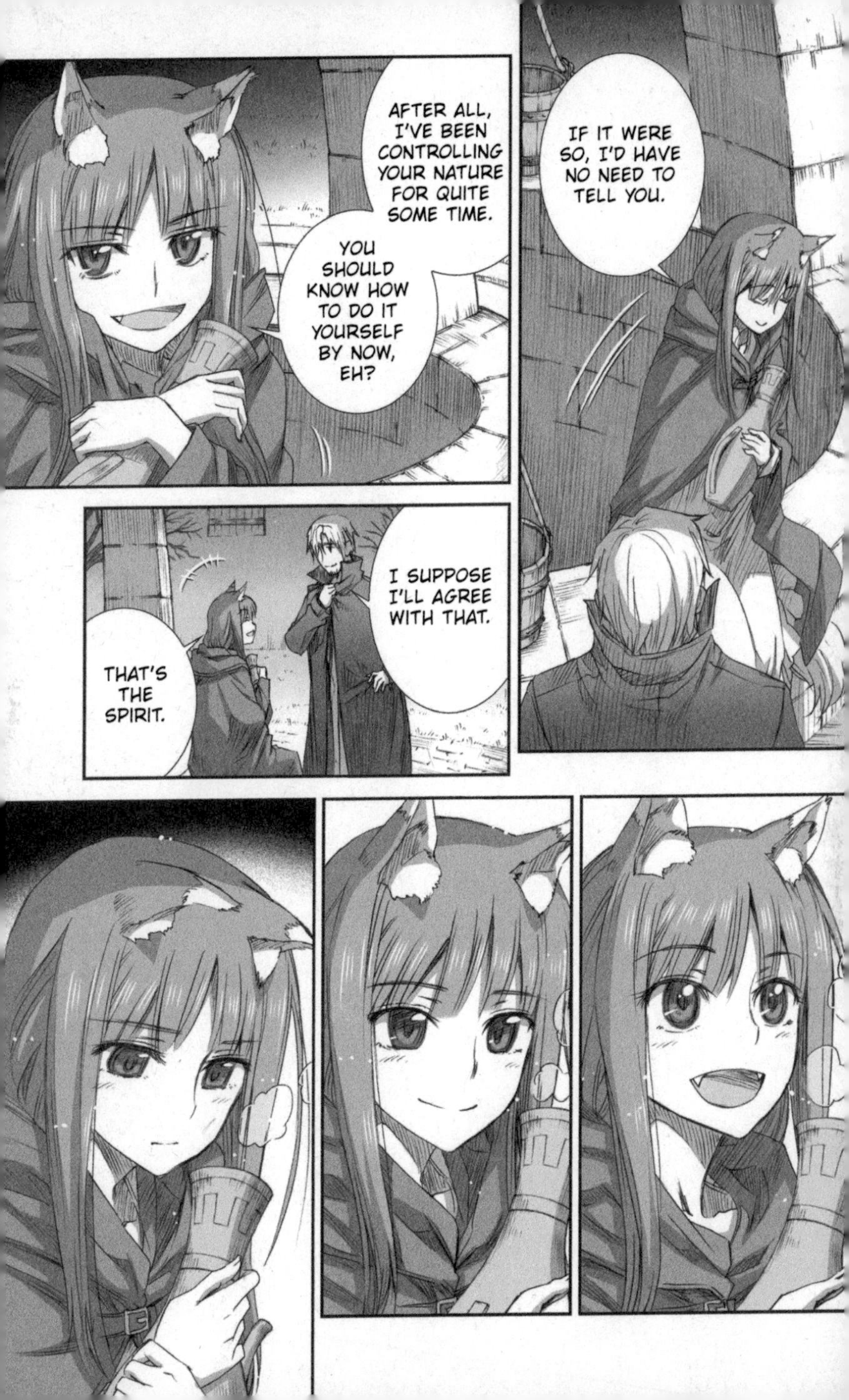
IF IT WERE SO, I'D HAVE NO NEED TO TELL YOU.
AFTER ALL, I'VE BEEN CONTROLLING YOUR NATURE FOR QUITE SOME TIME.
YOU SHOULD KNOW HOW TO DO IT YOURSELF BY NOW, EH?
I SUPPOSE I'LL AGREE WITH THAT.
THAT'S THE SPIRIT.

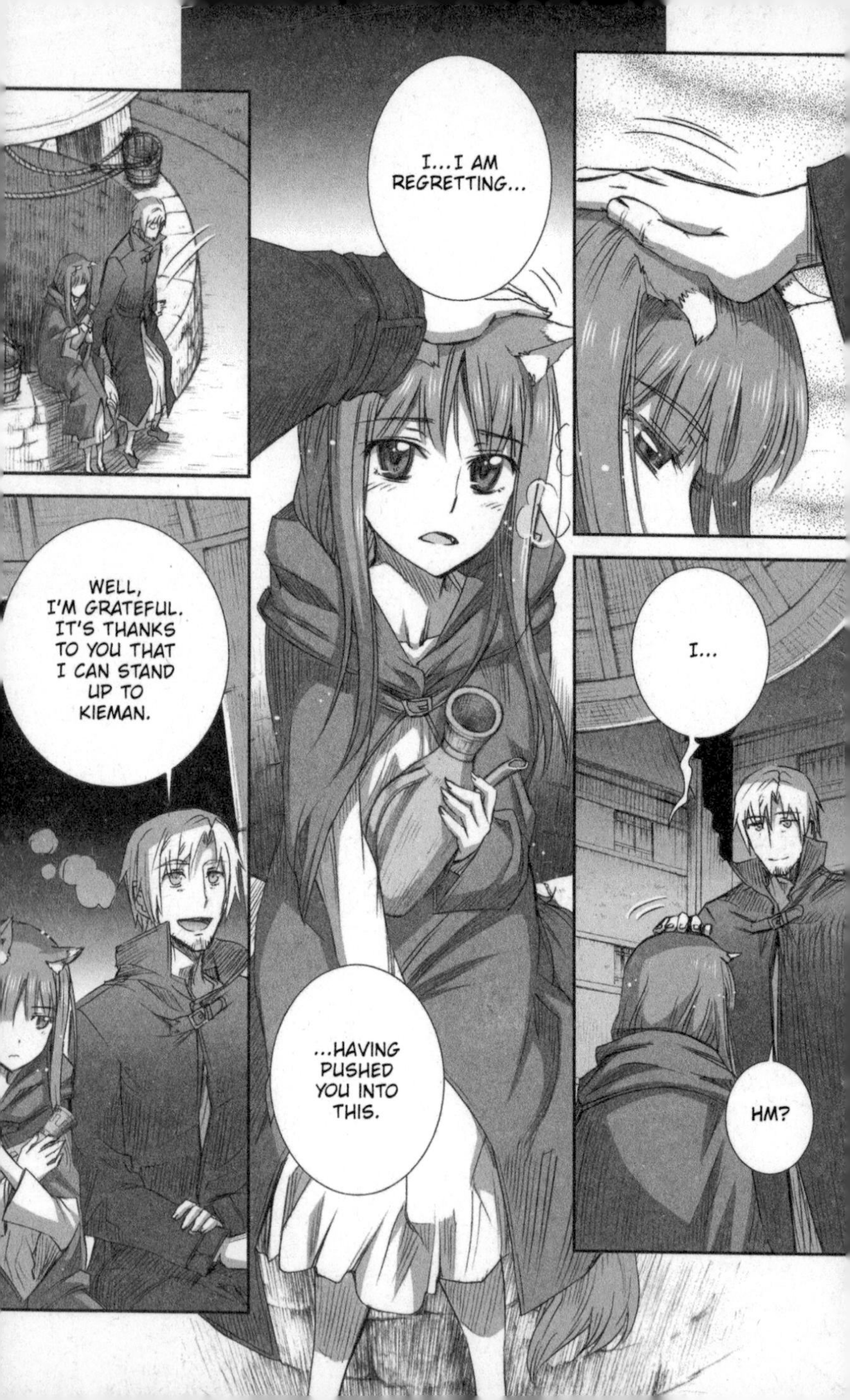
I...
HM?
I...I AM REGRETTING...
...HAVING PUSHED YOU INTO THIS.
WELL, I'M GRATEFUL. IT'S THANKS TO YOU THAT I CAN STAND UP TO KIEMAN.

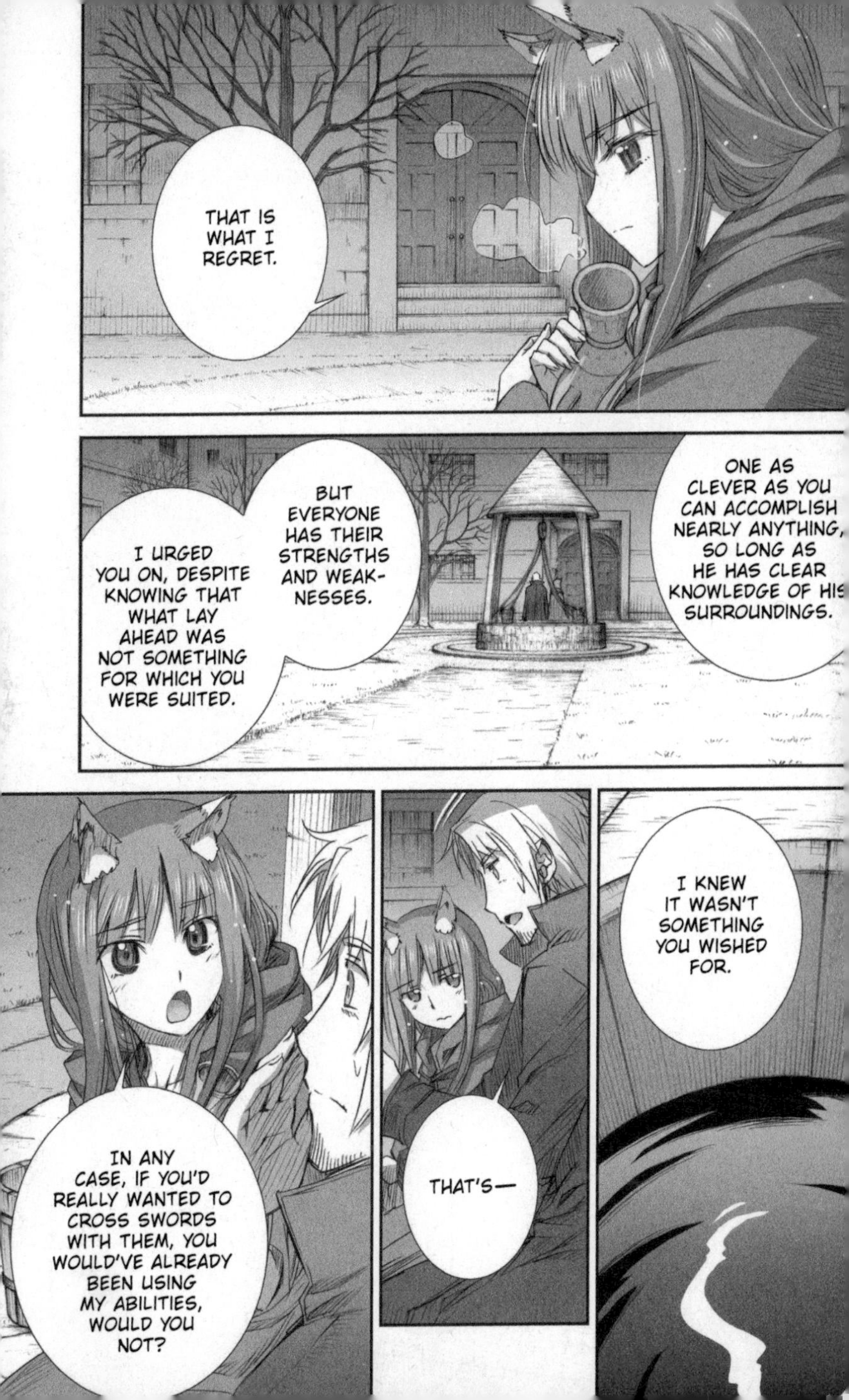
THAT IS WHAT I REGRET.
ONE AS CLEVER AS YOU CAN ACCOMPLISH NEARLY ANYTHING, SO LONG AS HE HAS CLEAR KNOWLEDGE OF HIS SURROUNDINGS.
BUT EVERYONE HAS THEIR STRENGTHS AND WEAK-NESSES.
I URGED YOU ON, DESPITE KNOWING THAT WHAT LAY AHEAD WAS NOT SOMETHING FOR WHICH YOU WERE SUITED.
I KNEW IT WASN'T SOMETHING YOU WISHED FOR.
THAT'S—
IN ANY CASE, IF YOU'D REALLY WANTED TO CROSS SWORDS WITH THEM, YOU WOULD'VE ALREADY BEEN USING MY ABILITIES, WOULD YOU NOT?

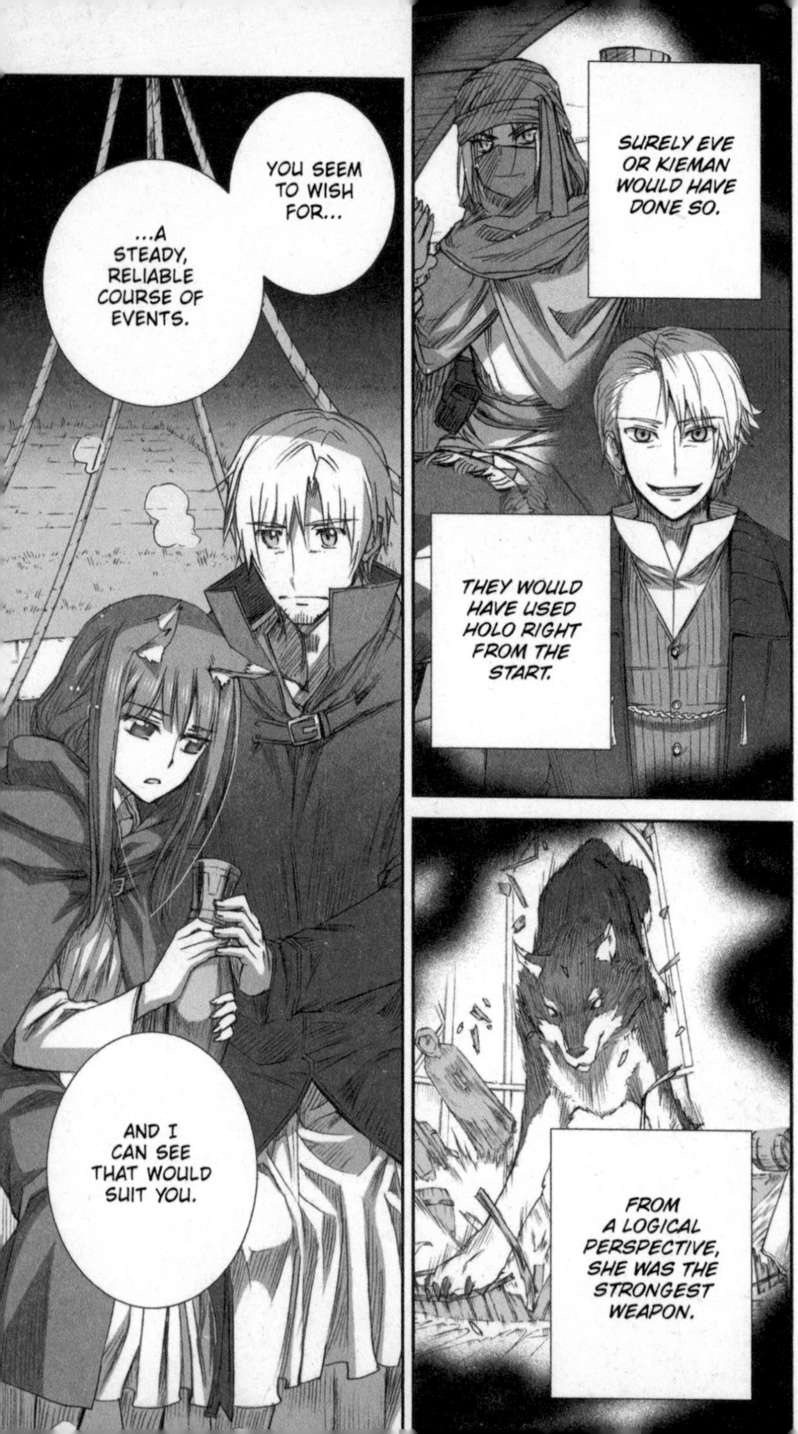
SURELY EVE OR KIEMAN WOULD HAVE DONE SO.
THEY WOULD HAVE USED HOLO RIGHT FROM THE START.
FROM A LOGICAL PERSPECTIVE, SHE WAS THE STRONGEST WEAPON.
YOU SEEM TO WISH FOR...
...A STEADY, RELIABLE COURSE OF EVENTS.
AND I CAN SEE THAT WOULD SUIT YOU.

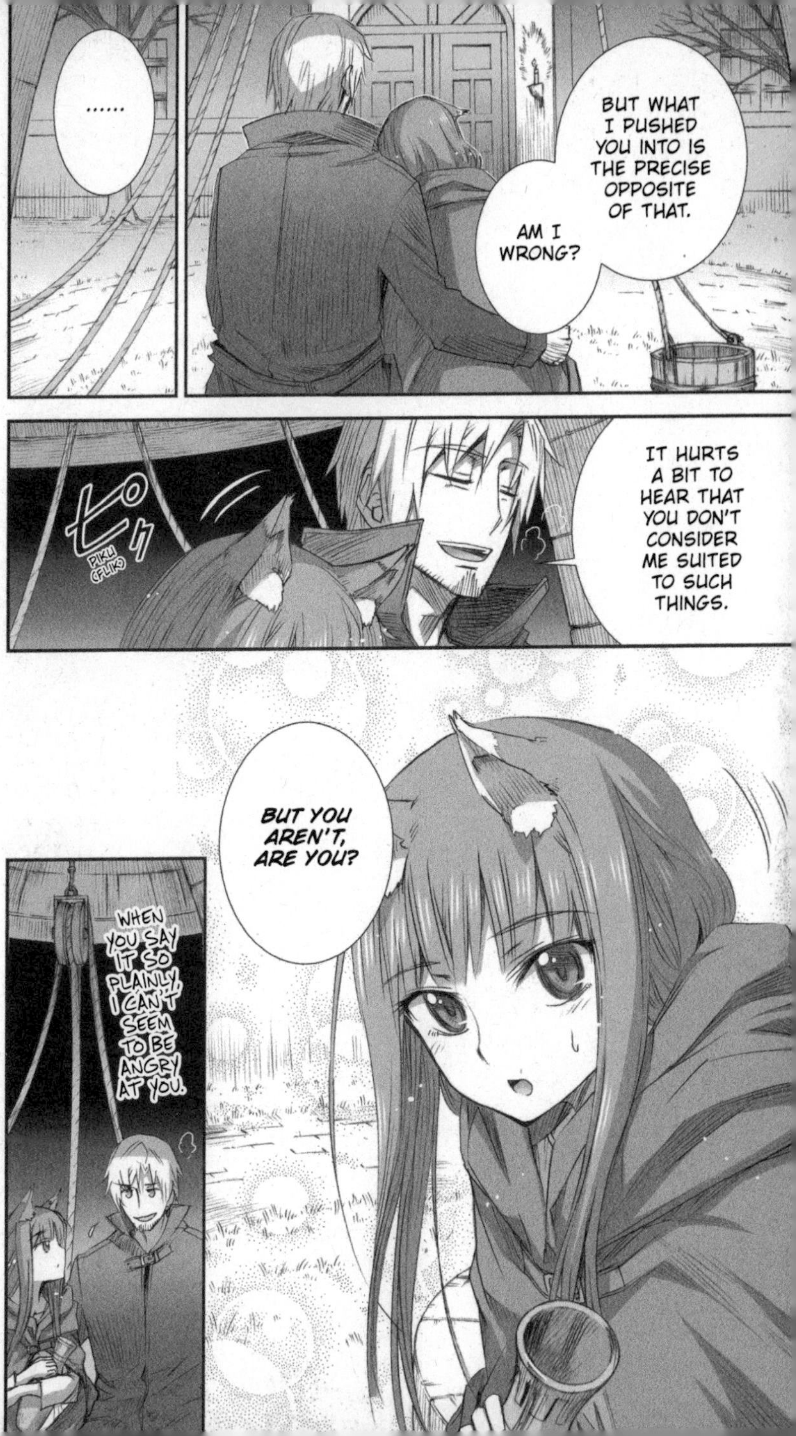
BUT WHAT I PUSHED YOU INTO IS THE PRECISE OPPOSITE OF THAT.
AM I WRONG?
......
IT HURTS A BIT TO HEAR THAT YOU DON'T CONSIDER ME SUITED TO SUCH THINGS.
ピクッ
PIKU (FLIK)
BUT YOU AREN'T, ARE YOU?
WHEN YOU SAY IT SO PLAINLY, I CAN'T SEEM TO BE ANGRY AT YOU.

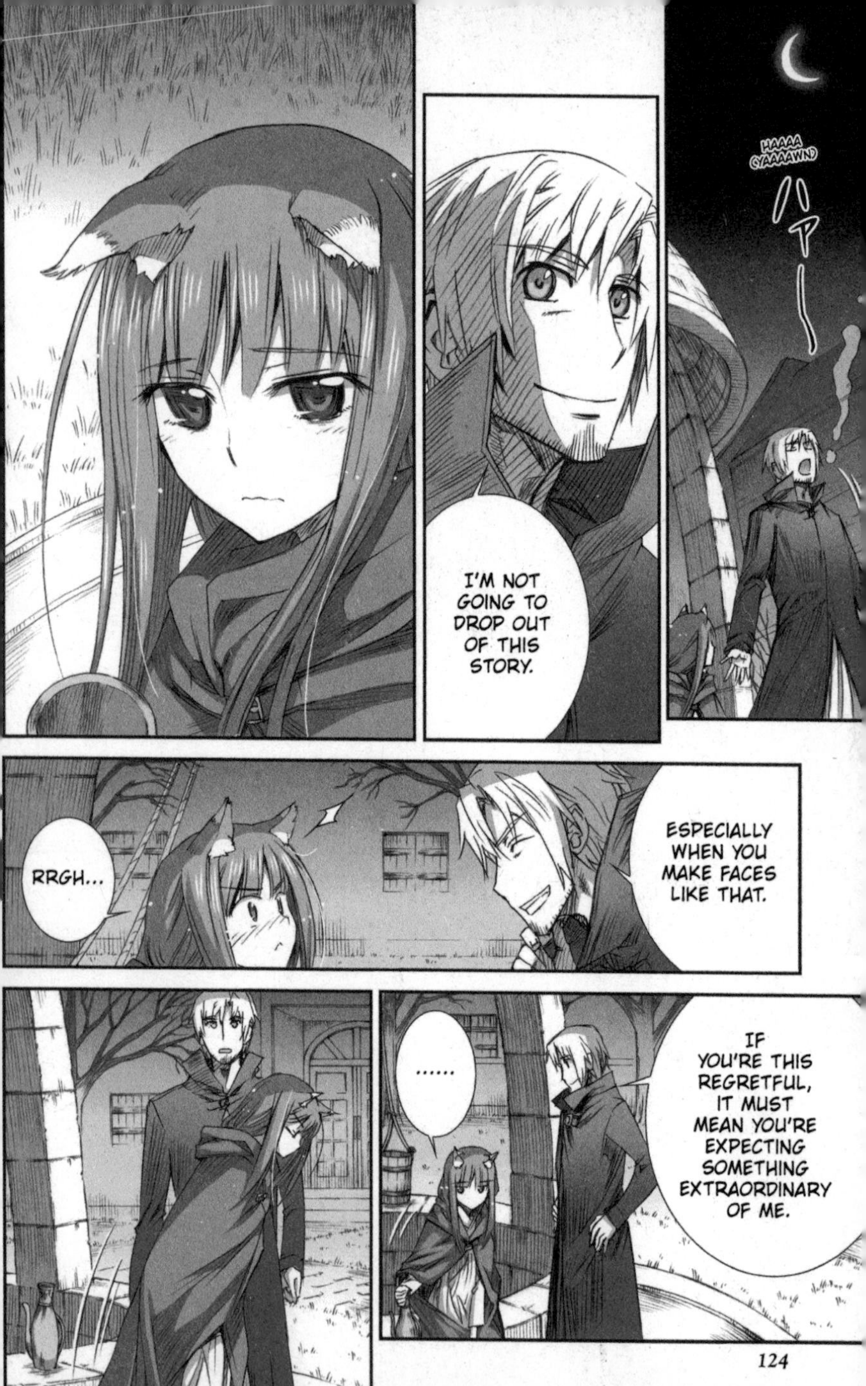
HAAAA (YAAAAWN)
ハアー
I'M NOT GOING TO DROP OUT OF THIS STORY.
ESPECIALLY WHEN YOU MAKE FACES LIKE THAT.
RRGH...
IF YOU'RE THIS REGRETFUL, IT MUST MEAN YOU'RE EXPECTING SOMETHING EXTRAORDINARY OF ME.
......

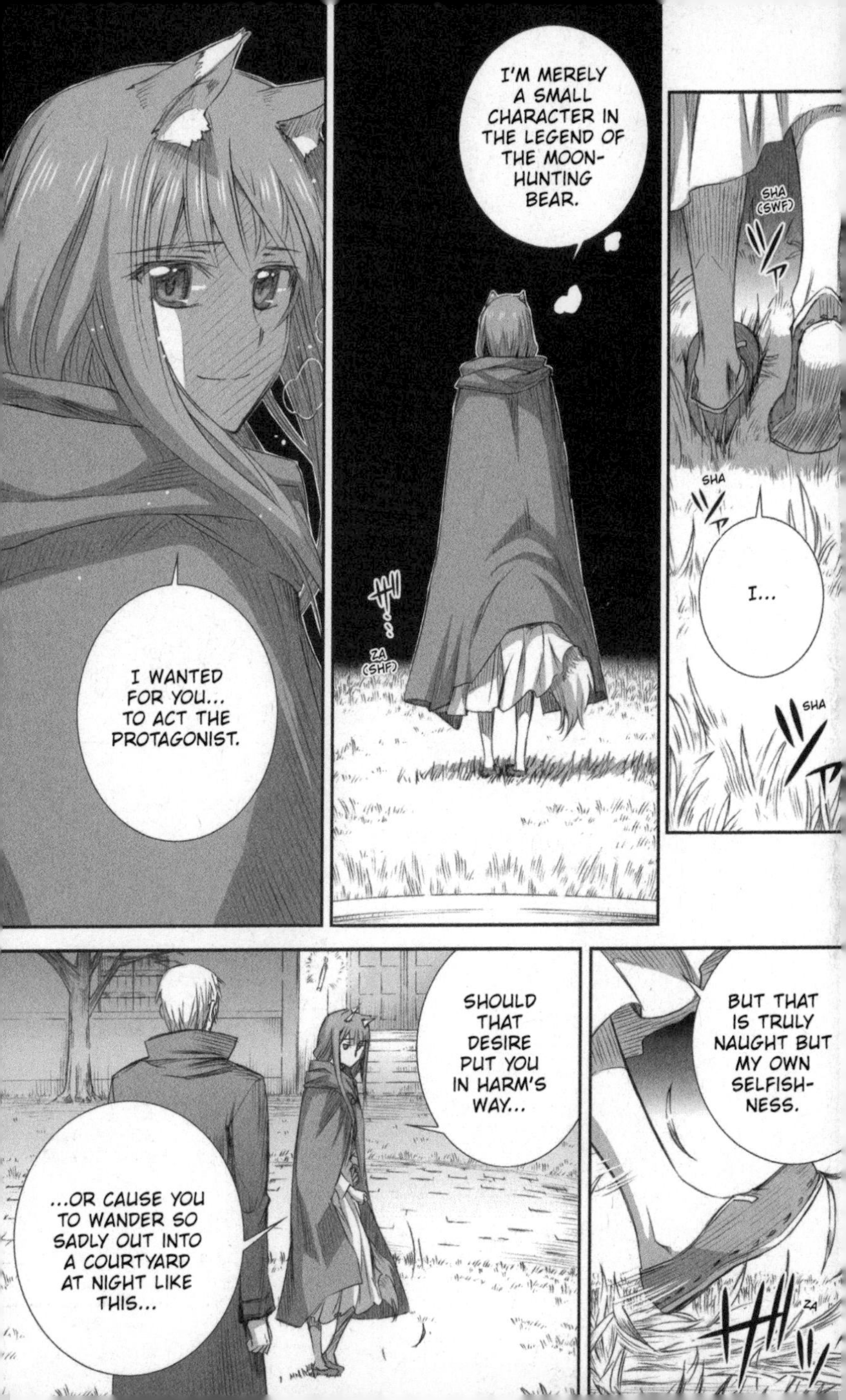
SHA (SWF)
SHA
I...
SHA
I'M MERELY A SMALL CHARACTER IN THE LEGEND OF THE MOON-HUNTING BEAR.
ZA (SHF)
I WANTED FOR YOU... TO ACT THE PROTAGONIST.
BUT THAT IS TRULY NAUGHT BUT MY OWN SELFISH-NESS.
ZA
SHOULD THAT DESIRE PUT YOU IN HARM'S WAY...
...OR CAUSE YOU TO WANDER SO SADLY OUT INTO A COURTYARD AT NIGHT LIKE THIS...

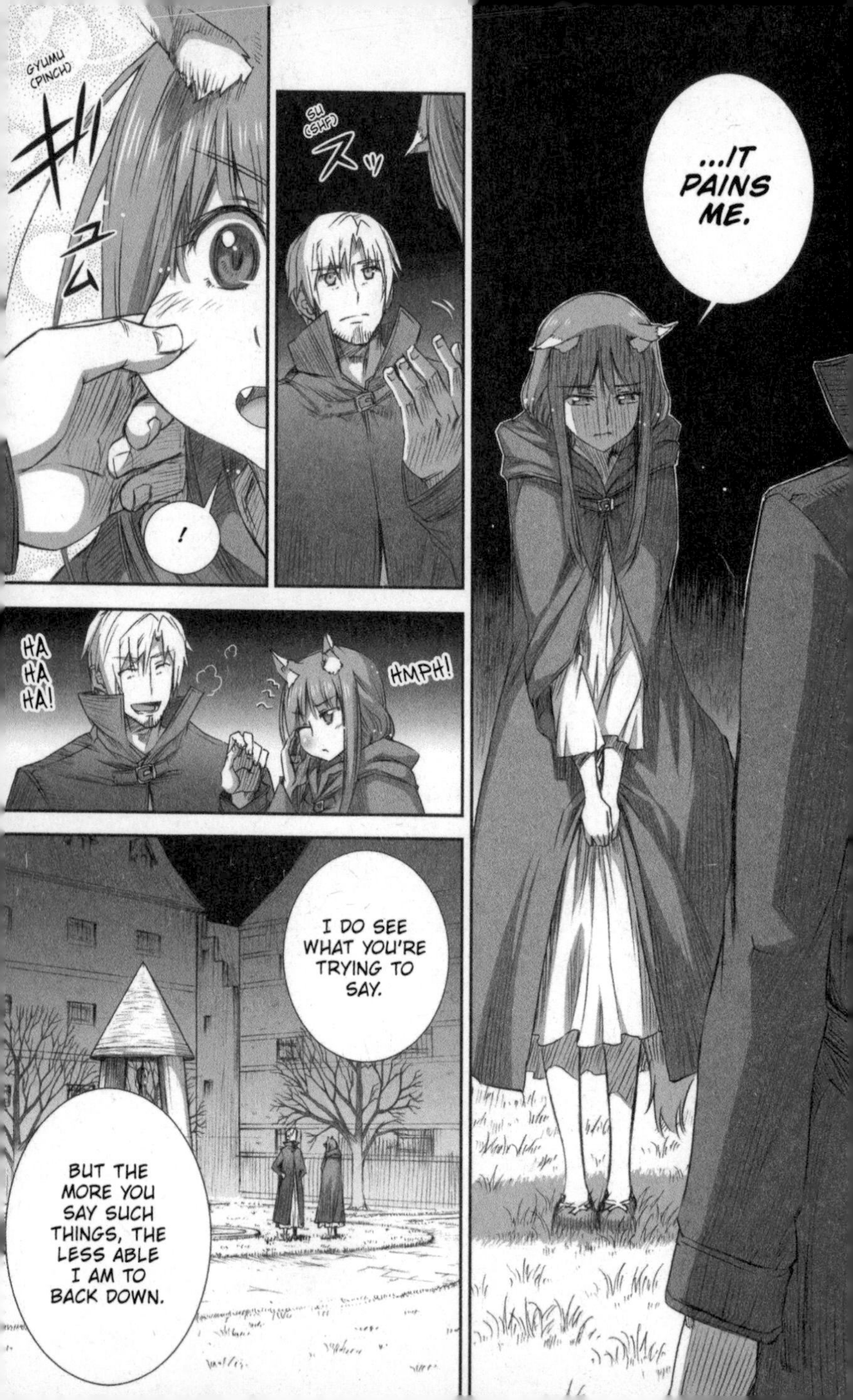
...IT PAINS ME.
SU (SHF)
スッ
GYUMU (PINCH)
ギュム
!
HMPH!
HA HA HA!
I DO SEE WHAT YOU'RE TRYING TO SAY.
BUT THE MORE YOU SAY SUCH THINGS, THE LESS ABLE I AM TO BACK DOWN.

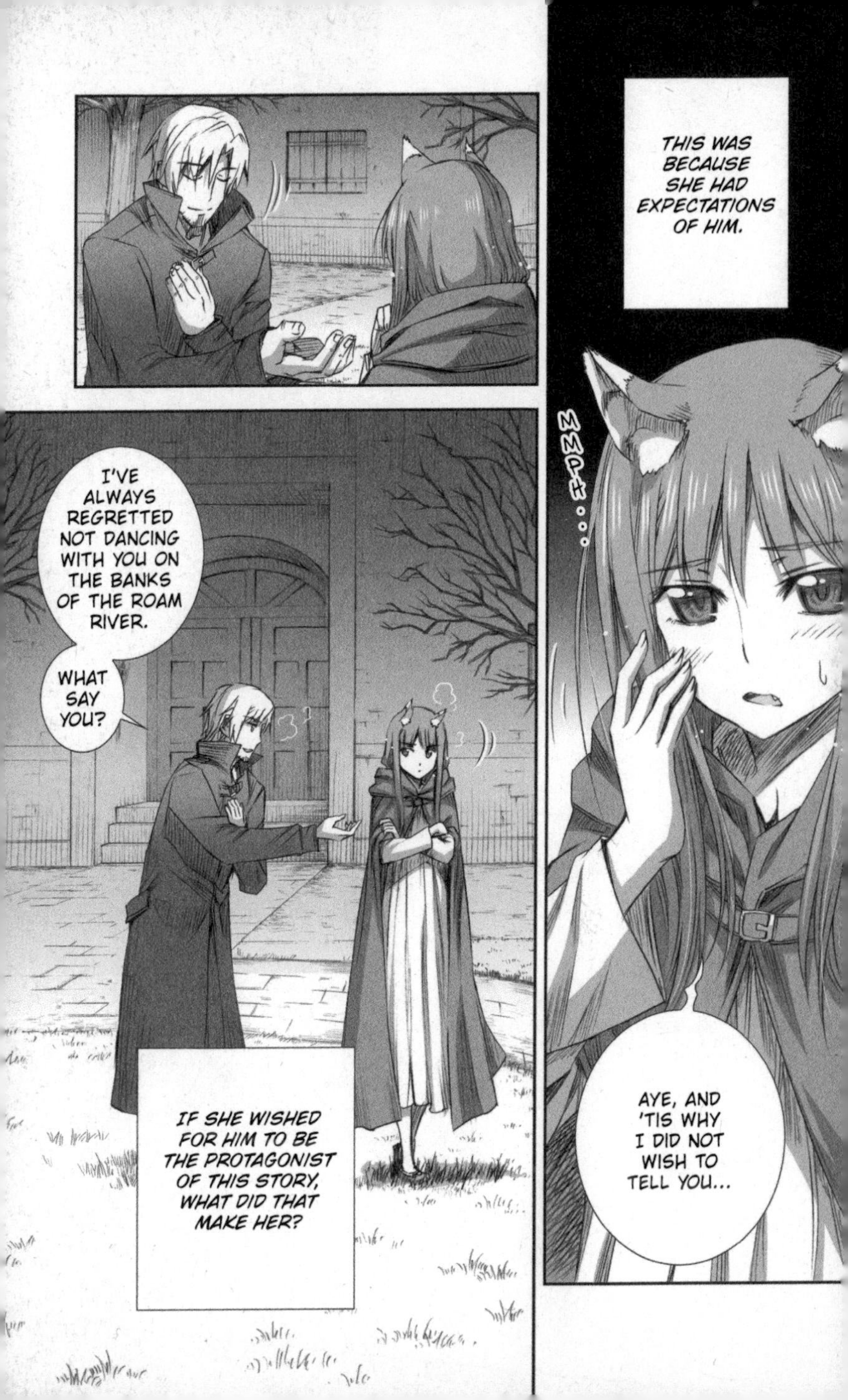
THIS WAS BECAUSE SHE HAD EXPECTATIONS OF HIM.
MMPH...
AYE, AND 'TIS WHY I DID NOT WISH TO TELL YOU...
I'VE ALWAYS REGRETTED NOT DANCING WITH YOU ON THE BANKS OF THE ROAM RIVER.
WHAT SAY YOU?
IF SHE WISHED FOR HIM TO BE THE PROTAGONIST OF THIS STORY, WHAT DID THAT MAKE HER?

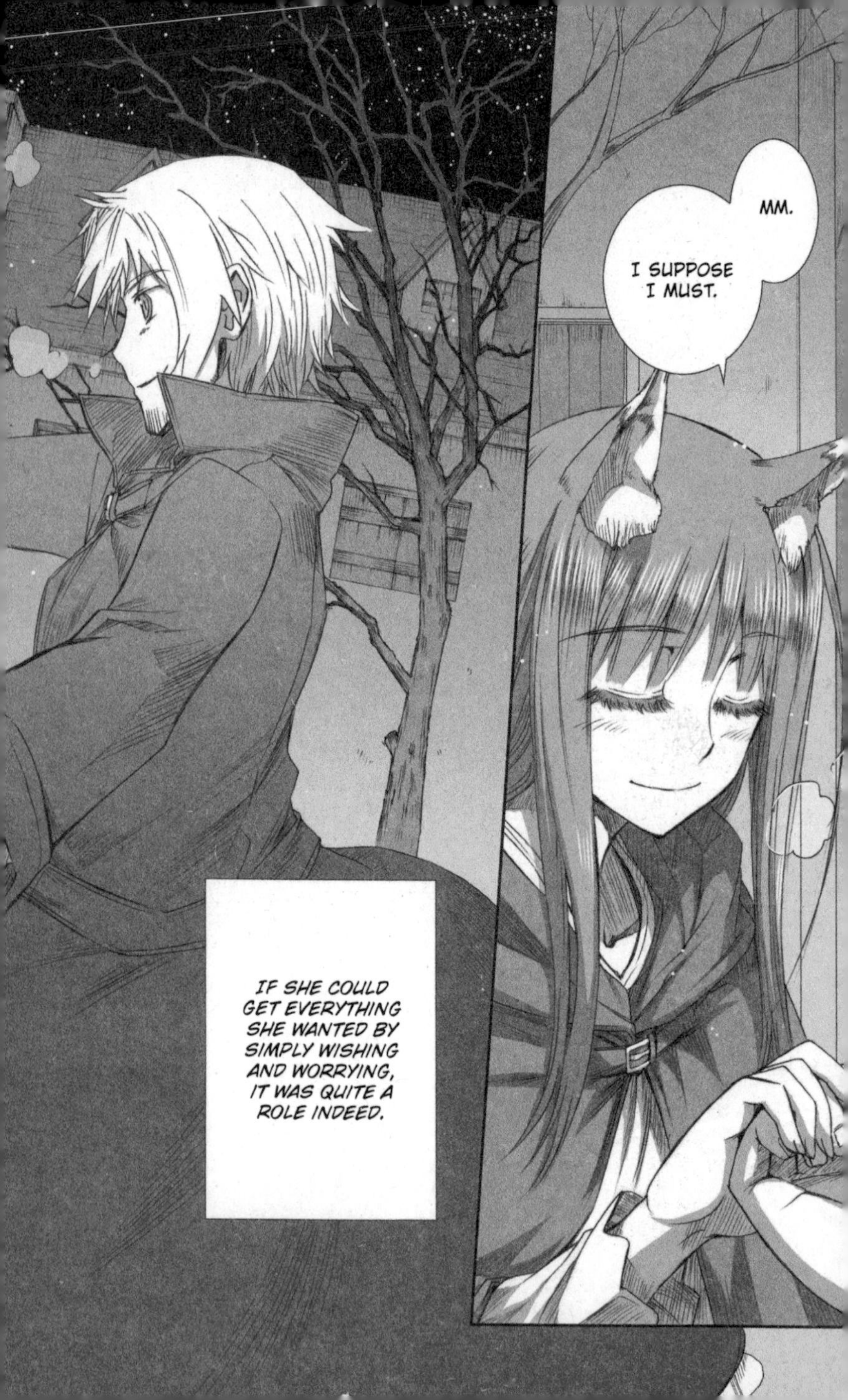
MM.
I SUPPOSE I MUST.
IF SHE COULD GET EVERYTHING SHE WANTED BY SIMPLY WISHING AND WORRYING, IT WAS QUITE A ROLE INDEED.

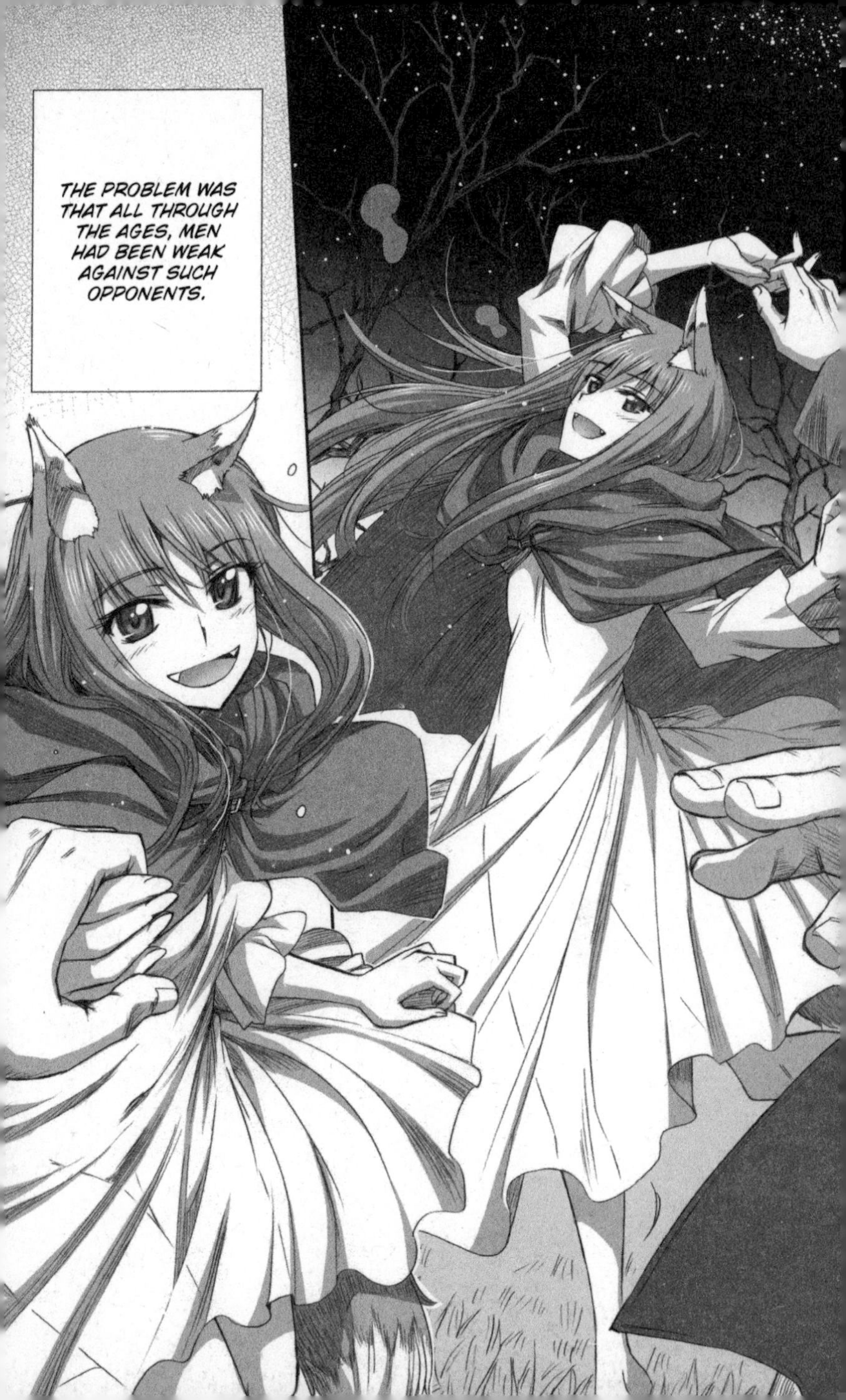
THE PROBLEM WAS THAT ALL THROUGH THE AGES, MEN HAD BEEN WEAK AGAINST SUCH OPPONENTS.

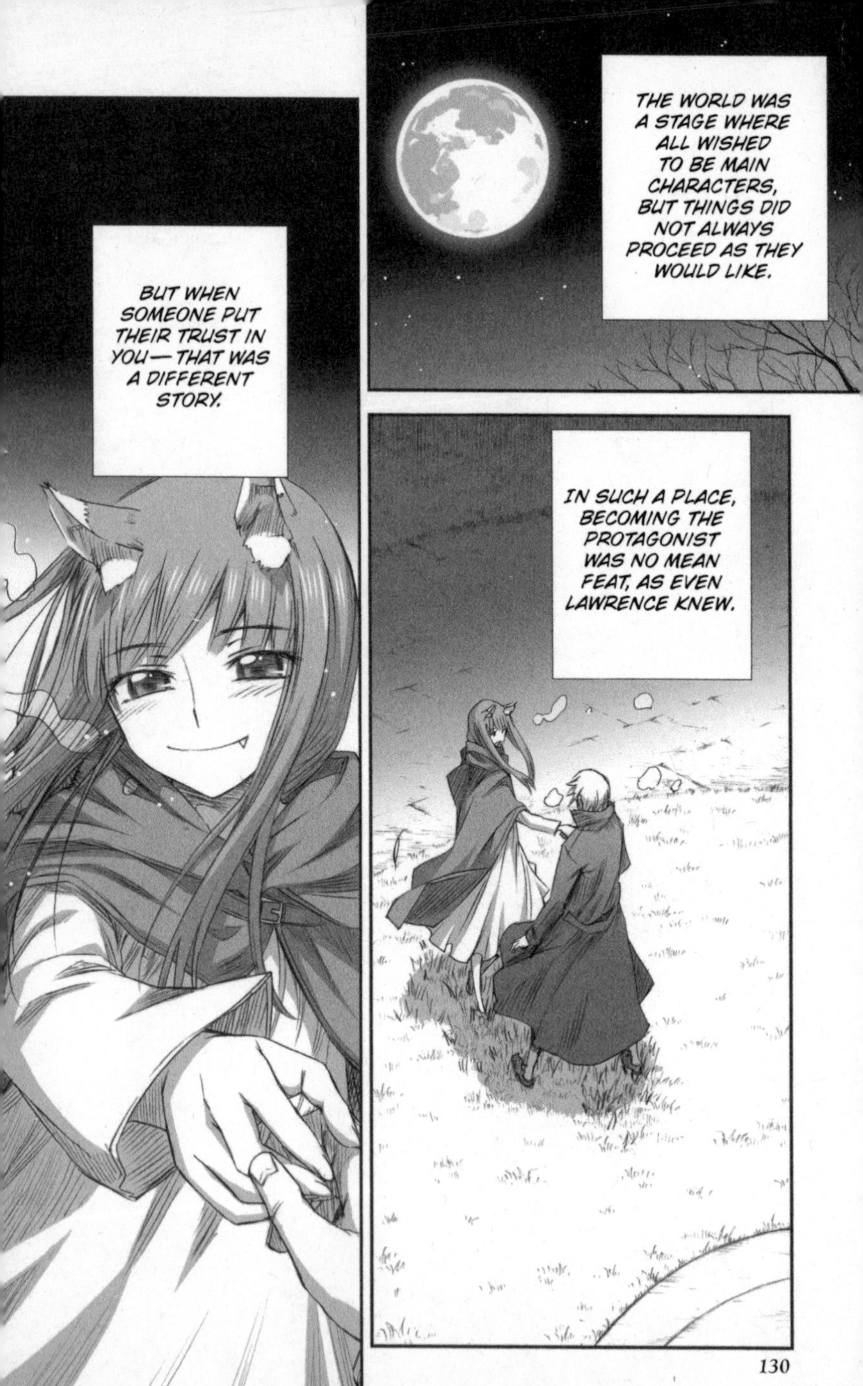
THE WORLD WAS A STAGE WHERE ALL WISHED TO BE MAIN CHARACTERS, BUT THINGS DID NOT ALWAYS PROCEED AS THEY WOULD LIKE.
IN SUCH A PLACE, BECOMING THE PROTAGONIST WAS NO MEAN FEAT, AS EVEN LAWRENCE KNEW.
BUT WHEN SOMEONE PUT THEIR TRUST IN YOU—THAT WAS A DIFFERENT STORY.

SPICE & WOLF

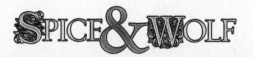

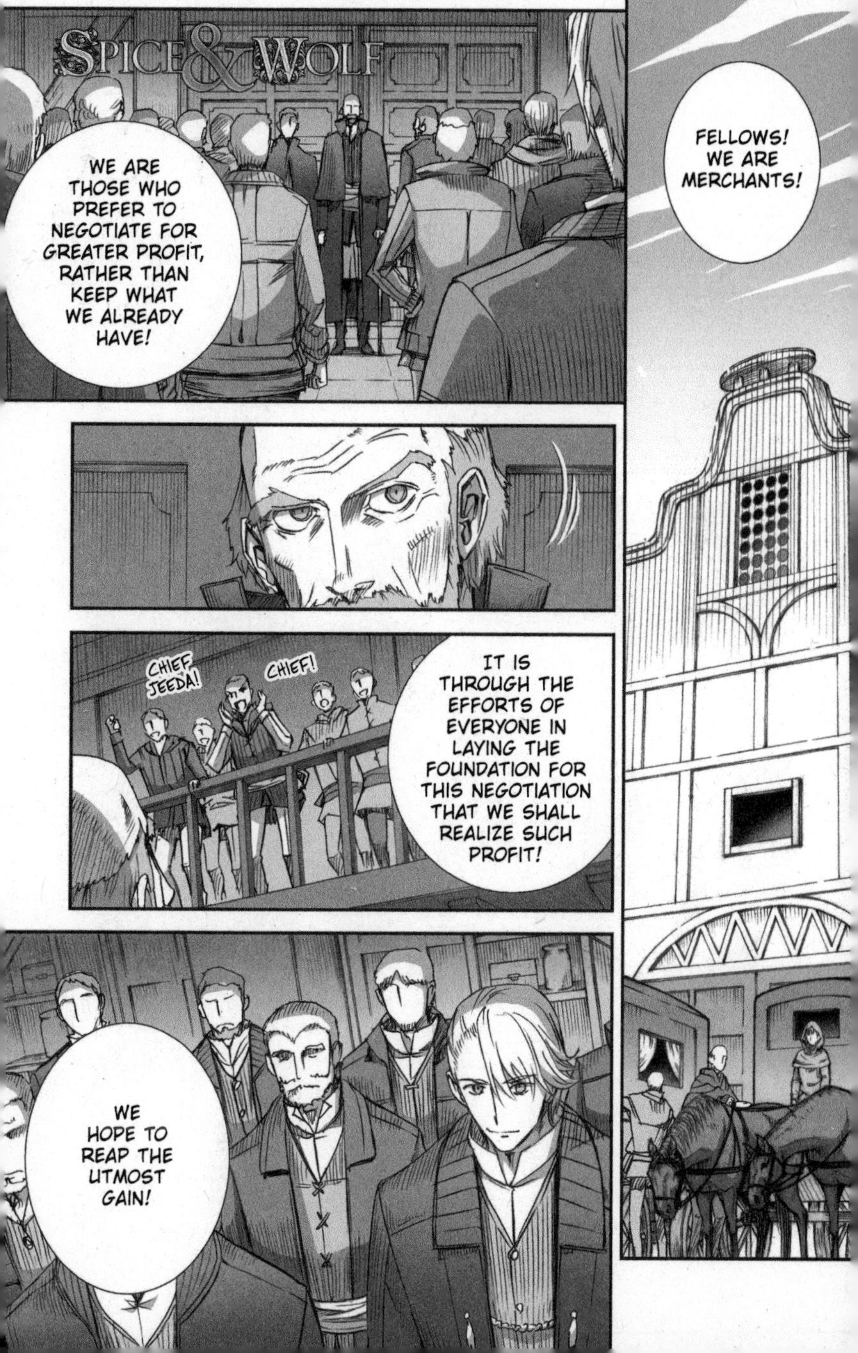
FELLOWS! WE ARE MERCHANTS!
SPICE & WOLF
WE ARE THOSE WHO PREFER TO NEGOTIATE FOR GREATER PROFIT, RATHER THAN KEEP WHAT WE ALREADY HAVE!
IT IS THROUGH THE EFFORTS OF EVERYONE IN LAYING THE FOUNDATION FOR THIS NEGOTIATION THAT WE SHALL REALIZE SUCH PROFIT!
CHIEF!
CHIEF JEEDA!
WE HOPE TO REAP THE UTMOST GAIN!

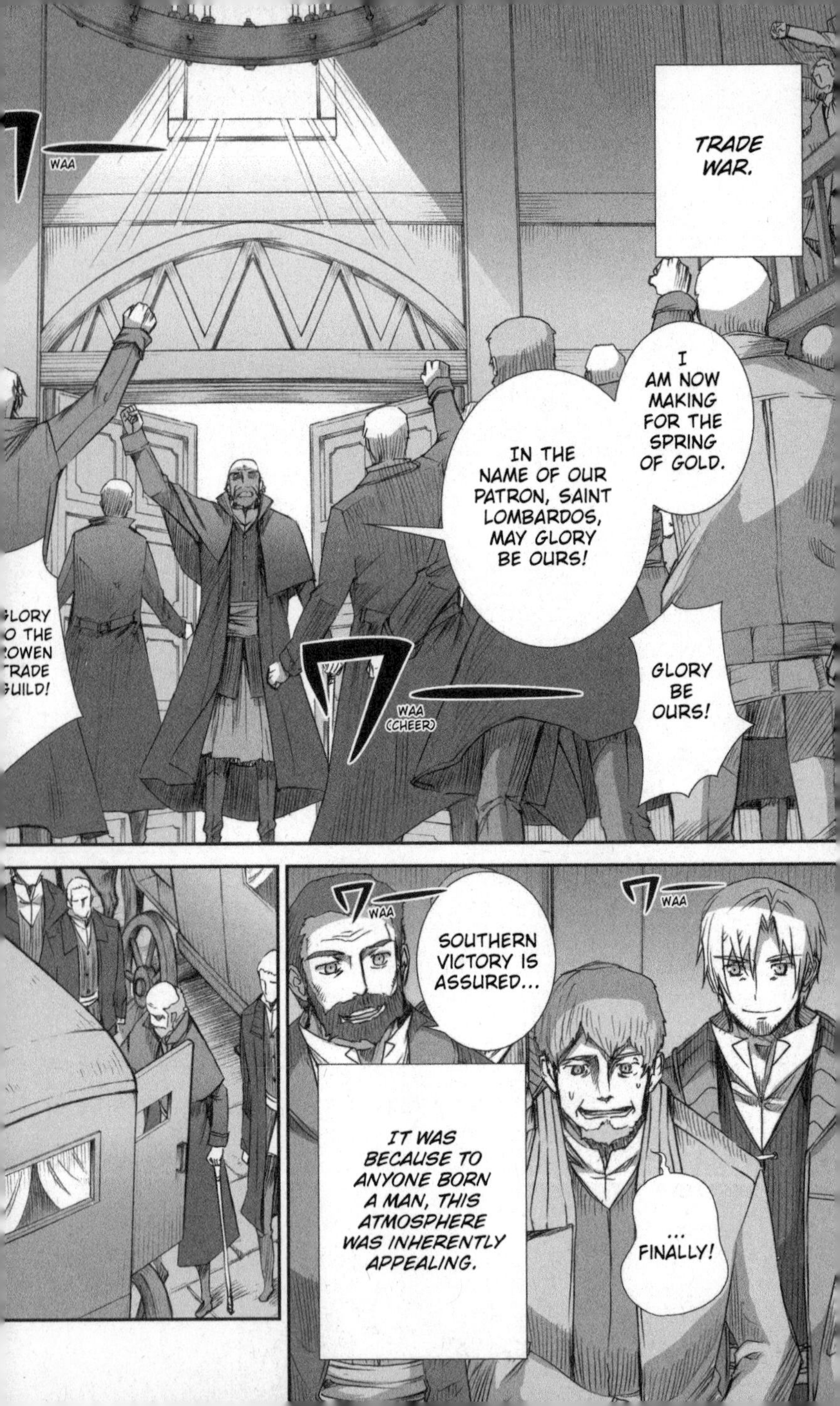
TRADE WAR.
I AM NOW MAKING FOR THE SPRING OF GOLD.
IN THE NAME OF OUR PATRON, SAINT LOMBARDOS, MAY GLORY BE OURS!
GLORY BE OURS!
WAA (CHEER)
WAA
LORY O THE OWEN TRADE UILD!
WAA
SOUTHERN VICTORY IS ASSURED...
WAA
... FINALLY!
IT WAS BECAUSE TO ANYONE BORN A MAN, THIS ATMOSPHERE WAS INHERENTLY APPEALING.

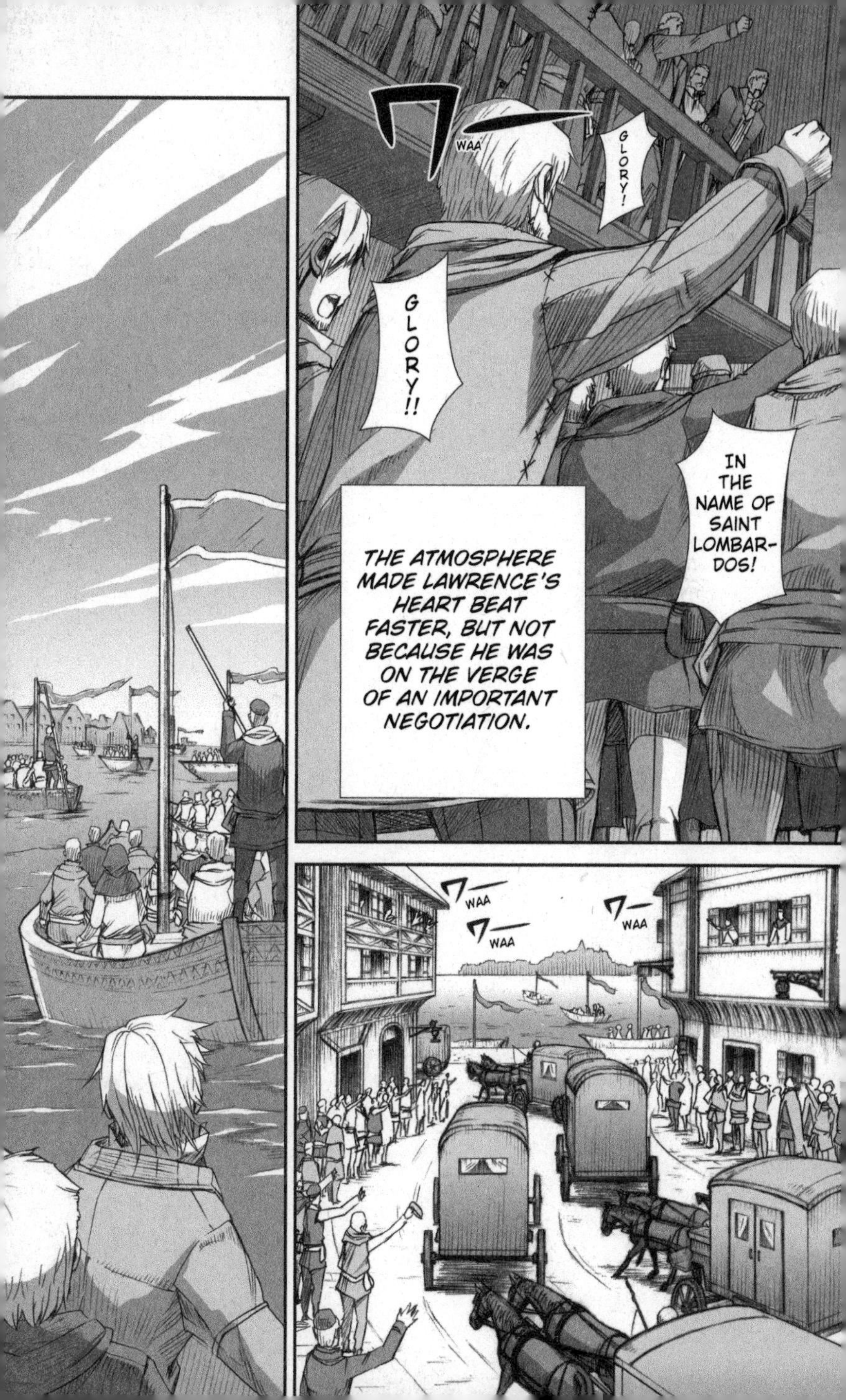
GLORY!
WAA
GLORY!!
IN THE NAME OF SAINT LOMBAR-DOS!
THE ATMOSPHERE MADE LAWRENCE'S HEART BEAT FASTER, BUT NOT BECAUSE HE WAS ON THE VERGE OF AN IMPORTANT NEGOTIATION.
WAA
WAA
WAA

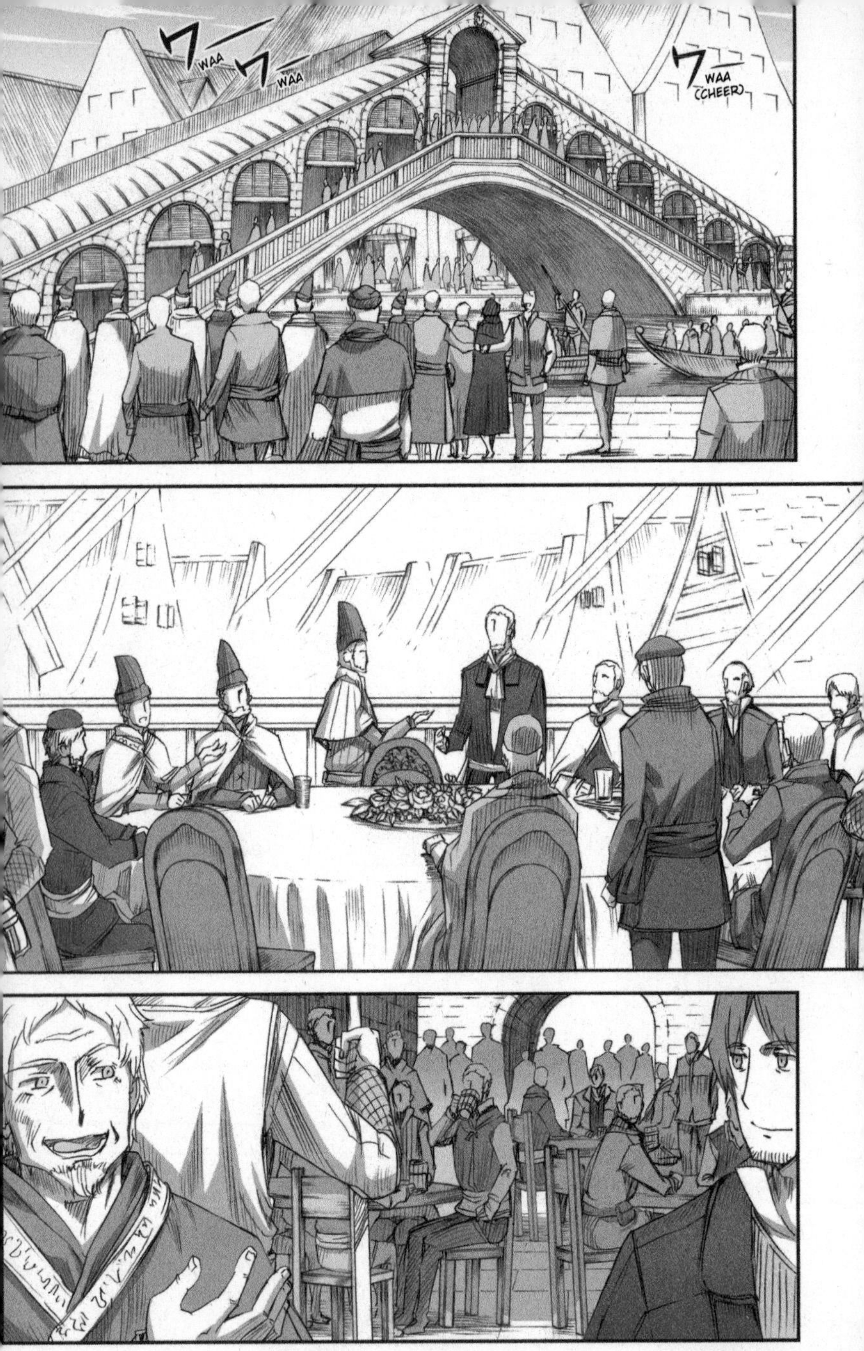
ワー
WAA (CHEER)
ワー
WAA
ワー
WAA

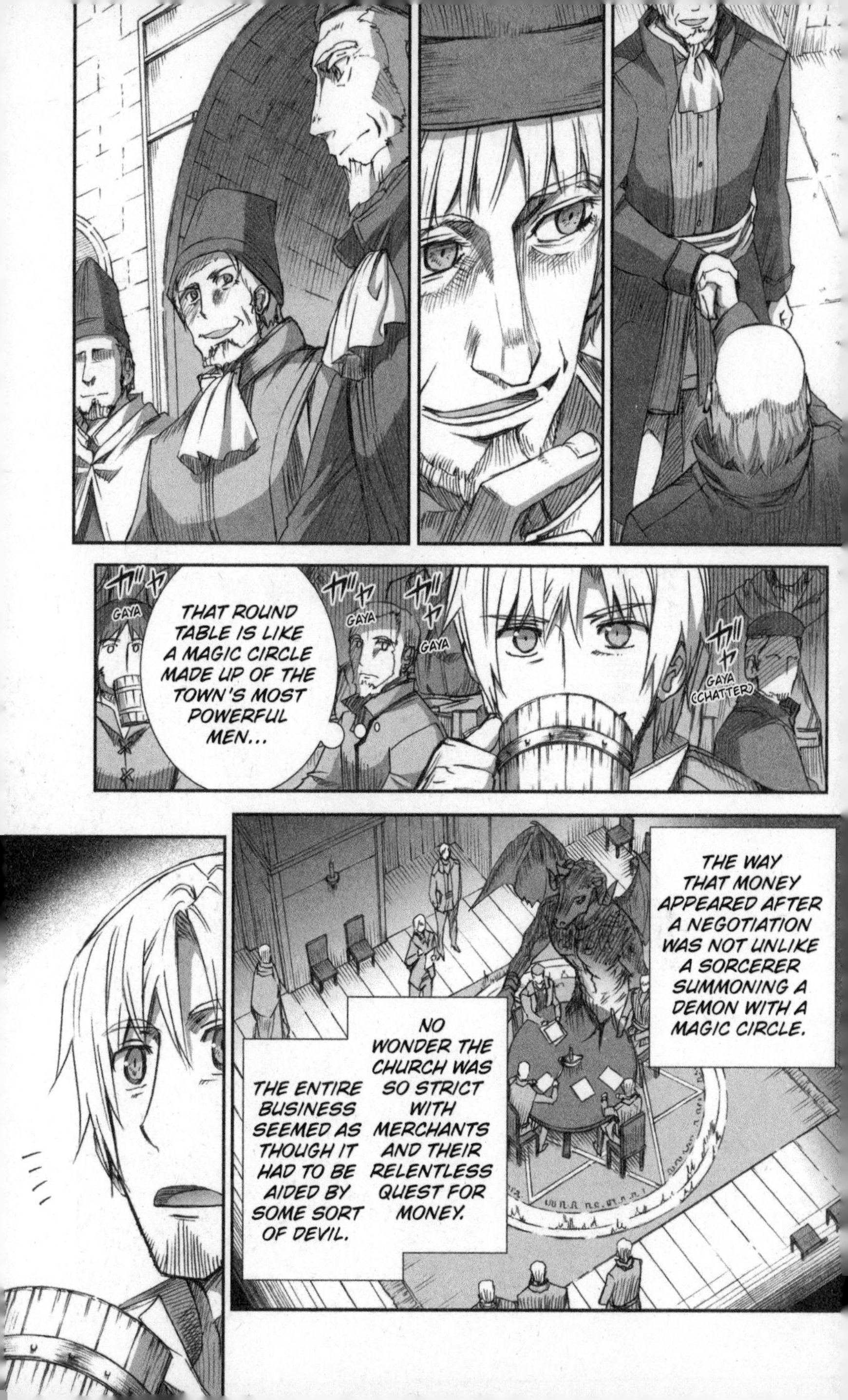
GAYA (CHATTER)
GAYA
GAYA
THAT ROUND TABLE IS LIKE A MAGIC CIRCLE MADE UP OF THE TOWN'S MOST POWERFUL MEN...
GAYA
THE WAY THAT MONEY APPEARED AFTER A NEGOTIATION WAS NOT UNLIKE A SORCERER SUMMONING A DEMON WITH A MAGIC CIRCLE.
NO WONDER THE CHURCH WAS SO STRICT WITH MERCHANTS AND THEIR RELENTLESS QUEST FOR MONEY.
THE ENTIRE BUSINESS SEEMED AS THOUGH IT HAD TO BE AIDED BY SOME SORT OF DEVIL.

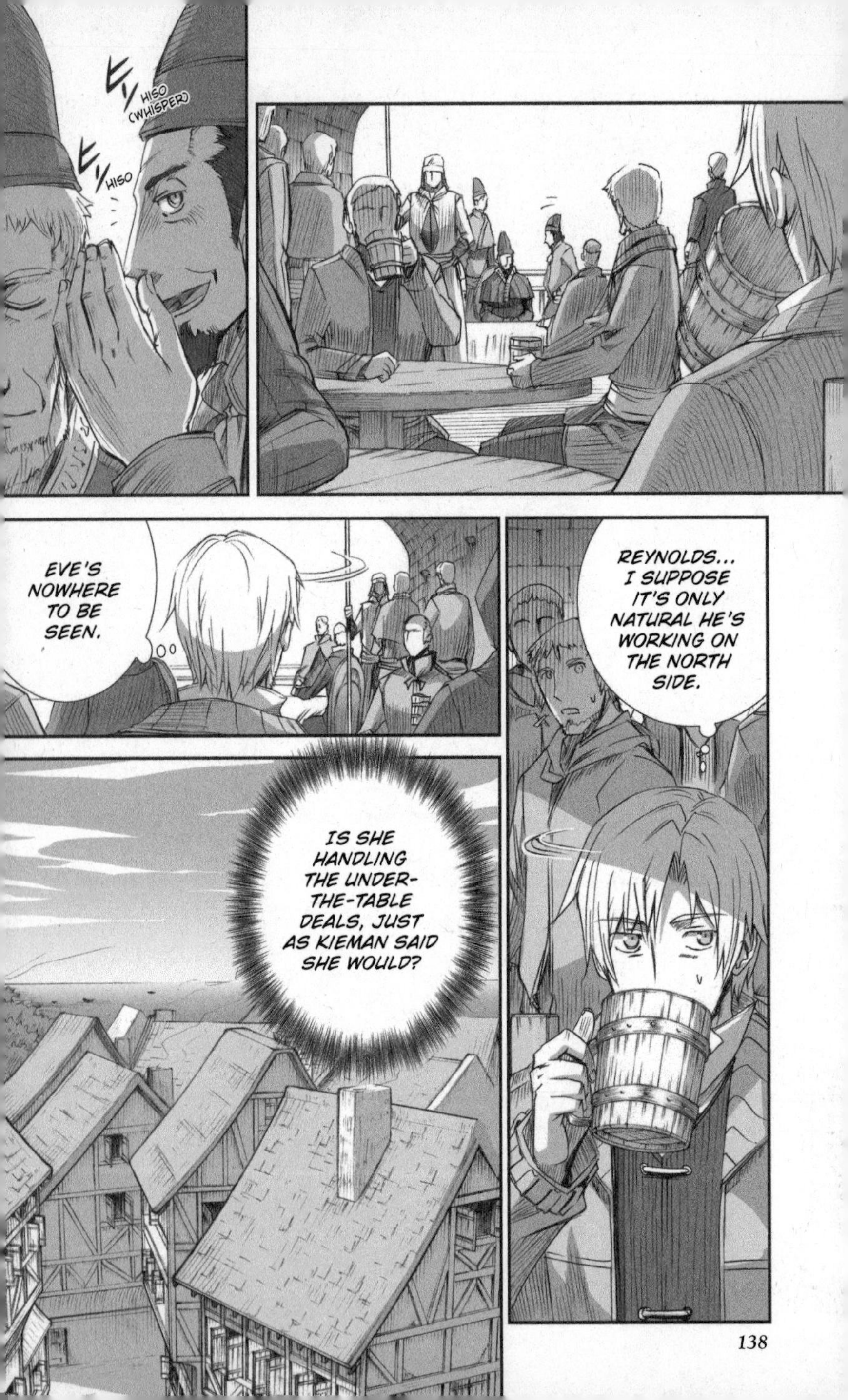
ヒソ HISO (WHISPER)
ヒソ HISO
REYNOLDS... I SUPPOSE IT'S ONLY NATURAL HE'S WORKING ON THE NORTH SIDE.
EVE'S NOWHERE TO BE SEEN.
IS SHE HANDLING THE UNDER-THE-TABLE DEALS, JUST AS KIEMAN SAID SHE WOULD?

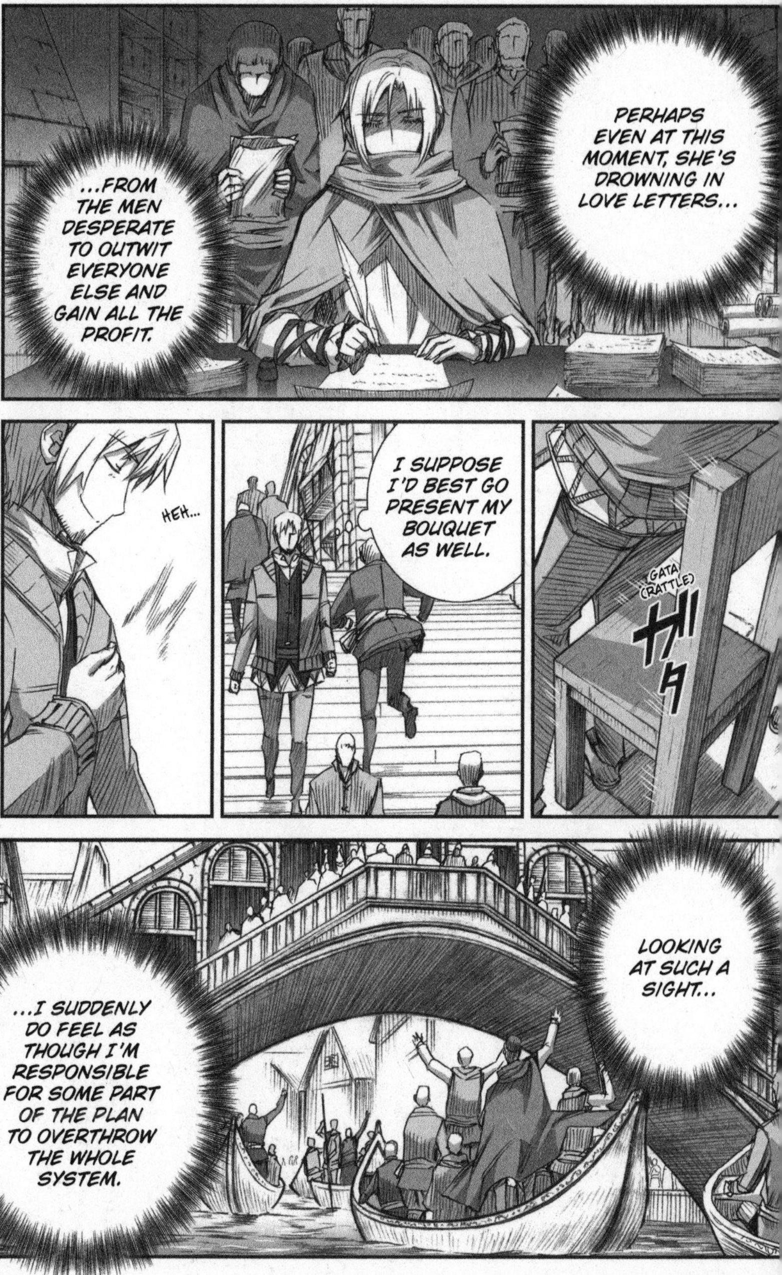
PERHAPS EVEN AT THIS MOMENT, SHE'S DROWNING IN LOVE LETTERS...
...FROM THE MEN DESPERATE TO OUTWIT EVERYONE ELSE AND GAIN ALL THE PROFIT.
GATA (RATTLE)
ガタ
I SUPPOSE I'D BEST GO PRESENT MY BOUQUET AS WELL.
HEH...
LOOKING AT SUCH A SIGHT...
...I SUDDENLY DO FEEL AS THOUGH I'M RESPONSIBLE FOR SOME PART OF THE PLAN TO OVERTHROW THE WHOLE SYSTEM.

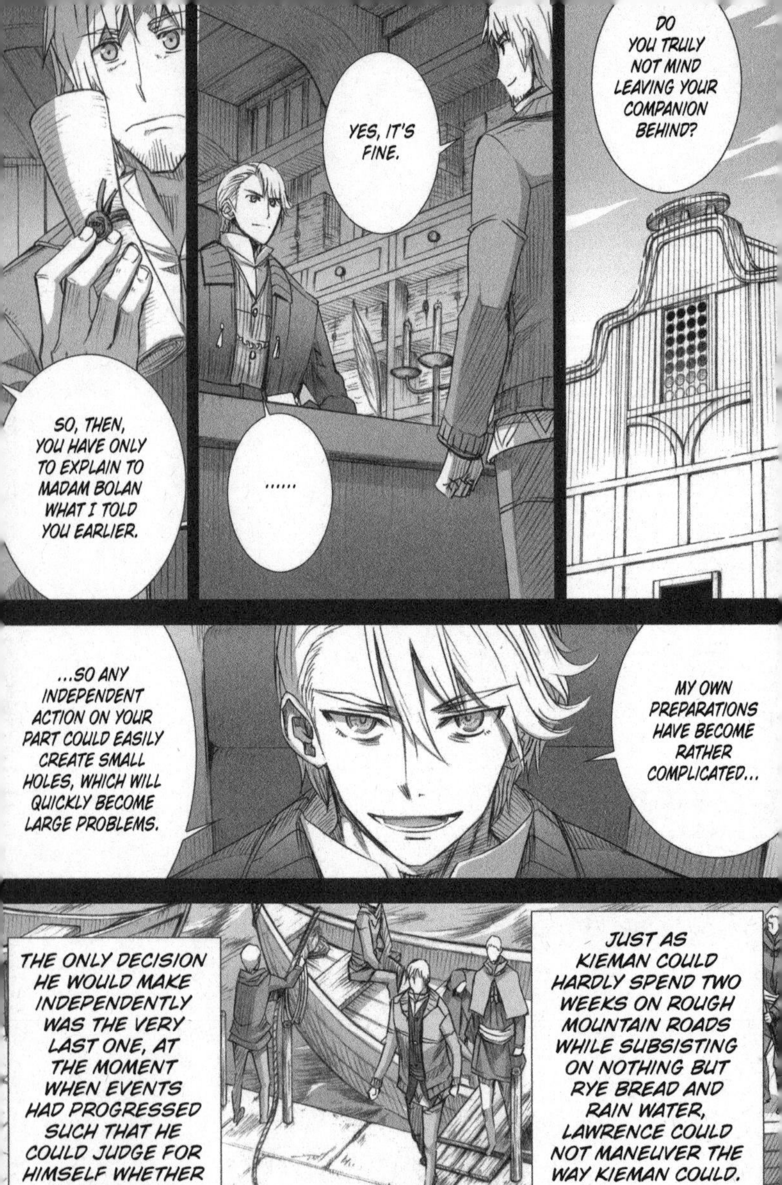
DO YOU TRULY NOT MIND LEAVING YOUR COMPANION BEHIND?
YES, IT'S FINE.
......
SO, THEN, YOU HAVE ONLY TO EXPLAIN TO MADAM BOLAN WHAT I TOLD YOU EARLIER.
MY OWN PREPARATIONS HAVE BECOME RATHER COMPLICATED...
...SO ANY INDEPENDENT ACTION ON YOUR PART COULD EASILY CREATE SMALL HOLES, WHICH WILL QUICKLY BECOME LARGE PROBLEMS.
JUST AS KIEMAN COULD HARDLY SPEND TWO WEEKS ON ROUGH MOUNTAIN ROADS WHILE SUBSISTING ON NOTHING BUT RYE BREAD AND RAIN WATER, LAWRENCE COULD NOT MANEUVER THE WAY KIEMAN COULD.
THE ONLY DECISION HE WOULD MAKE INDEPENDENTLY WAS THE VERY LAST ONE, AT THE MOMENT WHEN EVENTS HAD PROGRESSED SUCH THAT HE COULD JUDGE FOR HIMSELF WHETHER TO COOPERATE OR DEFECT.

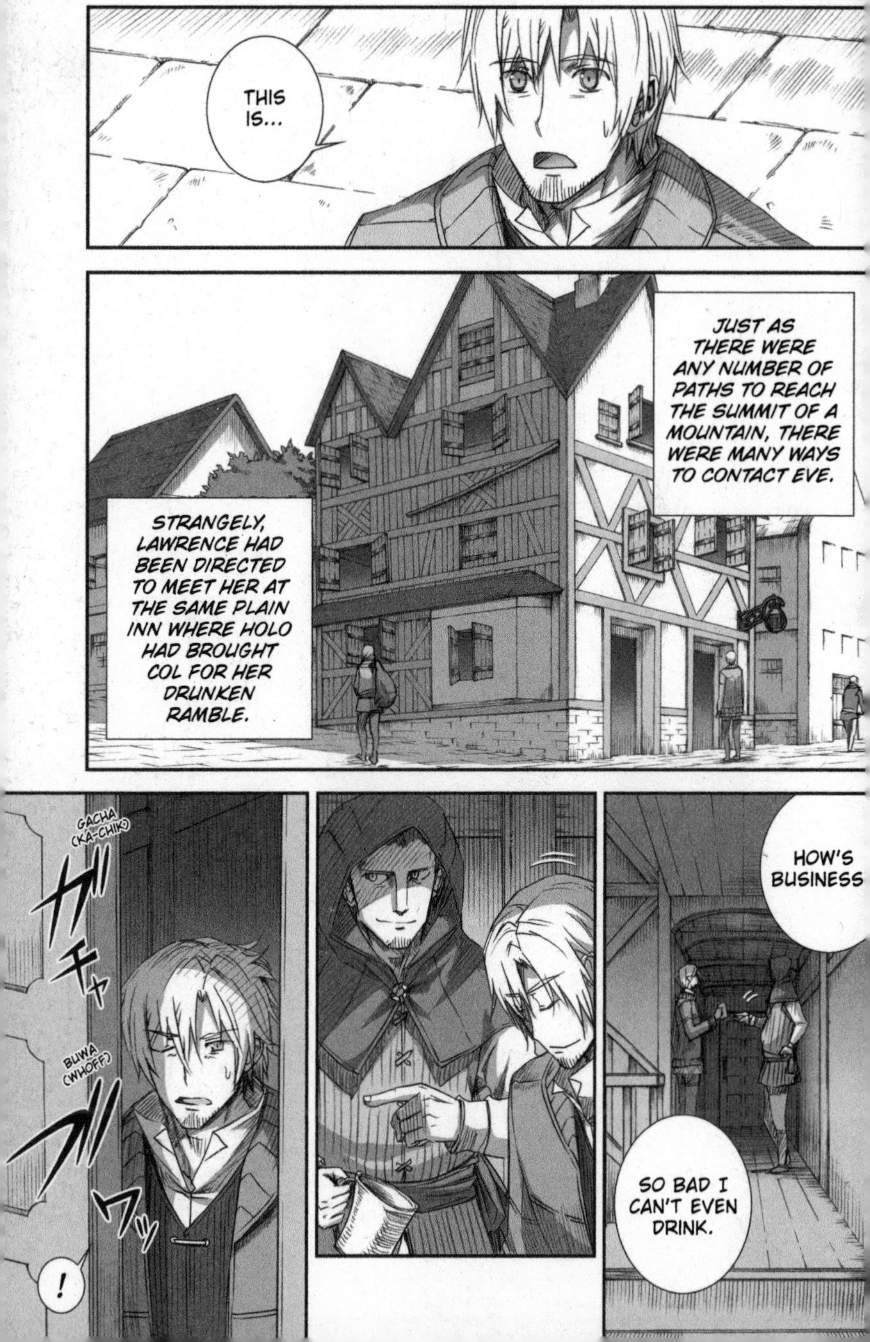
THIS IS...
JUST AS THERE WERE ANY NUMBER OF PATHS TO REACH THE SUMMIT OF A MOUNTAIN, THERE WERE MANY WAYS TO CONTACT EVE.
STRANGELY, LAWRENCE HAD BEEN DIRECTED TO MEET HER AT THE SAME PLAIN INN WHERE HOLO HAD BROUGHT COL FOR HER DRUNKEN RAMBLE.
HOW'S BUSINESS
SO BAD I CAN'T EVEN DRINK.
GACHA (KA-CHIK)
ガチャ
BUWA (WHOFF)
ブワッ
!

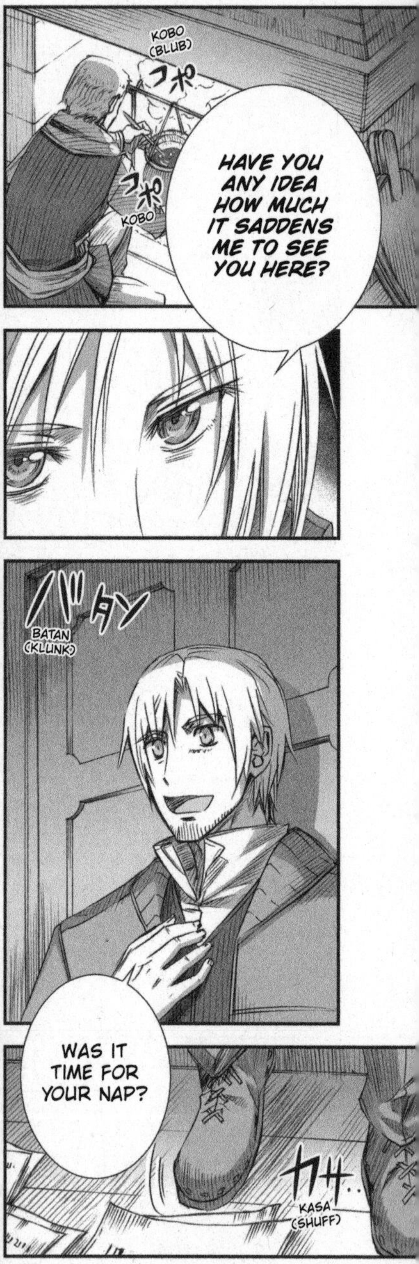
コポ
KOBO (BLUB)
コポ
KOBO
HAVE YOU ANY IDEA HOW MUCH IT SADDENS ME TO SEE YOU HERE?
バタン
BATAN (KLUNK)
WAS IT TIME FOR YOUR NAP?
カサ…
KASA (SHUFF)

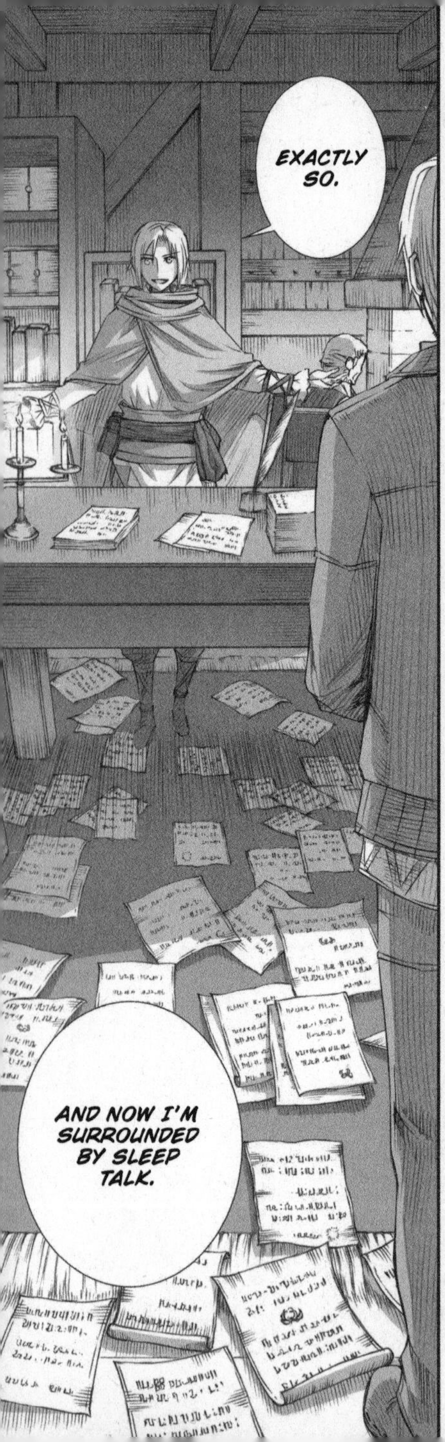
EXACTLY SO.
AND NOW I'M SURROUNDED BY SLEEP TALK.

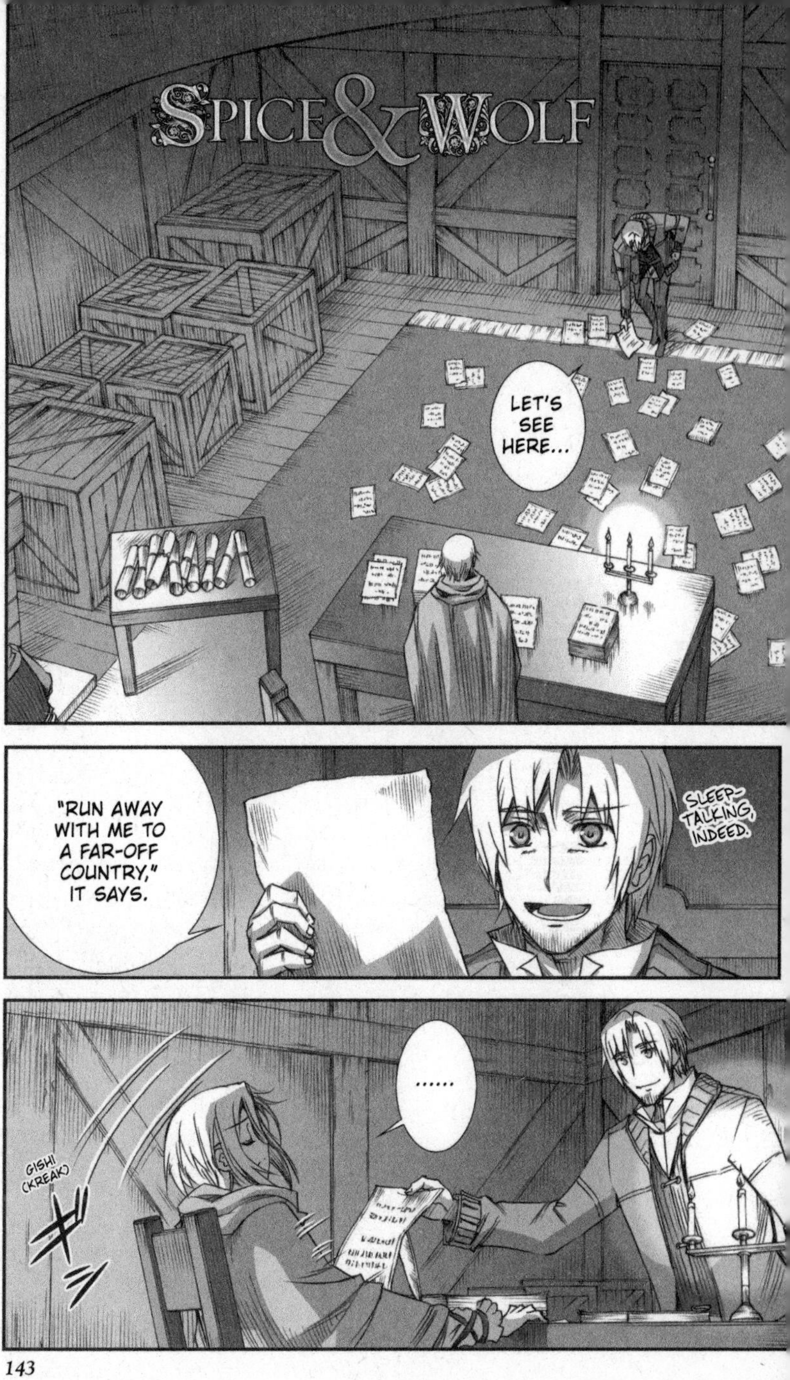
SPICE & WOLF
LET'S SEE HERE...
SLEEP-TALKING, INDEED.
"RUN AWAY WITH ME TO A FAR-OFF COUNTRY," IT SAYS.
......
GISHI (KREAK)

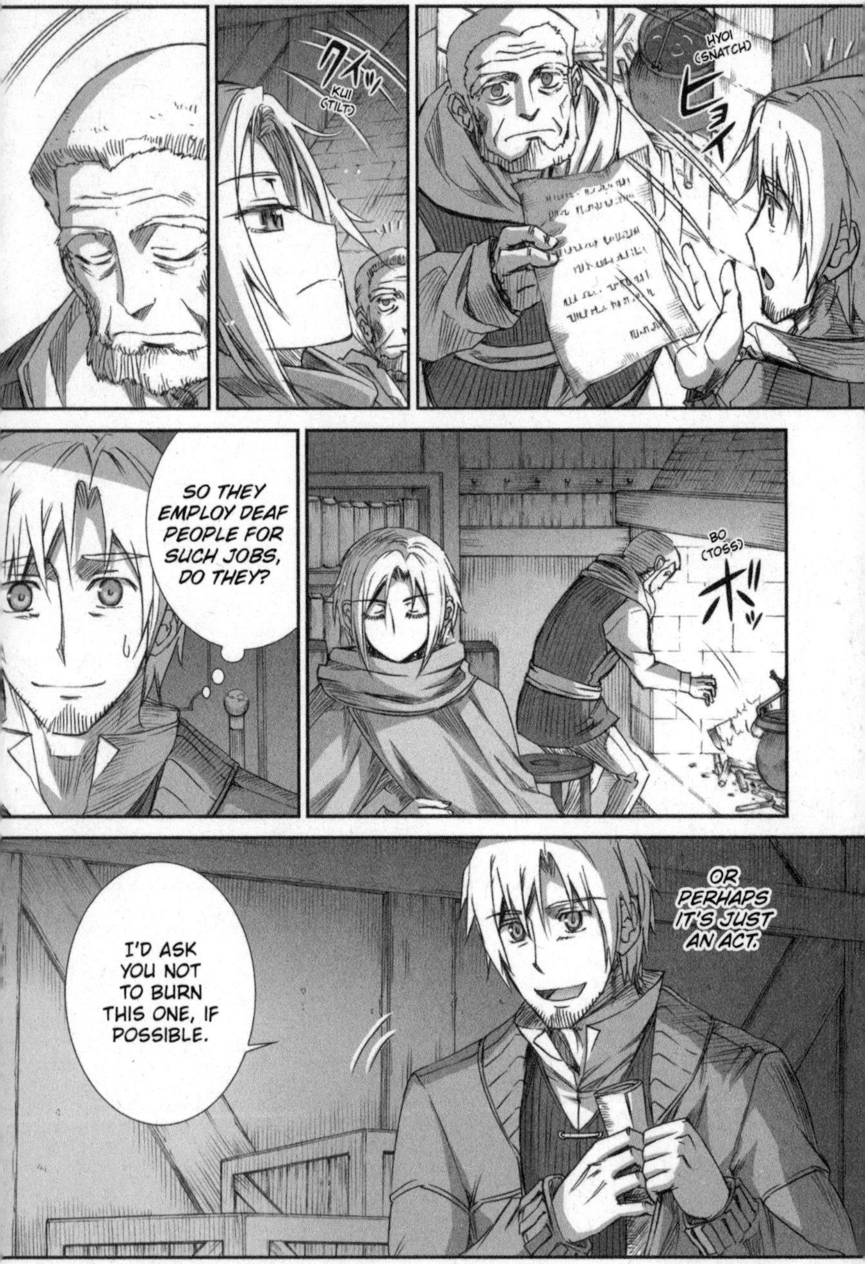
HYOI (SNATCH)
ヒョイ
KUII (TILT)
クイッ
BO (TOSS)
ボッ
SO THEY EMPLOY DEAF PEOPLE FOR SUCH JOBS, DO THEY?
OR PERHAPS IT'S JUST AN ACT.
I'D ASK YOU NOT TO BURN THIS ONE, IF POSSIBLE.

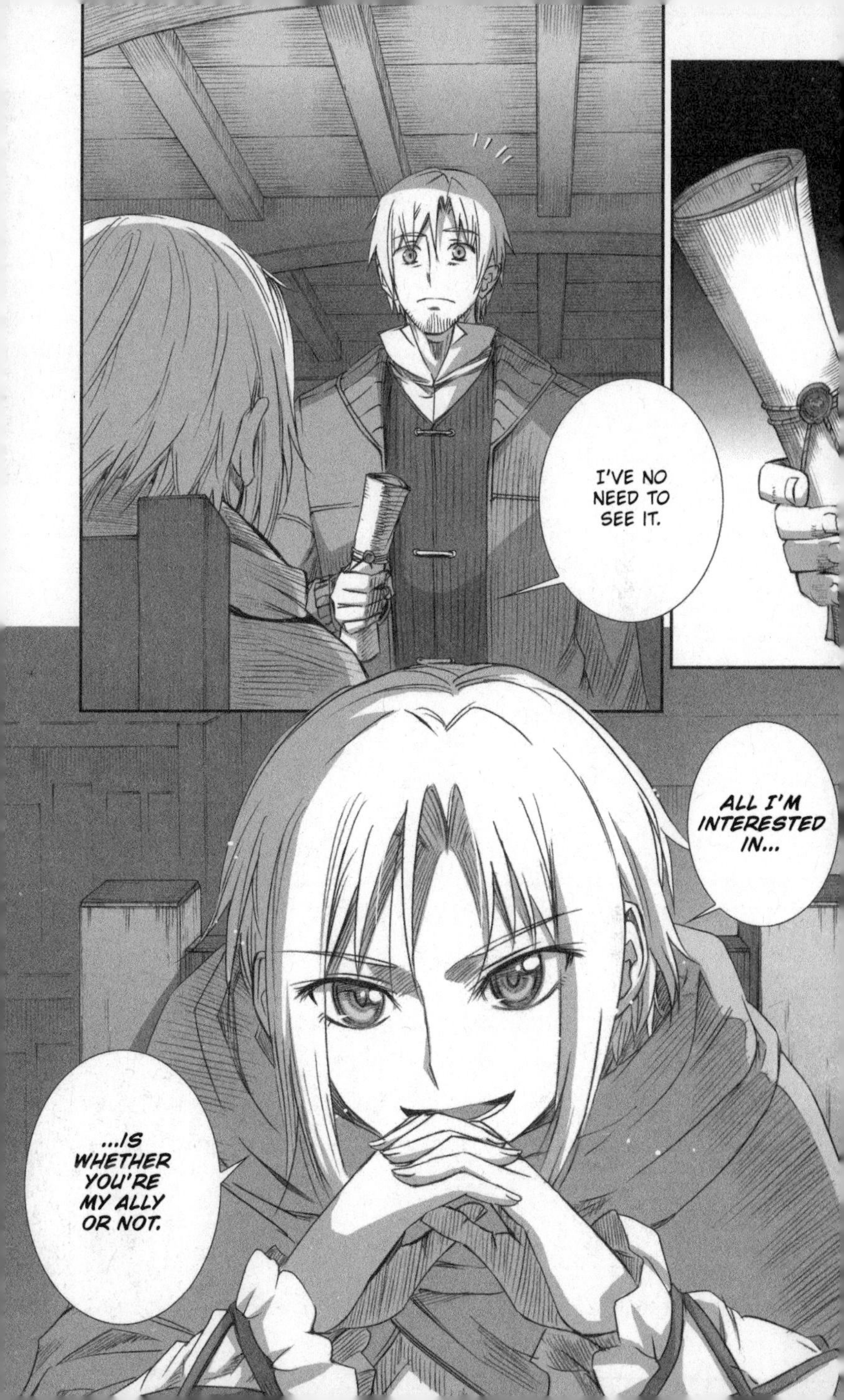
I'VE NO NEED TO SEE IT.
ALL I'M INTERESTED IN...
...IS WHETHER YOU'RE MY ALLY OR NOT.

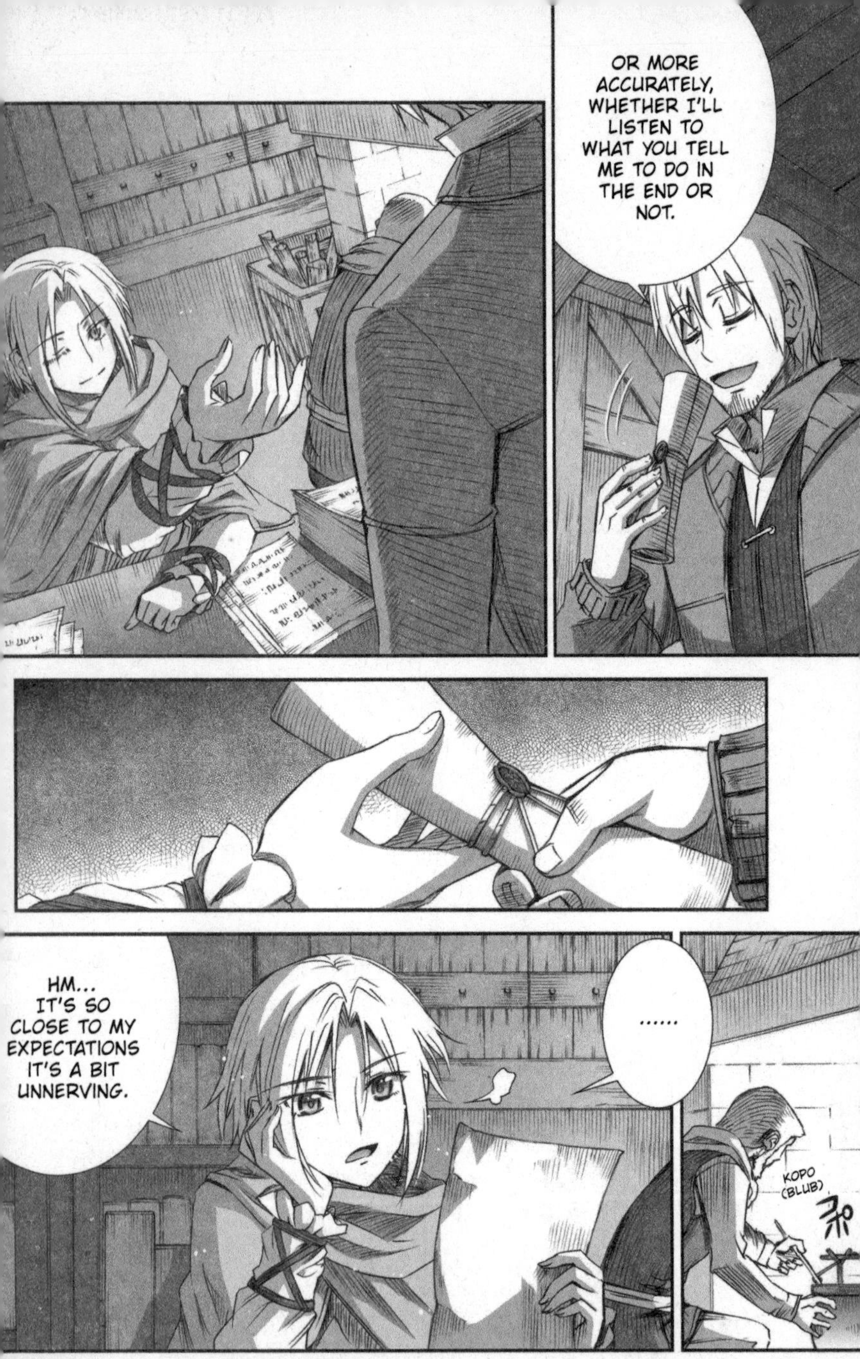
OR MORE ACCURATELY, WHETHER I'LL LISTEN TO WHAT YOU TELL ME TO DO IN THE END OR NOT.
KOPO (BLUB)
コポ
......
HM... IT'S SO CLOSE TO MY EXPECTATIONS IT'S A BIT UNNERVING.

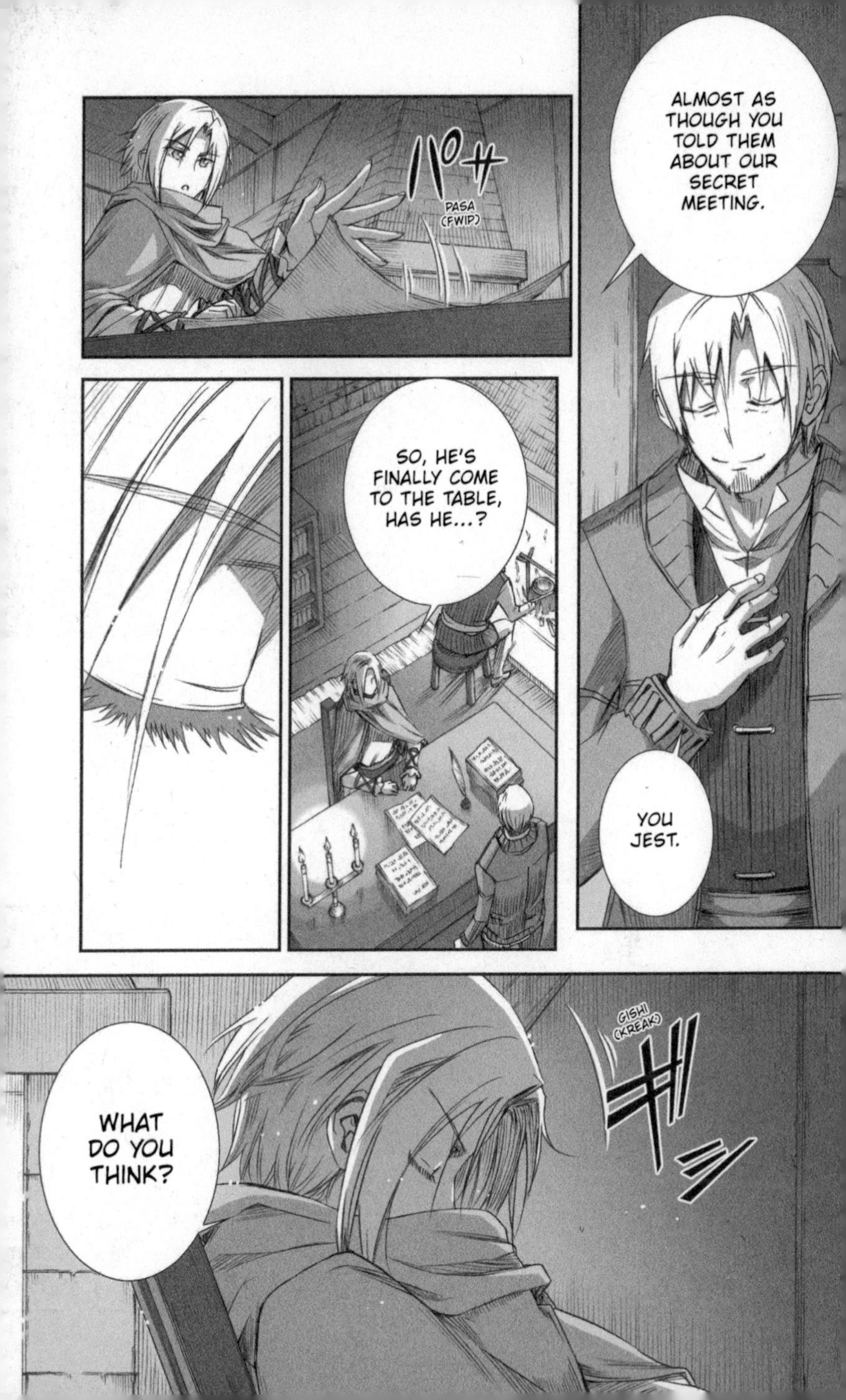
ALMOST AS THOUGH YOU TOLD THEM ABOUT OUR SECRET MEETING.
YOU JEST.
PASA (FWIP)
SO, HE'S FINALLY COME TO THE TABLE, HAS HE...?
GISHI (KREAK)
WHAT DO YOU THINK?

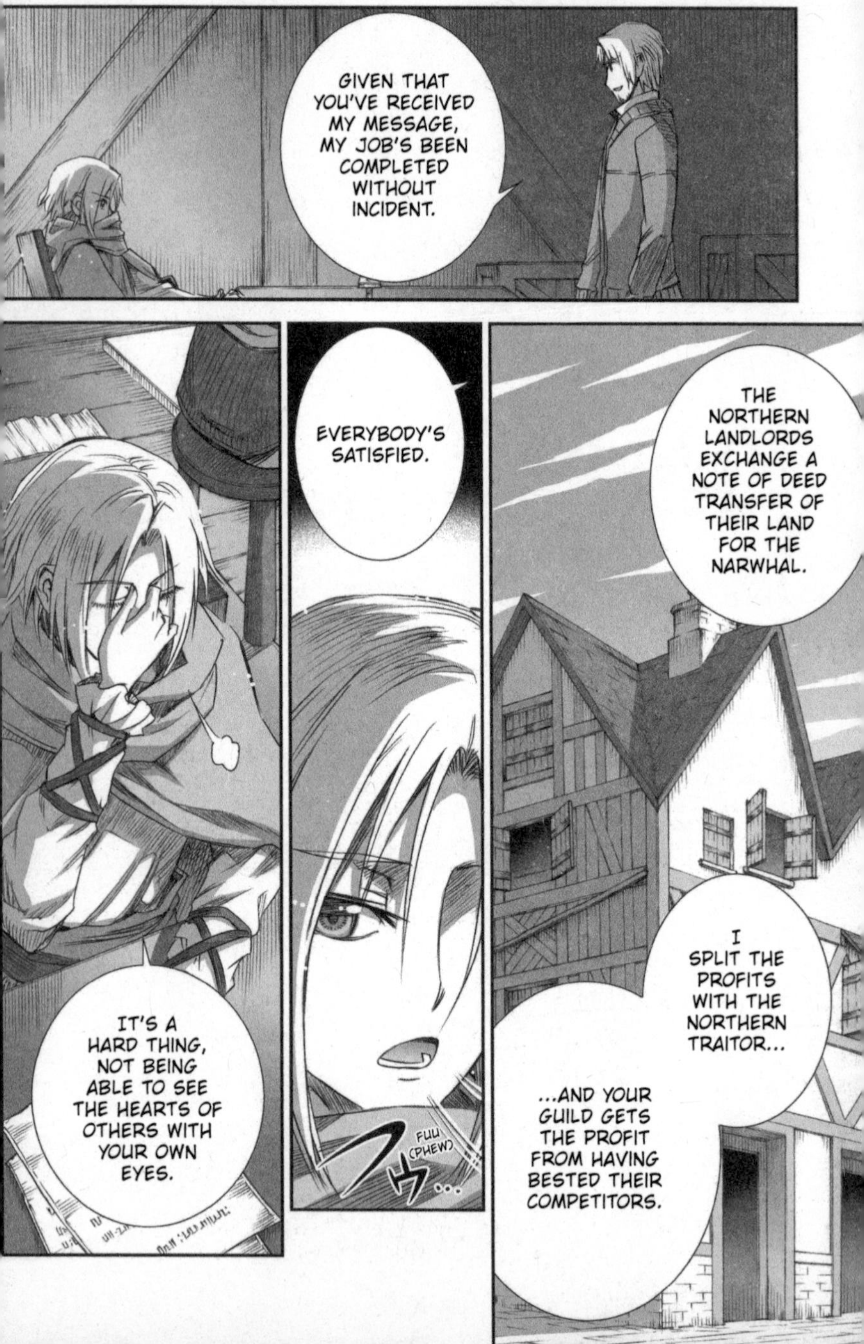
GIVEN THAT YOU'VE RECEIVED MY MESSAGE, MY JOB'S BEEN COMPLETED WITHOUT INCIDENT.
THE NORTHERN LANDLORDS EXCHANGE A NOTE OF DEED TRANSFER OF THEIR LAND FOR THE NARWHAL.
I SPLIT THE PROFITS WITH THE NORTHERN TRAITOR...
...AND YOUR GUILD GETS THE PROFIT FROM HAVING BESTED THEIR COMPETITORS.
EVERYBODY'S SATISFIED.
FUU (PHEW)
IT'S A HARD THING, NOT BEING ABLE TO SEE THE HEARTS OF OTHERS WITH YOUR OWN EYES.

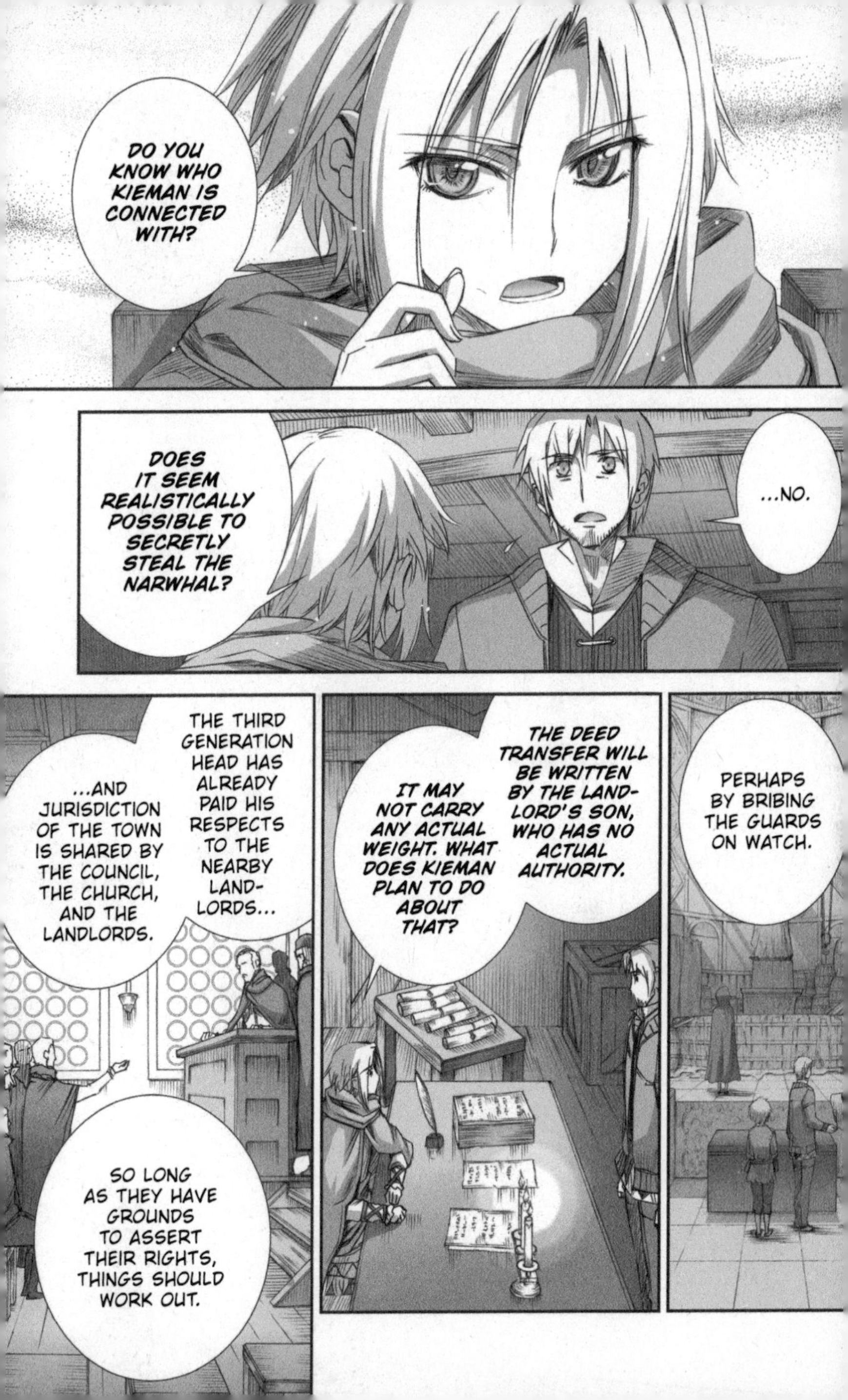
DO YOU KNOW WHO KIEMAN IS CONNECTED WITH?
DOES IT SEEM REALISTICALLY POSSIBLE TO SECRETLY STEAL THE NARWHAL?
...NO.
PERHAPS BY BRIBING THE GUARDS ON WATCH.
THE DEED TRANSFER WILL BE WRITTEN BY THE LAND-LORD'S SON, WHO HAS NO ACTUAL AUTHORITY.
IT MAY NOT CARRY ANY ACTUAL WEIGHT. WHAT DOES KIEMAN PLAN TO DO ABOUT THAT?
THE THIRD GENERATION HEAD HAS ALREADY PAID HIS RESPECTS TO THE NEARBY LAND-LORDS...
...AND JURISDICTION OF THE TOWN IS SHARED BY THE COUNCIL, THE CHURCH, AND THE LANDLORDS.
SO LONG AS THEY HAVE GROUNDS TO ASSERT THEIR RIGHTS, THINGS SHOULD WORK OUT.

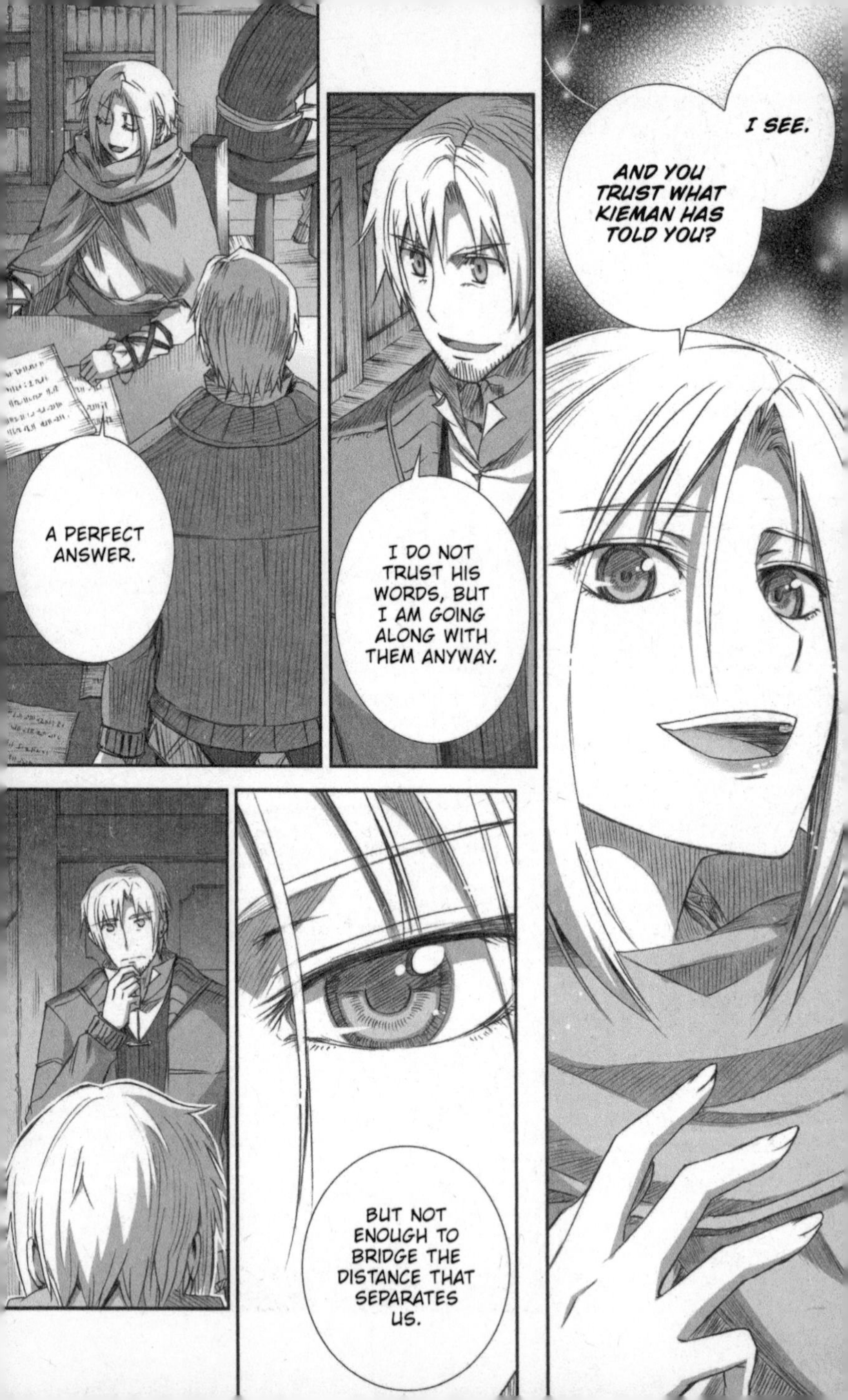
I SEE.
AND YOU TRUST WHAT KIEMAN HAS TOLD YOU?
I DO NOT TRUST HIS WORDS, BUT I AM GOING ALONG WITH THEM ANYWAY.
A PERFECT ANSWER.
BUT NOT ENOUGH TO BRIDGE THE DISTANCE THAT SEPARATES US.

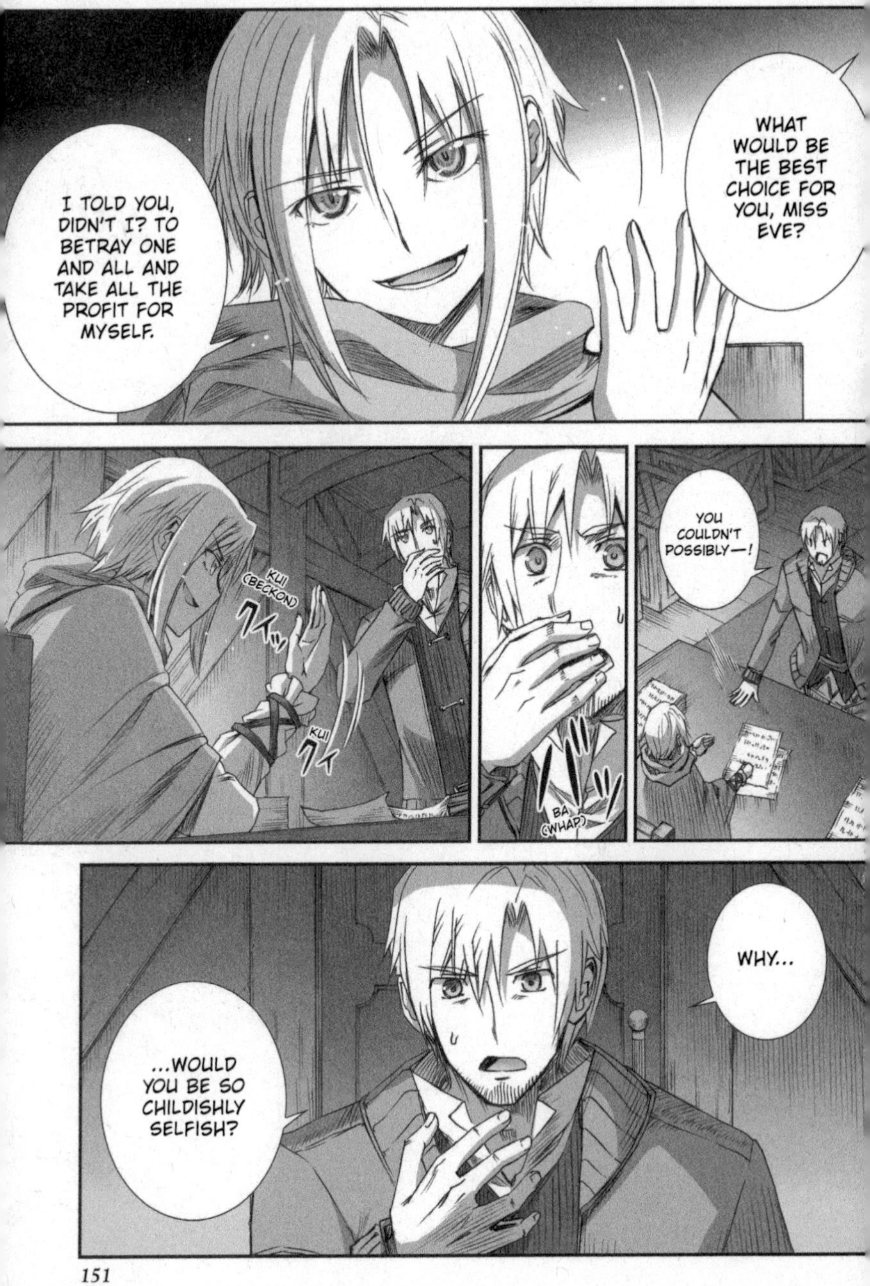
WHAT WOULD BE THE BEST CHOICE FOR YOU, MISS EVE?
I TOLD YOU, DIDN'T I? TO BETRAY ONE AND ALL AND TAKE ALL THE PROFIT FOR MYSELF.
YOU COULDN'T POSSIBLY—!
BA (WHAP)
KUI (BECKON)
KUI
WHY...
...WOULD YOU BE SO CHILDISHLY SELFISH?

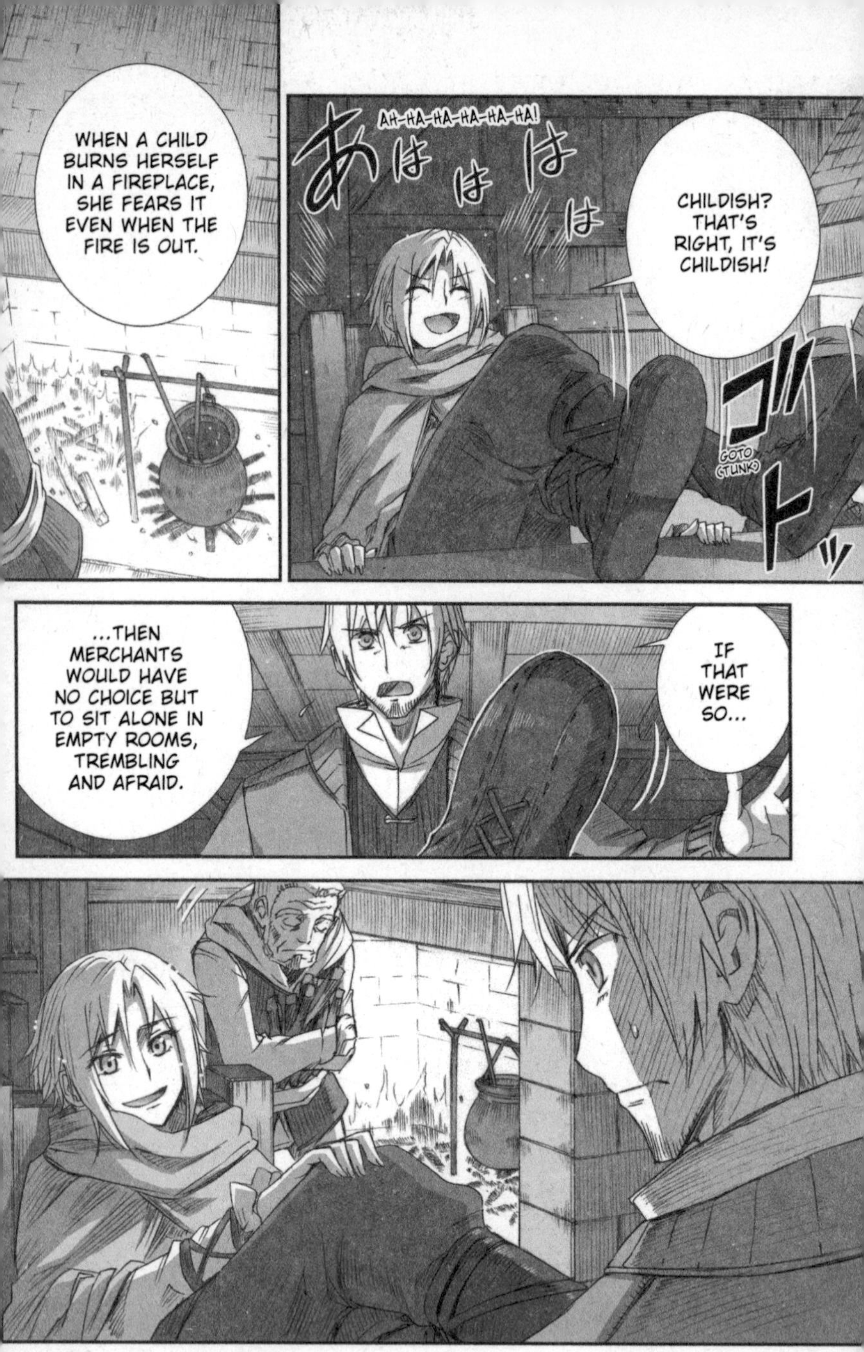
AH-HA-HA-HA-HA-HA!
あはははは
CHILDISH? THAT'S RIGHT, IT'S CHILDISH!
ゴトッ
GOTO (TUNK)
WHEN A CHILD BURNS HERSELF IN A FIREPLACE, SHE FEARS IT EVEN WHEN THE FIRE IS OUT.
IF THAT WERE SO...
...THEN MERCHANTS WOULD HAVE NO CHOICE BUT TO SIT ALONE IN EMPTY ROOMS, TREMBLING AND AFRAID.

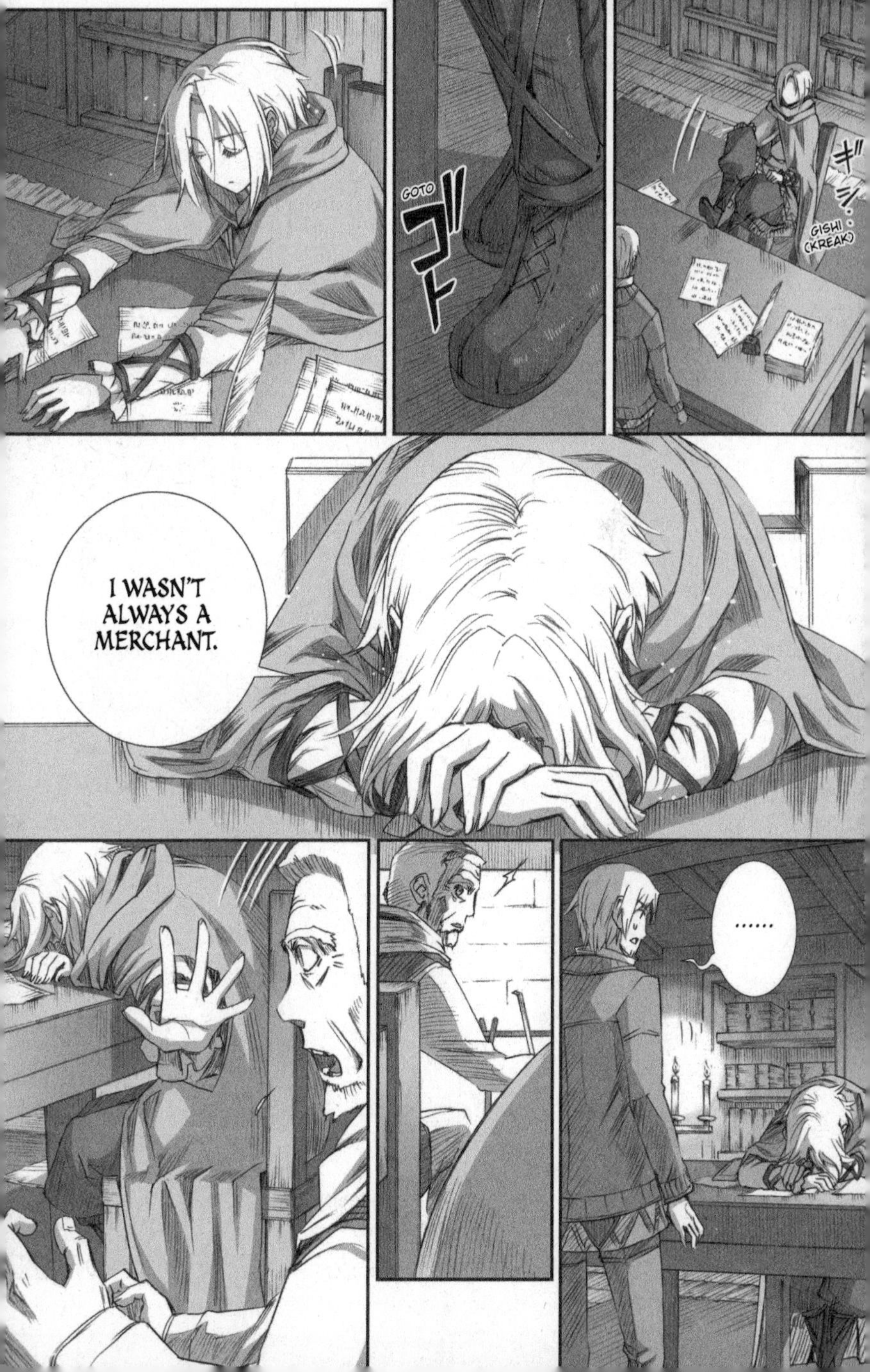

ギシ・
GISHI (KREAK)
ゴト
GOTO
I WASN'T ALWAYS A MERCHANT.
......

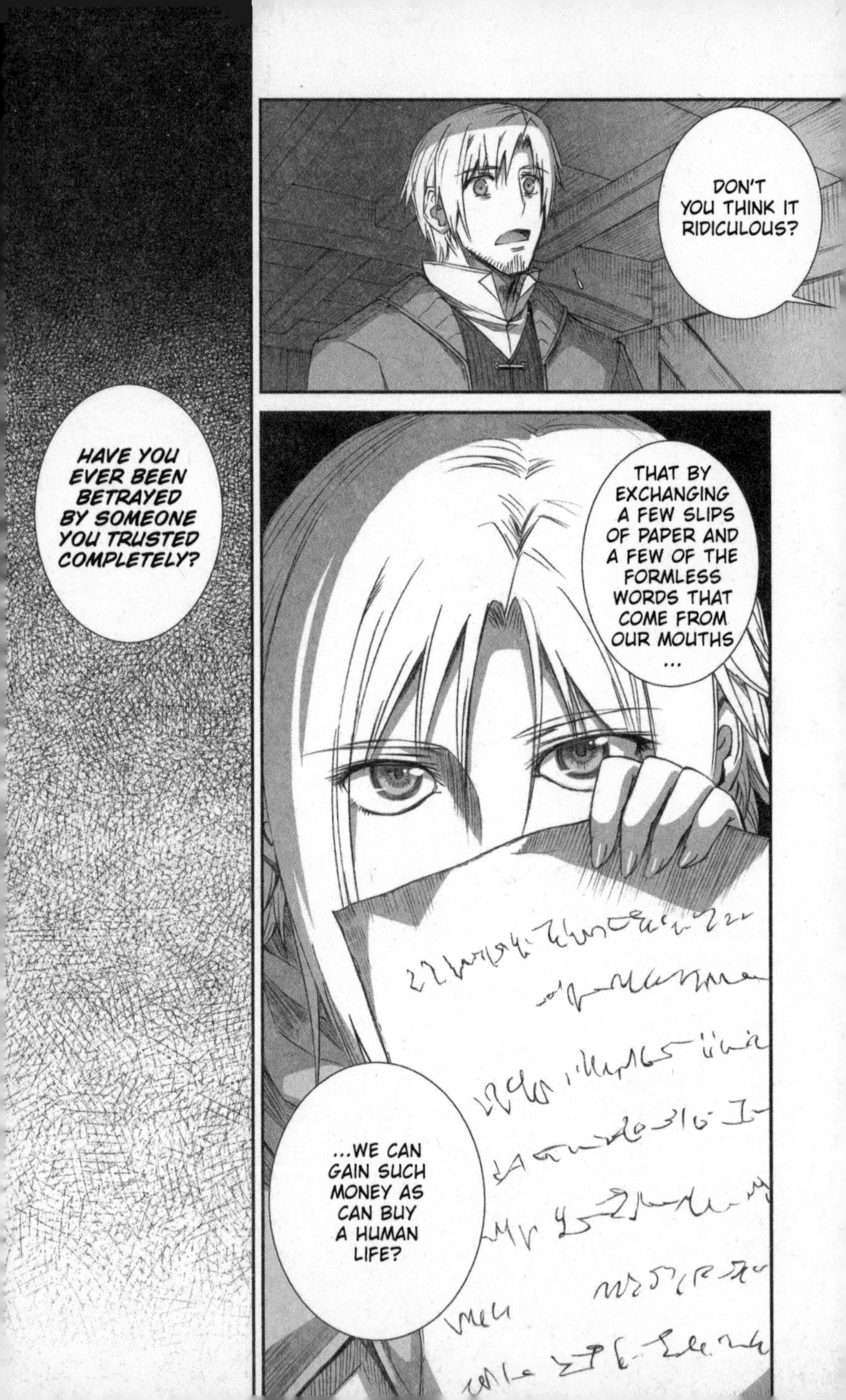
DON'T YOU THINK IT RIDICULOUS?
THAT BY EXCHANGING A FEW SLIPS OF PAPER AND A FEW OF THE FORMLESS WORDS THAT COME FROM OUR MOUTHS...
...WE CAN GAIN SUCH MONEY AS CAN BUY A HUMAN LIFE?
HAVE YOU EVER BEEN BETRAYED BY SOMEONE YOU TRUSTED COMPLETELY?

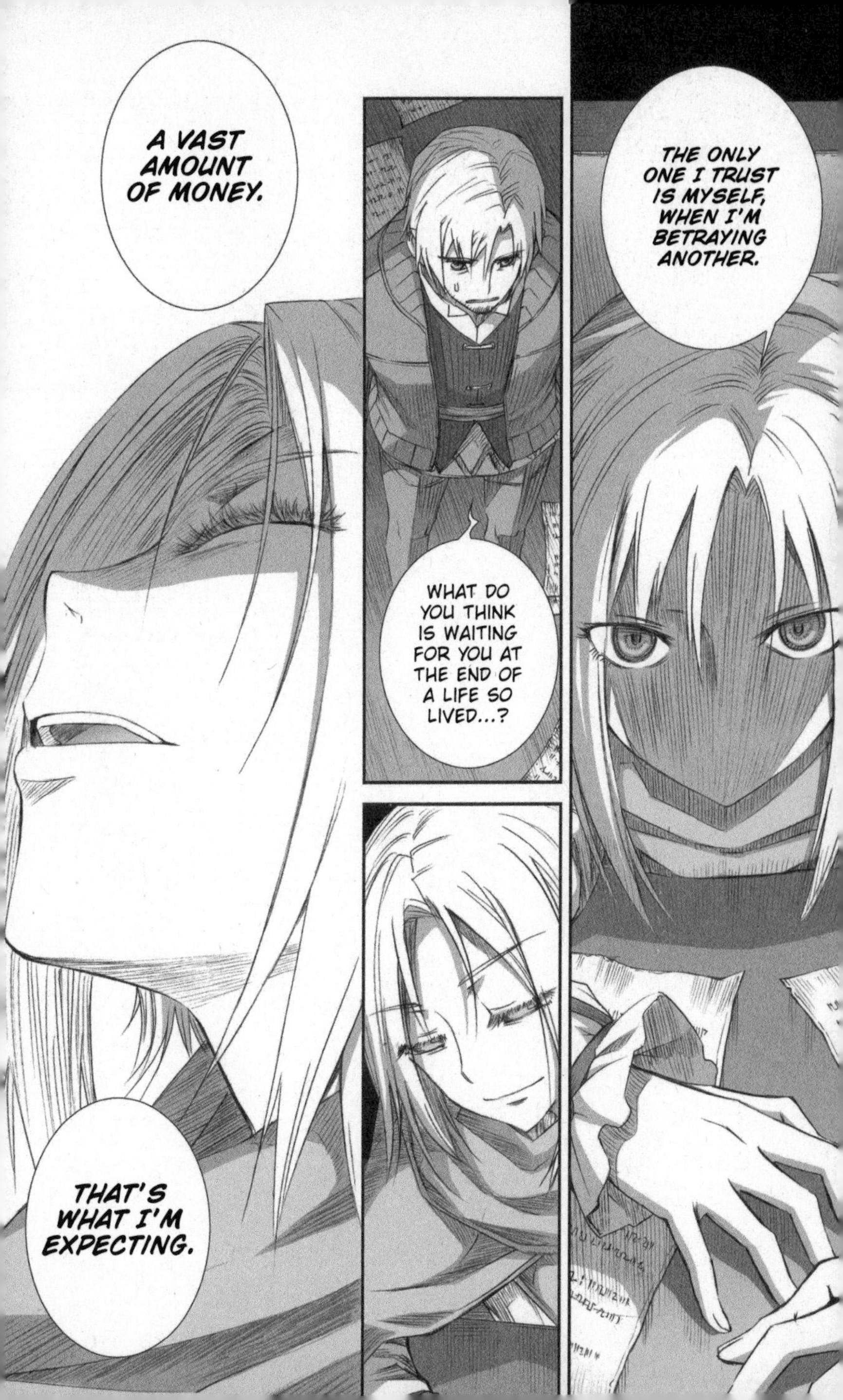
THE ONLY ONE I TRUST IS MYSELF, WHEN I'M BETRAYING ANOTHER.
WHAT DO YOU THINK IS WAITING FOR YOU AT THE END OF A LIFE SO LIVED...?
A VAST AMOUNT OF MONEY.
THAT'S WHAT I'M EXPECTING.

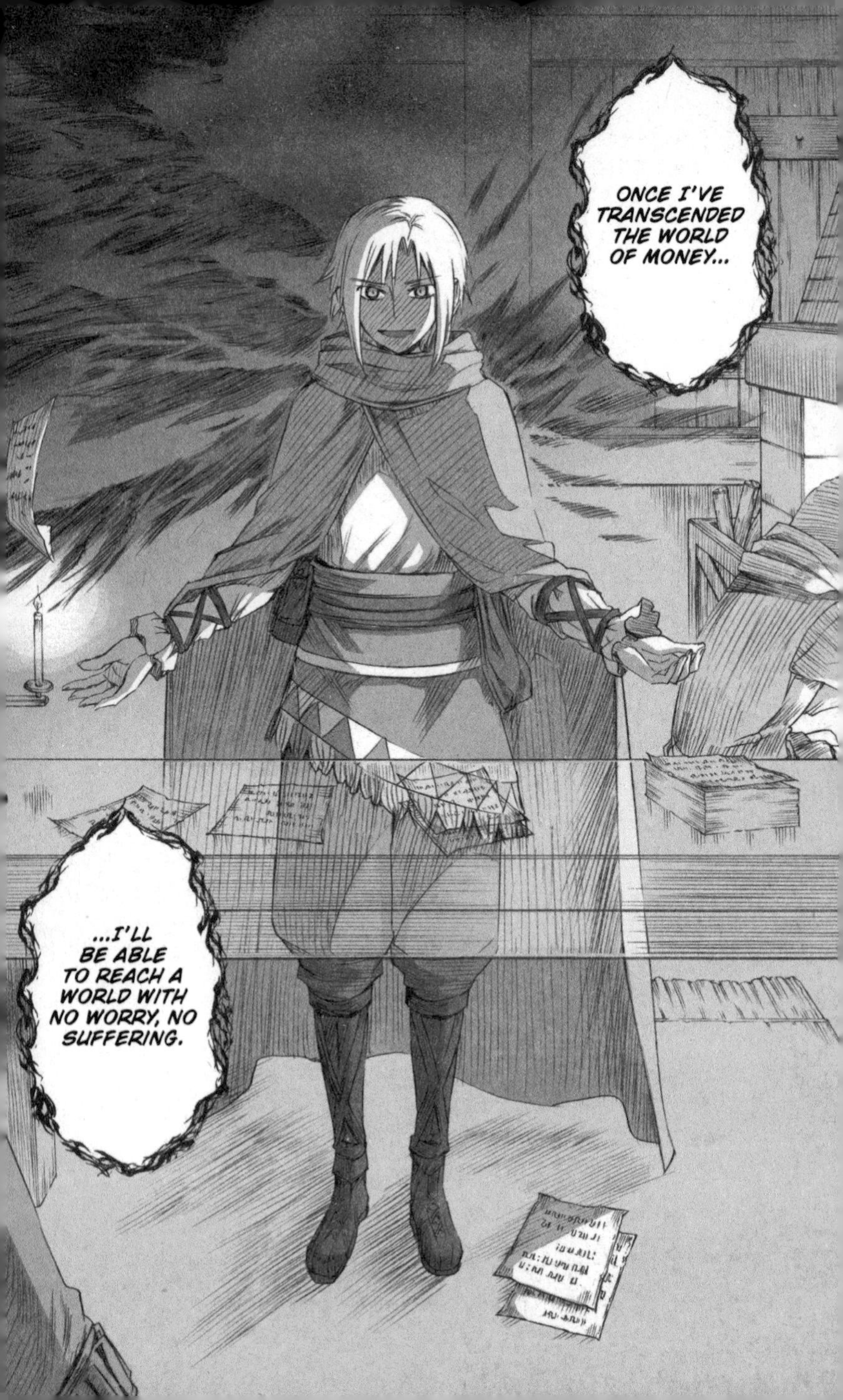
ONCE I'VE TRANSCENDED THE WORLD OF MONEY...
...I'LL BE ABLE TO REACH A WORLD WITH NO WORRY, NO SUFFERING.

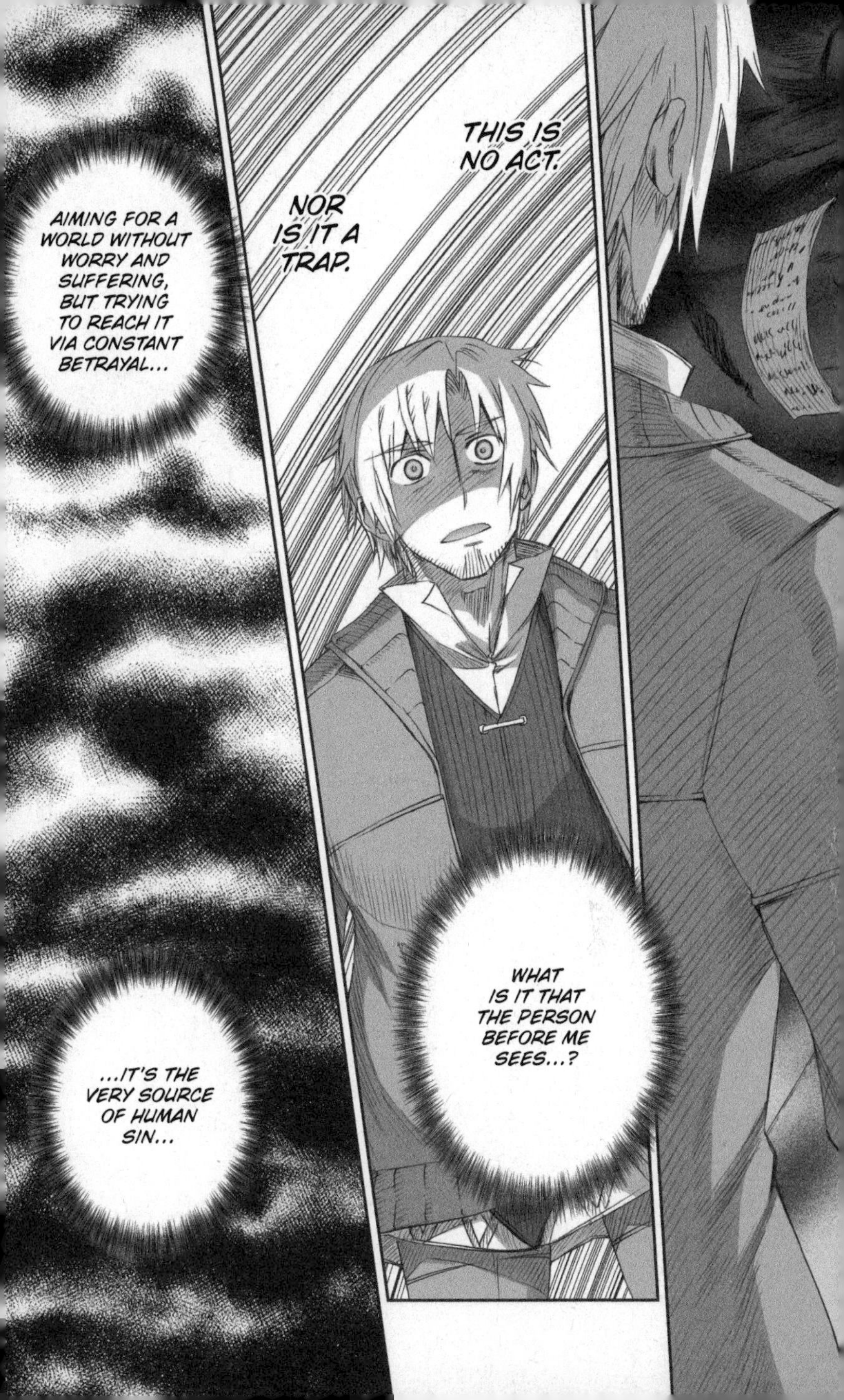
THIS IS NO ACT.
NOR IS IT A TRAP.
WHAT IS IT THAT THE PERSON BEFORE ME SEES...?
AIMING FOR A WORLD WITHOUT WORRY AND SUFFERING, BUT TRYING TO REACH IT VIA CONSTANT BETRAYAL...
...IT'S THE VERY SOURCE OF HUMAN SIN...

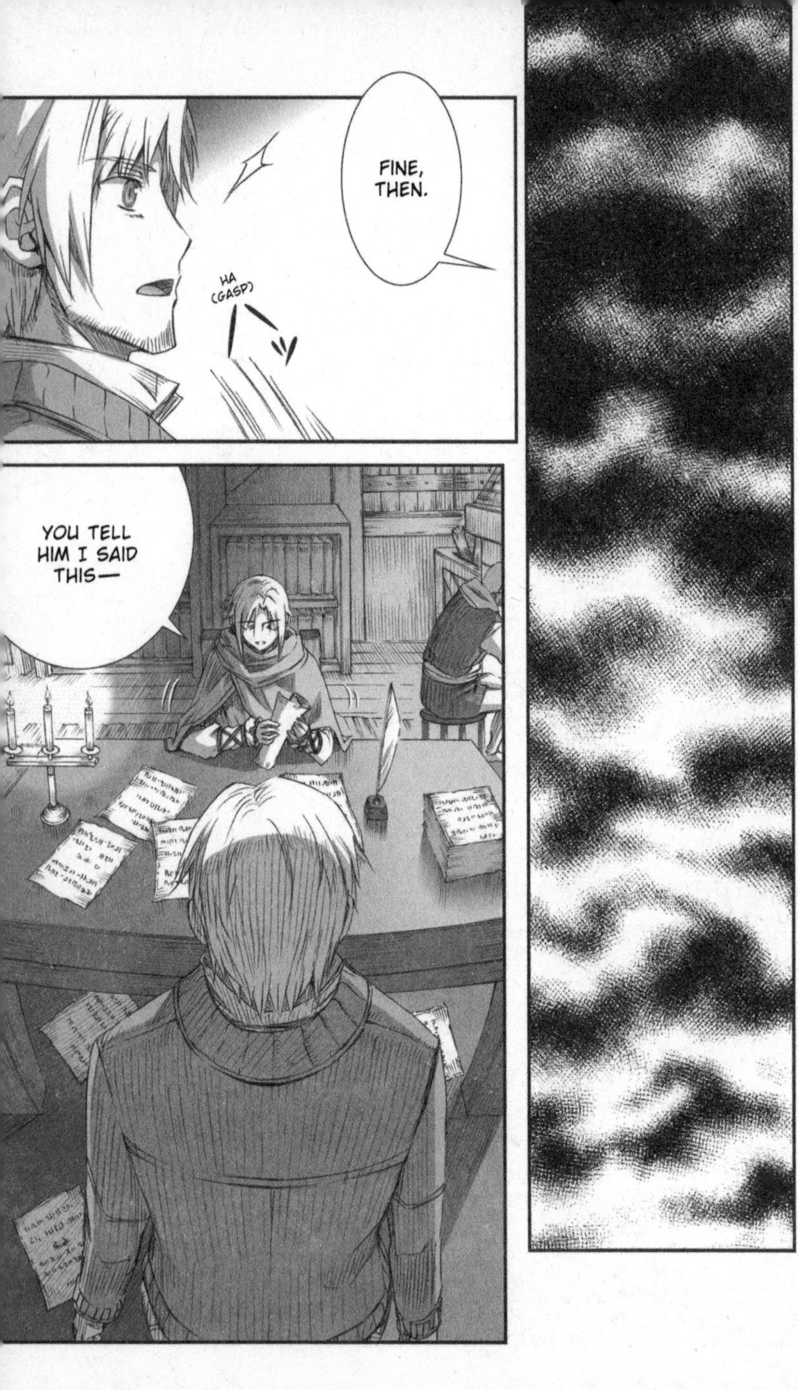
FINE, THEN.
HA (GASP)
YOU TELL HIM I SAID THIS—

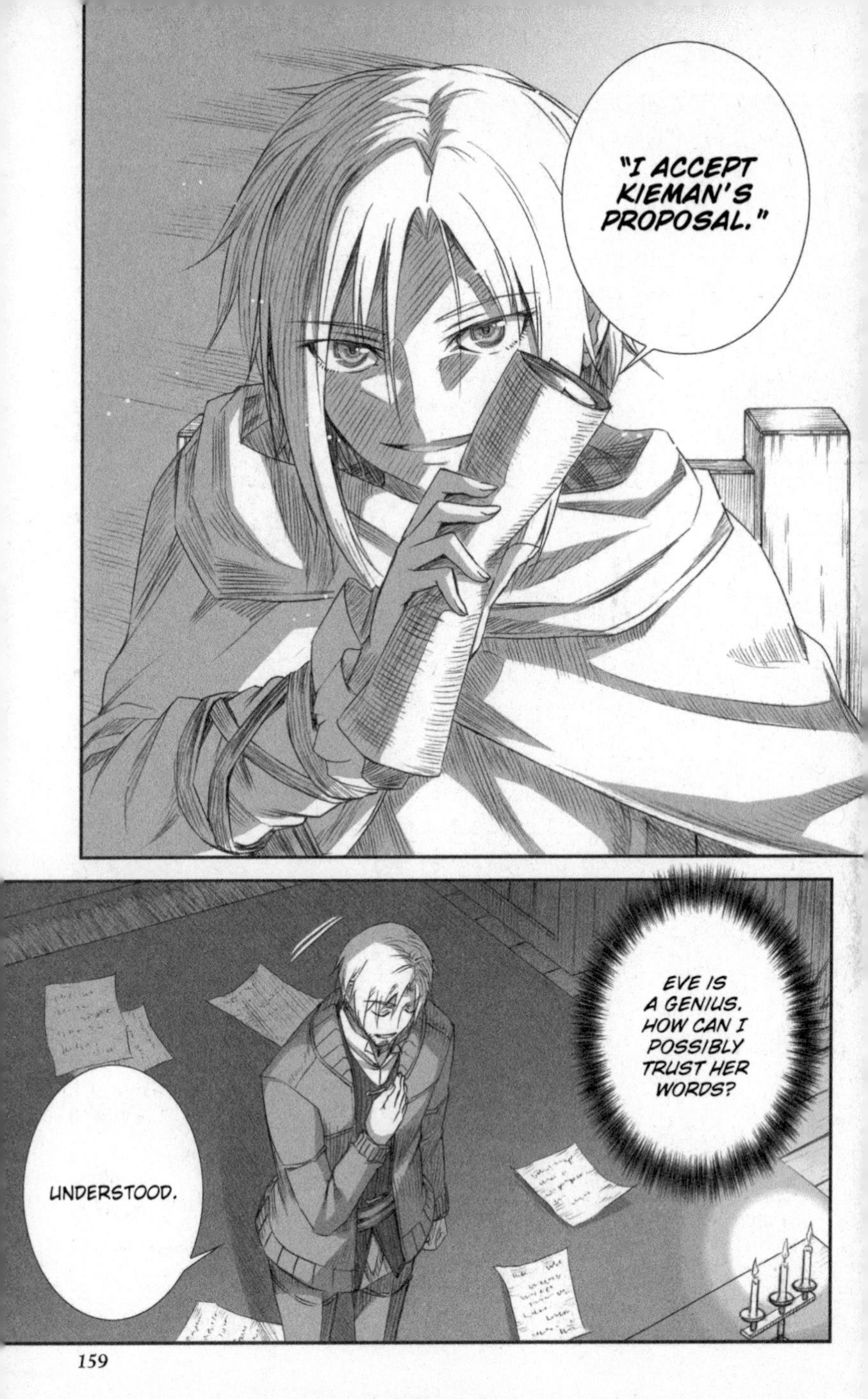
"I ACCEPT KIEMAN'S PROPOSAL."
EVE IS A GENIUS. HOW CAN I POSSIBLY TRUST HER WORDS?
UNDERSTOOD.

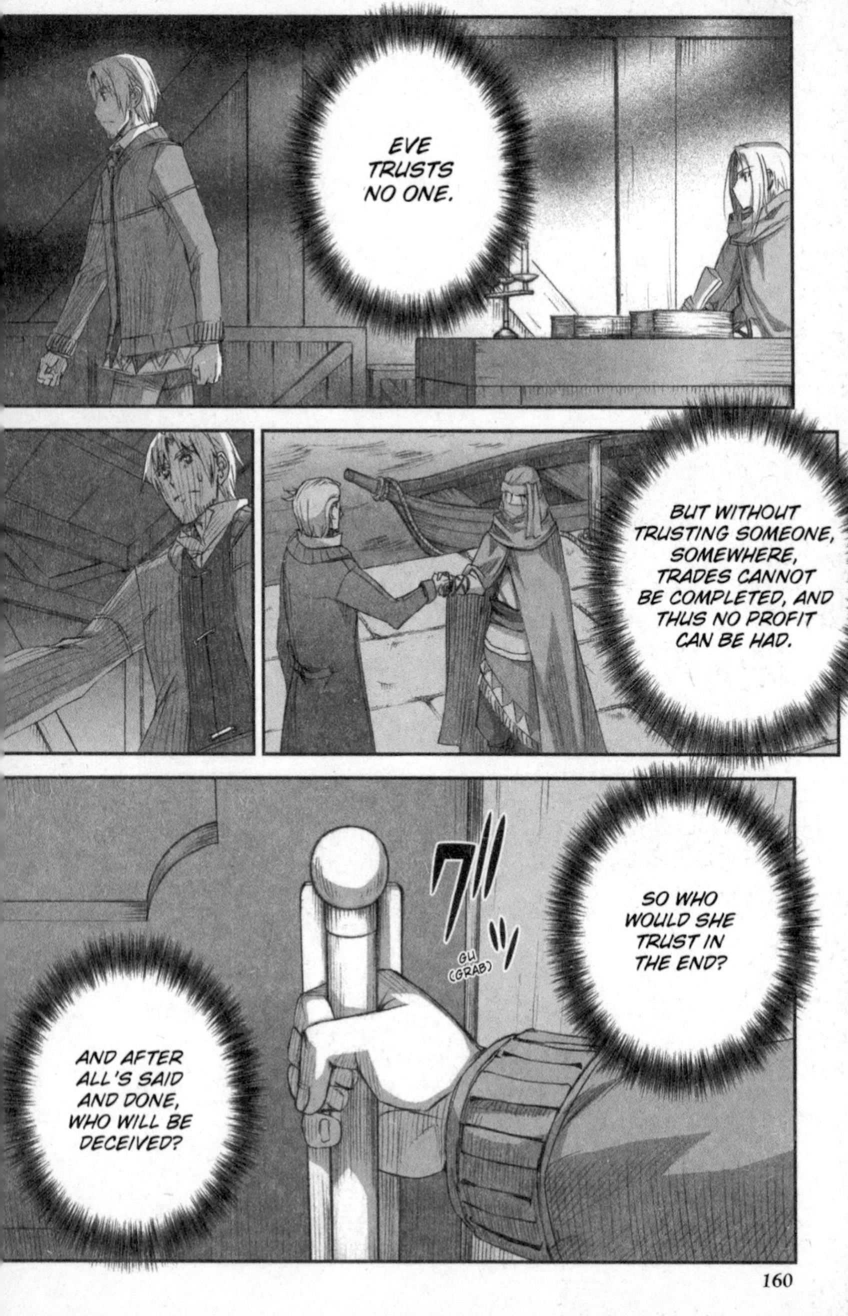
EVE TRUSTS NO ONE.
BUT WITHOUT TRUSTING SOMEONE, SOMEWHERE, TRADES CANNOT BE COMPLETED, AND THUS NO PROFIT CAN BE HAD.
SO WHO WOULD SHE TRUST IN THE END?
グッ
GU (GRAB)
AND AFTER ALL'S SAID AND DONE, WHO WILL BE DECEIVED?

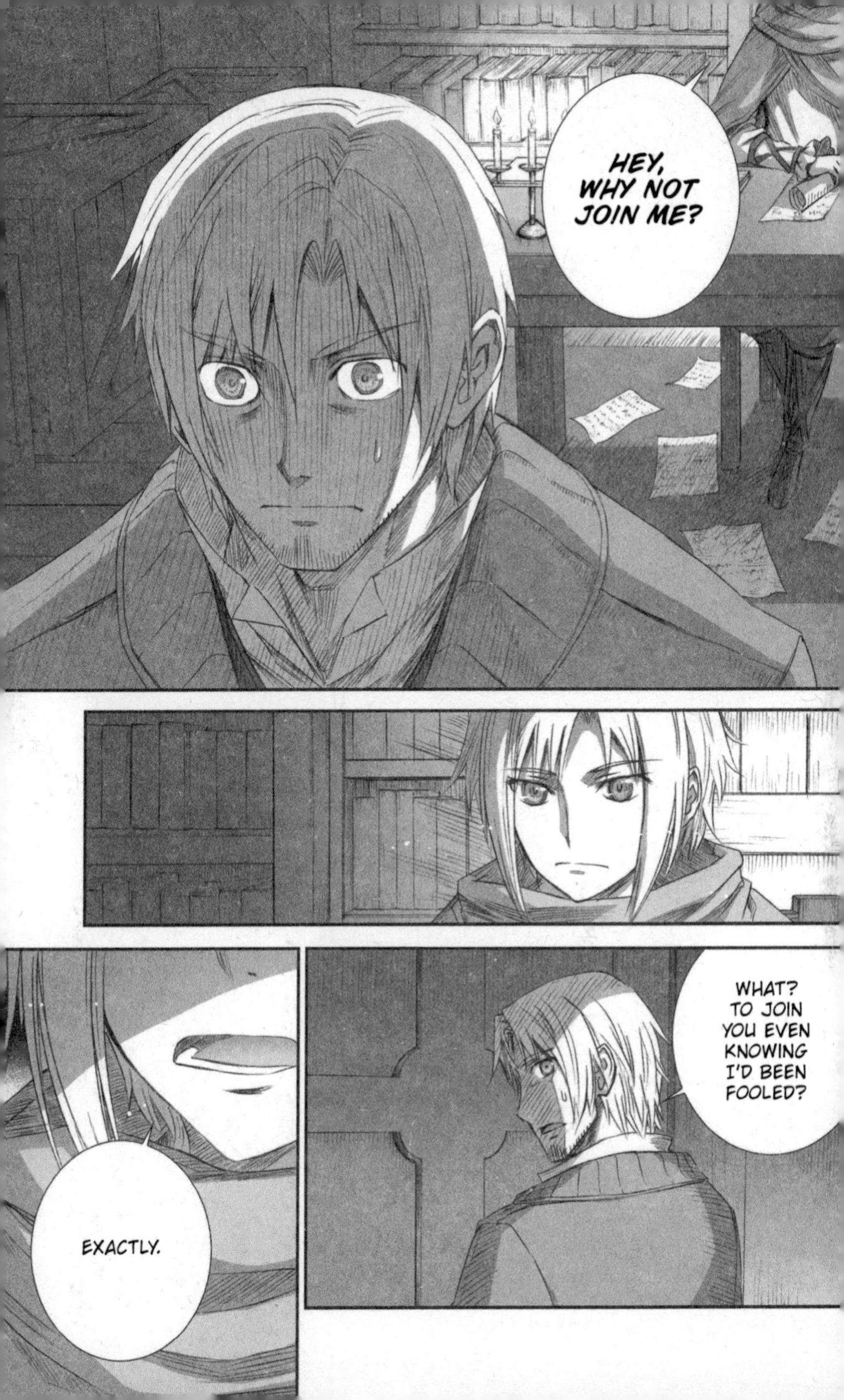
HEY, WHY NOT JOIN ME?
WHAT? TO JOIN YOU EVEN KNOWING I'D BEEN FOOLED?
EXACTLY.

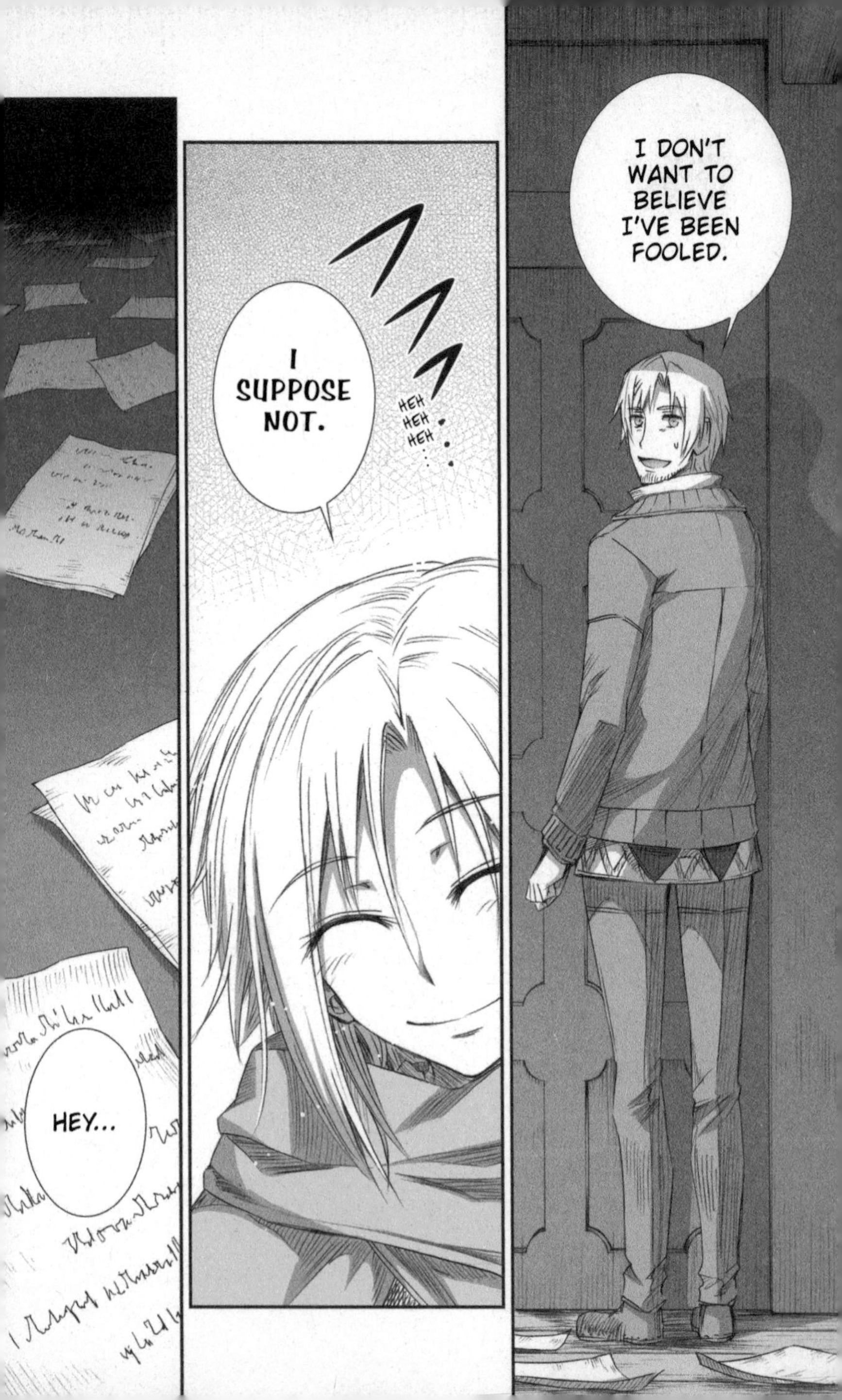
I DON'T WANT TO BELIEVE I'VE BEEN FOOLED.
HEH HEH HEH...
I SUPPOSE NOT.
HEY...

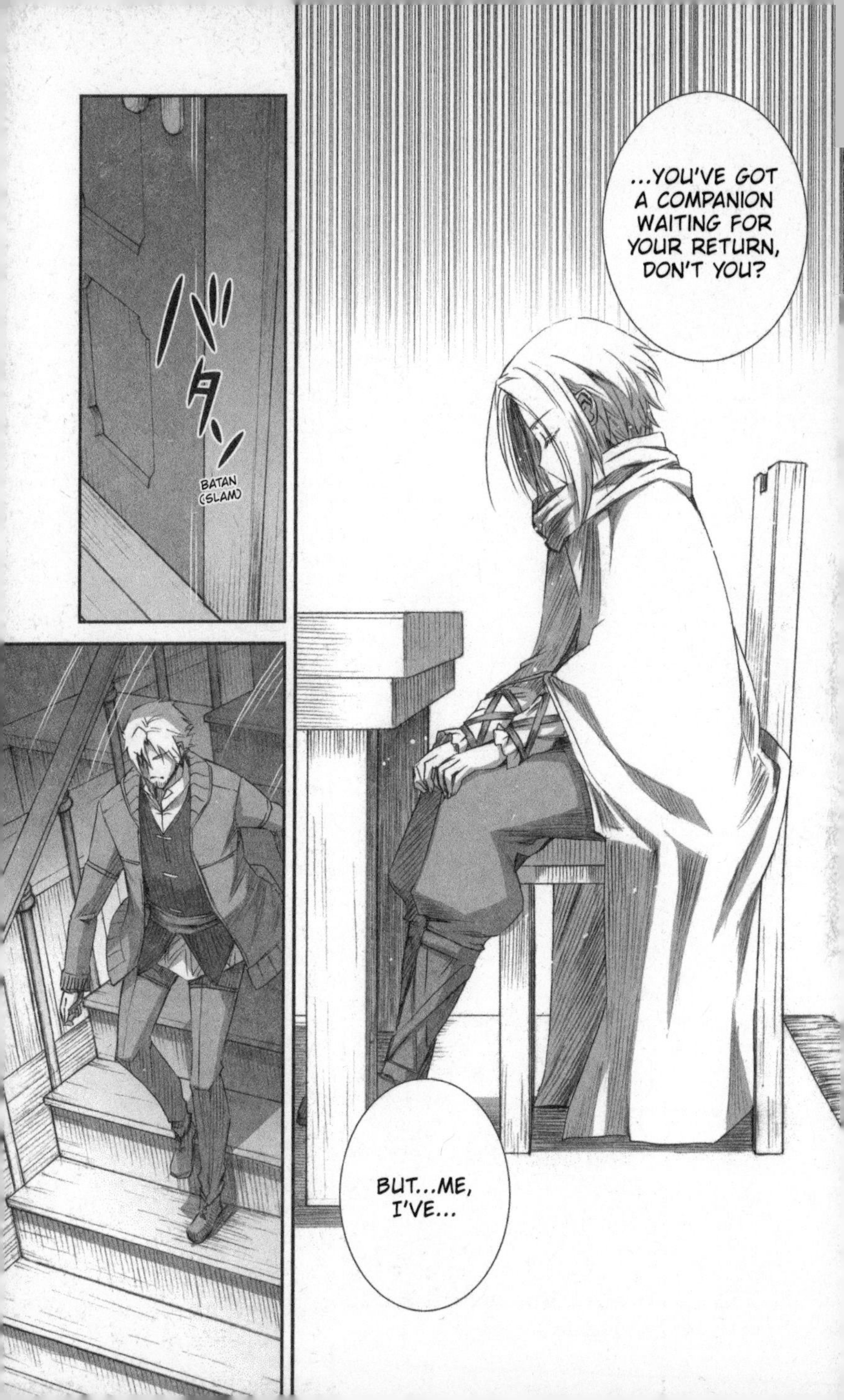
...YOU'VE GOT A COMPANION WAITING FOR YOUR RETURN, DON'T YOU?
BUT...ME, I'VE...
バタン
BATAN (SLAM)

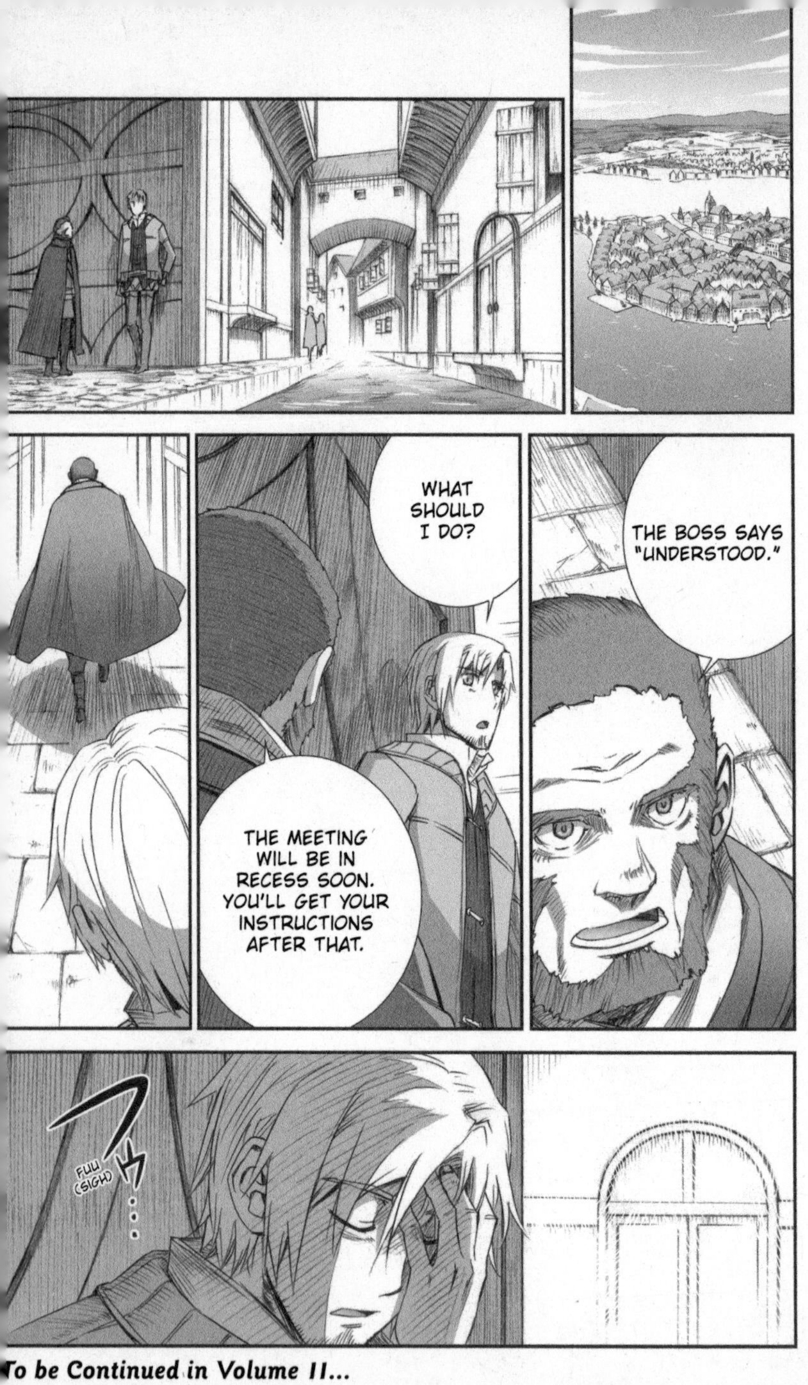
THE BOSS SAYS "UNDERSTOOD."
WHAT SHOULD I DO?
THE MEETING WILL BE IN RECESS SOON. YOU'LL GET YOUR INSTRUCTIONS AFTER THAT.
FUU (SIGH)
...

To be Continued in Volume 11...

SPICE & WOLF

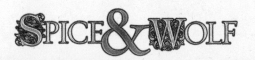

Thanks for 10 volumes!

words of Appreciation

THANK YOU ALL SO MUCH. I'M KEITO KOUME. WE'VE COME TO VOLUME 10 OF *SPICE AND WOLF*. DURING THE SEVEN YEARS IT'S BEEN RUNNING, I'VE BEEN HONORED TO DO SIGNING EVENTS IN TAIWAN AND FRANCE!

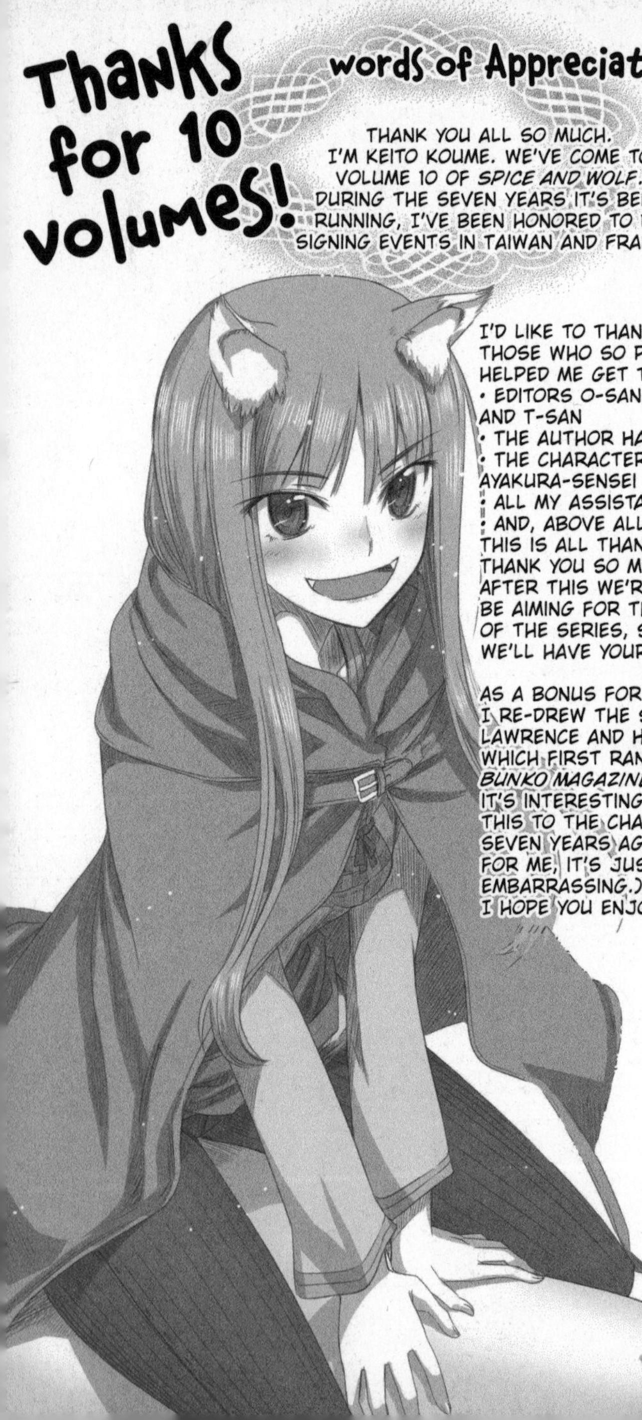

I'D LIKE TO THANK ALL THOSE WHO SO PATIENTLY HELPED ME GET THIS FAR:

- EDITORS O-SAN, A-SAN, AND T-SAN
- THE AUTHOR HASEKURA-SENSEI
- THE CHARACTER DESIGNER AYAKURA-SENSEI
- ALL MY ASSISTANTS
- AND, ABOVE ALL, THE READERS.

THIS IS ALL THANKS TO YOU! THANK YOU SO MUCH! AFTER THIS WE'RE GOING TO BE AIMING FOR THE FINISH OF THE SERIES, SO I HOPE WE'LL HAVE YOUR SUPPORT.

AS A BONUS FOR THIS VOLUME, I RE-DREW THE SCENE WHERE LAWRENCE AND HOLO FIRST MEET, WHICH FIRST RAN IN *DENGEKI BUNKO MAGAZINE*. I HOPE IT'S INTERESTING TO COMPARE THIS TO THE CHAPTER I DREW SEVEN YEARS AGO. (ALTHOUGH FOR ME, IT'S JUST TERRIBLY EMBARRASSING.) ANYWAY, I HOPE YOU ENJOY IT!

Special Thanks!!

MR. OKAMOTO ITTOUHEI,
MR. TENTSU TOI,
MR. YAKKUN,
MR. N-TA,
MR. YUU,
MR. A.

The First Meeting of Holo and Lawrence, Special Edition!
SPICE & WOLF
ZA (RUSTLE)
ZA
ZA
ZA
WHAT'RE YOU...? HOW DID YOU GET IN MY WAGON-BED?
I AM HOLO THE WISEWOLF.
THE NIGHT A TRAVELING MERCHANT PASSED THROUGH THE VILLAGE OF PASLOE ON ITS HARVEST FESTIVAL DAY, HE FOUND A GIRL HIDDEN AWAY IN THE BED OF HIS HORSE-DRAWN WAGON.
IT HAS BEEN SOME TIME SINCE I'VE TAKEN THIS FORM, BUT, WELL, IT IS QUITE NICE.

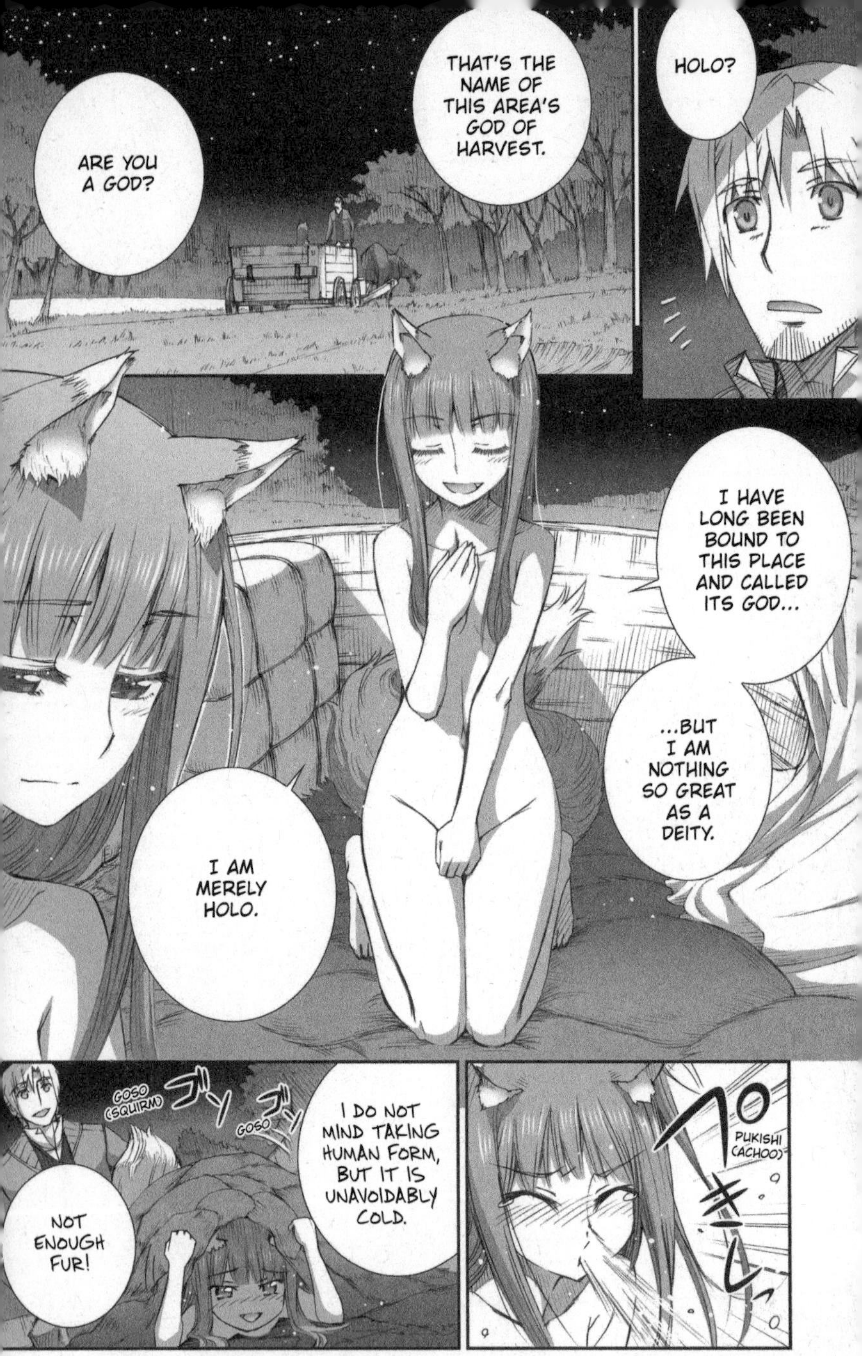
HOLO?
THAT'S THE NAME OF THIS AREA'S GOD OF HARVEST.
ARE YOU A GOD?
I HAVE LONG BEEN BOUND TO THIS PLACE AND CALLED ITS GOD...
...BUT I AM NOTHING SO GREAT AS A DEITY.
I AM MERELY HOLO.
PUKISHI (ACHOO)
I DO NOT MIND TAKING HUMAN FORM, BUT IT IS UNAVOIDABLY COLD.
GOSO
GOSO (SQUIRM)
NOT ENOUGH FUR!

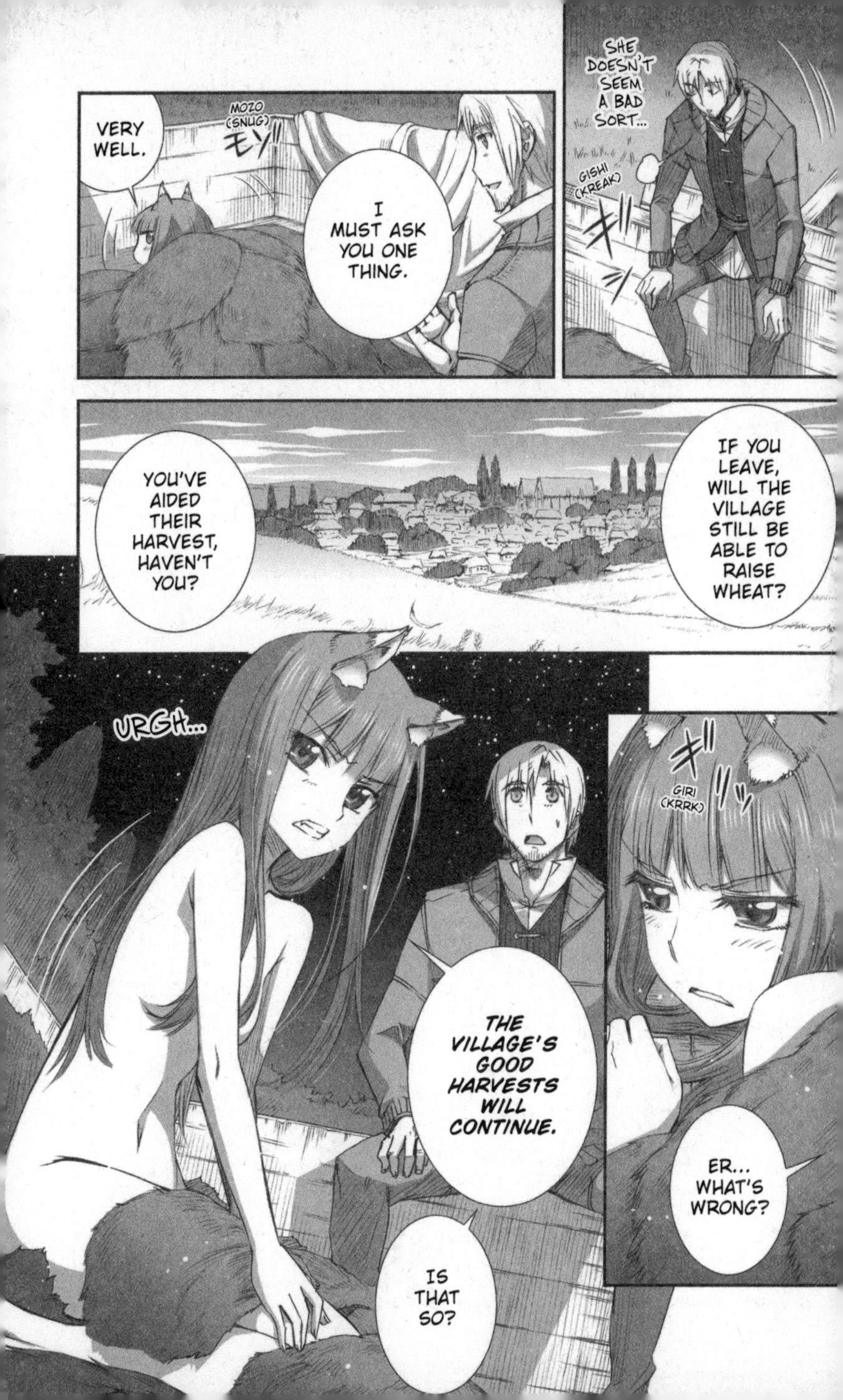

SHE DOESN'T SEEM A BAD SORT...
GISHI (KREAK)
I MUST ASK YOU ONE THING.
MOZO (SNUG)
VERY WELL.
IF YOU LEAVE, WILL THE VILLAGE STILL BE ABLE TO RAISE WHEAT?
YOU'VE AIDED THEIR HARVEST, HAVEN'T YOU?
GIRI (KRRK)
ER... WHAT'S WRONG?
URGH...
THE VILLAGE'S GOOD HARVESTS WILL CONTINUE.
IS THAT SO?

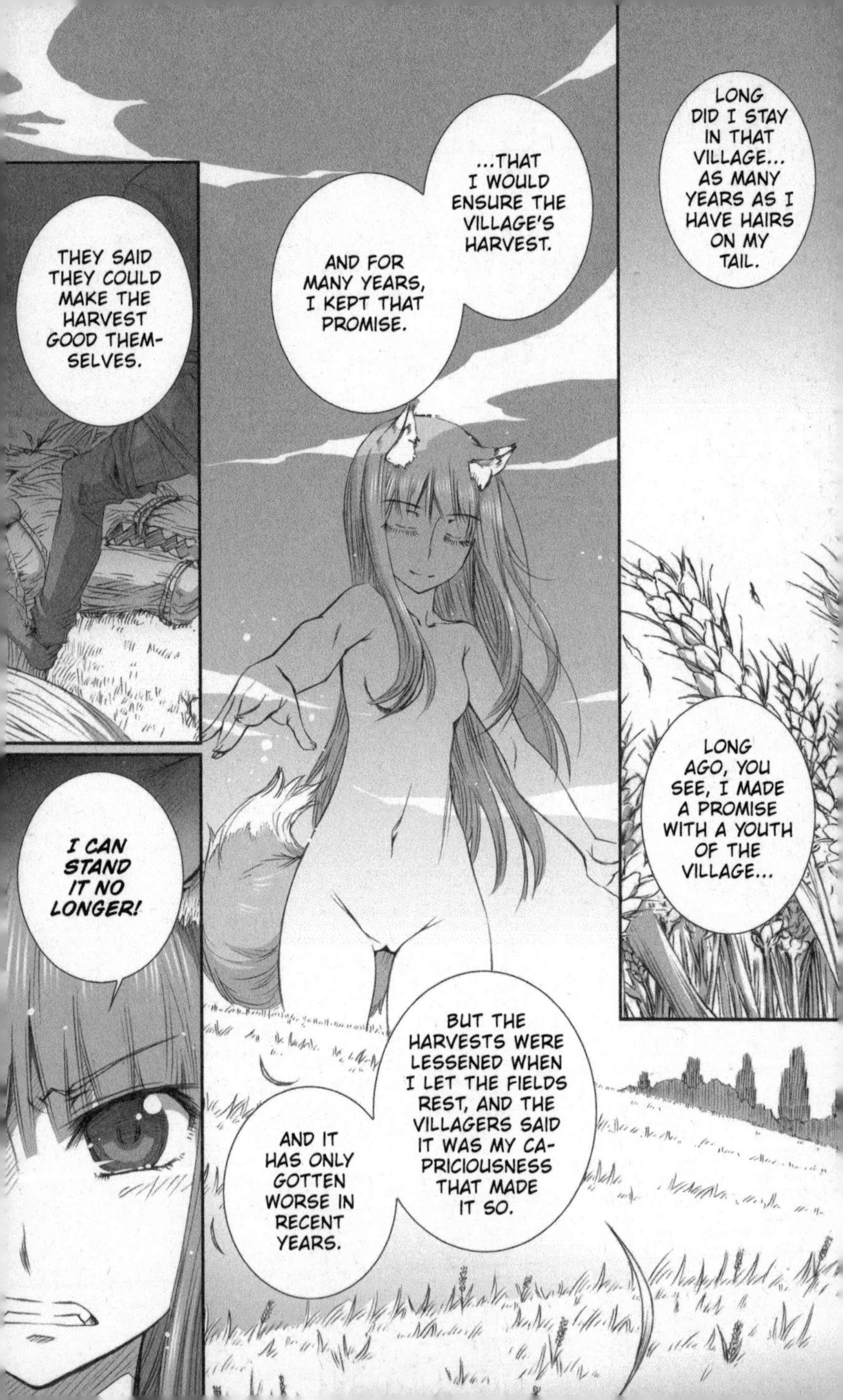
LONG DID I STAY IN THAT VILLAGE... AS MANY YEARS AS I HAVE HAIRS ON MY TAIL.
LONG AGO, YOU SEE, I MADE A PROMISE WITH A YOUTH OF THE VILLAGE...
...THAT I WOULD ENSURE THE VILLAGE'S HARVEST.
AND FOR MANY YEARS, I KEPT THAT PROMISE.
BUT THE HARVESTS WERE LESSENED WHEN I LET THE FIELDS REST, AND THE VILLAGERS SAID IT WAS MY CA-PRICIOUSNESS THAT MADE IT SO.
AND IT HAS ONLY GOTTEN WORSE IN RECENT YEARS.
THEY SAID THEY COULD MAKE THE HARVEST GOOD THEM-SELVES.
I CAN STAND IT NO LONGER!

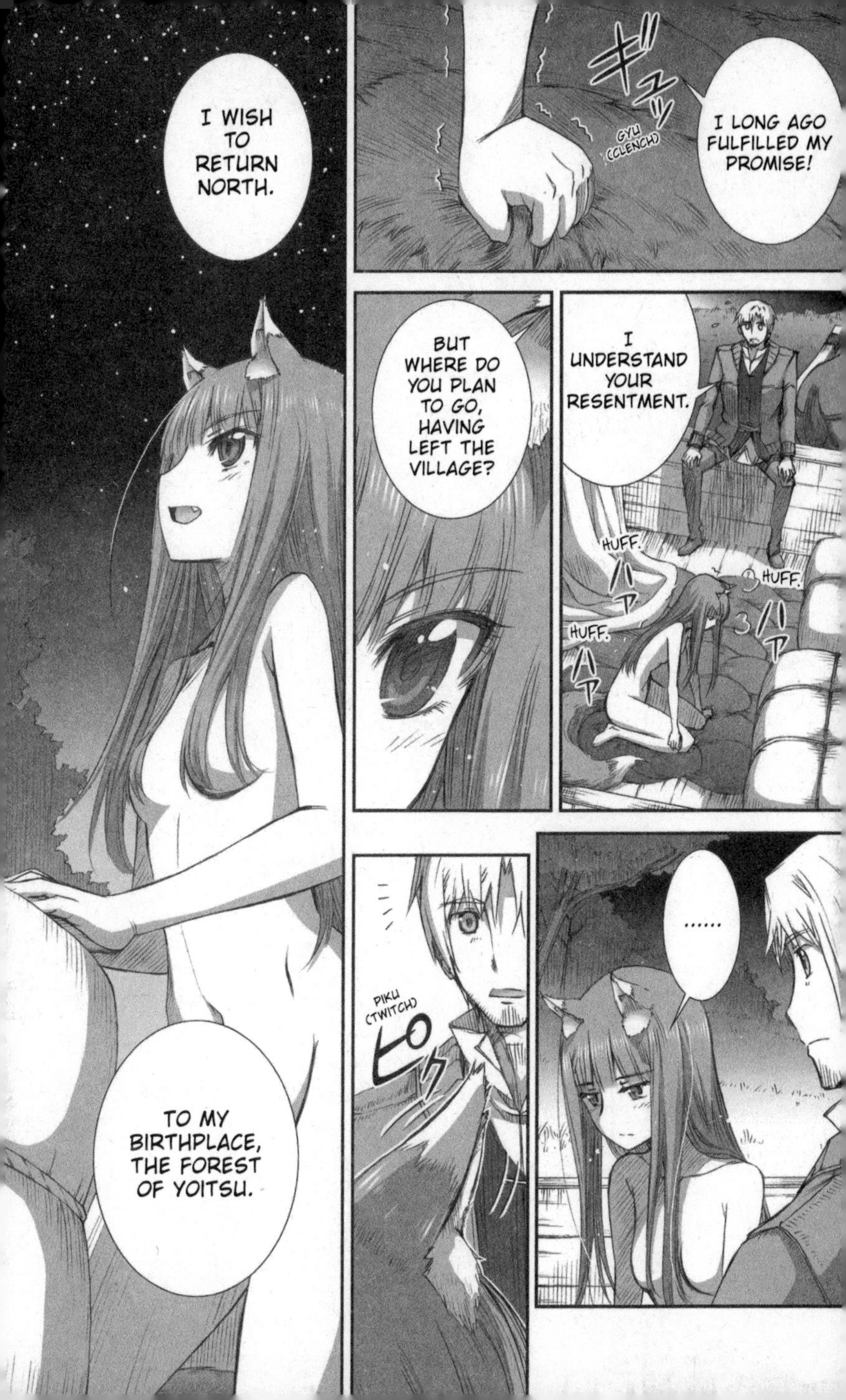

I LONG AGO FULFILLED MY PROMISE!
GYU (CLENCH)
I UNDERSTAND YOUR RESENTMENT.
HUFF.
HUFF.
HUFF.
BUT WHERE DO YOU PLAN TO GO, HAVING LEFT THE VILLAGE?
......
PIKU (TWITCH)
I WISH TO RETURN NORTH.
TO MY BIRTHPLACE, THE FOREST OF YOITSU.

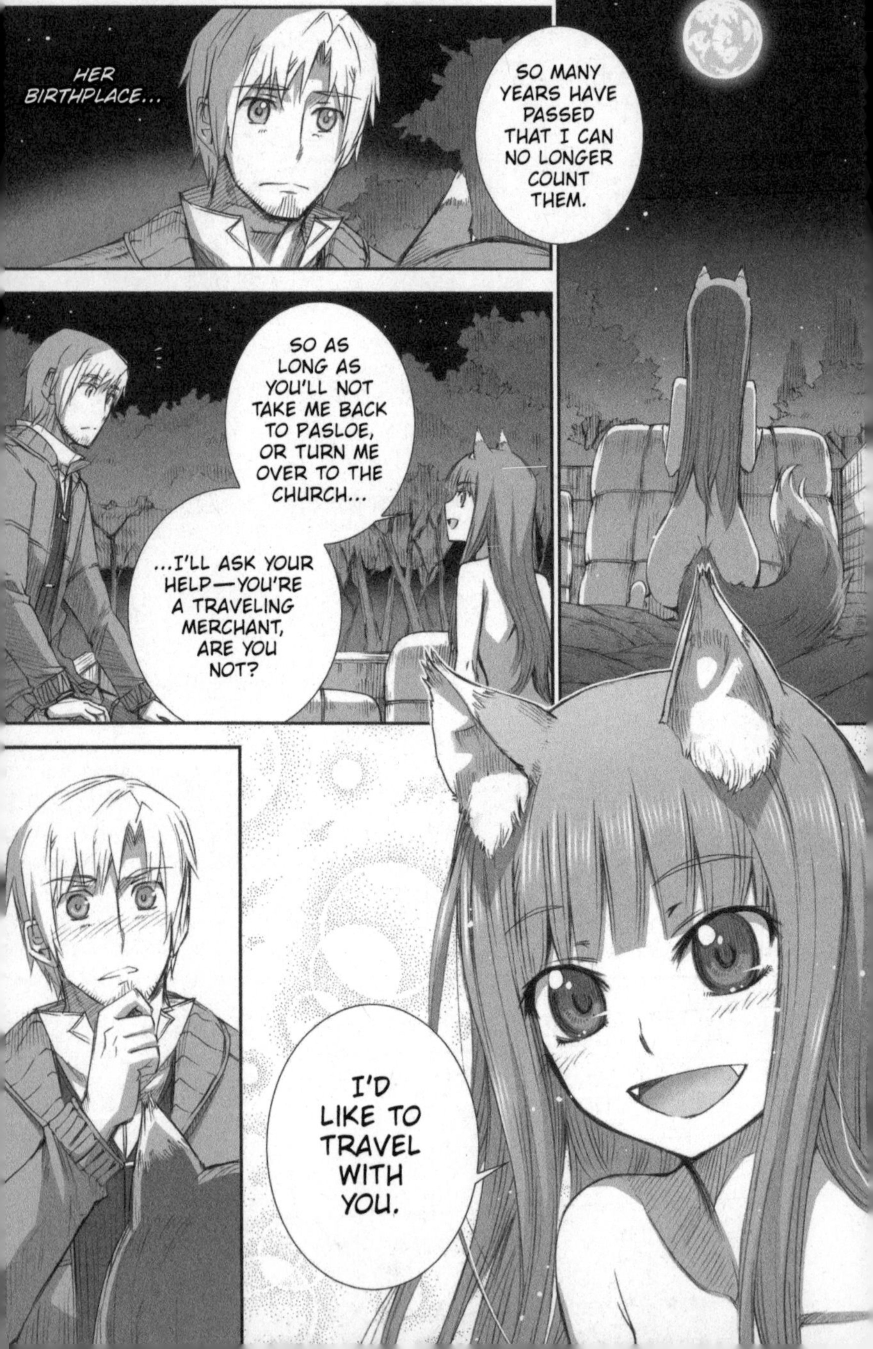
SO MANY YEARS HAVE PASSED THAT I CAN NO LONGER COUNT THEM.
HER BIRTHPLACE...
SO AS LONG AS YOU'LL NOT TAKE ME BACK TO PASLOE, OR TURN ME OVER TO THE CHURCH...
...I'LL ASK YOUR HELP—YOU'RE A TRAVELING MERCHANT, ARE YOU NOT?
I'D LIKE TO TRAVEL WITH YOU.

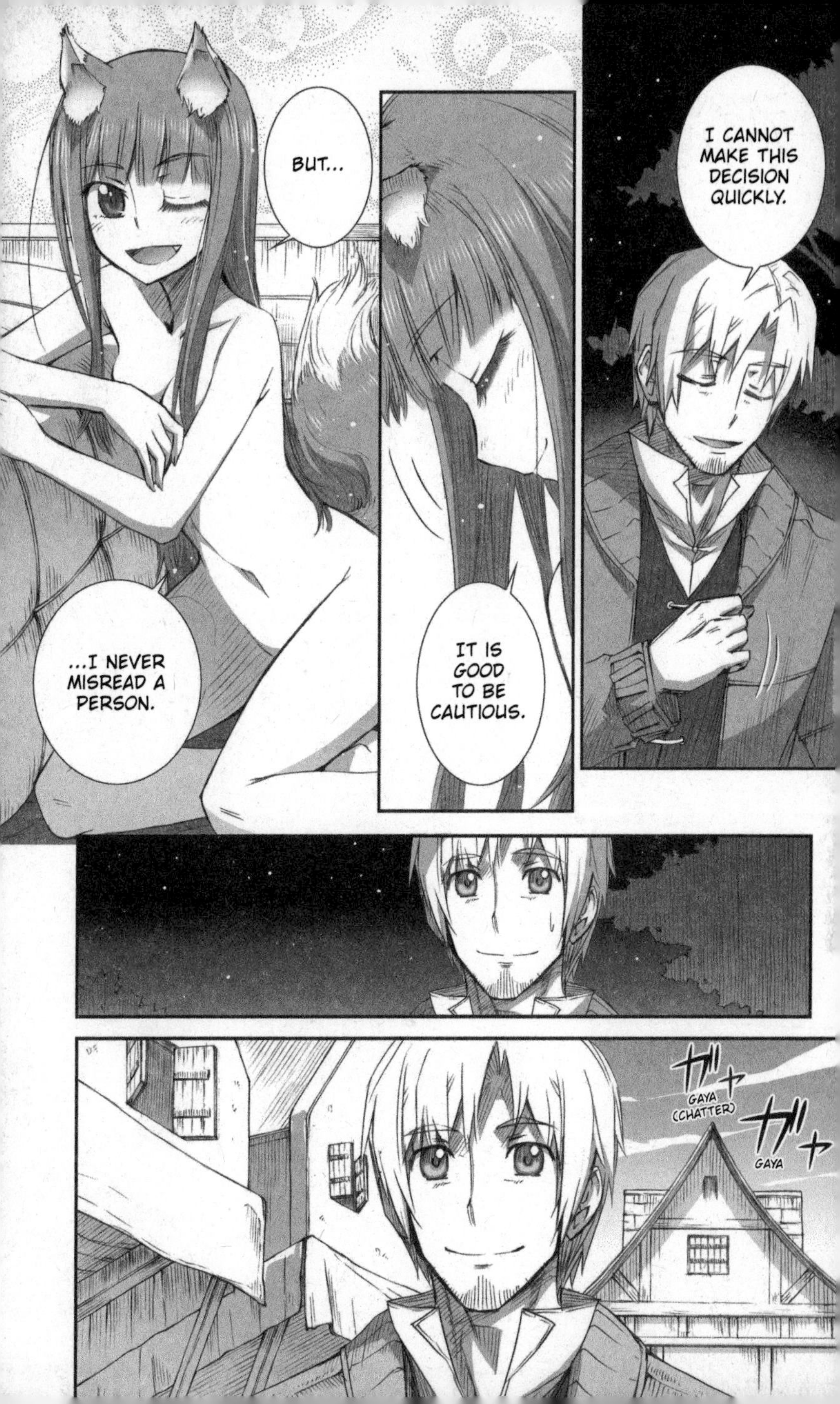

I CANNOT MAKE THIS DECISION QUICKLY.
IT IS GOOD TO BE CAUTIOUS.
BUT...
...I NEVER MISREAD A PERSON.
ガヤ
GAYA (CHATTER)
ガヤ
GAYA

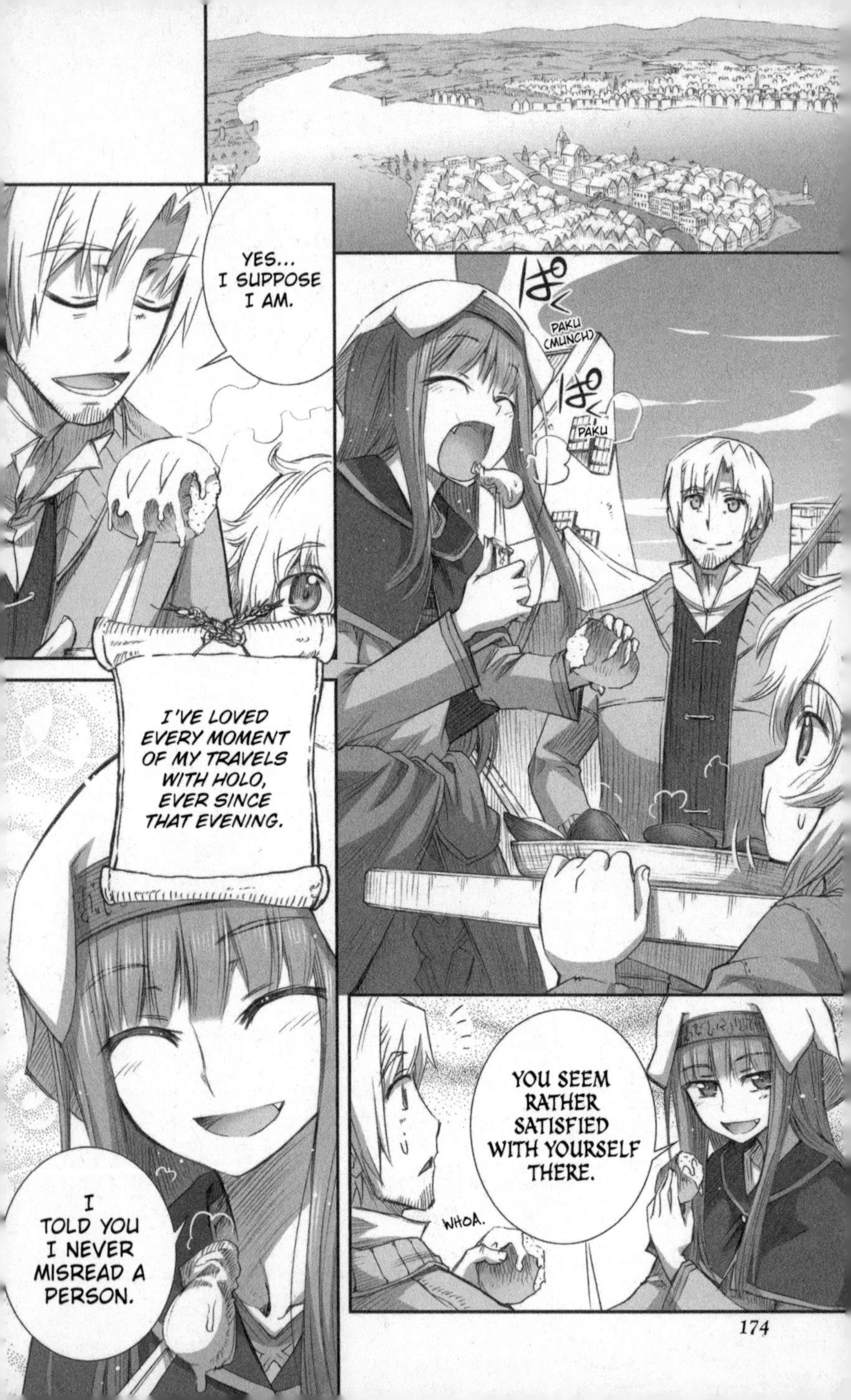
ぱく
PAKU (MUNCH)
ぱく
PAKU
YES... I SUPPOSE I AM.
I'VE LOVED EVERY MOMENT OF MY TRAVELS WITH HOLO, EVER SINCE THAT EVENING.
YOU SEEM RATHER SATISFIED WITH YOURSELF THERE.
WHOA.
I TOLD YOU I NEVER MISREAD A PERSON.

Finally, Volume 10! Congratulations!
Story-wise and plot-wise,
it's such an important point,
so I just can't tear myself away!
And as usual, Eve is terribly charming.
I cannot wait for her more
vulnerable scenes!

支倉凍砂
ISUNA HASEKURA

SPICE & WOLF

HOORAY!

■ Congratulations
on Volume 10! Finally,
double digits! Thanks for
all your hard work for so
long. I'll be cheering for
you with ever-increasing
anticipation!

JYUU AYAKURA

SPICE & WOLF ❿

Isuna Hasekura
Keito Koume
Character design:
Jyuu Ayakura

Translation: Paul Starr

Lettering: Terri Delgado

OOKAMI TO KOUSHINRYOU Vol. 10
©Isuna Hasekura/Keito Koume 2014
Edited by ASCII MEDIA WORKS
First published in Japan in 2014 by
KADOKAWA CORPORATION, Tokyo.
English translation rights arranged with
KADOKAWA CORPORATION, Tokyo,
through Tuttle-Mori Agency, Inc., Tokyo.

Translation © 2014 by Hachette Book Group

Yen Press
Hachette Book Group
1290 Avenue of the Americas
New York, NY 10104

www.HachetteBookGroup.com
www.YenPress.com

Yen Press is an imprint of Hachette Book Group, Inc. The Yen Press name and logo are trademarks of Hachette Book Group, Inc.

First Yen Press Edition: December 2014

ISBN: 978-0-316-33660-4

10 9 8 7 6 5 4 3 2 1

BVG

Printed in the United States of America